1921

Elizabeth Barrett Browning

FOR MY FRIEND
MARGARET CROSTHWAITE MADDERN
TO CELEBRATE
THIRTY YEARS' CORRESPONDENCE
IN THE BEST EBB
TRADITION

From a daguerreotype taken at Le Havre in 1858

Margaret Forster

Elizabeth Barrett Browning

A Biography

Chatto & Windus
LONDON

Published in 1988 by
Chatto & Windus Limited
30 Bedford Square
London WC1B 3RP

A CIP catalogue record for this book is available from
the British Library
ISBN 0-7011-3018-0

Copyright © Margaret Forster 1988

Designed by Humphrey Stone

Photoset by Rowland Phototypesetting Limited
Bury St Edmunds, Suffolk
Printed in Great Britain by
Redwood Burn Limited
Trowbridge, Wiltshire

Contents

Acknowledgements

The encouragement and help extended to me by the officers and members of the London Browning Society, and of the Browning Institute, made the research involved in the writing of this biography most pleasurable. I learned a great deal from attending the meetings of the society which are stimulating and varied.

Philip Kelley has been unstinting in his advice, never once failing to answer any of my many requests for guidance, and his own dedication to Browning scholarship has been a continual inspiration.

Edward Moulton-Barrett's courtesy and enthusiasm has been greatly appreciated and so has his hospitality.

Elaine Baly (Vivienne Browning) has spared the time to discuss many baffling aspects of Elizabeth Barrett Browning's personality and I have found a warmth and insight in her observations which have been illuminating.

My thanks are also due to Mary V. Altham for allowing me to read Surtees Cook's Diary; to Edward McAleer for assistance on the subject of Wilson; to A. R. N. Scott and Martin Roberts of Durham City Planning Office; to John and Patricia Hegarty for making me welcome at Hope End; to John Murray, for permission to see transcripts of material in the Harry Ransom Humanities Research Center, University of Texas at Austin; to Teresa Leiferman, temporary curator of the Casa Guidi when I visited it; to John Robson, Joan Leach and Sarah Miller.

List of Illustrations

Frontispiece. Elizabeth, aged 49, from a daguerreotype taken at Le Havre in 1858 (Courtesy of Edward R. Moulton-Barrett)

17. Elizabeth, aged 34, with Flush (Water-colour by her brother Alfred; courtesy of Edward R. Moulton-Barrett)
18. Surtees Cook (Miniature; courtesy of Mary V. Altham)
19. Henrietta Moulton-Barrett (Miniature; courtesy of Mary V. Altham)

Between pages 272 and 273
20. Mary Russell Mitford (Miniature by A. R. Burt, 1832; courtesy of Folger Shakespeare Library, Washington DC)
21. John Kenyon (Drawing; courtesy of John Murray Ltd)
22. Anna Jameson (Lithograph by R. J. Lane after the painting by H. P. Briggs; courtesy of Macdonald & Co. Ltd)
23. Robert Browning (Portrait by Dante Gabriel Rossetti, 1855; courtesy of the Fitzwilliam Museum, Cambridge)
24. Sonnet XLIII, *Sonnets from the Portuguese* (Courtesy of the British Museum)
25. Robert Browning, Senior (From the Browning Photograph Album; courtesy of the Master and Fellows of Balliol College, Oxford)
26. Sarianna Browning (From the Browning Photograph Album; courtesy of the Master and Fellows of Balliol College, Oxford)
27. Casa Guidi, interior (Painting by George Mignaty, 1861; courtesy of Rare Books & Special Collections, Mills College, Oakland, California)
28. Pen Browning, aged 9 (Photograph, 1858; courtesy of Wellesley College, Wellesley, Massachusetts)
29. Elizabeth with Pen, Rome, 1860 (From the Browning Photograph Album; courtesy of the Masters and Fellows of Balliol College, Oxford, and of the Browning Institute, Inc.)
30. Casa Guidi, exterior
31. Robert Browning, Rome, 1860 (From the Browning Photograph Album; courtesy of the Masters and Fellows of Balliol College, Oxford)
32. Elizabeth, Rome, May 1861 (Photograph; courtesy of the Browning Institute, Inc.)
33. 'My fig tree', Siena, 1860 (Drawing by Elizabeth; reproduced from Sotheby's Catalogue, 1913, courtesy of Philip Kelley)

Drawings in text
p. 15 A cricket game seen from the schoolroom window (Pencil sketch by Henrietta Moulton-Barrett, 1831; courtesy of Mary V. Altham)
p. 295 Pen's drawing of Robert Browning, 1853 (Courtesy of the British Museum)

The author and publishers would like to thank Philip Kelley and Edward R. Moulton-Barrett for their invaluable help in providing prints and details of the attribution and whereabouts of illustrations.

Author's Note

Any biographer faces the problem of which name to use to refer to Elizabeth Barrett Browning. To refer to her in the first half of this book as Miss Barrett and in the second as Mrs Browning would be correct but clumsy; to refer to her as Ba, the name by which she was known to her family and friends, would seem impertinent and inappropriate; to refer to her as EBB, which was how she signed herself in most of her non-family letters, would be the most fitting but it reads awkwardly; to refer to her as Elizabeth, which hardly anyone ever did, seems formal and stiff but it is the name I have decided to use as a result of this process of elimination.

Introduction

The case for a new, full-length biography of Elizabeth Barrett Browning
is quickly made. The standard work has remained Gardner Taplin's *The
Life of Elizabeth Barrett Browning* since it was published in 1957
(shortly after Dorothy Hewlett's *Elizabeth Barrett Browning* in 1953)
but in the intervening thirty years there have been exciting discoveries of
new material which have added a great deal to the knowledge of her
life. In addition, modern feminism has inspired a new interest in
Elizabeth Barrett Browning's poetry – *Aurora Leigh* was reprinted in
1978 for the first time since 1902 and acclaimed as a feminist epic.

One of the problems for biographers up to now has been the dearth of
material on Elizabeth Barrett Browning's early life and so, because of the
limitations of the available material, what has come to dominate
biographies of her are those brief though fully documented twenty
months during which Robert Browning courted, married and secretly
spirited her away to Italy. The source of all information during this
period is of course the love letters which are indeed so fascinating that
biographers can hardly be blamed for choosing to plunder such riches
and make extravagant use of their findings. But the new material
discovered in the last three decades includes hundreds of letters covering
Elizabeth Barrett Browning's childhood, adolescence and her adult life
before she married, and many more written during her marriage. These
inevitably change perceptions of her.

The discovery of these letters is in a great measure due to the efforts of
one man, Philip Kelley. While a student at Baylor University in Texas,
Philip Kelley worked in the Armstrong Browning Library there, helping
to prepare a checklist of all known Browning letters. In 1959, after
graduation, he came to England and worked in various antiquarian
bookshops, all the time pursuing his now avid interest in both
Brownings. During that year he was introduced to Edward Moulton-
Barrett, the great-grand-nephew of Elizabeth Barrett Browning. With

Edward Moulton-Barrett's encouragement and help Philip Kelley began contacting other family members and tracking down their collections of papers. By the end of his first year he had turned serious sleuth. More than four thousand unpublished documents relating to the Brownings had been located. Philip Kelley was convinced that there were still many more Browning letters in existence if only he could accede to them. To do this he had to attract attention to his project: commemorating the centenary of Elizabeth Barrett Browning's death, on 29th June 1961, seemed the ideal way of doing so. The exhibition, sponsored by St Marylebone Central Library, opened on 31st May 1961. Before it ended Philip Kelley made a dramatic and unexpected discovery.

On June 29th itself, the anniversary of the day of Elizabeth's death, Philip Kelley was looking through some documents in a solicitor's office, in company with some members of the Barrett family, hoping to find those letters written by Elizabeth Barrett Browning to her father and known to have been returned, unopened, to her. Instead, he found a diary, written by Elizabeth mostly during her twenty-sixth year. It was in two parts. The first, covering June to December 1831, was wrapped in manila paper and enclosed in a black silk slip-case. The second, covering January to April 1832, was in the centre of a volume bound in Russian leather used by Elizabeth to make notes on her reading. This second part had been tampered with. Eighteen pages were cut in half, fifty-six completely excised. Philip Kelley edited this diary with the help of Ronald Hudson and it was pubished by the Ohio University Press in 1969. John Murray published Elizabeth Berridge's abbreviated version in 1974.

By now, Philip Kelley was a man obsessed. His original aim – to provide a checklist of all known Browning letters – had widened alarmingly into a desire to collect and publish all the unknown ones. In order to do this he eventually set up his own press in 1979, the Wedgestone Press. He made his home in Winfield, Kansas, into a kind of Browning factory, where helpers literally clocked in and out as they worked on deciphering, transcribing and computerising the Brownings' correspondence. Later the whole project was transferred to a downtown business building. The work has been funded for the last ten years by a variety of grants. The first volume off the Wedgestone Press was *The Brownings' Correspondence: A Checklist*. It was this volume which gained the grant (from the National Endowment for the Humanities) desperately needed to start funding the publication of the actual correspondence. Volume One (1809–1826) appeared in 1984. To date, five volumes have been published, bringing this correspondence up to 1842. Suddenly, the whole of Elizabeth Barrett Browning's childhood and adolescence can be explored – no longer is the frail invalid of Wimpole Street a puzzle to us as she waits to hear Robert Browning's step on the stair. We now are in a position to know her rather better than she knew herself. We can smile at some of the things she tells Robert, knowing exactly what she has glossed over, and frown at some of her more extravagant denials, knowing she has contradicted herself in making them.

Any biographer presented with all these formerly inaccessible letters to and from Elizabeth would feel rich indeed. But there is even more wealth, enough to satisfy the greediest, in these first five volumes. As well as impeccable notes and appendices they contain a checklist of Supporting Documents. Many extracts from these documents are given (they consist mostly of letters to and from various relatives and family friends). The additional information they contain is substantial. People immensely important but up to now shadowy come to life, and it is most helpful and illuminating to have the letters of Mr Barrett to some of his other children during the various crises in Elizabeth's life. It is Mr Barrett who gains most through this imaginative publishing of these supporting documents. But the Browning correspondence in its glorious entirety – it will cover the whole lives of both poets – has as yet been published only up to 1842. It will be immediately obvious that, although superbly fed on juvenilia and given immense aid to understanding Elizabeth Barrett before she met Robert Browning, the biographer now finds the source material for Elizabeth's pre-marriage days to be much fuller than for the post-marriage ones. Fortunately, some of the letters which will be published in the complete correspondence have already been published elsewhere. The first volume of selected letters was published in 1958 – *Letters of the Brownings to George Barrett*, edited by Paul Landis with the assistance of Ronald E. Freeman. George was Elizabeth's lawyer brother. Elizabeth expected George to side with her upon her marriage but to her intense distress he supported his father. She was estranged from him until 1851, when after a reconciliation, their correspondence resumed. Then there are Elizabeth's letters to Mrs David Ogilvy, edited by Philip Kelley and Peter N. Haydon and published in 1974. Mrs Ogilvy was a young Scots woman, a poet herself, who briefly lived above the Brownings in Casa Guidi in Florence. One of her sons was almost exactly the same age as Pen, the son of Elizabeth and Robert, and the two mothers enjoyed a pleasant if not deep friendship based on this connection. There is also the three volume edition of Elizabeth's letters to her friend Miss Mary Russell Mitford edited by Meredith B. Raymond and Mary Rose Sullivan and published in 1983. After her marriage Elizabeth's letters to her friend were neither as full, nor as frequent and free in expression as before it, but the last of these three volumes contains a great deal of new material on the marriage years. There is also a huge amount of fascinating domestic trivia in a book published in 1979 by the Browning Institute. This is Edward C. McAleer's *The Brownings of Casa Guidi*, which covers only the marriage years. Volume Five of the Browning Institute Studies is also full of extracts from Elizabeth's letters to Arabel (her other sister) from Italy.

*   *   *

One of the aims of this biography is to stimulate more interest in Elizabeth Barrett Browning's poetry. This being so, it was a shock to discover that this is largely inaccessible outside a good library. Barely any of Elizabeth Barrett Browning's work is in print. Walk into any bookshop and all you will find on the shelves (if you are lucky) is the Women's Press edition of *Aurora Leigh* (1978) and a slim selection chosen by Malcolm Hicks for Carcanet (1980). Beyond that, nothing. Turn to anthologies and you will fare little better – the *New Oxford Anthology of Victorian Verse* (ed. Christopher Ricks 1986) has four Elizabeth Barrett Browning poems and one of those is an extract from *Aurora Leigh*. In order to be able to direct any interested reader to something more substantial I have published in conjunction with this biography a selection of Elizabeth Barrett Browning's poetry in which her development as a poet can be traced and some of her finest forgotten poems read.

PART ONE

1806–1846

Chapter One

PLACES haunted Elizabeth Barrett Browning from the beginning to the end of her life. "Places are ideas, and ideas can madden or kill," she once wrote to a friend.[1] But about her own birthplace she had no recollection – her memories began, most suitably for a poet, in the magical palace of a house which her father had built in Herefordshire. Here, in a secret valley, she thought of her life as beginning. She never realised the significance of where it had actually begun: in the county of Durham, among her mother's family, surrounded by the traditions and values of her mother's people. Her inheritance was Graham-Clarke as well as Barrett, something which popular mythology does not take into account. It is Elizabeth's reputedly tyrannical father, the supposedly terrifying Mr Barrett of Wimpole Street, who has dominated what is known about her. Her mother is hardly mentioned.

Mary Graham-Clarke was the eldest child of John and Arabella Graham-Clarke. She was born on 1st May 1781 in Newcastle-on-Tyne, the first of five girls and two surviving sons. Her father, a rich merchant who also owned land in Jamaica, was a man of considerable local standing. In Newcastle itself he owned two fine houses, both substantially more splendid than anything the Barretts owned at the time. One was in the heart of Newcastle, in Pilgrim Street, where he had a vast cellarage in which he stored his merchandise, and the other, Kenton Lodge, was in Gosforth on the outskirts of the city. As well as ships and land, he owned breweries and glassworks and all kinds of businesses stretching from Newcastle into Yorkshire. In his prime his total assets were estimated at £170,000.[2] There was never any question of young Edward Barrett Moulton-Barrett, when he proposed to Mary Graham-Clarke in 1805, finding favour simply because he was a good catch. The Graham-Clarkes neither needed nor wanted such a match. It was far more important to them that their much loved daughter should be happy.

Edward Barrett Moulton-Barrett[3] was a suitor whose background was as complicated as his cumbersome name. He was the grandson of Edward Barrett, an immensely wealthy Jamaican plantation owner usually known as Edward of Cinnamon Hill (the name of his house in the north part of the island). The young Edward and his brother Sam, sons of Edward of Cinnamon Hill's only daughter, Elizabeth, were thirteen and eleven when their grandfather died in 1798 and became his heirs because his three sons had all died before him. John Graham-Clarke was in the curious position of knowing rather more about this supposedly magnificent inheritance than either of the Barrett boys. He knew just how threatened it was in spite of the four years Edward of Cinnamon Hill had spent trying to make his will watertight. The aim of their grandfather's will had been that the family should continue to maintain and if possible augment the vast properties he had secured: he wanted no arguments. But no sooner was he dead than the first challenge to his will was filed, a mere seven days afterwards. The clause under dispute was an apparently trivial one: Edward of Cinnamon Hill was alleged to have removed 92 slaves and 50 cattle from the estate of his deceased eldest son and transferred them to his own. The beneficiaries of this son's will claimed them back. On 2nd July 1801, three years after the grandfather's death, there began thirty-six years of legal wrangling which effectively destroyed all his careful planning. The shadow it cast over young Edward's future was seen and anticipated by John Graham-Clarke who had himself been appointed an executor of the will of the late eldest son.

Apart from knowing these complicated financial and legal details, Graham-Clarke was well acquainted with Edward Moulton-Barrett's upbringing. He knew how different it was to his own daughter's. Mary had been brought up in a prosperous and enviably stable family deeply rooted in the local community, with all the accompanying social responsibilities this implied. She and her sisters were not allowed to be unfamiliar with poverty: they helped to dole out soup to the poor twice a week from the kitchen in their Pilgrim Street house and assisted in the free school their father had established in which girls were taught to sew and thereby given some prospect of earning a living. They saw how active a part their father took in local affairs and how respected he was. His concern for his daughters was as strong as for his sons. He went to great pains to see that this was reflected in his will which left them protected fortunes and gave more to his unmarried than to his married daughters. He was, in short, an exemplary family man and Mary was fortunate to have had such a happy home.

Edward Barrett Moulton-Barrett's experience was dramatically different. His father was not a respected man. Charles Moulton was the son of another plantocracy family in Jamaica about whom no one ever seems to have had a good word to say, though his faults have never been precisely enumerated. He married Elizabeth Barrett in 1781 when she was only eighteen and before the marriage failed they had four children – Sarah (born 1783), Edward (born 1785), Sam (born 1787) and a fourth who died. Elizabeth went home to Cinnamon Hill in 1789 with her three young children who were from then on, to all intents and purposes, fatherless. With their absent father's agreement they took their grandfather's name which, since they already had Barrett as their second name, gave rise to the repetition. John Graham-Clarke, who had added the Clarke to his own name for similar reasons, arranged the necessary royal and legal permission.

The atmosphere in Newcastle, where young Edward Barrett visited the Graham-Clarkes soon after he arrived in England in 1792, at the age of seven, was of course quite different from what he had known in Jamaica. Cinnamon Hill Great House (called "great" to distinguish it from the slave houses and not because of any immense size) was a place of exceptional beauty. It stood, and still stands, half way up a hillside rising above the coastal plain stretching from Montego Bay to Saltmarsh Bay. Surrounded by trees, it has even thicker woods and higher hills behind, and in front, far off, the long rollers of the Caribbean break in a thin white line on the coral reefs which guard the coast, a strand of white streaking the deep blue. In Edward's day there was an English lawn lovingly maintained in front of the house and a garden in which English lilacs mixed with spice trees, roses with pomegranates and everywhere the bright yellow logweed flowers studded the grass. But the life he and his sister and brother led there was one in which the overpowering loveliness of nature contrasted violently with what man was making of it. No child, however privileged or protected, could escape knowing about the savageries of slavery. The sugar cane, its green swathes forever rustling in the trade wind breezes, was harvested at the cost of floggings and brutal suppression. Thirty-nine lashes of a thick cattle whip was the standard punishment for any misdemeanour and spiked dog collars could be forced onto slaves who had tried to escape. More haunting than any of the bird songs was the long, mournful, eerie blast on the conch shell that signified the hunt for an escaped negro. Edward, leaving this life at the age of seven, had memories which were impressionistic, fragmented, heavily influenced by his own immature perceptions. The most important thing to him was not that he was leaving Jamaica but that he was leaving his mother whom he adored. All Jamaican white children left their mother sooner or later to go back "home" to be educated – it was a fact of life. Edward and his older sister Sarah and younger brother Sam sailed for Bristol in 1792 in the company of a Dr James Archer, a chaplain. Though he was no milk sop, Edward gave to Dr Archer, who was to return soon to Jamaica, a present to take back to his mother: it was a glove soaked in his tears.

For Edward, arriving after the gruelling two-month voyage, England was a shock. The Barrett children were plunged into a culture totally different from the one they had left – nothing had prepared them for the reality of Marylebone's grey, grim-looking streets where they stayed with relatives whom they did not know. Sarah was sent to Greenwich, to a young lady's school with strong Jamaican connections, and Edward and Sam were for the time being tutored at home before Edward was sent to Harrow. Their mother soon followed her children to England, together with her companion Mary Trepsack (Treppy).[4] At first, Elizabeth Moulton and Treppy moved about between hordes of distant Barrett relatives and until she bought a house of her own she often arranged for her sons to stay with her father's old family friend, John Graham-Clarke in Newcastle.

Few men have the opportunity to observe their future sons-in-law at close hand in this way. The Barrett boys fitted in with his own sons very well. John Graham-Clarke junior was three years older than Edward, and James was three years younger than Sam. It was obvious from the first visit that the Barrett boys relished the kind of family life which the Graham-Clarkes offered. Edward, aged ten, wrote in 1795 to his mother from Newcastle, "we are going to have holidays and be merry at Christmas." It was clearly a great relief to Elizabeth Moulton, who at that time had just experienced the tragic death of her twelve-year-old daughter Sarah, to know that her sons were so happy. On yet another occasion, after Edward had gone to Harrow, aged twelve, her boys stayed with the Graham-Clarkes and she wrote to Newcastle in the most fulsome terms saying, "My boys have written to me and seem rejoiced at the idea of being with you these holidays. I am myself happy as they will be under your own eye . . ." – the eye of a father substitute, the perfect family man such as their own father had never been. (They had a guardian in England, James Scarlett, the 1st Lord Abinger, but he was not the figurehead she had in mind.) Elizabeth Moulton knew that Edward in particular needed such an influence, especially after he was suddenly withdrawn from Harrow. There are no records to indicate exactly when he was withdrawn nor why but his stay there appears to have been not more than a year. According to family legend he left because he was flogged by the boy for whom he was fag because he let some toast burn. With Edward, pride was all. To be asked to toast bread was servile, to be beaten for failing to do it properly the ultimate in humiliation. His mother at least appreciated this. So he was withdrawn and thereafter tutored again at home until he went up to Trinity College, Cambridge, in 1801. He did not take a degree – many people did not at that time. He seems to have laid down the beginnings of a good library and met some interesting contemporaries such as John Kenyon, son of another Jamaican family and a distant cousin.[5] In the vacations Edward went back to the Graham-Clarkes. The lure by then was not so much that of jolly family life as the attractions of Mary – fourteen and far removed from him when he had met her at the age of ten; twenty-three and not so ridiculously above him when he was nineteen and in love with her. All he had to do was convince his guardian and her father that, though he was still a minor, the marriage should be permitted. James Scarlett demurred only until he had met Mary. When he did, he knew who was the luckier of the two. Mary herself had a free choice: John Graham-Clarke was in no hurry to rid himself of his most beautiful and charming daughter. If she could accept Edward knowing so much about him, after observing him over such a long period of time, then no one could argue that she did not know her own mind.

Mary Graham-Clarke and Edward Barrett Moulton-Barrett were married on Tuesday 14th May 1805 in Gosforth Church, an event reported in the local newspapers together with the information that "the Prisoners of Newgate (the Newcastle prison) return their most sincere thanks to Edward Barrett Moulton-Barrett for his benevolent donation of three guineas". The bridegroom, in marrying a local girl, was wisely following local custom. Mary was the first of John Graham-Clarke's children to marry, which gave her wedding particular importance. Her beauty and charm together with the dark handsome looks of her young bridegroom added a certain glamour to a naturally glittering occasion.

She had been twenty-four on May 1st and Edward would be twenty on May 28th.

After the wedding, the couple had a short honeymoon in the south of England but then returned to the county of Durham to take up residence at Coxhoe Hall which Edward had leased.[6] It was an imposing house built in 1725 in a castellated Gothic style and situated on a hill among thick beech woods, five miles from Durham. The views from the house, of open countryside, though partially obscured by the trees which protected its privacy, were extensive. Here, nine months later, at seven in the evening of 6th March 1806, Mary and Edward's first child was born, and named Elizabeth.

From the moment he became a father Edward Barrett was eager to get away from Durham. His wife's family, once so precious to him, were now less attractive, nor were relations with his powerful father-in-law as happy as they had been – his guardian had warned him that there was a suspicion that John Graham-Clarke was not paying to Edward money which was owing to him.[7] Money, in any case, was already of concern to Edward who had just come into his inheritance. His guardian warned him about general spending, pointing out that, as expected, the price of sugar was beginning to fall – "it is certain that since your grandfather's death in 1798 sugars have sold very low." Then, of course, there was the contested will. From the time of Elizabeth's birth her father had financial worries, but they were not so serious that thoughts of buying a property of his own was out of the question for Edward Barrett. He spent most of his time dashing off to look at properties, the further away from Durham and Newcastle the better. He did not even want to be near his brother Sam who had settled near Richmond in Yorkshire or his mother who was in Surrey or in London's Baker Street when not staying with him.

Before he found a place to make his permanent home, another child had been born, a boy named Edward, on 26th June 1807, a mere fifteen months after Elizabeth. No particular orders for celebrations had been given on his daughter's birth but on his son's the young father ordered a holiday for the slaves back home on his Jamaican plantations. Elizabeth and Edward were baptised together (though Elizabeth had been baptised privately at home by a family friend in her first weeks) in February 1809 at nearby Kelloe Parish Church. Before the Barrett name in the register stood the local names of a farmer, a labourer, a pitman and a shoemaker alongside whom Edward Barrett Moulton-Barrett, esq, of Coxhoe Hall, native of St James, Jamaica, looked both odd and exotic.

Edward's brother Sam wrote wittily that he was glad to hear his little niece had been properly christened at last and hoped "she still promises as well as when she was under my direction. Mary allowed that she was an Angel and I thought her so much like her uncle I gave my assent . . ." He was the only Barrett, apart from her grandmother, who saw the baby Elizabeth regularly. The visitors who came and went with such ease were Mary's sisters – Arabella, Charlotte, Frances and Jane – ranging from the age of twenty-one to eleven and all enchanted with their niece. Then of course there were the Graham-Clarke grandparents, the aunts, the uncles, the cousins – all temptingly near and all used to seeing Mary often.

At the start of 1809 all this changed. Edward Barrett gave notice at Coxhoe and moved his family down to London even though his wife was again heavily pregnant. First they stayed in London, where Henrietta was born on March 4th, and then in a rented house at Hammersmith before moving once more to join his mother in Surrey. Within weeks of arriving at her mother-in-law's home Mary was writing wistfully to her own family that the "thought of a journey to the dear North" was "the Summit of Happiness". Her husband had no intention of letting her anywhere near the north. He was furiously house-hunting, applying to every property he saw his own extremely exacting standards. Left at his mother's home in Surrey, with three children aged three and under, Mary could only hope and pray that he would find something soon and that they would become properly settled. She wrote to her mother in May, with something of an edge about her tone, "I well know that it will be a satisfaction to all parties when Edward gets happily settled in a place to his wishes." In September, as she was beginning to despair, a letter came from her husband to his little daughter ("my dear puss") which gave exciting news. Edward had found an estate he liked. It had the rather ominous name of Hope End (though this only meant "closed valley" in old English) and was near Ledbury in Herefordshire, an area of the country entirely unknown to Mary and a long way from the north. The note was charming but short on solid information. Edward wrote of being "completely fagged out" after touring the estate so it was obviously large; he mentioned that there was "no fruit this year" which suggested orchards; and he made a passing reference to inspecting "the Timber" which implied woods. But his enthusiasm was unmistakable – "the more I see of the place the more I like it," he wrote and added touchingly, "and the more I think I shall have it in my power to make yourself, Brother and Sister and dear Mama happy." He was not too preoccupied to remember that Elizabeth had had a cold and hoped that by the time he returned there would be no "symptoms of that lurking cough". With that sense of history which was one of her most attractive attributes Mary solemnly docketed the short letter with the words "First letter from her dearest Papa, Sept. 6th 1809, to Happy Ba!"

Ba (so called as an abbreviation for Baby and the "a" pronounced as in "pa") was about to be very happy indeed for ten whole years after her father bought Hope End. This took some negotiating. The asking price was £27,000 for the house (including furniture) and 475 acres of land. Edward offered £24,000, which was accepted, and by the end of the autumn the deal was concluded. Mary, arriving in November with her three children, was not at first as enraptured by Hope End as her husband though of course delighted to have come to the end of her travels. She could see how pleased her husband was and agreed with him that the deer in the park were pretty and the stream running through it "most attractive" but there were other aspects of Hope End that made it an acquired taste: Edward's taste. It was almost buried alive. From any of the quiet country roads surrounding the estate it was not only impossible to see the house but impossible to believe it existed. The paths leading to this house from the roads twisted and turned so cunningly and folded themselves so securely into the flanks of the small hills surrounding it, that when the visitor finally confronted a habitation there was a sense of shock. Once there, any awareness of an outside world disappeared. The silence was complete, except for the birds. The greenery even in winter was so thick it appeared impregnable. Treppy, when she visited with Elizabeth Moulton, wrote rather nervously that "this situation is rather retired". She also mentioned that another visitor from Jamaica had thought it rather like the parish of St Ann's there, which does indeed have the same kind of dense foliage. Brother Sam was so horrified at what he heard that he refused to visit until the summer came and made the prospect a little more attractive.

As far as the new owner was concerned it was already ideal. He was in his element, "up to his chin in brick and mortar" as Treppy put it, supervising the building of his new and extraordinary house (he converted the existing Georgian mansion into stables) which was to be Turkish in design. He requested from his architect minarets and all manner of outlandish features quite unknown in such a rural backwater. The neighbours were vastly intrigued, such grandiose, flamboyant architecture smacking all too clearly of the nouveau riche. But Mary was impressed by her new home as it gradually took shape and wrote to her mother that she thought it was "beautiful and unique" and that it was altogether like something out of "the Arabian nights tales". Once the external edifice was up – quite a performance because the walls of the minarets were solid concrete and cast iron was used for the tops – Edward became obsessed with making the interior perfect. No detail was too small for him. Mary described to her mother how the balustrades in the hall were brass, the mahogany doors inlaid with mother-of-pearl, the dining room papered in crimson flock, the drawing room "*circular*" and the fireplaces exquisitely carved. It took seven years to complete and after that there were the grounds to be landscaped. Before Edward had finished there were ponds and grottos, cottages and kiosks, an icehouse, a hothouse and a subterranean passage leading from the house to the gardens. It was no wonder that sightseers came from Malvern to gape.

Throughout this time – a decade – while Edward had been overseeing the building work and going off to London at frequent intervals to attend to his Jamaican business interests, Mary had been doing her work too: bearing children. By the time house and gardens were complete, so was her family of three girls and eight boys. The first baby born at Hope End the year after they arrived, a girl called Mary, had died aged four, a grief so secret it was never written about. Elizabeth was eight at the time and highly impressionable but no written mention of this death of a sister was ever made. The rest of Mary's large brood were all survivors. For eighteen years, from 1806 to 1824, Mary was in a state of almost continual childbearing. She endured this with fortitude and her children were all healthy. The gaps between births were short – on average, eighteen months – but the four older ones, Elizabeth, Bro, Henrietta and Sam, tended to think of themselves as distinctly separate from the clutch of brothers who came after Arabel, the next in line. The younger brothers – Charles, George, Henry, Alfred, Septimus and Octavius – have often been conveniently lumped together, as though they had one hybrid personality, but the differences between them both in character and in their relationship with Elizabeth were enormous. Nobody was more attached to or involved with their siblings than she was and she was never isolated from them even when she was ill. It was impossible for her to be in danger of becoming reclusive at any stage of her childhood, surrounded as she was by such a boisterous, demanding, talented group of brothers and sisters. It was their continual noisy presence which prevented Hope End from being the lonely place nature had conspired to make it. Nor was Elizabeth the remote, superior eldest separated from the rest by her intellectual inclinations. On the contrary, until she was about fifteen she was in the thick of their many activities, dominating, organising and inspiring them all. It was she who put on plays – a cousin remembered "*all* the squabbling delights of the green room" – created a camp in the grotto (from which letters were sent to her mother with urgent requests for "a few saussages") and led expeditions which ended in picnics. She was maternal, too, towards the little ones, begging most passionately to be allowed to play nurse for the day and take charge of the current baby. Dolls were important to her: she loved the doll Grandmother Moulton had sent her when she was as old as eleven and described appreciatively its "pretty fur cap and a cloth coat nightgown". Her precocious intellectual gifts, it is clear, never prevented her from having a great deal of fun. The child who reported reading Racine at ten also confessed to exhaustion after romping in the hay.

Part of discovering Elizabeth lies in discovering her brothers and sisters. Most of them had nicknames which complicate the process. Edward, the beloved brother nearest to her in age and every way, began life as Buff but by three was Bro, only to become Brozie on occasions of affectionate teasing. Henrietta was Addles. She had no interest in books or learning and her prettiness and sociability made Elizabeth a little jealous and contemptuous. Henrietta liked to play the piano, which Elizabeth professed to "abhor" (she was not good at it), and best of all she liked going to parties and dressing up, from which Elizabeth turned disdainfully away. Not surprisingly, as a child Henrietta suffered at her sister's hands (or tongue) and turned to Sam, three years her junior. Just as Elizabeth and Bro formed a partnership so did Henrietta and Sam. Sam, all agreed, was a card. He was witty and light-hearted and easy going. "Funny Sam," Elizabeth once commented ". . . he amuses us all . . . by his odd tricks." Like Henrietta, he was interested in clothes – quite the dandy if given the chance. Poor Arabel (christened Arabella), only a year younger than Sam, had no obvious ally. She was delicate as a child and spent three vital years away from the family recuperating her strength at the sea-side with her nurse. She was quiet and patient, lacking the strength of Elizabeth's character or the gaiety in Henrietta's. There was from the first a good deal of the martyr in her make-up – she was too ready to suffer for the sake of others and was inevitably exploited, especially by Elizabeth, even though she loved Arabel dearly. Elizabeth became upset when someone once referred to Arabel as an icicle and defended her staunchly with the explanation that "there are flowers that blow in the frost . . . and she is one of them, dear thing". All the Barretts persuaded Arabel to do things for them, usually tedious tasks they were too lazy to perform themselves, and she obliged so uncomplainingly that afterwards they felt uncomfortable. She liked drawing and walking and was deeply religious. Elizabeth came to depend on her more and more, not liking Arabel to go away on any kind of visit and clearly aggrieved when she did so.

The six brothers who followed Arabel ("the brats" Sam called them) began with Charles John, called Storm (or Stormy, or Stormie) because he was born in a storm at Christmas 1814.[8] Stormie was shy, sensitive and had a stammer. Elizabeth was protective towards him and readily provided him with security in her room at the top of the house. She was proud of being able to comfort him when no one else could. George, the next brother, needed no comfort. He was a model Barrett son – none of Bro's wildness, none of Sam's frivolity, none of Stormie's nervousness. From the beginning, George was solemn, serious, dependable and hard-working. He had rigid standards and principles, just like his father. Elizabeth was inclined to mock his stuffiness – she sometimes called him Pudding – but was quick to realise that George alone of the brothers showed signs both of earning his exacting father's respect and of being able to stand up to him. Elizabeth admired that. Henry, who came after George, annoyed her. She was always arguing with him, to little effect, and thought him self-willed (which of course she was herself). Alfred, inexplicably known as Daisy, bothered her less but he was closer to Henrietta. Elizabeth admired his drawing but disliked his general air of apathy – "he does not often fall or rise into enthusiasms," she reflected and if there was one quality Elizabeth demanded all her life in others, it was enthusiasm. She adored her two youngest brothers, Septimus known as Sette and Octavius known as Occy. Sette had the sweetest of dispositions – his mother saw him giving up his pencil when he was three to Alfred, aged five, so that his brother could draw, and commented "never was there such a Chesterfield in petticoats". Like Sam, Sette was a wag whose entertaining company Elizabeth relished. But it was Occy, born when she was eighteen, upon whom she lavished most affection. With him, she was openly demonstrative, rushing to kiss him if she had been away and loving to take him on her knee and cuddle him while she read him stories. She called him her "enchanting little beast" and when he grew old enough not to want to be kissed she hatched all sorts of plots to ensnare him.

All these children loved both their parents passionately. Their love for their father was no less restrained, in childhood, than was their love for their mother. There is no evidence that the tinge of fear which came later ever clouded their relationship with their father as children. On the contrary, they were more bold and cheeky in their demands upon him than was considered respectful for the times. Elizabeth referred to her father as "the monarch of Hope End" but told him not to "knit your brows or your glass eye may tumble off". The signal for endless games was the sight of Papa riding up the drive after a business visit to London. Mary described such an arrival late one evening: ". . . the windows were all shut and the school room and nursery were at tea when his anxiously expected voice was heard! Never was he more welcome . . . we sat down directly to our soup and chicken and half an hour basking in the armchair before a blazing fire enabling him to get thro' the evening very comfortably roasting chestnuts till the rioters all went to bed . . ." The picture is of a popular, energetic father, one for whom the children waited eagerly and from whose presence they were not dismissed but stayed, "rioters" though they were and the journey he had made exhausting. Writing to him on one of his birthdays Sette summed up the general feeling when he said, "You are a funny old fellow and I hope you will be as funny when you are a nice old man and play with me at Grand Mufti." Life, as Elizabeth recorded, was no *fun* without her father.

It was no fun for Mary either. Her husband was in London more frequently and for longer spells, which she found hard to endure particularly since she did not fully understand the business which kept him there. This was not her fault. In her husband's mind work and home were sharply separated: he did not want one to taint the joy of the other. Around Hope End he threw an imaginary *cordon sanitaire* which he would never allow to be breached. His wife and family were to be kept out of the sordid financial concerns which preoccupied him. This was a gesture of selflessness not selfishness but it meant that, while his wife was spared the strain that sharing his anxieties would have brought, she was subjected to another strain which he failed to take into account or even recognise. She was obliged to go along with his game that nothing was wrong, that everything when he was at Hope End was perfect, and she was obliged, too, to repress her own feelings about her loneliness when

From the schoolroom window, Henrietta's sketch of her brothers playing cricket

he was away. Only in her letters to her mother could she say how trapped she often felt, bereft of adult company for weeks on end and surrounded by eleven small children who seemed to leapfrog each other endlessly with measles and colds. Like most mothers in such a situation, she often felt she existed only to bathe hot foreheads and soothe coughing chests. Even writing a letter was a labour of Hercules – "I assure you it is by mere stratagem that I have scribbled thus far . . . here sits Alfred on my knee doing all he can to get the pen into his own hands . . . Stormy, George and Henry are running round the table . . ." Her only diversion was lengthy family visits paid by her sisters, especially Arabella (known to the children as Bummy). She was grateful, otherwise, if chance callers, not realising Edward was away, came on business and stayed to dine and play backgammon with her, as a Mr Hilton once did – "him excepted I have not seen a single soul since Edward's departure". It was all very well for Treppy to point out that Hope End, though secluded, was in "a very centrical situation to many gay places – Bath–Gloucester–Worcester –Cheltenham". These towns might as well be on the moon as far as Mary was concerned.

Yet Mary was not truly discontented or unhappy. Her children made her very happy and absorbed her – she was not the sort of mother who found their company tedious. On the contrary, she was keen to teach and stimulate them and made their education very much her prime concern. Nor was she easy to please. Sending one of Elizabeth's early efforts to her mother Mary commented, "This Elegant Scratch you will I know be glad to have . . . bad and illwritten as it is." Elizabeth recognised her mother's critical ability and begged her, "I hope you will tell me *exactly* the truth . . ." It was for her mother that she wrote little stories, which she asked her to buy "and if you would . . . write copys to be sold for the public". Mary controlled the schoolroom for many years and all the children found her strict. She would stand no laziness. She was annoyed with Bro for not concentrating: "we looked over some Maps yesterday with a very wandering and unsteady gaze." Once the older two boys were at school she supervised their homework diligently and was indignant if she thought they were not being well taught: "I am surprised to find that Sam's Latin exercise consists merely of *copying* from the grammar . . . which anyone can do who can write." Real application always pleased her. Stormie's progress was gratifying because he worked so hard on "the most advanced stage of exercises on the united noun adjective and verb". She was intensely ambitious for all her children. She wanted them to work hard, to have thorough educations and most of all to do themselves justice. Far from being a weak, feeble partner to the entirely dominant Edward, she was, so far as her children were concerned, a decisive presence in their youth. She guided them not only through their early lessons but into habits inculcated in her as a child. She made sure they realised that to help the poor was their responsibility. When Uncle Sam sent money, Elizabeth wrote back saying it had been spent on clothes for the poor and that they also intended "to have a soup shop for which they pay a penny a quart".

But in any conflict it was true that Mary's first allegiance was to her husband. When in August 1819 Edward wished her to accompany him to Foxley during an election campaign in which he was involved (though not a candidate) Mary went, though she "wished I had my dearest children with me", and stayed much longer than she wanted to.[9] She worried about not having news of them – "it is sometimes not sufficient consolation to believe no news good news." It did not help her maternal anxiety that Elizabeth wrote letters telling her "I felt TRUELY MISERABLE when you departed." But Mary saw her role as one, above all, of making her husband happy: she wished to ease his burdens and lighten his spirits. When he was at Hope End she noted with satisfaction that "our quiet and early hours seem to agree to admiration with dearest Papa". She encouraged him to play his fiddle and to sing and after a spell of such domestic bliss would report with pride "I never saw him look better in his life."

In such a mood, he could show himself staggeringly indulgent to his wife's wishes, as he did over a trip to Paris in 1815. The Napoleonic wars, which had kept English travellers out of France for more than ten years, had just ended and the Barretts were in the vanguard of the new wave of tourists. Mary described to her mother what happened as she and Edward were about to depart: ". . . dear Ba seemed so unhappy at our going that it increased my idea that it would be a material improvement to her to do so: and she jumped in the carriage with us." To her relief the nine-year-old Elizabeth behaved perfectly. She was not seasick on the crossing to Calais and arrived there in better shape than her father. At thirty, Edward had never been to Europe and was "rather rebellious" as Mary tactfully put it at having to give in to the Frenchmen who met their boat and insisted on carrying him on their shoulders through the shallow water to the pier. He did not speak a word of French, "a terrible deprivation" as Mary rightly said, and had to depend on his wife to be interpreter which did not please him either. But once they reached Paris, where Uncle Sam joined them, the holiday was a great success. Mary bought a new hat, and took Elizabeth with her to the Louvre. Eventually, Mary grew tired of Paris which in spite of its magnificence and excitement she found dirty, and wrote to her mother that she would be glad to get back to the "comforts of dear England". Unfortunately, on her return dear old England was found to have its share of dirt: "my dear Bro and Addles are suffering from the filthy complaint, ringworm on the head."

Naturally, Paris had made a deep impression on Elizabeth and she was only too eager to follow her mother's wish that she should capitalise on it. A French governess was engaged soon afterwards and Mary encouraged her daughter to write to her in French (even when they were both in the same house). Elizabeth found this hard but since she wanted both to become proficient and to gain her mother's approbation she struggled on, commenting (in French) that she was remembering her mother's words, "one day of hard work is worth two of idleness." Her own deficiencies in the French language annoyed her as she confessed to her mother: "I hope that you do not say oh there are always mistakes in

Elizabeth's notes but I hope that you will say well done my dear you do not always write so badly." To make writing more fun, Mary suggested Elizabeth should comment on the novels she was reading, all of which she had chosen for her. Mary, like Jane Austen and unlike most mothers at that time, approved of novels. Even in her imperfect, laborious French Elizabeth's own enthusiasm made itself felt. Mary had given her two of Maria Edgeworth's novels – *Patronage* and *Manoeuvring*, as well as Walter Scott's *Rob Roy*. What she made of them was revealing.

She liked *Patronage* but not *Manoeuvring*. Her taste was good. *Manoeuvring* was entirely to do with the desperate and too deliberately comic attempts of a Mrs Beaumont to marry her two children to fortune and titles. Elizabeth wrote, "Excuse me, I do not like at all Manoeuvring." She thought Mrs Beaumont a "silly woman schemer" whose strength went into "a servile ambition for gaining rank, for gaining wealth". *Patronage*, which she liked, was a strange novel to give to an eleven-year-old. It consisted of four volumes and contained long passages entirely concerned with detailed political plots. But it gave Elizabeth her first acknowledged fictional heroine in Caroline Percy. The admired Caroline – Elizabeth wrote that she was "perfection" – was beautiful, talented, clever, good, highly moral and most important of all devoted to her parents, especially her father. In the course of the novel she turns down three suitors before finally marrying the man of her choice. This is the excuse for long discussions on love and marriage: Caroline's view is that to marry without love is a crime. Nor is she in any hurry to find love and marry because she is quite happy improving her mind. The love of her parents is sufficient for her until she meets her ideal and even when she does, and gets married, she leaves her newly wed husband to accompany her father to a debtor's prison. (Elizabeth particularly mentioned loving this passage.) But as Elizabeth confided in her mother, Caroline, though perfection, was not a true heroine in the sense that Scott's heroine, Diana Vernon, was in *Rob Roy*. Diana was a lady after Elizabeth's own heart. She bursts on to the scene riding a black horse, with her black hair streaming in the wind. She is a female character far more powerful than any other in the fiction of the time. Whether or not Elizabeth understood all the machinations of the complicated plot, she certainly appreciated the originality of Diana. Diana's sentiments were also hers – "compliments are entirely lost on me" . . . "I can neither sew a tucker nor work cross stitch nor make a pudding." Diana studies Latin and Greek, thinks the library paradise and has it said of her that her knowledge was all the more extraordinary when measured against her total ignorance of actual life. As well as her spirit, daring and learning Diana has another noble attribute: her father is the most important man in the world to her and she proudly proclaims she will "never leave her dear father".

Novels were already, before Elizabeth was adolescent, her "most delightful study". They opened to her the contemporary world about which she had an insatiable curiosity and made her feel part of it. She begged her mother for more, vowing that far from preventing her reading more worthy books the novels would only serve to complement them and she would work harder at her lessons. Her mother did not doubt this: it was obvious that her daughter already worked very hard indeed. Both parents were proud of her intellectual tastes and did all they could to foster them. Unlike many a nineteenth-century set of parents they had no fixed ideas about girls' brains being inferior to those of boys – Elizabeth shared Bro's tutor and learned Greek with him. They knew she was clever and that she was perfectly aware of her own ability. But as she reached adolescence Elizabeth began to see the distinction between being a clever girl and being a clever boy. It could be summed up in one word: school. Boys went to school, girls on the whole did not, mainly because there were few reputable schools to which to send them.[10]

The day Bro entered Charterhouse School, in the spring of 1820 when Elizabeth was fourteen and he was thirteen, the difference between them was exposed for what it was. Sam was still at home, there were plenty of other brothers coming up behind him, but for Elizabeth an era had unmistakably ended: she was being left behind, treated differently. She stayed at home, never going anywhere except on visits to the family, those long extended visits nobody worried about because girls had no education to interrupt. Soon after Bro had gone, Elizabeth wrote to her father begging him to let her come up to London: "My dearest, dearest Puppy grant my request! ONE week in London! . . . Imagine yourself my age once more, how your heart would beat with joy at the prospect of an excursion to the metropolis!" Her request was refused. She was left to burn with envy of Bro, even though Bro was envious of her and left her with no illusions about life at Charterhouse. He told her that he worked till he sweated, was ever fearful of brutal canings and reported that his hands were "so cut and quartered with chops that I can hardly bend a finger". But Elizabeth cared nothing for such suffering when he was learning so much more than she was. Her suspicion that he was surpassing her academically led her to tell his old tutor that she was sure he could read Latin better than anyone in Britain now – something Bro denied furiously, saying it was an "atrocious, barefaced, unprecedented, impudent, abominable" lie. But she was not convinced.

Bro's being sent to Charterhouse was, of course, only one of the factors which influenced the change in Elizabeth from being a profoundly happy child to becoming an increasingly unhappy adolescent. Her own growth and development and an illness which left her weak and depressed made the period from fourteen to twenty a difficult one. But it was out of this "difficulty" that her poetry was born.

Chapter Two

THE Barretts, in Hope End days, were a healthy family. There were eleven surviving children, in itself no mean feat, and the recordings of minor ailments show that the general health of the family as a whole was good. Nobody in nineteenth-century correspondence ever seems to have been absolutely well, least of all the women, but the Barretts succeeded in this for long stretches of time, apart from childhood infectious diseases like measles and mumps. The only delicate child was Arabel. At the age of four she was left behind with her nurse Minny Robinson at Ramsgate, where the family had been holidaying. Minny sent back regular reports, often through Elizabeth to whom the four-year-old invalid tried to write. "Tell your dear Mama," wrote Minny of Arabel in November 1817, "her face is much better her Arm improves but very slowly. It is much less but still is stiff in the Joint she has not the least Pain in it and uses It very well but cannot touch her shoulder with it . . ." Mary was hopeful that Arabel would soon be home but the intended three extra months of sea air stretched into three and a half years. With memories of his daughter Mary's death at the same age, only three years earlier, Edward Barrett took no chances: he was quite willing to maintain a separate little establishment at Ramsgate if Arabel benefited. This kind of arrangement was unusual but not abnormal. Great faith was placed in the recuperative powers of sea air in an era when medical care was limited. In the summer of 1819, when the family were on holiday at Worthing, Arabel and Minny joined them there and again stayed on. They returned home at last in the autumn of 1820. Arabel was well for almost a year before all three girls fell ill.

The girls – aged fifteen, twelve and seven – all had headaches, pains in their sides, and suffered from "convulsive twitches of the muscles" as well as a general feeling of malaise. Arabel and Henrietta recovered quite rapidly but Elizabeth did not. Her worried father wrote to Mr Carden, a Worcester doctor, about her. He replied at some length. It appeared he had already seen the three girls when they first fell ill and that he had prescribed tincture of Valerian (a medicine made up from a common European plant and used in the treatment of neurosis at that time, though there is no evidence that it has any pharmacological effect at all). He now advised Mr Barrett to increase the dose for Elizabeth and get her out into the fresh air. He professed himself unworried – "I hope and expect you will see a progressive amendment . . ." – but added that if desired "a *tight* flannel roller" round the abdomen could be tried. This was in April. By June, still suffering from headaches and the pain in her side, Elizabeth developed measles. It was after this illness, still plagued by the other mysterious ailment, that Elizabeth began to show what would seem to be classic symptoms of hypochondria if they had not been so common among girls of her day. From the onset of menstruation, middle-class women were encouraged to regard themselves as delicate creatures who must take great care of themselves. Vigorous exercise was discouraged, rest encouraged. Every ache and pain was taken seriously.

At thirteen, Elizabeth had written to her mother that "my constitution and my appetite is as *bad* as ever" and referred to herself as having "natural ill health". This was the first mention of such a thing. All the available evidence, with the exception of occasional references to a cough, points to a particularly robust childhood. But at thirteen, Elizabeth decided she had "natural ill health" and when her spring illness of 1821 was followed by measles, she suddenly became obsessed with her health. (There is no mention of any fall from a horse at this point or of being kicked by one or of straining to saddle or mount a horse – all cited at one time or another as the reason for the onset of her invalidism.) She entered into correspondence with Dr Nuttall, her Grandmother Moulton's doctor in London, in which she described the "paroxysms" from which she was suffering. During them, her heart beat wildly and she swooned. These attacks were "agony" and came on several times a day. She also experienced constant pains around the right side of her chest which stretched round to her back. Dr Nuttall's theory was that it was all to do with the bowels. He urged her to show "no false delicacy" but to observe whether her bowels evacuated anything "clay coloured or greenish or blackish or frothy or mucous or yeasty. . ." To her anxious enquiry as to whether something might be wrong with her heart the good doctor said he doubted it, but kindly gave her a series of tests to carry out on herself. She was to time her pulse and her heart beats and report back. But he told her he was more inclined to think that her "active turn of mind and *inactive* state of body", together with her age, lay at the root of her sufferings. What he prescribed for her were mere purgatives. They did no good. Elizabeth languished until her father decided drastic action was called for and had her removed to the Spa Hotel in Gloucester where she could be under the care of the rising medical star of the region, one Dr Baron.

The Spa Hotel was in a green and attractive road on the fringe of Gloucester, opposite the spa itself. Here, a kind of family encampment was set up, enough rooms being taken, at considerable expense since the Gloucester Spa was fashionable then, to enable several relations to stay with the young invalid. Grandmother Moulton, Treppy and Uncle Sam took their turn as well as her mother and father, Henrietta and brothers and assorted Graham-Clarke aunts. Dr Baron examined her, confined her to a bed or sofa, told her always to use a pillow and, she wrote, on no account to get up until "VERY LATE". Though Dr Baron was the specialist, Mr Carden still visited her, and Dr Nuttall was by no means done with his correspondence-course cure. It was Dr Nuttall who told yet another specialist about Elizabeth's case. This was a Dr Coker who also visited and examined her. It was to this doctor that Elizabeth first seems to have mentioned that her spine felt "swollen". His résumé of her case was lengthy and more revealing than any other available. He went over the history of her illness, relating that it began, he was told, with a pain in the head which continued at intervals for seven weeks then transferred to various other parts of the body, finally settling "about the centre of the angle formed by the greatest pro-jection of the ribs, the umbilicus, and the anterior superior spinous process of the os ilium". This pain caused the troubling paroxysms which resulted in "convulsive twitches of the muscles" particularly affecting the diaphragm. There were on average three attacks a day but none at night. The patient's feet were cold, her pupils dilated, but the tongue was clean and her bowels unaffected (though "an aperient is required"). Dr Coker wrote to Dr Nuttall that he had written to Mr Barrett in "the hope of soothing" him and was of the private opinion that all three girls had originally "taken something deleterious" but, whereas the other two had recovered quickly, Elizabeth was simply taking longer. He really could not see that there was anything seriously wrong, and certainly nothing which corresponded to the invalid's complaint that her spine was "swollen". He examined her spine carefully and wrote, "this by no means seems to be the fact". He could detect "nothing obviously wrong with the spine".

Yet, paradoxically, he thought Elizabeth should be treated "as for a diseased spine" even though he said he had to "confess the positive proofs are wanting of the existence of diseased spine". He could find nothing else to treat. Her "uterine system", he noted, was "not materially affected", which was lucky since many nineteenth-century girls had their illnesses blamed on their wombs and suffered torment from the resulting treatments. So Elizabeth was promptly strung up in a spine crib – a kind of hammock – and told to wait and see if a spine disease would show itself.

It is at this point that it is first stated that Elizabeth was taking opium. She was only fifteen, but nobody considered this alarmingly young for such a drug to be administered. On the contrary, doctors advised opium from babyhood onwards in the form of cough medicines (Mother Bailey's Quieting Syrup, one of the most popular, was heavily based on opium). It was the equivalent of aspirin or paracetamol today. The form in which it was prescribed for Elizabeth, which was the most common form, was as laudanum. Opium, a hard, dry brown powder in its pure form (made when the gum from poppies dries out), was dissolved in alcohol to make it palatable and the mixture was called laudanum. Naturally, the strength of the laudanum varied according to the amount of opium (or morphine, an opium derivative) in it and according to the strength and amount of the alcohol in which it was dissolved. A certain number of drops were prescribed per day and if they were taken in water the opium content was further diluted. No doctor at this time states either Elizabeth's precise dosage nor how often she took it but at least it was clear why it was prescribed: to enable her to sleep.

This is not as obvious as it might seem because opium was used, confusingly, as both a stimulant and a sedative – it was the panacea for all ills. There were many contradictions in its effects according to the personality of the patient and their symptoms. Some patients instantly relaxed (Elizabeth was one of these) but others reported a feeling of heightened sensibility. For Elizabeth, in adolescence, it worked as a sleeping draught taken at night. From then onwards, she was never without it but it is likely that the dosage was weak because she showed none of the cumulative effects of large doses of opium taken frequently.

The entire Barrett and Graham-Clarke families followed the progress of Elizabeth's illness with the greatest concern and gave her strong support throughout it. Her mother, trapped at home initially because Henrietta had measles which was expected to sweep the nursery, wrote constantly "under the soporific dominion of a wet day and sick room". She was upset to hear Elizabeth had been "obliged to submit to Cupping" because she knew how terrified her daughter had been at the prospect. Cupping consisted of wiping the inside of a glass with methylated spirits, setting it alight then applying the upturned hot cup to the flesh (usually the back) where on contact it brought blood to just beneath the skin and therefore, theoretically, away from the affected tissues. It was used in the treatment of nephritis and also bronchitis both of which the doctors thought worth treating "as if for" in the hopes of eliminating the cause of the pain. Fortunately, in spite of the cupping, Elizabeth had decided she liked Dr Baron who was in overall charge. His orders – "great quiet and a recumbent posture" – met with her approval. She was not so keen on the cold showers he prescribed and did not like baths as hot as she could bear. Better results were obtained with the use of setons – a bizarre process consisting of passing pieces of thread or tape with a needle through folds of skin with the aim of discharging matter. Bro was on holiday from Charterhouse and staying with his sister in Gloucester at the time and wrote home cheerfully that this treatment had helped: "Hope speaks eloquently . . . with the delightful visions of returning health." The spasms were less frequent and appetite had returned. By the time it was her mother's turn to stay with her in September, three months after the move to Gloucester, Elizabeth was making even greater progress. Mary wrote home that although the pain in the ribs was still there at the end of each spasm, it was not as severe and these spasms were "the *mildest* yet seen". She was sleeping well (with the help of opium of course), and was in good spirits. Her father arrived in October and agreed that Elizabeth seemed much better, although while he was with her she had "some little difficulty in making water" and had to have a blister put on her back to aid "the Parts to do their proper office".

Neither her family nor her many doctors nor Elizabeth herself were really any nearer to knowing exactly what was wrong with her. Bro wrote to Henrietta that it was obvious she still had spasms, still had the pain and that none of the various treatments provided more than a temporary and sometimes illusory alleviation. He himself thought only "time and patience" would cure his sister. More than any of her puzzled family Elizabeth longed for a precise diagnosis of a precise disease: she resented deeply any suggestion that her suffering was in any way imaginary. She was enraged to be told to try to get better, as though she were not already trying to do so. She wrote quite bitterly to her mother,

"I HAVE exerted all my energy all my locomotive intellects all the muscular power of MIND and I HAVE found that though in some degree bodily anguish may be repressed from APPEARING yet it has failed to overcome." But by the autumn she was referring to herself as definitely having "a spine complaint", showing that Dr Coker's advice to treat her *as if* for a spine complaint had been only too successfully and dangerously followed. Elizabeth believed it implicitly and acted accordingly. Though she wrote to Henrietta, "I am unwilling to enter on the subject of my illness – it is an endless theme," she showed every sign of being unable to think of anything else, even though doing so made her feel "thoroughly unintellectual".

Mary tried hard to cheer her daughter up. Pregnant again, at the age of forty, with her seventh child, she was herself in need of cheer. She wrote to Elizabeth in November, telling her how she envied her sister Jane who had just married Robert Hedley and was on an extended honeymoon in Italy from where she had written to say she was on her way to see the bay at Genoa. "I have a longing," wrote Mary wistfully as winter closed in on Hope End, "to see that beauteous bay." She knew Elizabeth had too as she lay day dreaming in her spine crib, four feet off the ground.

Christmas that year was dreary at Hope End. The toasts on New Year's Day were painful to her mother, containing as they did so many hopes for Elizabeth. She told her daughter she preferred ordinary days because "when those we best love are not near the heart is most at ease when nothing occurs to excite its sympathies". Elizabeth, still in Gloucester, wrote gloomily to her aunt Bummy that "I fear many months must pass ere I change my position and tho' I endeavour to be as patient as I can yet dearest Bum the prospect is melancholy." What she failed to mention was that Dr Baron, expressing himself most tactfully, had told her that there was no reason at all why she should not return home, but she had declined the prospect because "illness casts a shade of apathetic gloom over scenes which in health and enjoyment were once so dear". She not only missed Christmas at home but spent her sixteenth birthday in the Spa Hotel, though there was no need for her to do so. Mary wrote her a poem in a trembling hand (Septimus had just been born) in which she called her "child of my fondest love" but Elizabeth stayed where she was, determined not to go home until perfectly well. In May, when she had been in Gloucester almost a year, she finally grew tired of waiting for this total recovery and returned to Hope End still convalescent. She could walk only a few steps after long months during which she had been immobilised most of the time in the spine crib. But it was now acknowledged that the "positive spinal disease" had not emerged. The doctors told her she could recover completely. The only activity they cautioned against was intellectual: excessive reading and writing were announced to be too exhausting for her debilitated constitution.

Elizabeth never believed this. As far as she was concerned, reading and writing were what made life worth living. Her enforced leisure had given her many extra hours in which to contemplate her future. Just before her illness, on her fourteenth birthday in March 1820, her father had had published *The Battle of Marathon*, her long epic poem in imitation of Pope.[1] The sight of these fifty copies with her work printed in them had marked the transition from liking to write poetry – which she had done ever since she was nine – to being a poet. The distinction was clear in her own mind. Suddenly, her life had meaning and she observed in an autobiographical fragment she wrote at the time, "Literature was the star which in prospect illuminated my future days . . . it was the spur . . . the aim . . . the very soul of my being." After she returned from Gloucester, the star burned brighter than ever.

She had learned Greek, with Bro, and now struggled to carry herself further into the language so that she could read all the poets she admired and benefit from them. Her past poetic efforts deeply dissatisfied her, even the ambitious *Battle of Marathon*, and her pleasure in writing family birthday odes certainly waned. The odes had originated in a joke of her father's who, when she was nine, had rewarded her with a ten shilling note in a letter addressed to the Poet Laureate of Hope End. Her mother explained what it meant and Elizabeth solemnly took the title seriously. From then on, Barretts were bombarded with odes. They were deeply gloomy in tone and spirit. Those to her mother always seemed to contain references to dead babies and watery graves, those to her father, though generally more cheerful, invariably described "Death's pale hand" hovering. Her brothers and sisters, whatever their tender ages, were treated to similar verses (Henry, at two, was given an ode inspired by Humility). In return, Elizabeth expected odes from them and duly received them. Bro was the only one with any wit and wrote some dashing, funny verses but grumbled about it being a form of slavery.

Elizabeth was well aware when she was writing her odes or verses or stories that she was straining to emulate those she admired and that she constantly looked to the accepted great for inspiration. Her desire to write went hand-in-hand with her love of reading, the one fuelling the other in a very obvious fashion. By the time she was sixteen and done with childish verse-making she had read, as well as the classics, Shelley, Byron, Keats and Wordsworth, of the more recent poets, and had been influenced by all of them. Her idea of a beautiful poem was Shelley's *Adonais* (published in 1821, the year of her illness). The poem was "perfectly exquisition" and Shelley one of those "sitting near the Gods without any doubt". His obsession with death was becoming Elizabeth's obsession, his way of bearing grief her way – ". . . on a cheek/the life can burn in blood even while the heart may break."[2] Nothing had made her heart break yet – the only death in the immediate family, apart from her four-year-old sister Mary's, had been that of her grandfather Graham-Clarke in 1818 to whom she was not close – but she instinctively anticipated what her feelings would be, how she would hold in her grief and pain. She continually analysed her own character and discovered things about herself she did not necessarily like. When she was twelve, she had written in a notebook a short description of herself which she entitled "My Own Character".[3] Remarking that "the investigation of oneself is an anxious employment" she went on to enumerate her faults. She was neither vain, cowardly nor obstinate but on the other hand she liked flattery, loved fame and was impatient. She hated needlework, drawing and learning the piano ("I sit down discontented and rise disgusted"). Above all else she knew herself to be of a passionate nature, only able to restrain herself by a strong effort of will. But three years later, at fifteen, after her illness and when Bro was at Charterhouse, she wrote another autobiographical fragment which was markedly different in tone.[4] She could no longer write proudly of being "very passionate". This passion she felt within herself was now a burden, the main struggle in her life was to curb, tame and hide it. She confessed how afraid she was of "the strength of my imagination which is now often too powerful for my control". It frightened her to admit that her mind "has ever been in commotion". She had forced herself to adopt a manner of "habitual restraint" which she knew often made her seem "to lack common feeling". Friends thought this, and she could see why, but knowing they were wrong gave her "a sort of mysterious pleasure". Equally thrilling was the strange feeling that "I always imagine . . . I was sent on the earth for some purpose". This was a nameless ambition so strong it almost amounted "to presentiment" that she would do something great.

Meanwhile, with the ending of childhood she was quick to mark her happy, carefree days as over: "my past days now appear as a bright star glimmering far far away."

This restlessness and depression, expressed in her notebook before she went to Gloucester, had increased by the time she returned home. During her illness she had also fallen into habits and attitudes – those of an invalid – difficult to shake off and which further complicated her outlook. She always said how she loved Hope End but now, at sixteen, she was far from content. As well as being frustrated with her own lot she was angry with her mother's. She had read Mary Wollstonecraft's *Vindication of the Rights of Woman*[5] and had told her mother she intended to support the author's conclusions. Her mother, amused, replied, "I would not put you out of conceit with it as long as it is your intention to belong to the sisterhood." What Mary did not appreciate was how, in her daughter's eyes, she herself was an example of a woman who suffered *because* she was a woman. Her daughter looked at her, forty-one with ten children and still not finished childbearing, and saw how the whole object of her life was to serve others, particularly her husband. From Elizabeth's point of view her mother's life was shocking and she did not herself wish to copy it. The child who had written, "I wish much to be like you," no longer wished this, if it meant having the sort of life she saw before her.

What Elizabeth was not mature enough to judge was the reciprocal love that existed between her parents. She was on the outside of it, a rebellious adolescent looking in and seeing only the external marks of what appeared to be her mother's total subservience to her father. "My mind," she had written in her notebook, "is naturally independent and spurns that subserviency of opinion which is generally considered necessary to feminine softness!" She saw that marriage was woman's fate and marriage meant subservience; therefore she was already beginning to despise the whole institution and reject it in favour of an alternative. The idea that, overwhelmed though she was, her mother loved her father and saw nothing subservient in either that love or her role in life was not entertained by Elizabeth. Love, romantic love, did not come into the equation she was furiously working out. Her views on women and their place in the scheme of things were still being formulated. Meanwhile, she was miserable and even bitter (about being a girl) and the sympathy she received because of her recent illness only fed her self-pity. But there are no indications that, at sixteen, she used her past illness and her continuing weak state as a psychological weapon against her family or that she wanted to be an invalid. Whatever the true nature of the illness that had afflicted her, she had spent a year of her life either in bed or in a spine crib and was debilitated from this treatment as well as from the malady. Her feebleness was genuine and her predicament no less real for being common. All female illnesses in the first half of the nineteenth century were supposed to be cured only if total inactivity was observed. This set up a vicious circle: the strictly enforced rest produced the weakness it was designed to cure and any possible physical improvement was more than cancelled out by the immense harm done to the mind. Women quite literally went mad with boredom (and it was boredom which had caused half their problems in the first place).

Bro, who wrote constantly from Charterhouse, became impatient with her. "Dab it but your a cool hand by Jove!!" he complained almost as soon as his sister was back at Hope End. "I have now written four letters and had from you ONE." He told her that now she was better he certainly was not going to write to her if she did not write to him – she *must* make the effort. His tone became bracing and jocular as he tried to coax her out of her depression. Her "impudence" he told her was "breaking out in fresh places and becoming more incorrigible than ever"; being in a spine crib four feet off the ground, he wrote, had only made this impudence rise with her head. Charterhouse was still painted in the most lurid colours to make it seem as unattractive as possible instead of that haven of scholarship she fondly imagined. "There has been another boy flogged most severely this week," wrote Bro, "a fourteen cutter for stealing a sovereign he screamed and bellowed most dreadfully . . ." Sometimes he sent her little presents: "I send you a very beautiful silver remember medal of Lord Byron which I hope you will value and preserve as it deserves, it struck my fancy last Saturday in Oxford St . . ." Teasingly, he added that maybe she would think it more like him than her idol Byron. When his efforts to amuse or please her met with no response he told her she should be "ROASTED" for her neglect of their correspondence. In spite of his joking approach Bro was deeply worried about his sister and sometimes could not conceal his anxiety. "I felt truly concerned," he wrote home after one holiday visit, "when I see so clear a proof of the great weakness which must yet exist in your legs and when I remember with what astonishing velocity they carried you downstairs on the memorable day when the school room chimney was on fire." But he tried not to refer to her weakness again, feeling that to dwell upon it was bad for her. Instead, he re-emphasised the horrors of Charterhouse, giving her detailed descriptions of the horrible food and his stomach ache after eating "some sliced, hard, dried beastly bits of beef with a sprinkling of cabbage passing . . . under the fashionable nomination of Bubble and Squeak . . ." The only mistake Bro made in his attempts to make his sister feel lucky instead of envious was in giving her details of all the hard work he had to do. It was unwise of Bro to groan over "the strict examinations in Homer" because that was what Elizabeth craved.

Elizabeth's letters back to Bro – far fewer, as he noted, than his to her – were full of only one thing and that was poetry. As she rarely went anywhere during the first two years after her return – not, as she was fond of saying, that there was anywhere to go – she could not give him any outside news and all the inside Hope End happenings were already catalogued by her mother and the rest of the family. So she talked poetry to Bro in her letters and told him what she was reading and writing. She also engaged him as her intermediary with literary editors as she began to aspire to publication in magazines and newspapers, a role Bro hardly relished, though he was happy to deliver his sister's manuscripts and letters. When Henry Colburn at *New Monthly Magazine* turned down one of Elizabeth's Greek epitaphs Bro wrote nervously, "I enclose Colburns note which he sent with the verses now dont be in a passion my friend Basy because all authors must meet with disappointment you know, I should advise you next time to send, a subject more interesting to the public." Later, that same summer of 1822, Elizabeth submitted some poems direct to Thomas Campbell, who had just taken over at the same magazine, and he wrote back at greater length. What he had to say was the first test of her own avowed liking for "genuine" criticism and she passed it without difficulty. He told her the poems were "the work of an inexperienced imagination" and that he objected "in general to its lyrical intermixtures" but he added that he would be "heartily sorry" if he were "to damp your poetical hopes and ambition". There was no fear of that. The sixteen-year-old poet grabbed her pen and sent Campbell another poem. This time he slapped her down smartly, saying he'd already been indulgent enough and adding he had "neither eyesight nor leisure" to go on criticising her work. Though it was a year before she dared to send anything else Elizabeth neither took offence nor gave up in despair.

She was still working hard at Greek verse, using Bro as her postal tutor. In response to her request, Bro gave her a lecture on hexameter verse: "An Hexameter verse consists of 10 feet, the four first feet may be either dactyls or spondees the fifth *must* be a dactyl the last *must* be a spondee, there must be three caesuras in every Hexameter verse . . ." But Bro's spell as his sister's mentor in Greek was coming to an end. In 1826, just after her twentieth birthday, Elizabeth published *An Essay on Mind* (at Treppy's expense this time). This was a much more ambitious project than *The Battle of Marathon* which, for all its cleverness, was only in the author's own words "Pope's Homer done over again or rather undone". *An Essay on Mind* was precisely what its title claimed: a poetic essay, in two books, on the qualities, elements and abilities of the mind. In her preface, Elizabeth challenged any idea that poetry was "not a proper vehicle for abstract ideas" or that it could not deal with "the argumentative". "Poetry," she wrote grandly, "is the enthusiasm of the understanding" and so it should "encompass everything". In the poem, she went on to justify her belief and in doing so demonstrated evidence of deep and wide reading. In poetic terms, her success was limited in *An Essay on Mind* – a heavy, pedantic tone imitative of Pope and Milton dominated the entire work – but with it she published fourteen shorter poems and here her own voice broke through. All these fourteen poems found admirers immediately. Her mother and father loved them (always important to her) and a distant cousin, the John Kenyon who had been contemporary with her father at Cambridge, wrote to congratulate her. He was a poet himself and also a wealthy patron of all the arts. He said that *An Essay on Mind* was "a bold attempt" but that what had delighted him were "the smaller pieces". Elizabeth was gratified but not half as pleased as she was when another admirer made himself known and, unlike Kenyon and everyone else, particularly praised *An Essay on Mind*.

This was Sir Uvedale Price, a classical scholar of nearly eighty who lived nearby at Foxley. He congratulated Elizabeth on her scholarship. She replied saying that she was overwhelmed but that what she craved was Sir Uvedale's critical comments rather than any congratulations. He promptly sent her a few observations and suggestions which was exactly what she had hoped. Eagerly, she pored over each criticism then replied saying she hoped Sir Uvedale would not think her presumptuous if she put up a defence. This she then proceeded to do, quoting Spenser and Milton and other classicists with the greatest of ease and breathtaking familiarity. Sir Uvedale, clearly astonished, told her she had "done right" in putting her case but that he was now, in turn, going to put his. And that was the beginning of what rapidly turned into a most extraordinary debate between a twenty-year-old almost entirely self-educated girl and a distinguished scholar of European renown. Elizabeth was at first feverish in her desire to prove herself, to show Sir Uvedale she was not just a girl who dabbled in Greek, someone whose learning seemed profound but was in reality shallow and showy. She marshalled the points of her arguments cogently, determined to show she knew her stuff. Told, for example, that the accents on some of her words fell wrongly, she was quick to cite her authority – "I think it may be observed that among our old Poets – Spenser especially – the established accent of a word is often changed with its position in a line" – and then she quoted exact instances from *The Faerie Queene*.

It was hardly surprising that in these circumstances of mutual intellectual pleasure Sir Uvedale wished to continue his dialogue with Elizabeth in person. He invited her to his home, Foxley, to her great consternation. She felt she could hardly refuse and yet she wanted to. Increasingly since her return from Gloucester she disliked social occasions other than those within her family, and even then nobody dreamed of inviting her to stay without promising, as her aunt Charlotte did, that she could have her "sanctum". On paper, she was extremely sociable; face to face, she felt constrained and ill at ease. This paradox fascinated her: she never tired of trying to analyse precisely why, on the one hand, she loved people and was fascinated by the minutiae of their lives and yet, on the other, could not bear to meet them. It was partly, she decided, that she lacked social poise (or felt she did). In her autobiographical fragment (at fifteen) she had said that "in society I am pretty nearly the same as other people only much more awkward much more wild and much more mad!!"

It was this self-styled awkwardness which now obsessed her. She was always referring to "one of my awkward curtsies" and bemoaning her inability to perform gracefully when "*obliged* to sing" at evening gatherings in other people's houses. So much of social life, she had decided, depended on affectation which she loathed. "What is called GOING OUT," she declared, "is the greatest bore in the world." She made a great fuss about going anywhere at all and professed exaggerated relief upon her return even if those who had been with her could have sworn she had enjoyed herself. Only if the attraction was great enough or the sense of obligation strong enough, as both were in the case of Sir Uvedale, was she prepared to push herself out of her house into someone else's. Even then, she almost always needed moral support. Henrietta, who never needed the least persuading, was ever at hand. In October 1826 they both went to Foxley. The visit passed off well but did not change her mind about visits in general. To her horror, she was made to accept an invitation on her own the next month to nearby Eastnor Castle, home of Lord Somers. She wrote to Henrietta that she had got on "*very ill*" without her. On her arrival, she was shown into the library which was occupied only by "an unknown gentleman" to whom she could think of nothing to say and that made her feel "even more awkward than I anticipated". Worse was to follow. After a formal dinner, there was music and "the conversation was down five degrees below *freezing*". The final humiliation was being made to sing. (She knew only one song – "Kathleen".) At eleven, when at last everyone retired to bed, she was sure it must be four in the morning. But at least when she returned thankfully home it was to find the previous visit to Sir Uvedale had been most fruitful: he had sent the proof sheets of his book *An Essay on the Modern Pronunciation of the Greek and Latin languages*, to be published the following year, begging her to read and criticise them for him. It was the ultimate accolade in her life at the time. She settled down to do so with enormous and unconcealed delight, perfectly happy to have real work to do at last.

She had by then decided that poetry, whatever language it was written in, was most certainly work. To write poetry was the most worthwhile work in the world because poetry was truth and there could be nothing more noble than trying to express universal truths. She did not feel shy about calling herself a poet – even when she recognised that she had only managed to produce "sickly poetry", she had absolute confidence that with time she would do better and that the struggle to do so was worthy in itself. A good poet was always "one of God's singers". Trying to become one of this select band was an ambition she was proud of and did not conceal. It had nothing to do with what she called "versifying", that scribbling in commonplace books so beloved of young ladies at that time. This she found contemptible and not to be confused with real poetry which was dignified, serious, sacred and pure. Her family accepted her interpretation of her vocation reverentially. Only her father was tempted to make the occasional facetious comment and he quickly came to appreciate that his daughter's poetry was no laughing matter. Nobody at Hope End sneered at or ridiculed the role of poet itself – in the first quarter of the nineteenth century poets were the most admired of all

creative writers. The end of the eighteenth century had seen the beginnings of the Romantic Revival, marked by the publication, in 1798, of
Wordsworth's *Lyrical Ballads*. In the decade of Elizabeth's birth Byron
published his first collection of poems (*Hours of Idleness*, 1807) and
when as a nine-year-old she was starting to write poetry herself, Shelley
had just finished *Queen Mab*. Playwrights no longer dominated
the literary scene though Drury Lane and Covent Garden were still
enormously popular theatres, and novelists, in spite of Jane Austen,
Richardson and Fielding, had not yet begun to do so. To be a "real" poet
was judged a most suitable occupation by Elizabeth's parents who had
no objections just so long as this did not tax Elizabeth's health.

By the time she was twenty-one and officially an adult – though
intellectually she had been mature since she was twelve – Elizabeth had
made a life for herself which might not be all she wished but which was
vastly preferable to the awful emptiness which had engulfed her during
her emotionally turbulent adolescence. She knew what it was to which
she wanted to devote herself: poetry. She had forced herself into
believing that this was enough to fill her life. But in this scheme of things
public acknowledgement was important: she was honest enough to
admit that it was not sufficient to write poetry but that having it read was
part of the process. It was more than that. Seeing her work in print
excited her and she did not underestimate the significance. Her excitement had nothing to do with feeling she was successful – she rated
popular success as shallow – but was more a feeling of intense joy that
here was tangible proof that she was communicating through her poetry.
The real thrill was attracting the attention of her peers, something she
positively craved. Stuck in Hope End in out-of-the-way Herefordshire she had no chance of coming into contact with any poets of
her generation now writing, such as Tennyson, Letitia Landon, Mary
Howitt, Thomas Hood and Richard Monckton Milnes. Her two books,
printed at the expense of relatives and distributed mainly among them,
came to the notice of few people. It was through publication in London
literary magazines and newspapers that she knew she could catch the eye
of other poets and those appreciative of "true" poetry. This, more than
anything, was what she wanted – to belong to that blessed company who
as she did regarded poetry as their being. To be known by them, to be
accepted by them and to communicate with them was what would give
her restricted life meaning.

Such recognition would also, though less importantly, give her work meaning in the eyes of her family who, though cherishing her talent and being fiercely proud of it, also needed the evidence that publication brought to show them that the world valued her. To have their own judgement endorsed by *New Monthly Magazine*, when it printed "Stanzas, Excited by Some Reflections on the Present State of Greece" in 1821, was reassuring. Each poem printed for public consumption and each new magazine which accepted Elizabeth's work was a victory for them all. *The Literary Gazette, The Globe and Traveller, The Jewish Expositor, and Friend of Israel* might not be normal Hope End reading but that did not matter: the Barretts were prepared to like and praise them all, if within the covers their daughter was acclaimed by the very fact of being printed. Her verses at this stage were unsigned but that was unimportant; *they* knew, and it added to the pleasure that it was a private one. Mary described in a letter to Elizabeth how her father had come into the drawing room as she was reading "Lines on the Death of Lord Byron" (which appeared on 30th June 1824 in *The Globe and Traveller*). With her best casual air, Mary asked him what he thought of the Lines and " . . . he said 'they are very beautiful indeed the only I have seen worthy the subject.' 'I cannot help thinking,' replied I, 'that we know something of the author.' 'They cannot be Ba's,' said he, taking the paper from me to read them again, 'tho' certainly when I first read them they reminded me greatly of her style – have you any idea they are hers?' 'I have a *conviction* of it,' said the conceited Mother, pouring out the tea with an air that threatened to overflow the tea tray . . ." Her mother, of all her family, was the most excited by her success. The publication of *An Essay on Mind*, even though the costs were underwritten by Treppy, convinced Mary that, as she wrote to Elizabeth, "you are launched on the world as Authoress." Thoughts of fame were firmly acknowledged; Mary began pressing for advertisements the minute she heard the volume was to appear. No parent could ever have been more involved in or delighted by the prospect of a child's burgeoning career.

Elizabeth's brothers and sisters were equally proud and impressed, though Bro risked being satirical more than once. He could not resist teasing her about her absurdly slow rate of output – how could she spend so long on one poem he wondered. "Your poem you say is coming on rapidly," he commented once, "and I am delighted to hear it but those hundred lines; they seem to me something like the hundred heads of Hydra except that your hundred lines remain the same through every letter from you . . ." And writing poetry, he observed, did nothing to sweeten her temper. Bro felt removed from the excitement which his sister's success was generating back home where copies of *An Essay on Mind* had arrived. Mary described the scene when it was announced that "a brown paper parcel was come for Papa from Worcester which '*felt very much like books*'". They were at dinner. Her husband went to get the parcel while she was obliged to wait, watching the butler "with his usual grace, stood at right angles with a napkin in his hand and the boiled leg of mutton and mince veal, nearly smoked their last . . ." In came Mr Barrett triumphant, book in hand, and declared, "There is your poem!" For once, Barrett standards were swept aside. The dinner remained untouched until a paper-cutter was procured and the pages slit open and then mouthfuls were eaten only between readings of the poems. In other rooms, the younger children – "for news ran like lightning . . . thro' the nursery" – were not content to wait their turn. Soon ". . . Seppy bounced in to say he wanted Ba's pome for Arabel and *them* . . ." When Mary joined "them" later, the twelve-year-old Arabel was reading aloud from her copy to an admiring throng. She thought the poems preceding the Essay "beautiful" but didn't understand a word of the Essay itself. Henry, aged eight, turned a few somersaults and announced he thought "every word of it was very nice indeed". Henrietta, already suffering from an inferiority complex, confessed later to her sister that "when I think who you are and what qualities you possess I am afraid I am going mad".

The minute *An Essay on Mind* was received, there was a rush by Barretts and Graham-Clarkes to make sure that booksellers in Ledbury and Gloucester, Newcastle and Cheltenham, Hastings and London – anywhere any family member lived or was staying – were well stocked. Mary wrote to Henrietta, who was staying with the authoress herself at their Grandmother Moulton's in Hastings, that "the poem cause quite a sensation in the North – nearly 50 copies sold in NC and more ordered". Grandmother Graham-Clarke had sent a copy "into Scotland" in the hope that it would do something for "the loved authoress's fame and pocket". A friend of hers sent two copies to Malta and a distant cousin sent one to the Netherlands. From London, family members wrote, "they all have *the* poem". Naturally, hopes of reviews were high. "What papers is it advertised in?" Mary asked Elizabeth. "I hope the London booksellers have copies: would that we could get it reviewed. I shall try if James has any means." James (Mary's younger brother) had not but, after a four month wait, two small reviews did appear. *The Eclectic*

Review mentioned it en passant saying, "this little volume is the essay of no ordinary mind – that it discovers considerable talents, informed by extensive reading no one, we think, can hesitate to admit," and *The Literary Gazette* said, "this poem is represented to be the production of a young lady and . . . we see much to admire." Not effusive praise, but it satisfied the Barretts. Mary was anxious that her daughter should understand what the publication of *An Essay on Mind* had meant to them: "there never was any circumstance, in the existence of your dearest Father or my own, that could afford us the same gratified feelings as this strong evidence that our beloved child has so well applied and cultivated the talents with which she is gifted."

Such fervent admiration was liable to turn anyone's head, but not Elizabeth's. She was remarkable in knowing, always, where she stood. She had no illusions about her so-called "success". It was not that she did not appreciate her parents' praise but that she knew they could not judge her work as she wished it to be judged. "No one," she had written, "can be more solicitous to obtain . . . a fair and candid criticism." To get that, she needed to assemble a body of work good enough to publish as a collection under her own name. She had grasped the nature of the publication game and was eager to play it. Publication brought recognition and recognition brought that company of her peers which she needed and wanted. This became her goal and gave her life a direction it had lacked: that nameless ambition to do something great was channelled.

Chapter Three

A T twenty-one, Elizabeth considered her life irrevocably set upon its future course. She was a poet, with two books published, drawing confidence and pleasure from the growing collection of her work appearing in magazines; she was a scholar, still working hard at Greek, reading widely and improving her knowledge through correspondence with other scholars; and she was a daughter, eldest of eleven children, involved in the collective life of a large and close family though choosing her role within it carefully. This role was not a traditional one. She taught the younger boys Latin but no longer pleaded to be nurse for a day or even an hour. She made it quite clear that being a poet was not a pastime but a serious, time-consuming business which did not allow her to be part of the household as her sisters were. And lastly she was, if not an invalid, a young woman known to be almost permanently in poor health.

By the time she was an adult it is no longer possible to assert that Elizabeth did not exploit this weakness of hers. In the four years since she had returned from the Gloucester spa she had resumed normal life, to the extent of getting up from her bed and walking around the house and gardens, but she had never again taken up any strenuous pursuits such as riding. She clearly relished the peace of her own room at the top of the house and the long, lazy mornings when she stayed in bed reading and writing. The exact nature of her weakness was not enquired into – there were no more visits from doctors. She was susceptible to coughs and colds but the main problem was this continuing mysterious "weakness". The whole family accepted it as a fact and conspired to protect Elizabeth from demands on her strength. This protection was certainly used by her to escape social duties – she neither liked to be visited nor to visit and her lack of strength gave her the perfect excuse – and there is no evidence of any positive determination by her to overcome her physical languor, as there had been initially.

She seemed, on the surface, content. Her main complaint was the lack of intellectual stimulation. Nobody in her day-to-day life could provide her with the quality of discourse she had in her letters to and from Sir Uvedale Price or Sir James Commeline (a local vicar, also a classical scholar). When she looked about at the people with whom her family socialised, she despaired. The Martins, the Cliffes, the Trants, the Biddulphs, the Paytons, the Knowles were all pleasant people but none of them could engage her mind on that higher plane she liked to inhabit. The little inter-house visiting she was compelled to share became more rather than less obnoxious the older she grew and she began to despise as well as dislike it. Sometimes there was a good deal of impatience and arrogance in her attitude. Forced to pay another visit to Eastnor Castle where the far from stupid Lady Margaret Cocks, the Earl of Somers' daughter, was always eager to meet her, Elizabeth raged at the "waste of time" this involved. She could not see the point of it all, describing to Henrietta the agony of "an hour's dull sitting" before dinner and then the boredom of having to talk to people with whom she scathingly said she had nothing in common. The greatest pain of all was "cards in the evening" which to her was "stupid". She preferred being at home even if this meant being pestered by Henrietta to do something for a church bazaar. The idea that she might meet some nice young man at Eastnor Castle never occurred to her. Sam was the brother who liked to tease his sisters about romantic attachments but even he could find no grist to his mill where Elizabeth was concerned. If she did meet any young men, she never mentioned them or only very briefly and dismissively. All her male friends were elderly scholars and her friendships with them conducted mainly on paper.

While she was on a spring visit to Eastnor Castle in 1827 Elizabeth received a letter from Henrietta which intrigued her greatly. It told her she had a new male admirer, a total stranger. He was a blind gentleman who had come to reside at Malvern. This was Hugh Stuart Boyd who brought to Elizabeth the kind of friendship she had long needed. He was married with a daughter and was four years older than their father. Boyd had studied Greek at Cambridge, where he began to write his own Greek tragedies. His blindness had not begun to threaten him until he was around thirty when he developed acute ophthalmia. Of independent means, Boyd never settled in any place for long – Malvern was only the latest in a long sequence of temporary homes. Learning that the author of *An Essay on Mind* was living locally he wrote offering his congratulations and expressing great interest in the work. It was the first unsolicited approach of this kind Elizabeth had ever received and as such was more valued than any other. (Sir Uvedale was a neighbour known by her family and John Kenyon was a relation, however distant.) Boyd was "hers". He was a scholar and poet himself, responding to her own scholarship and poetry, the first of those "like minds" out there in the greater world waiting for her. Within a remarkably short time she had formed a relationship with him of the greatest importance for her future.

When she replied to Boyd's letter, Elizabeth made it clear that what she wanted from him was help. She was grateful for the compliments he had paid her but wanted him to be her teacher. Cautiously, she warned him she could not meet him, partly because they lived too far apart (untrue) and partly because it was winter (it was in fact early March, the beginning of spring). These were transparently feeble excuses: she simply had no desire to meet new people until they had been well and truly tested on paper. Boyd rapidly passed all the tests. He responded precisely as she wished – lecturing her, correcting her, endlessly adding to her knowledge, flattering her by asking her opinion, arguing fiercely and in general providing the exhilarating company she had lacked. Soon he became bold enough to deviate from the discussion of Greek into those of a more commonplace, if still intellectual, kind. At the start, he had laid down conditions about there being "no confidences" between them but after a while, in direct contradiction, his curiosity about her and her family surfaced. Whatever he said, he was clearly fascinated by the Barretts. Few of his letters to Elizabeth survive but hers to him reflect the pressure Boyd exerted to have the rules and regulations that governed Hope End life explained to him, particularly regarding visits.

Elizabeth predictably took refuge in her health once summer had come and she could not cite the weather – "my health . . . is not bad; but deficiency in strength makes me quite incapable of much exercise" – but Boyd quickly sensed there was more to her refusal to meet him than that. Finally, she confessed the real reason was that her father did not approve. He said it would be unseemly: "my Father has represented to me that, whatever gratification and improvement I might receive from a personal intercourse with you, yet, as a *female* and a *young* female, I could not pay such a first visit as the one you propose to me without overstepping the established observances of society." Even that was not the whole truth. She was only too willing to hide behind her father's disapproval and use it to explain the inexplicable, her great desire to meet Boyd which conflicted with her dread of first meetings.

Six months after their correspondence began, Elizabeth had to admit to herself that Boyd had become too interesting to resist. One of the biggest obstacles to their meeting was her father's views on her health, views carefully cultivated by Elizabeth. For five years Mr Barrett had watched over his eldest daughter's precarious health with the greatest concern and sympathy. He had condoned her way of life – the excessive rest and seclusion – because he thought she needed such care. He had, on the whole, respected her wish to be excused social intercourse partly because he could see it tired her and partly because he disliked it, in most forms, himself. But now, as Elizabeth perfectly well understood, he was being asked to believe she was suddenly capable of riding several miles to visit a man she had never met. Her father would inevitably say she was not strong enough to do so. Anticipating this reaction, she at first took refuge in subterfuge, quite unable, out of embarrassment and appre-hension, to say she was as strong and fit as she wanted to be, and equally unable to admit the deeper implications of her wish to meet Boyd. She began to concoct plans for contriving to meet Boyd without having to ask her father's direct permission, which involved her Grand-mother Moulton and Treppy renting a cottage near him and thereby providing her with the perfect alibi for a visit. These plans came to nothing. Boyd, who thought the whole thing ridiculous, especially considering he was blind and married with a daughter of his own around Elizabeth's age, began to grow impatient and talk of moving on from Malvern. From being glad that her father's curious standards as well as his wish to protect her health gave her a reason for not visiting Boyd, Elizabeth now became frantic to persuade him he was being unreason-able. She forced herself to confront him and, once she had assured him she was well enough to meet Boyd, to persuade him also that a visit to Boyd was perfectly proper and even a duty. She emphasised that she wanted to meet Boyd only in order to learn more from him and that since he was suffering under such a permanent disability it was beholden upon her to go to him. Her father, deeply suspicious about whether she was really well, and of the likely consequences of her excitable state, was further distracted at that stage by his wife's illness. Mary was in bed, ill, both physically and emotionally. In November 1827 Grandmother Graham-Clarke had died very suddenly and Mary had been devastated. She wrote to a sister, "I never heard of my sainted mother's illness till I was told of her death." At the time she received the news, which prostrated her, she was suffering "very severely from rheumatism" but reflected "after all the long enjoyment I have had of health I cannot complain". But it made it difficult for Elizabeth to choose to leave her mother and indeed, in the circumstances, she did not want to.

By the spring of 1828, Mary Barrett was pronounced by Elizabeth to be "tolerably well", well enough to be left for half a day at least. She began again to plead with her father to let her go and meet her poor, blind, scholar friend who had been so kind to her over a whole year. Again and again she asked for reasons why it was not permissible. None were forthcoming, other than the original one she had repeated to Boyd. There was no argument: her father simply refused to discuss the matter. But then in March, soon after her twenty-second birthday, fate played into her hands. She wrote an account of what happened to Grandmother Moulton (but seems not to have posted it). One day, when she and her sisters were on their way to visit the Trants[1] in Malvern, they passed Mr and Mrs Boyd whom Henrietta and Arabel knew by sight. During the visit Elizabeth also went to a neighbouring house. Unknown to her, she was seen by Mrs Boyd who told her husband.

When she got home Elizabeth worried aloud that Boyd would know she had been so unkind and rude as to pass him on the road without acknowledging him. Her father sneered at her conceit, saying, "How could he know it was *you*?" But of course Mrs Boyd had known, recognising Elizabeth from descriptions she had heard and the other Barrett girls by sight. She had also seen her visit the Trants – curious, when Miss Barrett repeatedly told Boyd she made no visits. The next day a letter arrived from Boyd, a stiff, angry letter saying that if she were capable of visiting anyone at all, then it made nonsense of her supposed inability to visit him, a respectable, married family man. He added that in any case he had decided he would be leaving the area so she need trouble no more about visiting him. Elizabeth flew to her father and showed him the indignant letter, "accompanying it with a running commentary of my own feelings and wishes". The furthest her father would go was to say she could do as she liked. This was the only sort of capitulation he was ever known to make. Pushed into a corner, made to see his position was indefensible, Edward Moulton-Barrett could never bring himself to say either that he had been wrong or that changed circumstances had altered his opinion. But all Barretts knew that if he said, "Do as you like," this was tantamount to victory for them.

Overjoyed, Elizabeth snatched her opportunity. She was much too nervous to visit Boyd alone so persuaded Bro to accompany her and her sisters who were to go with her as far as the Trants to keep her courage up. All the way along the road from Hope End towards the ridge on the Malvern Hills where Boyd lived she was trembling "at seeing my unknown correspondent . . . in whose nearness and conversation I expected something particularly awful and abrupt". Her sisters tried, without success, to soothe her. Before they got to the Boyds' house, there was a very steep hill – the Wyche – known to need care on the descent. There was no drag chain on the light carriage but the girls assured Bro that it was quite safe without one and that they had negotiated the hill many times before. But as the pony began to trot down the hill the carriage pushed against its legs and the trot rapidly turned into a panic-stricken gallop. Bro shouted that no one was to touch the reins but Elizabeth, in her fright, grabbed them and they were all catapulted out onto the bank when the carriage over-turned as it whirled round a corner. Nobody was seriously hurt, but Henrietta damaged her ankle slightly. Luckily, another carriage passed at that moment and carried her off to the Trants. The other three trudged along, the girls very shaken, until they came upon the pony again, caught and held by some work-men. Bro was all for getting back into the carriage but Elizabeth was too scared so he tied the pony to a tree and gallantly put himself in the shafts to pull his sisters along. Hardly had he begun than they rounded a corner, and there were the Boyds. Elizabeth was appalled: "my frights of all descriptions made me tremble from head to foot." She was covered in dust, her hat was torn and she knew terror had made her even more ashen than normal. It was no good reminding herself that Boyd could not actually see her. She was trapped and there was no way out. She managed to dismount, introduce Bro and explain about Henrietta's injury, saying that of course the accident meant that their visit must be cancelled and her sister collected and taken home at once. She could think of nothing more to say. Boyd spoke not a word. They all walked to the Trants with only Mrs Boyd chattering away. Once there, they shook hands and all went their separate ways.

Mr Barrett was highly amused. He even accused Elizabeth of contriving the whole incident "for the sake of dramatic effect" and pointed out as evidence that she had taken care not to injure herself. Boyd was kinder. He wrote to her as soon as he got home, enquiring after her welfare: Elizabeth was touched. Now that she had seen Boyd, she was even more drawn to him. She thought him much younger looking than she had expected – "his features are good, his face very pale with an expression of placidity and mildness" – but also much more tragic. The "quenched and deadened appearance of his eyes" shocked her. His blindness now struck her as utterly pitiful. Twice she repeated in the account written for her grandmother that Boyd was "totally blind" as though it had never occurred to her before exactly what this meant. She found herself both moved and troubled by the realisation of his position: seeing him being led along, entirely dependent on the support and guidance of his wife, she admired him even more. She was impatient not only to receive help from him but to give it to him. She could read to him, especially Greek which few could manage. All the excuses she had flourished to explain her inability to visit – the weather, her health, her mother's illness, the lack of suitable transport – now became obstacles that must and should be swept aside by her own will power whenever humanly possible. Within a month, she had contrived another visit which passed off without a hitch and thereafter she managed to visit her friend roughly once a week throughout the summer. Mrs Boyd visited Mrs Barrett and Boyd's daughter, Annie, visited Henrietta. From being opposed to the very idea of Boyd coming within his magic family circle, Mr Barrett even became tolerant enough to go so far as to enquire after his welfare.

That summer was one of the happiest Elizabeth had yet known. Her friendship with Boyd developed along delightfully satisfactory lines as she discovered what he liked and disliked and she could "hardly trust myself to speak" when he soon let it be known he received "great comfort" from her acquaintance. Her own usefulness charmed her: she felt so privileged to be allowed to read Greek to him and worked hard preparing passages selected by him. But what increased her happiness was that as well as having a new friend to stimulate her she also had Bro at home. He had left Charterhouse at the age of eighteen and had returned home the year before. Among her other brothers and sisters Elizabeth had pleasant companions but none, as yet, her intellectual equal. Bro was that equal in her own opinion if no one else's. At fifteen, she had written as well as her autobiographical essay another entitled "My character and Bro's compared". Bro, she thought, was "more solid and profound" than she was and a far better critic. He reflected more than she did and depended more on reason than emotion. But she realised he had one possibly fatal flaw: he was "satisfied with mediocrity" whereas she "burned to excel". By the time they were both adults, Elizabeth accepted Bro's opinions as she did few others. There was no one else to whom she could show her poems and he was the only one who could appreciate Boyd's wit, displayed in his Greek verses. It made her very happy to have her brother always with her at Hope End.

But Bro was not as happy to be there. He seemed to spend half his life shooting pheasants and the other half acting as courier for his sister. The height of excitement was attending a political meeting in Ledbury. He and his father were passionate advocates of parliamentary reform and later great supporters of Hoskins, "our Hereford Reform hero" as Elizabeth referred to him. (When Hoskins was eventually elected in May 1831, Bro made a speech at the official dinner which was flatteringly reported in the local paper.) Bro read *The Times* diligently and was forever expounding on current matters of importance. He, his father and Elizabeth spent many evenings round the fire talking politics, discussing what was meant by "a free nation". Their ideas were similar: they all had a very clear notion of the right of the great mass of people to have a say in the affairs of the country thereby ensuring its democratic freedom. They had all been proud, too, when Uncle Sam was elected, in 1820, to the House of Commons to represent Richmond in Yorkshire (he had written to Elizabeth soon after that it was "the most blackguard hole a man can be found in"). But, though interested in politics on both a national and local level (he was a High Sheriff of Herefordshire before he was thirty), Edward Moulton-Barrett did not groom his eldest son to follow in his uncle's footsteps. There was no sign, even though he was now twenty-one, of his being groomed for anything at all.

What Bro was destined for was one of the many mysteries of the Barrett household. He was employed, to a certain extent, as paymaster of the estate during his father's absences in London. In May 1828 Mr Barrett wrote to Elizabeth, "you should demand of Bro £20 to forward to me here in order to enable me to pay and return to you". He was also to "give Mama what she wants to pay the wages that are due". In addition, Bro now taught the younger boys Latin, a task Elizabeth was glad to relinquish. But these two roles were hardly enough to occupy a young man of Bro's ability and no one doubted that his father had other plans for him. The popular guess was that Bro would be sent out to Jamaica to help manage the Barrett estates there. But he dreaded this, and his father had always been aware that Bro had no interest in estate management. Once, when Bro went to visit his grandmother in Hastings, his father asked him to report back "on the state of the Hop yards on his way to Hastings; but not a line from him have I received".

Bro did not seem to notice such practical matters. Uncle Sam did not think highly of his ability in general, writing to Henrietta while Bro was still at Charterhouse that he was cross with her brother for wanting more "cloathes" when he had plenty. He should not, thought Uncle Sam, bother his overburdened father with such trivial requests but, he added, "I excuse however anything from Bro, he neither knows better nor can he do better." It was a fairly damning indictment of the family's heir. Everyone agreed Bro was charming, fun, intelligent, well-read (if not in the same league as his sister) but that he had little sense of purpose or direction. It was expected that his powerful father would give him one.

Burdens sat heavily on Mr Barrett at the time. None of the Jamaican plantations was yielding the usual profit and, in addition, rumours of rebellion among the slaves grew daily more threatening. The famous law suit lingered on: the Jamaican court, after twenty years, had ruled against those who had challenged Edward of Cinnamon Hill's will but an appeal was being lodged and until it was heard nothing was settled. His brother Sam, who had resigned his parliamentary seat to go to Jamaica, initiated reforms on the plantations, but he also knew that in a sense he could only stem the tide. By 1830 the abolition of slavery was, it was generally felt, only a matter of time.

Mr Barrett was at the same time concerned about his wife, though reluctant to admit there was anything seriously wrong with her. Mary was forty-seven and she had not regained her strength since the birth of her twelfth child, Octavius, in 1824. After her mother's death, her low condition was attributed to shock and grief. Elizabeth had written to a family friend with an unexplained confidence supporting this view – ". . . the mind of my poor mother has subsided from the first agony of grief . . . she has been relieved though somewhat exhausted by her frequent bursts of tears . . . I do not think her general health injured." Mr Barrett would have no doctors but Elizabeth confessed, "if a decision respecting medical advice were to depend on *my* feeling and judgement *no* delay should take place in procuring it." When, some six months after Grandmother Graham-Clarke's death, Mary still had not recovered, her grief could no longer be held to be the cause. Mr Carden was finally sent for. He diagnosed rheumatoid arthritis. Elizabeth, writing in August 1828, said her mother was "very, very unwell". By September, she was less worried and wrote that her mother's illness was clearly not as serious as her own had been seven years before. When Mr Carden suggested his patient would aid her recovery by a change of air, everyone was pleased:

the crisis was over. Elizabeth, with her pronounced dislike of anyone at all leaving Hope End for any reason, was sanguine, writing to console herself that "the separation from her will not be a very long one". Mr Barrett made arrangements for his wife to go to Cheltenham, where she had often stayed, in the charge of her sister Bummy and Henrietta, before he himself left for London and the complicated business concerns which needed his attention.

Mary always enjoyed going to Cheltenham – only the thought of Elizabeth's "tearful eyes as I parted with her yesterday have hung somewhat heavily on my heart". But that ordeal over, the journey had been a delight. She had enjoyed everything – "the scenery, the roads, the carriage" – and she was sorry when it was over. Arriving at 14 Montpelliers Terrace she was a little disappointed to find it a bit of a back-water but quickly comforted herself with the thought that her "rustic brain" would survive better out of the fashionable hurly-burly on the main square. The house was perfect: "the beds luxurious and cleanliness unrivalled – pretty entrance with painted lamp – nice dining room and drawing room . . ." She felt "delightfully comfortable and well". Henrietta, who requested her silk band and shoes to be sent on at once, was delighted to find that she had no need to be constantly with her mother. Sam, still at Charterhouse, hearing how much better his mother was and how much Henrietta was enjoying herself, wrote, "I suppose the next thing I shall hear will be that Mama has been to one of the dashing Cheltenham balls and then I shall hear that you are gone off to Gretna Green with some dashing young man." In fact the next thing he heard was that his mother was dead.[2]

Mary died on October 7th, but Mr Barrett did not hear of her death until the next day. He set out at once from London for Cheltenham and by four in the morning of October 9th he was just outside the town. He stopped at the Plough Inn and wrote to his brother-in-law James. His mind at first was filled with urgent practical necessities. He wrote that he wished his wife to be buried in Ledbury, where their little daughter Mary lay, but was worried that the vicar might refuse because "he is odd and unfortunately I have been opposed to him". His next concern was for his "poor, bereaved children", in spite of his own torment which was bitter: "I cannot tell you what I have felt, to be deprived of one associated with everything that was in the way of a rational life and enjoyment for so many years . . ." His only solace, which was powerful, was religious. He firmly believed his wife to have had "the true saving faith which cometh from God alone". His head ached, he wrote, and he could not go on, except to tell James he was "beloved" because Mary had loved him. Before leaving London he had written to his children: "This morning has the afflicting dispensation of our Heavenly Father been made known to me . . ." The entire content of his letter to them was religious, the prevailing sentiment "Lord, not my will but thine be done, Thou knowest best." It read like a prayer, frantic and painful, desperate in its desire to find meaning in random tragedy. He dreaded most that his "beloved ones" would feel "without hope". They must not. He enjoined them to weep "but within bounds". They must remember that their mother was now with God to whom she had always belonged. Of his own feelings he could not, as ever, speak: "I can scarcely define my sensations, the blow is too recent." He was their "attached however afflicted" father.

During his frequent and often lengthy absences in London Mr Barrett had taken to visiting the newly built chapel in Regent Square where he greatly enjoyed the preaching of Edward Irving, the Scottish founder of the Catholic Apostolic Church. Irving's writings had been approved Hope End reading ever since 1823 when Elizabeth was given his "For the Oracles of God, Four Orations" by her father. She wrote to Boyd that although she could not recall "a single word" of it, Irving "as a Preacher" had "affected me more than anyone I ever heard" (though she did not say where she had heard him). Irving affected Mr Barrett even more. His sermons, which attracted great crowds, were dramatic, powerful and even frightening denunciations of the world. He believed God spoke through him and that he was an instrument of divine retribution. Mr Barrett's own religious feeling, always deep, became even more intense after the death of his wife. This letter to his brother-in-law was the first indication that Mr Barrett was beginning to interpret God's word in his own strange way. He was becoming obsessed with the idea that the world in which he and his children lived was corrupt and that salvation lay in keeping pure for the next world.

Elizabeth did not weep when told of her mother's death. She envied those around her who openly sobbed. Most of all she envied Henrietta, who had witnessed it. This was "the deepest affliction" of her life and it had taken away all feeling. She was mute. Sympathy was loathsome to her. Her grieving was an inward horror which she could reveal to no one. All around she saw the black clothes – her father had ordered heavy mourning for everyone, including the servants – and tear-stained faces and yet she could not be part of the general sorrowing. Her notes written to Henrietta, still in Cheltenham, on the 9th and 10th, immediately after receiving the dreadful news, were composed, stilted, frigid. She regarded the letters of condolence which began to flood in with indifference.

Watching her, Bro was alarmed. He noted that she read the letters from Cheltenham giving details of the death "without its producing the slightest effect on her". Her refuge was in reading books – the theological writings of St Gregory of Nazianzen (one of the four fathers of the Christian Church) and her bible. She accepted her father's advice to think of God as always right – ". . . all *must* be right since He doeth all!" But it was not until her father arrived home that she could begin to contemplate the future. He gave to all his children during this traumatic period the comfort, strength and hope that they needed and sought. He talked with them, prayed with them, encouraged them to believe that in their mother's death there was some purpose, that it was not as pointlessly cruel as it seemed. His own distress was kept hidden, but Elizabeth measured the depth of his agony silently and marvelled at his self-control. She knew he repressed his grief for their sake and acknowledged this: "it is an inexpressible comfort to me to witness his calmness." She, of all his children, knew what such control cost. She was inspired by his example: "my father's fortitude has assisted mine. After all, *his* is the greatest affliction and *he* has taught me to use exertion – and God had enabled me to do so successfully." She convinced herself that God had indeed shown mercy by releasing her mother from "disease and weakness" and in doing so had removed all the family from that wicked state of being "too happy". Being "too happy" was not what man had been put on earth for and it should consequently be guarded against. She was grateful that, unlike Sette and Occy who were only six and four, she had known the joy of having such a mother as theirs throughout her childhood. Everywhere she looked she assured herself there were more and more things for which to be thankful.

It was a brave response but unconvincing even to herself. Her mother's death was the first to put to the test Elizabeth's own personal philosophy, in so far as it had evolved by then, and also her religious beliefs. Both were changed. Her early poems, attached to *An Essay on Mind*, had already reflected her conflict about the nature of life. "Trust not to Joy," she had advised and had recommended the past as the only safe place. Memory had already obsessed her: she saw it as fighting with death to win ascendancy but losing in the end because "Life came by Death". Now she had to believe what she had put forward as a theory. If what she had written in these early poems were true – written when no death had touched her as her mother's did – she ought to be rejoicing, not inconsolable. But her adolescent crisis of faith, which had been relatively minor, had left her not absolutely confident that a belief in God's goodness explained and excused everything. She decided that what she had failed at the time to take fully into account was the question of divine retribution. Now she realised its power: "all the kindnesses and excellences of this earth must be paid for by grief."

She would not be caught off her guard again; from now onwards she was vigilant, forever weighing happiness against its built-in cost. In addition, it became an absolute rule of hers always to imagine that the worst would happen in any case where there was uncertainty. She felt her nature change. From saying she thought herself naturally optimistic she went to the extreme position of declaring, "There is no kind of enjoyment which one can have on this side of the grave without paying its price in pain." She never stopped calculating that price. For a young woman of twenty-two it was a bitter lesson to assure herself she had learned. It made her wary, cautious, much too suspicious. She lost the last of the spontaneity she had had as a girl. Believing that round every corner lurked some tragedy, she refused increasingly to risk going round any corners at all. Like her father, she reinforced her innate resistance to all change: keep everyone at home all the time and nothing terrible would happen. She reminded herself constantly that lightning had struck out of a clear blue sky and that therefore she must never look up and glory in such a sky again; but all her ambitions were to look skywards and find some purpose in life beyond mere existence. The resulting dichotomy within her was deeply painful.

No one outside her immediate family circle helped Elizabeth to fight her own despair as much as did Boyd, who treated her with great intelligence and an insight she had often suspected him of lacking. When he heard the news of Mary Barrett's sudden death he wrote instantly but his letter was put away with all the others which she refused to read. Her eventual reply, some weeks later, thanked him for "feelings which have already sympathised with mine". She appreciated both his reminder that at least she had not lost her mother in infancy and that her "remaining earthly consolations" should not be despised. His letter, she wrote, had soothed her and his "unaltered regard" comforted her. But Boyd realised diversion would be of more use than comfort. He adopted his best stern, schoolmasterly tone and urged her to study a particularly difficult text.

His instructions were precise and peremptory: "I should like to know what you think of Gregory as a poet. In the first passage, you will find a description of a storm at sea and a Prayer to Christ. Tell me what you think of them . . ." Elizabeth could not resist any request for her opinion. She began to read and concentrate on the selected poetry and in doing so filled her mind at least for a while with thoughts other than of her mother. By June, eight months after her mother's death, Elizabeth was once more visiting Boyd regularly and their friendship had entered a new phase.

So had her entire life. Mary Barrett, gentle and self-effacing though she often appeared, had been more of a pivot upon which the Barrett family life turned than the members of it realised. It was true that Mr Barrett had always been the ultimate authority but he had not been an ever-present one. When Mary died, the gap was enormous and obvious. Elizabeth was twenty-two, Bro twenty-one, Henrietta nineteen and Sam (who left Charterhouse soon afterwards) sixteen. They were the adults at home trying to re-adjust while their father was in London. They all had to assume new roles and relate to each other differently. Elizabeth simply reinforced her existing role: she was a poet and her health was delicate. Long before her mother's death she had established that it was her right to stay in her room at the top of the house and have nothing to do with the running of it. Nobody expected that she would now stand in for her mother. Instead, Aunt Bummy came to do that. Bummy was the same age as Mr Barrett, forty-three, and the only one of the four Graham-Clarke daughters who had not married. But Bummy was not like Mary, particularly where Elizabeth was concerned. Whereas her mother had smiled indulgently at her daughter's need to stay in her sanctum, and even encouraged her to do so, almost in awe of her, her aunt had no such feelings. She muttered that Elizabeth took more looking after than anyone in the house and she was not nearly as reverential about her poetry. But at least Bummy loved her and, equally important, she took charge. With her at Hope End, Elizabeth managed the transition from life with her mother to life without her better than the others on a practical level. This unwelcome transition was much more difficult for Henrietta and Arabel. Unlike Elizabeth, they had been involved, under their mother's direction, in domestic tasks which had to continue but which, until Bummy's arrival, seemed overwhelming in the responsibility they suddenly represented. But, though Bummy took this weight off their young shoulders, emotionally she could not as easily replace their mother. Bummy was very different. She had strong notions of duty and was much more decisive than her sister had been. Without Elizabeth's intellectual resources, her sisters were at first even more desolate than she was, and to them their father was not as great a consolation.

Elizabeth had always hated her father to go away. His absence frightened her, even when the house was full. Now, his trips to London became unbearable for her. Even when he was merely out of reach of the house – in the grounds, sawing trees – she was nervous and uneasy. If he rode to a Bible meeting in Ledbury or Hereford, she could not sleep until she heard him return. Any illness of his caused her not simply concern but terror – what would become of them all without him? She regularly wept when he went to London and then wept again with relief when he returned. If he came home unexpectedly, his arrival was made to sound like a divine visitation: "Can you imagine *part* of the surprise and happiness?" She repeatedly tried to make her father promise not to go away and when he neither would nor could she accepted the necessity of his departure with ill concealed reluctance. At this period, Mr Barrett was undoubtedly the less possessive of the two. His daughter's clear dependence on him was a heavy responsibility and even a strain. It was difficult for him to understand, since there was no justification for the insecurity she had apparently felt since childhood. She wrote of being left alone but had in fact never been left alone: when her parents were away together she had ten siblings and numerous servants at home with her. But Mr Barrett had always accepted that Elizabeth was unduly sensitive and, together with his wife, had consistently shown sympathy with her fears. He did not judge her as he did his other children.

But his concern was still primarily for his daughter's health; he had no desire to keep her captive. It was Elizabeth who holed up in her sanctum and refused to move except to visit Boyd. Mr Barrett, who had grown used to Boyd, prohibited visits to him only if Elizabeth was clearly ill. Apart from these excursions, she wanted only to stay at home. She craved her father's companionship, but she did not delude herself into thinking she could be a substitute for her mother. Observing her father minutely, she saw how much he missed his wife – "Papa seemed a little tired having only us to talk to" – and how great was the strain to be cheerful at all costs. She wrote that he wore "a thick mask of high spirits" and was aware that behind it was a troubled, lonely soul. She noted that his anti-social behaviour became, like her own, more extreme. His horror of visiting or being visited by anyone but the family (and sometimes even by some of them) grew deeper. If Elizabeth was feeling malicious, she would torture him by gravely insisting some visit or other was inescapable. Once, Sir John Conroy, secretary to the Duchess of Kent (Queen Victoria's mother), left a visiting card at Hope End after calling and finding Mr Barrett away. "I suggested," wrote Elizabeth to Boyd, "(out of spitefulness) that he clearly meant ... Papa to return the visit." Papa did no such thing.

The love and affection between Elizabeth and her father was at this time, on the surface at least, free-flowing and almost untroubled. Mr Barrett called all his children "dear and beloved" and did not hesitate to let them know how much they meant to him. He wrote in a letter to Elizabeth and Henrietta, "I know and feel the congratulations are due to myself in having been blessed above all desert with such dear beloved and affectionate children." They were his "pets". They, for their part, felt secure in his love. "I feel how dearly he loves us," wrote Elizabeth, but, significantly, she began to think he loved them "too well". His relationship with her was so harmonious that even what she clearly saw as his faults were presented in an attractive light. She was proud that "of all particularly particular people he is the chief" and gloried in his uncompromising nature. His anger against inefficiency and incompetence was notorious but when it operated on her behalf she was proud of him. Papa's sense of honour was the highest in the land and Elizabeth found it deeply impressive. There was, for example, the incident over the proposed publication of letters to Sir Uvedale Price after his death in 1829. Elizabeth, when approached by the person wishing to collect and publish the correspondence, had no objection but her father was outraged by her lack of any sense of propriety: ". . . the giving . . . possession of the correspondence in opposition or in ignorance of the wishes of the family upon the subject would be a dereliction of all I know you to feel towards the memory of Sir U.P. . . .' he told her. She ought, he added, to be "over-scrupulously delicate" in the matter and he found that even writing to her on the subject had put him into "a passion".

Passion, of course, was a quality Elizabeth realised that, like herself, her father possessed in abundance. He was capable of sustained outbursts of passionate anger which upset her not because they frightened her but because she saw them, correctly, as symptoms of extreme distress on his part. Fortunately, in the period immediately after his wife's death, Mr Barrett's diatribes were directed against church and state. It was easy to agree that some election candidate was a fool, easy to concur that some sermon had been wicked, easy to join in general condemnation of the government. Yet Elizabeth worried that her father appeared to have no other outlet for his violent feelings. She knew he was plagued by business worries (though of the particulars she knew no more than her mother had done). It seemed to her that her father had neither anyone with whom to share his burdens nor anyone with whom he could truly relax. He played with his sons when at home – cricket was his favourite game – and worked machinery on the farm but this eased only his physical tension. In London, he did not even have that sort of diversion. There, Mr Irving's extraordinary "hellfire" sermons were the only entertainment he allowed himself. His only close friend appeared to be his mother and when she died two years after his wife the blow was severe. From London he wrote to his family, themselves shocked, that "I will not speak of her whom we loved living and love dead, for I cannot venture on the subject". When he returned after the funeral to Hope End his face showed such evident pain that Elizabeth broke down in a most uncharacteristic fashion, unable to "resist natural grief". (Usually, extreme grief made her silent.) She was bound more than ever to him and could neither contemplate nor imagine ever leaving him. In this context, the changing nature of her friendship with Boyd seemed to her unimportant. But it was not. Death, her mother's death, had been faced and challenged; love, her first love outside the natural love of parents and siblings, had not.

Chapter Four

H UGH BOYD was the only man outside her own family for whom Elizabeth had ever cared but he was a safe recipient of her affections. Nevertheless, he was not quite so safe as Mr Barrett had come to believe. If there were only Elizabeth's letters to him upon which to depend, then the degree of attachment she felt for him would remain obscure: he would remain a scholarly friend who probably aroused no deeper feelings than admiration and interest. But Elizabeth kept a diary between June 1831 and April 1832 which makes it plain that, although she may not have been in love with Boyd, in the generally accepted sense of that phrase, love was there and its presence, its alarming presence, recognised by her.

Contrasting what Elizabeth wrote to Boyd in her letters with what she said about him in her diary is a painful business. The ruthless honesty of the diary underlines the extent to which she was performing every time she composed a letter, however apparently direct the letter might seem. There was no pretence in the diary: it was intimate, confided in, the only place she could release the tension she was experiencing. In her first diary entry, 1st June 1831, she is filled with anguish because she cannot decide whether Boyd does or does not like her to write to him. She worries over whether she has made it too plain how much it matters to her that Boyd should stay in the area: "could I help appearing so when I was so? Could I help *being* so? Had I felt a less strong regard for him I should neither have *been* nor *appeared* –". The writing is tortuous and angry, the tone distressed. She despised herself for caring so much what Boyd thought about her but could not stop herself from minutely analysing his every word and expression and reading significance into them. The difference in attitude between letters and diary revealed itself on June 22nd when she wrote him a delightful letter, apparently in the best of spirits; but on the same day she was consumed with fury in her diary because Bummy had said, "really *all* the young ladies in the neighbourhood seem to me in

[56]

the habit of going to see that poor man." Elizabeth did not see herself as a competitor but on the other hand, since she had sworn the diary would contain "the thoughts of my heart", she had to admit that Boyd did seem to play her off against Miss Henrietta Mushet, Miss Heard, Miss Steers and even her own friend Miss Eliza Cliffe (who was currently painting her portrait). She railed against all of them, and against Boyd, in her diary. "The society of that Miss Hurd is as much valued as mine – as much! *at least as much*." Boyd had excused himself from walking out with her because of what he felt was his untidy appearance but "Miss Steers walks out . . . he is not afraid of disgracing *her* by his slovenly appearance".

But her real venom was reserved for Henrietta Mushet who, like her, could read Greek. In November, she assured her diary she would no longer go to see Boyd at all if Miss Mushet were there because "shant be wanted and *wont* be wanted", though she denied contemptuously Annie Boyd's malicious and unbearable allegation that she was jealous because she suspected Miss Mushet knew more Greek than she did. "If her knowledge were double what it is," Elizabeth fumed, "I should not be jealous of that." Impatiently, she waited to hear that Miss Mushet had departed but instead came a message from Boyd which she found unbelievable: "Mr Boyd . . . expresses himself 'sorry at my not having come over yet, *as*' (what force there is in some words!) 'he wishes the two rival Queens to meet!'" She cried with humiliation: "the coolness of Mr Boyd's expressions and the indifference he shows about writing to me went to my heart; and when I was in the room by myself I could not help shedding actual tears. He did not deserve one of them – and yet *they were shed*." She was forced to meet Miss Mushet or look churlish. It helped only a little to discover that she was "five foot ten and plain". Elizabeth was five foot one and pretty.

Yet there were times when Boyd seemed to care for her and made her very happy during this generally unhappy period. Rumours that Hope End was to be sold had begun the year before but, true to form, Mr Barrett told the family nothing. As usual, he saw it as his job to protect them from all unpleasantness, to keep them out of any difficulties he was in: he was their father, it was up to him to make decisions. In the case of selling Hope End, the shame and distress he felt were acute: he had failed his family. Elizabeth and all his other children and the entire anxious household knew that "perhaps" Hope End was to be sold because of some terrible financial reversal to do with Jamaica. Where they would go if the rumours turned out to be true, nobody knew. To ask their father outright was both unthinkable and too simple. In this atmosphere, it was a relief for Elizabeth to get away for a few hours and forget the threat hanging over her. There were days when she left home before breakfast (enough in itself to arouse comment, given that her normal rising hour was noon) and rode over to Ruby Cottage, ready to be with Boyd as soon as he had been shaved. She would remain closeted with him, while his wife and daughter came and went to see to his needs, reading Greek to him and discussing what had been read. Boyd was sharply, fiercely critical and she relished the rare chance to pit her own intellect against a worthy opponent. If their friendship had been solely intellectual, she would have returned to Hope End satisfied but she herself was aware that her feelings of frustration when she left Boyd arose because she was always expecting, and failing to receive, something more. She knew it was unreasonable of her to do so. Boyd was giving her what he had offered: he was teaching her, sharing his scholarship with her, feeding her hungry mind. But she was looking for her own warmth to be reciprocated. She wanted an emotional response, a spiritual recognition that was entirely lacking. Boyd's coldness appalled her. "I am not of a cold nature," she reminded her diary, "and cannot bear to be treated coldly." Furthermore, "when cold water is thrown upon hot iron, the iron *hisses*." Unfortunately for her own peace of mind, she rarely gave vent to any actual hissing in Boyd's company. More often, she hissed in her diary and then cried. It was very unusual indeed for her to "speak out". The nearest she came to it was in July when he had kept her waiting for hours before admitting her to his room. During the waiting she had "sate and sate and talked and talked and thought and thought until I was boiling over". The people she had been obliged to spend this time with were Mrs Boyd, Boyd's sister and a friend called Nelly Bordman. When Boyd eventually condescended to call her in she wrote that "I could restrain myself no longer – and overflowed – gently, with you seem to have thought a great deal about what *they* like but very little about what *I* like!" (This was because Boyd had said he thought the ladies would be enjoying her company.) It was not much of a reprimand but this "hissing" made her feel better, although she was proud that she had managed to control her real passion and remain cool.

What she could not conceal from herself was how easy it was for Boyd to hurt her. He had only to tell her that her sister Henrietta had a much nicer voice for her to be upset even though she knew this to be true. She knew she was being "morbidly and foolishly sensitive" but she could not help it. Boyd had her in his power. Her aunt Bummy recognised this of course. It was Bummy who suggested that perhaps Elizabeth was overestimating his need of her. Bummy had stayed at Hope End for a year after Mary Barrett died, returning eighteen months later, in May 1831, to find her niece obsessed by Boyd. She asked Elizabeth if she had ever considered she might sometimes be outstaying her welcome at Boyd's house. Elizabeth was furious and said in her diary that she had replied that, if she thought Boyd did not "like my going *very often*", then she would not have dreamt of going at all. Occasionally, when a visit to Boyd was for some reason or other cancelled, Elizabeth on her own admission went into "near hysterics" with disappointment. Bummy saw and understood rather more than Elizabeth liked. She wrote bitterly in her diary that Bummy could "see through a post" where Boyd was concerned. What Bummy saw did not please her. She saw that Elizabeth was making herself ill over a man who was not only unobtainable but also unworthy of such devotion and most probably unaware of it. It upset Bummy to witness her niece making herself so vulnerable. In August, Elizabeth wrote that she had been "goose enough" to tell Bummy she and Boyd had been quite alone in the evening on her last visit learning lines from *Prometheus*. Bummy declared Boyd's conduct, in allowing such intimacy, had been "ungentlemanly and disgusting". Elizabeth was "lighted up into a passion" at this absurd allegation and afterwards reflected she could not understand "Bummy's evident aversion to my dear friend and everything and body connected with him". She was shocked when Bummy even went so far as to refer to "those nasty Boyds".

It was not only the perceptive Bummy who was becoming heartily sick of Elizabeth's adoration of Boyd – so was Henrietta. She objected that Elizabeth now despised all their other friends and thought only Boyd worth visiting and talking to. Whether her sister liked them or not, in Henrietta's opinion the Martins, the Trants, the Cliffes and the other local families were part of their social circle, offering the only social life available, the life Henrietta liked and needed, those teas, dinners and all-too-rare parties which Elizabeth scorned. "Henrietta always wishes to go everywhere," Elizabeth wrote disdainfully in her diary, and, "I wish Henrietta would estimate people more by their minds than she actually does and that she were not so fond of visiting for visiting's sake." It annoyed Elizabeth that Henrietta tried to push her into an active social life when ". . . I do not attempt to oppress her with my influence". The socially acceptable pattern of visiting infuriated her and so did the role society decreed for young women like herself and Henrietta – one to which Henrietta was happy to subscribe.

At twenty-five years of age, Elizabeth knew what society expected of her: marriage, sooner rather than later. Marriage, motherhood and a domestic life. During the period covered by her diary she liked two novels in particular which dealt with this topic so absorbing to her: the fate of the clever girl who does not wish to marry. One was *Self-Control* by Mary Brunton, published in 1810, and the other *Destiny* by Susan Ferrier, which had just appeared in 1831. In *Self-Control* the heroine, Laura, has an indecent proposal made to her by a handsome colonel: that she should be his mistress. Laura, who had expected an offer of marriage, is revolted. The whole novel is taken up with Laura's determination to remain pure. The only love she wants is her father's, the only love she feels is for him. She is "hopeless of happiness" in any other respect until she meets a young aristocrat her love for whom she struggles to deny. In the end, she grows to realise that passion is as much part of love as "spiritual sympathy" and marries her young man. Elizabeth approved of *Self-Control*. It was "well written and interesting" and showed "a combination of fortitude and delicacy" which "always interests me in a particular manner".

She liked *Destiny* even more. Reading it made her forget Boyd's coldness for at least two days. It is a story about marriage, its dangers and pitfalls, and Susan Ferrier leaves the reader in no doubt that her own view of marriage is cynical. Elizabeth felt exactly the same: her own experience, extremely limited though it was, had been enough to show her what a mockery the institution of marriage normally was for a woman. She dreamed sometimes that she was married herself and it was always horrible. "I dreamed last night that I was married, just married; in an agony to procure a dissolution of the engagement," she wrote in her diary. "Scarcely ever considered my single state with more satisfaction than when I awoke! – I never *will* marry." But on other days this would be qualified to a less vehement "Certainly, if ever I were to make up my mind to marry I would fancy my selection to be an angel at the very least."

She saw few signs of men being angels around her. None of her brothers were angels. She might adore Bro but knew he was not angelic, and nor was Sam. One night in September, Sam was brought home from a cricket match "in an irrational unchristian state" – drunk. Henrietta, who woke to hear her favourite brother being carried upstairs, was "very much frightened". She was so disgusted she said she would not speak to him for a fortnight but Elizabeth thought this was silly. She was proud of her own tolerance and worldliness, writing, "Nobody is immaculate; and young men are more inclined to a fault of this kind than to many others: and our sullenness wd. no more do good in such a case than Xerxes' whipping did to the sea." She did not admire such behaviour; it was merely excusable in young men who were tiresome anyway. "It is very extraordinary", she reflected pompously in her diary, "but I never was acquainted with a *young* man of any mind or imagination . . ." (presumably excluding Bro). Young men were simpletons who only served to annoy. One in particular currently annoyed her, Dominick Trant (the very distant Barrett cousin who lived nearby with his widowed mother). She had known this young man most of her life but in his twenties she thought he grew "very forward" and that he was "gliding into a taste which is most unmanly and ungentlemanly – that of exciting confusion of countenance *in order to enjoy it*". Dominick took a delight in making her blush, teasing and flirting with her until he had the satisfaction of making her look "confused". This was labelled "impertinence" and found "quite intolerable". She wanted none of it. Let Henrietta get excited by such attentions; she would not.

She was not, all the same, totally immune to personal compliments though she tried hard to be. It hurt (though only the diary knew) when Henrietta's looks were admired more than hers. Boyd told her how pretty someone had thought her sister. Elizabeth wrote, "She *is* certainly – very pretty." There were few aspects of her own appearance which pleased her, though she was not vain enough to worry. She liked her own hair, thick and dark, and her eyes, large and brown. But she did not like being quite so small and thin and she detested her high, squeaky voice. Clothes interested her more than she cared to admit publicly: she was always thrilled when her father sent or brought her new things to wear. But she was contemptuous of women who spent hours on their appearance and contemptuous too of those who whiled away hours with so-called feminine occupations. Henrietta incensed her when she spent almost a day binding music: "after consecrating about twelve hours to the binding business Henrietta's music book is bound almost as well as if she paid 6s. for it. How much is time worth? Sixpence an hour?" There was an arrogance in this attitude: the implication was that she had better things to do and so ought everyone else to have. It made her hard to live with for those like Henrietta who always humbly conceded to her sister and consequently under-valued herself. What Henrietta failed to appreciate was that this kind of righteous anger was also a symptom of her sister's own discontent: she might not bind music books all day but she was no more satisfied with her lot.

Elizabeth had long since passed through her feelings of contentment at being a poet, working hard, with no need of anything other than family life and her friendship with Boyd. Her ambition and restlessness had begun to plague her again almost as much as it had done in adolescence. The present failed to interest her: she was always, she told Boyd, "enjoying the past and dreaming of the future", and was accused on all sides of "*never enjoying the present moment*". But what was there to enjoy? She felt more and more sure that Hope End would be sold – there had been a letter from London which had made her father turn ghastly pale – and less and less sure that Boyd even noticed her. He was definitely leaving, in any case; by the spring of 1832 he was tired of Malvern. That would leave her with the irritating Trants, the annoying Cliffes, the Martins (with whom she said she did "not amalgamate") and Lady Margaret Cocks whom she "dreaded like a thunderstorm". And what future was there to dream about? It looked empty and black. She reflected that all her good luck in life seemed to be over and that she might as well give up hoping for a change in her fortunes. She knew that the first thing she ought to give up was hoping for any change in Boyd before he left.

In the spring of 1832 Elizabeth's diary reveals that her greatest need was some assurance that Boyd cared for her. It was a hideous weakness in her own opinion but she could not help it. For a proud young woman, who thought herself above "feminine frivolity", it was mortifying to have to admit in her diary, "I wish I had half the regard which I retain for him impressed on this paper that I might erase it thus [an ink blot]." But she could not deny that regard and could not erase it. She remembered how replies to her letters had come readily only a year before, whereas now she had to wait days and even follow one letter with another before he wrote back to her. Sometimes when she visited him, he would ignore her: "would he have had the paper read to him when he could have talked to me – *at one time*?" A year ago, on a walk with Bummy and her sisters, she had played the game of "trying our fate by daisies": picked the heads off as she held them in a bunch, reciting "il aime – un peu –

beaucoup – point du tout. And there are the degrees of my philosophy –
un peu – beaucoup – *point du tout*!!!" Now she was even more sure
Boyd did not care for her at all. Henrietta, who was unwise enough to
say that she thought it improper that her sister should care more for Mr
Boyd than for anyone outside her family, was furiously corrected. Boyd
was merely her "dear and intimate friend", her only one. But she was not
even sure of that. "It is evident to me sometimes that to have me with him
is his greatest happiness," she wrote in her increasingly over-burdened
diary. Yet on some days she felt "it was evident from his manner that he
would prefer me being out of the room. So I went – of course! Went – of
course!" She resolved to "ice over" her letters to him and make her
behaviour equally cool. Both resolutions were immediately broken. She
could not play a part she did not feel, could not go against her own
nature. And all the time she was confused, self-doubting, emotionally in
turmoil. She still missed her mother desperately and missed too the love
she had so unstintingly been given. "I would barter all other sounds and
sights . . . for the love, the exceeding love which I never, in truth, can find
again."

Her father saw what a fever she was in. He dreaded intensity in her, of
any sort. It was bad for her, he felt, to become over-excited, it would
undoubtedly make her ill. The year before, she had seemed so well. At
the start of her visits to Boyd she had enough energy to think nothing of
scrambling up and down the steep path from the road to his cottage. She
had mentioned in her diary, in the course of 1831, such feats as climbing
"a very high railing with rather a deep ditch at the other side" (to escape
a bull) and "cantering" on her pony as well as walking "miles" on a
picnic outing. One observer who was on an outing with her and some of
her family to the Herefordshire Beacon in September had even remarked
to her brother Sam, after watching Elizabeth "run and slip" down the
hill, "what immense spirits your sister has". She had put this proudly in
her diary, agreeing she felt about ten years old. But by the following
spring the joie de vivre had disappeared. Worry over Boyd's feelings for
her coupled with concern about the still rumoured departure from Hope
End combined to make her nervous and depressed with the usual result
of loss of appetite and energy. Mr Barrett, who had a liking for simple
and obvious solutions when situations were at their most complicated,
decided that his daughter's sudden return to poor health was connected
to Boyd and would improve if Boyd were removed from her life. He
began to object once more to the frequency and duration of her visits to

Boyd: "What! You were there yesterday – and did you write today?" Recording this outraged query in her diary Elizabeth added that when her father then asked her, "What for?" his question was "unanswerable". She knew her poor health gave her father apparent justification. She was, she confessed, becoming a shadow through reading long, difficult passages of Greek to Boyd. When she asked permission to go and stay from Monday to Thursday with the Boyds, in order to write out an essay for her friend, her father refused to give it. He said she looked "worse and worse". On a recent visit to Mrs Martin she had fainted "fairly away" and felt "very, very unwell". While her sisters were out riding she had experienced an attack of "fainting and hysterics". Miss Commeline had told her "½ of me has vanished away in thinness".

It is impossible to over-emphasise how tension of any kind – pleasurable excitement just as much as unpleasant – had an immediate physical effect on Elizabeth. She was, as she described herself, "intensely nervous". The response of her body to the state of her mind alarmed her. Delight as well as dread made her heart race, rapture as well as fear could make her faint. The explanation for this lay in her vivid imagination: she could empathise so completely with a sufferer, for example, that she could feel their pain. It was this acute sensitivity which made her a good poet but the penalty was that it also made her the victim of her own violently experienced emotions. When she was mentally in turmoil, her body was affected. She did not wilfully choose not to eat but was simply incapable of forcing down food. Anorexia nervosa, the first of the female nervous disorders to be labelled in the nineteenth century, was not identified until 1873 but there were elements in Elizabeth's response to her father's ban on seeing Boyd so often which make it tempting to think such a diagnosis correct. Naturally, her inability to eat, with the resulting loss of weight and fainting, enraged Mr Barrett and, as is usual in anorexia, his rage only made Elizabeth feel even less hungry. It was hardly surprising that her father, Elizabeth wrote, was "in a panic about me all at once". She had to cajole and plead with him to allow her to visit Boyd at all: he accused her of holding a pistol to her head. He granted it only because he knew what she did not: Hope End *was* to be sold. They would be leaving and her relationship with Boyd would suffer a natural termination.

Mr Barrett's faint hope that his brother Sam, out in Jamaica still, might come up with some last minute rescue plans for their financial state had been dashed. Sam had enough troubles of his own without saving his brother's fortune. His young wife Mary had died in July 1831, then in the spring of 1832 there had been a slave rebellion. The complete abolition of slavery was reckoned only to be months away and when it finally happened Mr Barrett thought they might as well sink the island of Jamaica: it would be finished. He knew that the cumulative effect of the long law suit, the poorer production rate and lower price of sugar, and the insurrections of the slaves meant that he must face his future as a moderately rather than an extremely wealthy man. He needed to cut back at once. Hope End was his biggest asset and its upkeep was the greatest drain on his depleted finances. To sell it was the sensible solution but it cost him dear to be sensible: his anguish, as all his children knew, was greater than their own. Hope End, and the life that went on there, had been his creation, his bulwark against the world. By selling it, he sacrificed his own security.

As soon as Elizabeth realised that she would be leaving Hope End, she thought only of persuading Boyd to move with them. He had been on the verge of moving for some time now: what could be simpler than to arrange to go wherever she was going? But, unfortunately for her plot, she had no idea where that would be. Her father, as usual, told her nothing. She read the signs, as everyone at Hope End did, but the signs were contradictory. He went to look at houses in Epsom but said nothing. When he was with the family, his good humour was so evident that Elizabeth shrewdly deduced that it did not arise naturally but from his determination to protect them by making them think that all was well. In the middle of July, there was a new red-herring: he went off to Devonshire. Elizabeth was not fooled by his cheerful words – "God bless you my love – I shall be with you again early next week" – even though he smiled as he said them. She noticed "his voice trembled". Her father's visible emotion was immensely distressing to her simply because it was so extremely rare. She knew that he prided himself on never showing emotion, especially not misery. For Mr Barrett to be seen to weep was too horrible to contemplate because of the loss of face it would mean to him. Confronted with her father so near to breaking down Elizabeth's one thought was to help him preserve his dignity: it was this anxiety that prevented her and everyone else from ever questioning Mr Barrett directly. All his children conspired to let him keep them in the dark not out of fear but out of respect and love. To challenge their father was to distrust him; to suggest he was failing them seemed cruel.

He returned on the 24th to tell his family they were going to Sidmouth.

Elizabeth wrote to Boyd that she was amazed; Devonshire had never been thought of by any of them. At least this laid to rest the most alarming rumour, which Bummy had told them was foolish, that they were all going to Jamaica. Devonshire, if surprising, seemed more attractive than Brighton, Eastbourne, Bath, the Isle of Wight and Wales – all mooted at one time or another – but knowing their destination did not give them any clue to the other big question: when?

The summer of 1832 dragged on and Elizabeth reported in her diary that her nerves were torn to pieces. She could hardly endure people coming to look round the house. Bro was furious and attempted to have one party of prospective buyers thrown out but the agent with them flourished his ticket of entry and could not be denied. He and the rest of the family crouched in an upstairs room, obliged to listen to the footsteps and vulgar laughter of the interlopers as they invaded the premises and made crass observations. An advertisement in the local paper told them what their father had failed to say: Hope End Mansion, adapted "for the accommodation of a Nobleman or Family of the First Distinction", was to be auctioned on Thursday 25th August at twelve o'clock.

Elizabeth's misery was complete. All around her were the happy memories upon which she survived: to move from them was to murder them. She had enshrined her childhood there as perfect and had wiped out entirely the memories of boredom and frustration. She could not be philosophical about leaving: fear gripped her, fear of the unknown where nostalgia might not be able to sustain her. The only way she could deal with the approaching calamity was to bow her head, submit, and remind herself that any open distress of her own would deepen her father's sense of failure and humiliation. It was her chance to show him that she stood by him. She wrote in her diary that her dread of upsetting her father "outgrew" all other fears. It was for his sake that she forced herself to concentrate on what she could take with her instead of what she was leaving behind. She still had her books, her "studious tastes" and best of all her family. It occurred to her, too, that "dear Papa's mind . . . will be more tranquil perhaps when he is away from a place so productive of anxieties."

At least there was not the additional agony of leaving Boyd. He had already left, to go to Bath. The letter telling her was read by Elizabeth "with many tears". She wrote back, "Oh Mr Boyd! I thought it would end in some way like this. I DESERVED it to end so . . . I often looked too much for comfort to you, instead of looking higher than you . . ." She begged and pleaded with him to forget her – "I entreat you never, never as long as you live . . . you will never never have another friend whose regard for you can be stronger or truer or more incapable of change than mine." He had asked her to visit him, when she was moved and settled herself, but she announced, "it is impossible". She was fatalistic: "what is done is done".

After Boyd left, Elizabeth stopped keeping her diary, which had in any case begun to disgust her, but in her letters to him she mentions her new way of trying to deal with her unhappiness: she was reading the Bible in the original Hebrew. This provided her with suitably hard work to take her mind off the coming upheaval but did not console her as a certain novel did. The novel was *Corinne, or Italy* by Mme de Staël (published 1807), which she had already read twice but to which she found herself returning to escape the stress she was suffering. *Corinne* describes a life far removed from Elizabeth's. The Corinne of the title was a famous poetess, actress and musician, idolised by all Rome. The novel contains enormously long discursive passages on art, religion and philosophy – all of which Elizabeth enjoyed – but the greatest attraction lay in the character and status of Corinne herself. She scorns conventions, is happy to travel with her lover without a chaperone, and values her free life too much ever to sacrifice it for love, although she is passionate by nature. Corinne leads the life she wants to lead according to the dictates of her own heart and not of society. But praiseworthy and enviable though this was, what most inspired Elizabeth about her was Corinne's career as a successful poetess. Corinne's life was the fantasy not just of Elizabeth but of a host of nineteenth-century aspiring female writers; the fact that in the end Corinne's lover marries someone else, and she dies, made not a bit of difference. Corinne had dared and won; she had broken out of the domestic, subservient role, and gloriously fulfilled herself and followed her own passionate nature to the bitter end.

While waiting to leave Hope End, Elizabeth was too disturbed to think of any self-fulfilment through creative work. Reading Greek and Hebrew and translating *Prometheus Bound* were easier ways of occupying her exacting mind. She wrote little original poetry at this time though occasionally she would be inspired ("Caterina to Camoens" was one instance). The chaos in the house affected her, even though she was away from it all in her sanctum, lying in the window looking out over the green trees to the even greener hills which shut her out from the world she had escaped for so long. She was worried about her books because her father "particularly desired us to take as few as possible" and half of these had to be lesson books for the younger boys. Only one box of her own was allowed to go to Sidmouth, the rest were to be stored until Mr Barrett decided on a permanent home. There was no room for any novels. After her packing was done, she returned to day dreaming, trying hard to shut out the noise of workmen hammering packing cases together. Her mind was full of "the desolating changes" which had fallen on her since her mother's death began the tragic sequence. But in keeping with her resolution to bear up for her father's sake she wrote to Boyd in her last letter from Hope End, "We *intend* to be very happy at Sidmouth." She held out the hope that soon she might be writing to him "more chearfully".

The departure from Hope End on 23rd August 1832 was not as traumatic as the days leading up to it had been. The rooms, stripped of furniture, were pitiful but somehow less theirs: Elizabeth discovered to her surprise that Hope End, beloved though it was, *was* just a house. Five cartloads of possessions had gone to the warehouse the week before and the noise of "hammering and men walking up and downstairs from morning to night" as the rest of their belongings were crated up further de-personalised the proceedings. When the morning of August 23rd dawned, Elizabeth was ill with apprehension. She could not bear the thought of saying goodbye to her suffering father and wished they could all leave together and never look back. But he was staying with Bro to supervise the final removal. Elizabeth was glad when, at the last minute, he also kept ten-year-old Septimus with him to be a comfort (Sette often slept with him).

The dreaded farewell over, the first hour of the journey proved the worst as one by one the familiar landmarks slipped past but, once through Ledbury, the agony subsided. After Gloucester, new sparks of interest were ignited, almost shamefully quickly. Elizabeth had always wanted to travel, even when paradoxically vowing she never wanted to leave Hope End. Now, forced into it, she was immediately stimulated. At Bath, the half way mark in their 130-mile journey, they stayed the night. She thought the town beautiful though dismissed the whole of Somerset as "hideous": how anyone could call this real countryside she could not credit. Devon pleased her more. As they rattled along the narrow lanes with their high hedges she admired the occasional thatched cottage and the many flourishing gardens. Sidemouth was pronounced a pretty "nest among the elms". She thought it small and "not superfluously clean" but the house Mr Barrett had taken was large and comfortable and best of all had a drawing room whose four windows directly overlooked the sea. Elizabeth was entranced by the sea, declaring it "the sublimest object in nature". She could, and did, spend hours just looking at it. The perpetual motion of the waves and the constantly varying colours of the water excited her. At Hope End, her view of green and yet more green had made her feel safe and secure but it always had a somnolent effect. Now, staring at the dramatic, ever changing sea, her heart literally beat faster. She paid it the greatest compliment in her power by declaring she was "almost as fond of the sea as of poetry" because the sea was "visible poetry". Every prospect seemed brighter: perhaps they really would be happy here without needing to pretend. Elizabeth wrote to Mrs Martin on August 28th that they all felt "inexpressibly relieved" and that the entire family was now "calmer, happier than we have been for very long". Most significantly of all she wrote in another letter two days later, "I am sure we shall be far happier than we have been for more than a year."

Chapter Five

THE Barrett contingent settled down quickly at Sidmouth and Elizabeth was indeed soon able to write "more chearfully" to Boyd. They had arrived at the height of the holiday season, finding the little seaside resort busy and lively. There seemed to be something of advantage for everyone except Bummy who, Elizabeth confessed, "does not seem *delighted* with Sidmouth". The younger boys were ecstatically happy on the beach. They were out all day long, standing up to their waists in the sea with their shrimping nets "looking like professors", as Elizabeth described it. Henrietta unfortunately had toothache when they arrived and was confined indoors with a swollen face. Arabel had taken to swimming in the sea (she kept this up even in December) and to sketching with the help of a sketching master. Sam, the resident Barrett male in charge, had no difficulty finding parties to attend. By the time Bummy had left them, and their father and Bro and Sette had joined them in September, Elizabeth and the others all looked extremely well. Elizabeth even boasted of her good health to Mrs Martin (with whom she had rapidly established a regular correspondence, finding that absence made her "amalgamate" better with this family friend whom she had said in her diary she did not like). "I am certainly much better in health – stronger than I was and less troubled with the cough," she wrote. She put this improvement down to the air and the bracing sea walks they all took as a family along the sea-front, Mr Barrett being a great walker. They also took donkey rides and enjoyed boat trips to Dawlish, ten miles away. It was little wonder that Elizabeth slept better than she had for ten years and that her appetite improved. Henrietta, in case Mrs Martin was still in any doubt, stated categorically, "Ba is no longer an invalid." There was a corresponding improvement in Mr Barrett's health and spirits. His only complaint about Sidmouth was, as Elizabeth told Mrs Martin, an odd one: "he complains of not having fish enough." He stayed with them until just before Christmas 1832 and

Elizabeth bore his eventual departure well: "as there is now no cause for very very long absences we ought to bear the short ones patiently."

But for all the health-giving properties of Sidmouth it did have one serious drawback. Bro and Sam might find plenty of parties and Henrietta plenty of people to visit (though once the season ended she was quickly dissatisfied with the general calibre of the residents) but for Elizabeth there was no one of any interest. She wrote sarcastically to Boyd that "so much quadrilling and cricketing" went on in Sidmouth "nobody can doubt its intellectuality". About eleven families had called on them but she could not be intimate with any of them: "They call on us and we call on them and then we bow when we meet them . . ." It was dreary and disappointing. Henrietta went to a ball and was "danc'd into a fever by a most animated German and came home at a quarter to three in the morning" but Elizabeth did not want such diversion. She wanted someone with whom she could talk and learn, someone as passionate about scholarship and poetry as she was. Writing to Boyd was no substitute for visiting him. "I suspected months ago that the pleasure which you once seemed to have in hearing from me was much lessened," she wrote to him in November. She was remarkably open about her feelings, explaining, "the charm of my intercourse with you was the power of communicating with a person who could feel like me and with me and of saying within myself – *I cannot tire him*". Now she felt she was doing just that, tiring and boring him. He seemed to her to waste endless pages upbraiding her for not visiting him in Bath. She felt he was angry with her when he had no right to be. Her explanation for this was painfully self-deprecating. "I have observed," she wrote, "that people in general who like me best have liked me better at first than afterwards." The fault, she concluded, "must be in me somewhere". Quickly, she finished this embarrassing self-analysis and passed on to what was always safe, a discussion of Euripides.

As usual, she turned to studying as a means not so much of escape as of satisfying her mind, filling it to capacity to block out the kind of rambling, repetitive thoughts about her own situation in which she now hated to indulge. She set herself once more to finishing the Old Testament in Hebrew. An earlier vow, made in her diary before she had resolved to try to like Sidmouth for her father's sake, was repeated – "I will seclude myself there and try to know nobody and like nobody – but live with my books and my writings and dear family." Yet another routine had been established, much like her Hope End one except that it included afternoon exercise but lacked the visits to Boyd. Every bit as much as her father, she concentrated on being self-sufficient within her family and her work and like him she made this effort appear entirely successful. Her pleasures were books and nature. Only one person in Sidmouth made any impression on her. He was the Reverend George Hunter, minister of the Marsh Independent Chapel at Sidmouth.

Elizabeth first heard him speak when she accompanied her father to his chapel. Mr Barrett liked Hunter's preaching "extremely" and so did Elizabeth, though it was a pale shadow of Irving's in London. She described him to Lady Margaret Cocks as "a very eloquent and scriptural preacher who is at once a man of literature and acquirements and a humble unassuming Christian". His preaching was not only eloquent and strong but had some current of feeling running through it with which both Elizabeth and her father identified. Coming into contact with him as she did, in the company of her admiring father, made him from the beginning an approved friend. Hunter had a daughter aged seven called Mary.[1] It was unprecedented for Mr Barrett to initiate friendships but he came as near as he could by making it clear that his daughters could invite Hunter home and offer to teach his daughter. Elizabeth, with two other ladies, also had his blessing to accompany Hunter to Bible meetings as far afield as Exmouth (they did not return until 1.30 in the morning). She discovered that although fiery in his sermons Hunter was otherwise "gentle and humble and simple minded". But what pleased her most was what she described as "a *feeling* (not that cold word *taste*) for poetry and literature". She was quite surprised to find him strongly critical of some of her Greek translations because he "sensed painful effort in them". Within a few months she had grown to like Hunter so much she was advertising his virtues to Lady Margaret Cocks (who, like Mrs Martin, had suddenly become a confidante now that Elizabeth did not actually have to see her) and trying to get her to find pupils for him to teach. She described him as "a gentleman of very high attainments and intellect" and "a dear and esteemed friend of ours".

But Hunter was never in any sense as important to Elizabeth as Boyd who still continued to plague her thoughts. Her hopes of resuming her former relationship with him were raised at Christmas when he moved to Sidmouth with his wife and daughter. She had been against such a move for his sake, feeling he would like neither the place nor the rather uncomfortable house he had taken, but could not of course prevent herself looking forward to it. When Boyd, whom she had not seen for four months, arrived, her pleasure was marred almost immediately by her realisation that she had not misinterpreted the tone of his letters: something *had* changed and she had to struggle to come to terms with it. It took her a long time to realise that perhaps it was not Boyd who had changed but herself and that because she was different she was seeing him differently. She decided she had been absurdly melodramatic in thinking that life without her beloved friend would be insupportable. It had not proved so. Now, when she was once more seeing Boyd regularly again, she decided she had been a little deluded. He was not after all the perfect friend. He was too self-centred, too demanding, not nearly sensitive enough for one of her tender susceptibilities. She pitied him but was no longer desperate to measure his regard for her. She felt the more powerful one, the protector, and her energies went into being indignant with his wife and daughter for not looking after him properly. She had never sounded more like her father than when she wrote to Mrs Boyd, "I certainly have been unable to see poor Mr Boyd so solitary in this strange place without wishing you had determined otherwise than you did." (Mrs Boyd and Annie were still in Bath where Annie conveniently fell ill, delaying their arrival.) In case Mrs Boyd might miss her point, Elizabeth added sharply, "I have been unable to help thinking that as soon as Annie was strong enough to attend Bath parties she was also strong enough to come here." She, Elizabeth Barrett, understood duty to parents better, she implied. In general, she was rather appalled to remember how large Boyd had loomed in her life and when, after a year, he returned to Bath, where his wife and daughter were happier, she accepted his departure with equanimity. The nature of their relationship had changed forever.

Other leave-takings upset her far more than Boyd's. In November 1833 three of her brothers left Sidmouth inducing in her feelings of panic. All departures induced an exaggerated response from Elizabeth. Her tears and faintings if any of her family were going away had always been the greatest encouragement to them to tell her nothing and skip the goodbye scenes. Perfectly aware of how embarrassingly melodramatic her behaviour was, she could only plead an over-awareness of the perils of travel. There was some justification for this – travel was perilous, especially to Jamaica (ships were regularly lost) – but she herself knew this was only part of the explanation for her panic. The truth was that her approach to all farewells was morbid: they were a rehearsal for death. She imagined never seeing again the person to whom she was bidding goodbye and could not control her terror. Perhaps, like her mother, they would never return. In the circumstances, it was no wonder Mr Barrett kept any news of approaching partings a secret. He spared those leaving as well as Elizabeth herself. Everyone was relieved to escape the terrible fuss, quite enough to make the traveller feel doomed before he had stepped out of his sister's room.

She wanted none of her brothers to go anywhere, for whatever purpose. It was only just bearable to have her father commuting between Sidmouth and London but to have Bro, Stormie and George all disappear was too much. Bro's departure, though it had been likely for a long time, naturally upset her most. He was twenty-five when they moved to Sidmouth and far too old not to be leading a more useful life. She knew that it was almost inevitable that he should be sent to Jamaica to learn to manage his inheritance but had always hoped this would go on being deferred. But Uncle Sam needed help. He was facing the approaching drama of the emancipation of the slaves – royal assent was given to the amended bill in September 1833 – and anticipated a crisis. Mr Barrett dreaded telling Elizabeth that the time had come for Bro to assume his responsibilities as eldest son but was aware that, providentially, his daughter was in a state better able to stand such a shock than she ever had been as an adult. It was a good time, if there could ever be said to be such a thing, for Bro to go. Mr Barrett practised a little subterfuge all the same, merely saying, at the beginning of November, that he was taking Bro with him to London for a couple of weeks. At the end of this fortnight, Bro sailed on the *David Lyon* from Gravesend to Jamaica. Mr Barrett was pleased with how she took the news, writing afterwards to his brother, "Our beloved Ba, upon the colour I put on the project, namely as being profitable to Bro's interest, has consented in a spirit that has if possible raised her still higher in my estimation . . ." Elizabeth herself wrote that a shade had passed over her heart but "it was otherwise willed by God". She bowed her head and submitted once more, reminding herself of the folly of being "too happy".

Her father, though she did not know it, was far more worried about Bro than she was, knowing exactly what temptations he would meet there. He worried about the climate and about the type of society, with all its evil habits, in which the impressionable Bro would mix. He wrote to Sam, "May the Lord keep him from the evil effects of both." He told Sam he had written a note to Bro "wherein I begged him to be more guarded than I am given to understand he is . . . I do not like to hear of his long rides in the broiling sun and perhaps subjecting himself also to the Evening Dews . . ."[2] Far from expecting Bro to toughen himself up, Mr Barrett told Sam that he wanted Bro to "get a gig or Phaeton to convey him. I beg you to procure such a conveyance for him immediately and let me see it in my account." He was also liberal towards his son, telling Sam to "supply him with what money he may require . . . he may feel some delicacy about this, I hope you have or will speedily anticipate his application to you." Sam wrote back that Bro was doing well: he had been impressed by his nephew's intelligent and astute reports on the estates which he had sent him to inspect. Mr Barrett expressed himself "gratified not a little" and felt vindicated in his sending of Bro. Clearly, the boy was developing much more satisfactorily out in Jamaica with proper work to do than he had been while hanging about his sister in Sidmouth.

Stormie and George, then nineteen and sixteen, did not go so far but Elizabeth resented their departure "notwithstanding the manifest advantage of such a plan". They left Sidmouth to go to Glasgow University – Glasgow because it was attended by Dissenters and Dr Wardlaw, under whom the boys were to study, was an Independent minister, a fact which met with their father's approval. Elizabeth was glad that George, though younger, was accompanying Stormie who, with his stammer, needed someone to give him confidence. (This was Mr Barrett's intention.) The only advantage in the sudden male exodus was that there was more room. But without the three elder boys Elizabeth was devoid of the kind of conversation she liked. Sam was with his father in London most of the time, leaving Henry, aged fifteen, as the oldest boy. Henry and Elizabeth still did not get on. She had little in common with him: unlike Bro he was not interested in politics and certainly not in any kind of studying.

But Elizabeth had her poetry to work on and was finding that her restored health gave her the energy she needed to write, while the calm and quiet of Sidmouth provided her with the right atmosphere for composition. Her father, when he left Sidmouth before their first Christmas there, had taken with him to London "in his pocket a mss of mine". This was her translation from the Greek of *Prometheus* by Aeschylus, which she had almost finished at Hope End; attached to it were nineteen accompanying shorter poems. Modestly, Elizabeth had said she did not suppose anyone would want to publish these but to her delight the publisher A. J. Valpy did. They appeared on 11th May 1833.

[75]

The themes in her poems were the same as in those attached to *An Essay on Mind* but her mother's death had darkened them further. Their message was that one should be prepared at all times for disaster; it was important to accept that everything was God's will and to find comfort in this and in the relentless force of Nature. But if the themes were similar though stronger, the style was developing. Her liking for eccentric rhymes, for strange uneven rhythms, for coining new words, for using archaic ones, all these tendencies were reinforced. They were very odd poems for a young woman to write – intensely morbid, violent, passionate – and hard for people to understand. "The Tempest" is the most striking. It is about the discovery of a corpse in a forest during a storm, a corpse the poet tries to bury under a tree which is struck by lightning. The entire poem struggles to convince that the fear of death is something we must, and can, overcome and that the best way to do so is with love which endures whereas death does not.

The volume appeared, without Elizabeth's name, as by the author of *An Essay on Mind*. Those who knew who this was were largely baffled: it was hard to equate the frenzy of poems like "The Tempest" with the pale, slight, quiet figure of Elizabeth leading her exemplary life in Sidmouth. The few reviews she received concentrated on her translation of *Prometheus* and did not bring her much joy. *The Athenaeum* was dismissive: "we advise those who adventure in the hazardous lists of poetic translation to touch anyone rather than Aeschylus; and they may take warning by the author before us."

Elizabeth was twenty-seven that summer and ready to settle for a dull but healthy life and be grateful. Commenting on her new found health she wrote there was "scarcely a ruin" of her cough left and added sarcastically, "my likeness to Hercules will in time be quite complete". All other expectations were firmly suppressed. She was afraid to have dreams and hopes; all her efforts were directed towards maintaining the status quo. She was, in this mood, proud of her indifference on the subject of their next move, sharing none of the feverish anxiety to be told as she had done at Hope End. Sidmouth was pleasant but disappointing and she had no loyalty to it. Since she disliked all upheaval and change she would have preferred not to move if given the choice but claimed that choice was the last thing she wanted: "I have often thought that it is happier *not* to do what one pleases." Her father would make the decision. She was content to say, "so be it". All she wanted was that the whole family should be together.

That year, her father was ill. "Oh! What security have we . . ." she wrote to Mrs Martin when she heard her father had cholera ". . . you know he is ALL left to us – and that without him we should indeed be orphans and desolate." This betrayed self-interest as well as concern for her father: Elizabeth, well versed in contemporary fiction, understood very well what their fate might be if Papa died. She and her sisters ought all to be caring for him instead of having to pack off Henry, as they did, to do so. She wrote to Mrs Martin that they had only been "so daring" as to send Henry, not renowned for his nursing talents, because they could not bear to think of their father "alone and suffering in a London Hotel". (In fact, he had moved to Treppy's house and was well looked after.)

Mr Barrett recovered and towards the end of 1835, after Stormie and George had returned from Glasgow and Bro from Jamaica, he made his decision. He felt that it was imperative for the future of his sons to have the family under one roof. London was the obvious place to live. George, who wanted to be a lawyer, could enter an Inn of Court; Bro and Sam could be trained to follow in his own footsteps in the family business; and all the others from Henry aged seventeen to Octavius aged eleven could be easily educated. The cost of living in London was not really a problem: Mr Barrett was not nearly so rich as he had been but he had not "lost his fortune". He had had to sell Hope End but he had not needed to sell the whole of the vast estate and, despite the dramatic fall in the yield from the Jamaican plantations, there still was a lucrative trade available.

Elizabeth could see the sense in her father taking a lease on 74 Gloucester Place (within the traditional area where Barrett relatives had always settled) while he looked for a more permanent residence. She saw, too, that being in London would give the family a better chance of staying together for many years. George in particular would not need to live without a proper home now that he had a specific career to follow in London. He had returned from Glasgow "much grown and improved" and she was amused to find she was "so vain of my brother". Stormie, whose stammer was so bad he had been unable to take his degree because he could not get through the viva part of the examinations, also needed a base, whatever he was going to do. And as for Bro, Elizabeth had no illusions. The leisurely atmosphere of Sidmouth would be bad for him and would encourage him to be idle. But what also attracted Elizabeth, though she was reluctant to confess it, was what she herself might gain. London was the centre of the literary world. It housed many of those writers she admired. All the magazines and newspapers to whom she sent her contributions were in London and, though sending things from Sidmouth theoretically made no difference to their fate, she had an instinct that it did. If she were actually in the capital, it crossed her mind that she might go out to something more interesting than a Bible meeting. She wrote to Lady Margaret Cocks, "After all, I shall not be pained in leaving Sidmouth as some time ago I should have been," and added, "I would rather go to London than a hundred places I could mention." The London the Barretts moved to at the end of 1835 was an exciting place, especially for young people who had spent almost their entire lives buried in Hope End so that the enormous changes taking place in the social and political structure of their country had hardly been felt by them. They had lived in a backwater where wars and social unrest were little more than rumours. But now, in London, they were made instantly aware of the violence of the changes taking place. The population of the capital soared, as thousands of agricultural workers flooded into the city in search of work now taken from them. From being a pleasant Georgian town London was erupting into a huge conglomeration of housing settlements. Where the Barretts lived, in Marylebone, was an exclusive new area of rapid development but elsewhere slum areas were beginning to create the "Infernal Wen". The year after the Barretts settled in London the first passenger railway opened and in 1838 Euston, the first of the great stations, was built. London in the 1830s was a city of visible drama: everywhere one looked there was something new happening and the tempo of the Railway Age was so insistent that its reverberations would be sensed even in Elizabeth's quiet back room.

London from which she expected great things did not fail her, if at first she was repelled by its physical aspect. She missed the green lanes of Devon, the beauty of the sea and the clarity of the air. The views in Gloucester Place were of bricks and more bricks, there was hardly a green leaf to be seen (and those she glimpsed were covered in soot) and worst of all was the eternal noise of carriages rattling along which made her head ache. That first winter the climate was a shock: "London is wrapped up like a mummy in a yellow mist so closely that I have scarcely a glimpse of its countenance since we came." She wondered what Dr Johnson could have been talking about: "Did Dr. Johnson . . . love . . . the pavements and the walls?" If so, she deduced he must have been blind. She thought it outrageous when people commented "What a lovely day". Loveliness was alien to the place. She yearned for the country and found little solace in driving to Hampstead Heath which, though pretty and pleasantly breezy, could not be confused with the real country. What made her irritable was that London's manifest disadvantages were not at first compensated for by any improvement in her social life. She told Lady Margaret Cocks that she was as isolated as she had always been and that congenial literary company was "as *distant* as when I was at Sidmouth". She doubted, too, her ability to profit, should it miraculously present itself, because she found she had grown "a double rind thicker and thicker on my spirit" which no one would penetrate. Defiantly, she announced there was no one in London "whom I would not rather *walk to shun* than *walk to see*". Inevitably her health, so exceptionally good at Sidmouth, was affected by her return to an indoor life. Her cough returned. She reported that she was "stuck to the fender" whereas at Sidmouth, where she had heard it was warm and sunny, she would have been promenading along the sea-front. Fear of contagious diseases, always prevalent in London, began to haunt her. In Sidmouth, they had been safe from the cholera and smallpox epidemics.

Yet in spite of these very real drawbacks Elizabeth began to appreciate London in a remarkably short time. By January 1836 she was telling Mrs Martin that, though half her soul was still on the sea shore, she was "*satisfied* with London, altho' I cannot enjoy it". Enjoyment was only a few brief months away, and meanwhile she was relishing George's success: "dear Georgie has entered the Inner Temple after passing triumphantly a classical examination." He was making something of being in London and she only wished she could have the chance to do so herself. In the spring, it came. John Kenyon, the distant cousin who had written to her after the publication of *An Essay on Mind*, came to pay his respects. This large, portly, balding, florid-faced man was fifty-two (a year older than Mr Barrett) and was renowned for his kindness and sociability. His house in Devonshire Place was a centre for many of the literati whom Elizabeth worshipped. Kenyon, by the time he met Elizabeth, was an eligible widower. There could have been no one more useful to have as a friend – Kenyon knew every literary and artistic person in London worth knowing – and also no one more respectable. He held that magic passport into the Barrett household: he was *family* (his great-grandmother having been the sister of Elizabeth's great-grandfather).

Kenyon knew his function. It was of the type he relished. Realising immediately the extreme shyness of his new friend he exerted all his tact and charm to draw her into the society which he could clearly see she needed and wanted. He was, reflected Elizabeth, "a difficult person to say *no* to" because he was "so very, surprisingly kind to me that every 'no' of mine would sound to me like a separate ingratitude". This was what Kenyon counted on. Throughout that first winter he visited Elizabeth often, always bringing with him new books or magazines which he would leave with her and then discuss on his next visit. He was impressed and amused at how strong her views were and also how independent. Wordsworth, for example, was generally thought no longer worth admiring but she admired him unreservedly. While others sneered that some of his narrative poetry belonged to a very low order indeed, she staunchly defended it. Measuring her adoration, Kenyon took her breath away by saying he was giving a dinner for Wordsworth and would be delighted if she would come.

The idea was both thrilling and terrifying. Elizabeth's reaction was to look around for excuses to explain why she could not possibly go. The weather? But it was May and sunny. Her health? The cough had gone. Her father's objections? He had none. He admired Wordsworth himself and respected Kenyon. There was no reason at all why she could not go and indeed she most passionately wanted to. As well as admiring Wordsworth's poetry the truth was that Elizabeth loved the thought of meeting him simply because he was famous. Fame attracted her in its own right. Not only the famous in person but all their memorabilia fascinated her: the mere sight of Keats' handwriting made her feel faint. Presented with the chance of sitting next to Wordsworth she never seriously persuaded herself that it was possible to decline. The usual panic at the thought of meeting a new person was present but her determination to conquer and control it was unusually strong.

But just before she met Wordsworth Kenyon introduced Elizabeth to someone else who was, in her own day, also famous. This was Mary Russell Mitford, author of *Our Village*, a series of sketches of country life published first in *Lady's Magazine* in 1819 and then, after their astonishingly successful reception, in volume form between 1824 and 1832. Mr Barrett admired *Our Village*. It contained a description of "a little world of our own, close-packed and insulated like ants in an ant hill" – very Hope End, very Barrett-like. It took the form of a diary, with descriptions of weather and landscape, in each season, and was permeated with the most obvious wholesome advice. The very chapter titles summed up its tone – "The First Primrose", "Violeting", "Nutting". Even if Mr Barrett had not approved of Miss Mitford's work, he could only admire, as everyone did, her devotion to her elderly, invalid father with whom she lived in her cottage at Three Mile Cross near Reading. It was to this fifty-nine-year-old gregarious, warm-hearted, gossipy literary lady that Kenyon presented Elizabeth on 27th May 1836, the day before the Wordsworth dinner party.

Afterwards, Elizabeth confessed to Miss Mitford how nervous she had been right up to the moment of introduction. She was aware that she had begun to weary Kenyon with the absurdity of her professed nerves until he began, she imagined, to feel "like a King beseeching a beggar to take a dukedom". He told her repeatedly that she was being foolish because Miss Mitford was as certain to like her as she was to like Miss Mitford. Trying to make the meeting as easy and natural as possible, Kenyon arranged for the introductions to be made on an outing to the Diorama and the Zoological Gardens. Elizabeth spent the morning walking up and down the house, too agitated to read or write, and when the carriage came her knees trembled so much she could hardly get into it. As ever, Elizabeth's acute nervousness translated itself into physical manifestations more often associated with shock. She worried so intensely about what she would say to a stranger and what would be said to her and most of all whether she would be liked, that her blood pressure soared and the trembling and palpitations began. It was shyness in its most painful and uncontrollable form, betraying a lack of social confidence and self-assurance hard to reconcile with the supremely confident intellectual Elizabeth. But, however difficult to credit, there is no doubt that this turmoil was genuine and that she was to be pitied rather than ridiculed or scorned for this reaction to meeting new people.

Once she met Miss Mitford, her terror disappeared and she was ashamed of having felt it. Nobody could be ill at ease with Miss Mitford. She talked all the time but her conversation was not idle chatter: she had met as many literary folk as Kenyon and had opinions about them all. Only the night before she had met a new young poet called Robert Browning, whose *Paracelsus* had been published the previous year and had been well reviewed. But Miss Mitford had thought it "one heap of obscurity confusion and weakness". She was far more interested in the shy, diffident young woman to whom Kenyon now introduced her.

Together they walked round the zoo and as they gazed at the giraffes Miss Mitford quizzed Elizabeth in the way she knew so well how to do. Out it all came: the story of Hope End, of her mother's death, of her father's devotion, of his financial setback, of her own precarious health and lastly of her work and ambitions. Miss Mitford was enthralled. She vowed in letters she wrote to friends that she "perceived at once a splendid talent". She had not read any of Elizabeth's work but was sure great things were in store. She was enchanted by her, "very pretty, very gentle, very graceful with a look of extreme youth which is in itself a charm". It was Miss Mitford's considered opinion, as expressed to Lady Dacre, that her new friend's "painful" shyness would disappear "if once brought forward in the society she is so fitted to adorn".

The circumstances of Elizabeth's meeting the next day with Words-worth threatened to be much more daunting: she would have to sit, trapped, at a grand dinner table. She could not have faced it without Bro as her chaperon and the knowledge that Miss Mitford was also to be there. In the event, the dinner was not as formidable as she had feared: nothing ever was. She said she was not disappointed in Wordsworth (who was by then an old man) but that perhaps she would not exactly have "singled him out from the multitude" as great. She thought there was a reserve in his countenance, that his eyes were meek rather than brilliant, and that his "slow, even articulation" lacked animation. She trembled "in my soul and my body" when put next to him but he was kind to her and even recited a sonnet of Dante's for her entertainment. She was far more impressed by Walter Savage Landor who talked "brilliantly and prominently", swapping epigrams effortlessly with her and Bro. When she got home she announced, "I never walked in the skies before; and perhaps never shall again, when so many stars are out!"

Sky-walking had proved more to her taste than she had ever envisaged but it was quickly over. No mad round of parties followed. But sitting on her sofa, her mind wandered again and again to that evening and every time she extracted another drop of delight. But she still automatically fought against suggestions to meet new people and even Kenyon became discouraged, though he was extremely fond of her and wanted to please and help her. Henrietta wondered if he was not more than fond, writing to her brother Sam, "How would you like him to be your *brother-in-law*? I w[oul]d very much – a kinder-hearted person and one more agreeable never existed – you must know that he is a great admirer of our dearest Ba – we torment her most terribly about him." Elizabeth wrote to Miss Mitford the following week, the beginning of a long and voluminous correspondence, that "in ending these happy days" she had been touched by her kindness. Already, nostalgia was the theme. The past now had yet another enchantment in it.

But as well as memories she had a new and worthy correspondent. Miss Mitford was put to the test swiftly. Elizabeth sent her a copy of her own *Prometheus Bound and Miscellaneous Poems* saying, "I wish that its worse fault were on its outside" (it was unbound). Miss Mitford reciprocated with a present of her own *Domestic Scenes, Sonnets and Other Poems*. Elizabeth was delighted, writing back, "There is not one being whom I know here except Mr Kenyon who ever says to me 'I care for poetry'." Now she had someone. But Miss Mitford was able to offer her more than a mutual liking for poetry: she, too, devoured novels, including the French novels Elizabeth relished, especially those sensational romances by Eugène Sue and Frédéric Soulie. It was such pleasure to be able to ask "have you read . . . ?" and be almost sure of an affirmative answer. Miss Mitford read widely, magazines as well as books, and was as quick to spot new talent as Elizabeth herself.

Ever since Miss Mitford had mentioned Robert Browning and his *Paracelsus*, Elizabeth had wanted to read it. Kenyon lent her his copy that summer of 1836, a summer so hot that "the pelting heat upon the pavement" bounced up and scorched her through the open windows of the house. The "burning London sun" had put her "into prison". In this prison she lay exhausted – "intense heat always enervates me" – and read this strange poem. Her comments to Miss Mitford were that she was "a little discontented" and that she would have liked "more harmony and rather more clearness and compression – *concentration*". But she recognised it as the work of "a poet in the holy sense" whose "palpable power" and "repressed gushings of tenderness" she sensed and admired. *Paracelsus* had "religious feeling" without which she thought poetry would "lose its elevation". This was something about which she and her father were in perfect agreement. He liked her to write with this feeling and disapproved if he felt she moved away from it. There were uncanny echoes of Elizabeth's own sentiments in *Paracelsus* too. *Paracelsus* tells his friend Festus that "from childhood I have been possessed by a fire", and so had she: she shared his restlessness, his hope that he would give something to the world. Like him, she knew she was weak but "felt somehow/a mighty power was brooding/taking shape within me". When he talked of "my strung, so high-strung brain" this

[83]

echoed her own description of her own brain at the opening of her diary. But it was Paracelsus' voice from within with which she identified most. This "voice" believed, as she did, that poets were intended by God to save the world.

Elizabeth's rather clumsy critical remarks to Miss Mitford masked the disturbance she felt. She was stirred by what she thought of as Browning's mystic voice and added him at once to those poets whom she revered, dead and alive. The subject of the poet's role was at that time obsessing her. That summer she finished working on a long poem of her own in which she tried to frame her concept of the poet. This was "The Poet's Vow", which appeared in *New Monthly Magazine* for September 1836. In it, a poet sits alone trying to make sense of the world and discovers he is, after all, not above other men but "A human creature found too weak/To bear his human pain." Elizabeth's uncle Hedley, her aunt Jane's husband, was only one of many who could not make much of it. She reported this with glee – "Uncle Hedley made a long pause at the first part!" – and was quite proud of causing such consternation. She hoped Miss Mitford would be "one of the six or so" who understood it, but she was disappointed: her friend upbraided her for sharing the same fault of obscurity as Browning. *The Athenaeum* was kind, if patronising, calling it "a too dreamy ballad" and asking in future for greater clarity. Far from being cast down, Elizabeth was confident. Charges of obscurity did not worry her. She had been facing them for a decade and they had never been more strongly made than by her father in 1827 when he had been furious with a poem of which she was proud called, eventually, "The Development of Genius" (not published till her death). "You can never please people," he had told her, "by this want of explicitness." She had not been brave enough to reply that pleasing people was no concern of the true poet, that effort was demanded of the reader to grasp truths. Now, as she entered a prolific period in her writing life, she was beginning to see that what people called her obscurity was *her* and that she should not be afraid of herself. There was no arrogance in this attitude. On the contrary, she was unfailingly modest, but nevertheless she recognised her own voice and was preparing to go on speaking in it.

Miss Mitford helped to take her in another direction. She was editing one of those albums so popular at the time, big, handsomely bound books with lavish illustrations, usually published in November to catch the Christmas trade. Elizabeth had always thought herself superior to such productions but once in London she realised that if the editor were famous enough it was considered an honour to be asked to contribute. Miss Mitford was famous enough. She asked Elizabeth to do her the favour of writing something for *Finden's Tableaux*, making no secret of the fact that she needed the money to support her father. She told her who had already promised contributions and Elizabeth was amazed by "some shining names near which I may well be awestruck at having to stand". She sent a ballad, "The Romance of the Ganges", apologising for its length (fifteen-year-old Sette told her in disgust that it was "so like singing all night when asked for one song"). Miss Mitford hardly appreciated how extraordinary it was that her friend had condescended to do this kind of "writing to order" which Elizabeth made no secret of despising; and, moreover, she had written to suit an illustration of quite nauseating silliness sent by Miss Mitford. The pleasure of helping her friend combined with the thrill of belonging to a group, if a loosely defined and temporary one, overcame her principles.

But she had much more serious work on hand, too. She had begun work on a long, dramatic poem about the crucifixion. It was called "The Seraphim" and "Papa fancies it". There was a vitality in her letters, reflecting her happiness in her work and in her new friendships, but there was also a growing impatience with her father for not finding a permanent residence. First Devonshire Place was looked at, then Wimpole Street, but in spite of his being "on the very threshold of a house in the former" and "almost past the doorstep" in the latter, 1836 and 1837 went by without a decision. Bro said sarcastically he did not believe people ever *did* take houses, "it must be a popular fallacy". None of them liked the Gloucester Place house. Henrietta, returning from a country visit, even said, "What a disagreeable smell there is here!" but she was prejudiced because, until they moved, she was not allowed a piano. The search for a permanent home had become such a joke that they fell to reassuring themselves that it did not matter. In December 1836 the collapse of a chimney persuaded them that it mattered rather more than they had thought: the chimney crashed through a skylight and proved to Mr Barrett what he had suspected. The rented house was in a shocking state of repair and the sooner they were out of it the better.

But at least they were all together except for Sam who had taken his turn in going to Jamaica and Henry who had been sent off on a modified Grand Tour of Europe. Since he hardly put pen to paper no one knew how he was enjoying it but Elizabeth was angry with him for causing their father anxiety. She wrote to Mrs Martin, in the strictest confidence, that Henry's tutor had written to say he was self-willed and difficult to manage – he had at one point taken off on his own in Switzerland – and that he did not know if he could continue to take responsibility for him. "Papa is displeased and disappointed," wrote Elizabeth, "and he *did* speak of having him home at once." It puzzled her that Henry could possibly cause such trouble when he knew how much his father loved him. She was relieved that Alfred showed every sign of doing as well as George since, at sixteen, he had enrolled at the new London University. She only wished Bro would spend his time so profitably but was forced to confess in a letter to Mrs Martin that the only exploit of Bro's she had to relate was his attendance at a party where "they all met for what I call the very foolish purpose of inhaling laughing gas". But there were good reports of Sam, to whom Henrietta wrote regularly. Her main news at the end of 1837 was that the only thing stopping their father taking 50 Wimpole Street was the lawyers fussing over deeds.

Lawyers had their uses that year, all the same. In August 1837 Uncle Sam had sent from Jamaica to his lawyers in London instruction to make out a Bill of Sale for his share ($\frac{1}{8}$th) of the trading ship *David Lyon* which he wanted to give to his niece Elizabeth. Before this transaction had been legally ratified, Uncle Sam died (in December) but Elizabeth received her share in the ship together with a legacy of several thousand pounds, which was invested for her. The annual income she received from her ship shares varied but usually yielded around £200. In addition, she had another £4,000 invested which had been left to her by her Grandmother Moulton in 1830. Naturally, since she was the only one of his nieces and nephews singled out, Elizabeth was overwhelmed by this evidence of her uncle's generosity. Henrietta, who, like the other Barrett children, received nothing, seems not to have felt a spark of envy, writing to her brother Sam that "such kindness melted poor Ba to tears" and Mr Barrett added that Elizabeth had maintained, "I am sure I did not want this." She constantly claimed she was not interested in money, pleading her inability to understand any kind of figures, and said she was grateful that her father managed her finances. Yet at the same time her awareness that she was a good way towards being independent had begun to please her: she was not so altruistic that money really had no meaning. Long ago, it had irked her to ask her father for little amounts like turnpike money and it had disturbed her that she could not buy a book for Boyd without counting the cost. She had come to realise by 1837 that it was foolish to boast about not caring if she had money and that the main good of it was "the freedom it bestowed of not having to think about it". Nevertheless, not only she did think about it but she had contradictory thoughts. On the one hand, she said she was careful with money – "this fussy and most unpoetical gift of mine" – and on the other that she had no idea how much she spent because "whenever I 'do' sums . . . I sit down by the waters of cocytus . . . and deserve all the immense contempt Papa serenely expresses for me". But she had worked out that money bestowed status, which was of increasing importance to her.

If having money of one's own brought status, especially for a woman, having work published under one's own name brought even more. This was the position Elizabeth was striving to reach in the spring of 1838. She wanted to come out of the shadows and publish a collection of poetry without remaining anonymous. She was tired, at the age of thirty-two, of having no clear literary identity. Fortunately, her father, who had before forbidden her ever to put her name to her work, was so proud of "The Seraphim" that he agreed to let Elizabeth B. Barrett appear on the title page. But before this excitement, there was the different one of moving into a real home at last. Mr Barrett had finally taken a twenty-four year lease on 50 Wimpole Street and, though the papering and painting was not complete, the family moved from their temporary lodgings in May of 1838. Elizabeth at last had some territory to make her own. The room she claimed was on the third floor at the back of the house overlooking the "high star-raking chimneys". It faced south-west, which meant it had the late afternoon and evening sun. In it she had a sofa serving as a bed, a table for her books and paper, a wardrobe, a chest of drawers, some bookshelves (made by her brothers), a washstand and an armchair. This made the room a little crowded but it felt comfortable. No sooner had all her beloved books arrived from storage, than her father delighted her by appearing with "a whole vision of majestic heads . . . busts of poets and philosophers". His thoughtfulness touched her deeply: ". . . in all his bustle and vexation of house furnishing to remember so light a thing as my pleasure!" It was further proof of his love that he had thought not of what would please himself but what would please her: she saw and appreciated the difference.

But the greatest pleasure, soon after she was established in her new sanctum, was the publication on 6th June 1838 of *The Seraphim, and Other Poems*. Her father was proud of her. In her preface, she stated that all her poems were "religious in their general character" and that she felt intensely "the solemn responsibilities of the poet". This was exactly what her father wanted her to be: religious, responsible, humble. The title poem, "The Seraphim", was not so humble. It consisted of long dialogues between two angels, "mid-air above Judea", who are looking down on the crucifixion. They swoop down, calling on God to avenge his son's death but the vision of the cross fades and Christ rises. The poet, in an epilogue, smiles to think that when she dies she will be permitted to see the heavenly host. Her readers did not smile with her. Yet again, her shorter poems were generally preferred, especially her ballads. All her poems contained the same vocabulary as her earlier work – not one without the obligatory deaths, corpses, shrouds and general parapher-nalia of dying – but they were much easier to understand and enjoy. The themes, too, were similar (the transitory nature of life, the appreciation of beauty) but the development of an innovative style was much more pronounced. Her pleasure in double rhymes, sight rhymes, and in half rhymes had increased. So had her much more questionable use of assonantal double rhymes – rhymes that cheat the ear and depend on the *resemblance* of sound only (such as "benches" rhymed with "in-fluences"). There was also a greater display of onomatopoeia and of refrain; she obviously believed rhyme had to be harmonic.

The opinions of readers varied widely – some thought her style irritating and affected, others found it refreshing – but it was not individual reaction so much as critical notice which she welcomed. She received enough this time to be gratified. *The Athenaeum, The Exam-iner, The Atlas, Blackwood's, The Quarterly Review* and *The Metro-politan Magazine* all, in due course, paid her considerable attention. Generally, the critics found plenty to dislike but always something favourable, too. Elizabeth showed herself most professional in caring more about the type of reviews she received – their length, their seriousness – than about the views expressed within them, though she did not scorn those either. Adverse criticism interested her more than applause. She was never hurt by abuse, nor did she personalise attacks. She was quickly fascinated in this, her first real trial, by how *wrong* critics could be in what they alleged. *The Literary Gazette*, for example, called her affected, a charge she denied absolutely. No one, she wrote to Miss Mitford, had ever written from a more "real natural impulse". The other criticism which puzzled her was the charge of plagiarism: she had "a nervous dread" of this. One reviewer suggested that in some of her ballads (the "Romaunt of Margret" was cited in *The Atlas*) she was imitating Tennyson, whereas she knew she had never read the poems she was supposed to have copied. It put her on her guard and she wrote that she was sometimes afterwards moved to alter lines if she suspected that they might be thought derivative. Her originality was above all things precious to her; the greatest compliment a critic could pay her was to say she was original. *The Examiner* therefore pleased her most by saying she was "indeed a genuine poetess, of no common order" (even if it went on to add that she was too ambitious for her own good). This pleased her: she wanted to be over-ambitious. However, just when she was ready to push forward in her work even more vigorously, her health let her down with a cruel sense of timing. 1838 was the year of her first real publishing success, but it was also the year of an illness so serious it had far reaching and unexpectedly disastrous consequences for her work.

Chapter Six

E LIZABETH'S severe illness in the winter of 1837–1838 had begun
with an ordinary cold which "turned into a cough" and kept her
confined to the house "in a very weak state". At first, she refused to see a
doctor, commenting to Miss Mitford that "their science conjectures
dimly and is at fault quickly", but, when by the spring she was not better,
her frightened sisters begged her to relent. Mr Barrett, no greater lover of
doctors than his daughter, called in the very best, Dr Chambers,
physician-in-ordinary to the newly crowned Queen Victoria. He came,
examined Elizabeth, and was reassuring, saying, "there is no DESEASE –
only an excitability and irritability of the chest which requires precaution". It was difficult to think how Elizabeth could be any more
cautious than she already was since she had not stirred from her room
for weeks, a room so warm that she actually hatched and reared a dove
there. "Everybody said," she wrote to Miss Mitford, "that nothing alive
cd. come out of an egg rolled backwards and forwards every day under
my fingers – and behold a little Dove!" But with Dr Chambers'
encouragement, she settled down to being even more immobile.

Naturally, she had novels to make her enforced idleness tolerable. She
lost herself and her cough entirely for a while in one novel in particular,
Edward Bulwer-Lytton's *Ernest Maltravers*. This, as the author assured
his readers, was a "whole sketch from life", the story of poor Alice
Travers, exploited mercilessly by her wicked father. She is rescued by
Ernest and becomes his adoring mistress until her father turns up again
and carries her off, pregnant with Ernest's child (though Ernest does
not know it). Elizabeth was enthralled and outraged by what happens
to Alice, who then escapes from her father again and bears a daughter.
More and more this theme of the wronged girl was creeping into the
novels Elizabeth read, but never had the case been so strongly and
plainly stated. Bulwer-Lytton's words – "the poor unfortunates who
crowd our streets . . . have rarely in the first instance been corrupted by

love; but by poverty . . . It is a miserable cant phrase to call them victims of seduction – they have been the victims of hunger, of vanity, of curiosity, of evil *female* counsels . . ." – made a deep impression upon her. She wrote to Miss Mitford that the novel had so gripped and disturbed her that "its presence will not pass from me! It is a splendid book!"

But however successfully she might be distracted by novels, Elizabeth's health did not improve. She had "very little pain" she told Miss Mitford but "the cough is wearing" and so was "the sense of lassitude". Her father, writing to his brother Sam in February, reported that Elizabeth had "a terrible cough that racks her but I am told she is all sound and fine weather will restore her." He did not know that Sam himself had already died of fever, a blow which set Elizabeth even further back. She had always adored her uncle, writing to Lady Margaret Cocks that he was "once to *me* Uncle, brother friend and nurse when I lay in the long weary sickness at Gloucester". She felt so much worse after the terrible news from Jamaica that in March Dr Chambers decided to apply a blister, a kind of poultice believed to draw off inflamation from the membranes. Elizabeth hated it and swore it did no good. She was struggling to prepare her poems for publication and only this made life supportable. Once they were finished and warmer weather arrived, she looked for an improvement in her wretched health but instead caught another cold and Dr Chambers was again called in. He was grave. This time he said the lungs *were* affected: "they did not respond as satisfactorily as heretofore to the latest application of the stethescope," Elizabeth relayed to Miss Mitford. This explicit mention of the stethoscope is important since doctors have argued ever since about whether Elizabeth did or did not have TB. There is no doubt at all that Dr Chambers, if he used a stethoscope, would have known.[1] But he pronounced his patient's lungs as "affected", not tubercular, and "affected" could mean a much less serious disease. The fact that he told Elizabeth that she had "not lost ground" and that she would soon be better is a further indication that he did not suspect TB. At any rate, Elizabeth had confidence in him. She pronounced him "a kind and skilful man" who did not dodge unpleasant truths by "calling things by cowardly names". When, soon after her poems were published in June 1838, Dr Chambers announced he was going to apply leeches, she submitted without a struggle though she loathed and feared them even more than she had done cupping. To her surprise, she felt much better

[91]

afterwards and came down to the drawing room for the first time for weeks. The "acute pain in the side" which had begun to torment her recently was now "diminished to the ghost of a *sensation*". Her recovery was short lived. By July she was back in bed and Dr Chambers prescribed digitalis for her erratic heartbeat. Her heart was duly quietened, though her cough persisted. She was the only member of the Barrett family who did not go to watch the processions on Queen Victoria's Coronation Day (28th June 1838). She would not have joined the crowds in any case but she relished the sense of being so near the centre of things and was avid for every detail of what sixteen-year-old Sette – who had been "on his feet, Queen-devoted, for thirteen hours" – could relay to her. Victoria was "very interesting" to her, ill though she was. She had written some verses to the new Queen the previous year, and continued to be fascinated by the very idea of such a young woman having so much power.

In August, Dr Chambers delivered an ultimatum: either his patient must winter somewhere warm or he would not answer for the consequences. He used "very strong language" Elizabeth told Miss Mitford and said, "there is not at present any ulceration of the lungs – only a too great fulness of the bloodvessels upon them." It appeared the left lung had haemorrhaged in the previous winter but he thought it capable of "recovering itself altogether" if she went to a south coast resort like Torquay. Mr Barrett took a good deal of persuading that Elizabeth needed to leave London. His attitude is not as callous as it may appear. His family had been together again under one roof for a comparatively short time and he was reluctant to separate it once more (as indeed was Elizabeth). Elizabeth could not go alone; she would need at least one sister in attendance and one brother as chaperon. But underlying his hesitation was a lack of faith in anything a doctor told him: he could not really believe Elizabeth would be better off in Torquay. It took Dr Chambers' ultimatum – she must go or he would not answer for the consequences – to make Mr Barrett grudgingly relent.

The going proved as hard as it always did. Elizabeth was in a state of constant anxiety until August 25th was fixed as the day of departure by boat from London to Plymouth. She wrote to Miss Mitford, "Oh! this going! It does cost me so much." She hated to break up the family and her exaggerated feelings of doom were further heightened by the sudden news that her maid would not go with her. A new maid had to be engaged at once, enough in itself to bring her to the edge of collapse. But this new maid was a great find. Her name was Elizabeth Crow, aged twenty-one, a farmer's daughter from Lincolnshire. She was the first servant to establish a close personal relationship with Elizabeth (as Minny Robinson always had with Arabel) and she managed to do so because of her talent for taking charge. Crow was eleven years younger than her new mistress but this did not inhibit her. She was cheerful, firm and confident, a combination Elizabeth greatly liked in people about her. Engaged just two weeks before the departure for Torquay, Crow helped to make the journey less of an ordeal. Having Henrietta, Bro and George as travelling companions helped even more.

But once in Torquay, the move seemed fated to fail right from the start. The Barretts stayed with the Hedleys, who had taken a house for the winter, until they could rent their own accommodation and be joined by the ever-useful Bummy, but Elizabeth was not happy. She disliked the régime imposed by Dr Barry, her Torquay physician. He scorned her London habit of not rising until noon and she was indignant that she was made "to get up at ten . . ." then "at one or two" she was sent out in a wheelchair. She complained that the barbaric early rising and the spartan fresh air made her "fit for nothing". Dr Barry, after only ten days, pronounced her greatly improved – "the stethescope was tried . . . and the report was more favourable". But Elizabeth actually felt worse: "such lowness of spirits that I could have cried all day if there was no *exertion* in crying!" What upset her most was that Dr Barry had forbidden her to write. She described to Arabel how he would ask her, "Have you been writing today Miss Barrett?" and, if she admitted she had, he would say, "You will be so good as not to do so any more!" If she confessed to having written not only letters but *poetry*, Dr Barry's distress was plain: "Well then! I may as well take my leave! I have told you the consequence . . ." Elizabeth felt ashamed – she was learning to like this serious young doctor even if she disliked his treatment – and agreed she would not commit such a heinous crime again. As a penance, she even agreed to wear "flannel waistcoats up to the throat".

By November 1838, the Barretts were installed, with Bummy in charge, at No. 3 Beacon Terrace. Elizabeth was no happier, even though Bro had been allowed to stay on when George returned to London. Her father had consented "plainly against his own wish", as Elizabeth admitted to Arabel. She felt guilty about keeping Bro. "His presence is not *necessary* in the strict sense of the word," she confessed to Arabel but added gloomily, "perhaps no happiness is . . ." She reported that she felt "so weak . . . as scarcely to bear without fainting even the passive fatigue of being carried from this bed to the sofa downstairs." The sea air did not make her feel better and the climate was not as mild as she had been led to believe it would be. Instead, a bitter east wind blew. When her father came down at the end of November she was distressed that he saw her "degree of amendment" was not good. His disappointment pained her. He wrote to his son Sam in Jamaica, where he had taken over from his uncle, that Elizabeth was "much the same". But in a burst of extravagant admiration he also told Sam "she is a handmaiden of the Lord . . . She is a blessed one, the most beautiful of Characters, of the highest attainments and possessed of the noblest Mind." He thought God had "truly blessed me in her . . ." When he left her, Elizabeth wrote emotionally to Miss Mitford that he had wept. She had a sudden, frightening realisation that he loved her "too dearly". On his voyage home, a fellow passenger described the fifty-three-year-old Mr Barrett as looking "little more than thirty" and admired not only his looks but his "frank, good natured countenance".

Once her father had gone, Elizabeth was unable to lift her spirits. At the beginning of 1839 a well known poetess, Mrs Hemans, died aged forty-two and she was "startled and saddened" into commenting, "the longest years do not seem to go to the lives of poetesses". In February, just as she was imagining she would never be well again, she contracted "a kind of bilious fever which necessitated the use of stronger medicines than my state cld very well bear". It turned out to be jaundice and left her with "the worst feelings of debility" she had ever experienced. Life seemed to consist of going from being very ill to merely ill and back again. She could not eat and felt "the whole machine was giving way everywhere". She reported that there was "an exhausting increase of haemorrhage". But by the time her thirty-third birthday came round there was, to her own surprise, some improvement and by April she was not only being carried regularly downstairs but was asking Arabel to send her satin bonnet to wear on the walks she was contemplating. She had been dreaming of walks with her father, who "led me over gates and stiles and palings of all sorts till I was quite out of breath . . . and then came a most tremendous rain in which Papa vanished away". She felt much better, but Mr Barrett was not convinced of her improvement. He wrote to his son Sam, "this terrible illness of my beloved Ba has unhinged everything with me, my mind, my time . . ." Her determination to return as soon as possible to Wimpole Street – "I MUST be with them this summer ... I MUST *indeed*. I keep saying that day after day" – was alarming to him. He had no intention of allowing her to return unless he could see that she was well.

Elizabeth's passionate desire to return to London was not entirely explained by her wish to have the family reunited. The truth was that she wanted to be back in London for other reasons too. Torquay bored her in a way Sidmouth had never done because she now had London as a comparison. "As to London," she wrote to Arabel, "I dont and wont deny the extent of my affection for it." That "affection" had mostly been won not because of her personal life there but her literary one. She had left soon after the publication of *The Seraphim and Other Poems*, just as she was beginning to make her mark. In Torquay, she felt remote from her own success. She knew her poems had not sold well and wondered if there should be more advertisements, not, as she hastened to add to Miss Mitford, that she craved popularity because she "wd. just as soon cry for the Pope's tiara – and as vainly!" Good weather in May made the seaside a little more attractive – she went on some outings and enjoyed them – but she was "in a fuss" about getting her father to fix a date for her return home. He came to inspect her in July but was not impressed: "I am told that I can't go back to London this winter without performing a suicide!" The only way she had of persuading her father was to look obviously healthy and so she redoubled her efforts to strengthen herself. She tried to walk a little further each day but in September succumbed to a chill; another winter in Torquay was unavoidable.

Bro was still with her. She was guiltily aware that it was not much of a life for him any more than it was for her. The only thing that made it bearable for him was that so long as he was needed in Torquay he could escape being sent back to Jamaica, a fate he dreaded. He spent most of his time that year painting water-colours. According to Bro himself, writing to Sam, these were "sundry ungainly efforts" but Elizabeth vowed he was a good artist and was proud of him when he sent some to London: she boasted to Sette that his big brother "does not falter or slacken yet in application". (The "yet" was a little too much of a give-away.) But Bro's main function was to support her and this he did. He encouraged her to write ballads for Miss Mitford's latest album, constantly brought her little presents to cheer her up ("such pretty blue *two* vases") and best of all flopped down "on the company side of my bed". There, he talked the dull hours away, "a torrent of a logical and liberal philosophy" as she described it. He always put her pleasure before his. He would have liked, for example, to see more of his brother Sam when he came on leave from Jamaica and paid only a brief visit to Torquay but he denied himself the pleasure of going to London because he did not like to leave his sister.

On 1st October 1839 Elizabeth prepared for the horror of another Torquay winter by moving house, to No. 1 Beacon Terrace "which is promised to be a warmer residence." It was also cheaper – by a guinea a week, as Bro told Sette – and such things were important because she was paying for her own household there.[2] Henrietta wrote to Sam that, as Dr Barry's fees stood at £125 and the druggists at £50, Elizabeth's finances "will hardly bear" the rent of the previous house. Elizabeth herself hardly cared whether it was cheaper or warmer; all she lived for was the post, with its precious letters, books, magazines and news of London. It was fortunate for her that in January 1840 the penny post was introduced by Rowland Hill, abolishing the old franking system and the payment on receipt of a letter. This had always inhibited Elizabeth but now, for the price of one penny, she could write as much as she wished and did not have to worry about burdening her correspondents with the expense. She was soon announcing that the penny post was "the most successful revolution" of her day and praising the "wonderful liberty" given by it.

She looked forward to the arrival of magazines and newspapers nearly as much as to letters. Occasionally, some running story in a newspaper would rouse her from her lethargy and produce energetic indignation (as well as revealing her insatiable love of gossip). The treatment of Lady Flora Hastings (a lady-in-waiting of Queen Victoria's scandalously reputed to be pregnant) made her furious. When Lady Flora submitted to a medical examination to establish her innocence Elizabeth was outraged enough to declare "if such limited measures" as her word "did not suffice to save her reputation if I had been she I wd. have lost it. Let it go." Lying on her sofa in Torquay she wished more than ever that she were in London to hear the latest developments more quickly. The only news in Torquay was of a depressing and not a stimulating nature: her doctor was ill. He had rheumatic fever and she was "anxious and saddened" and worried about his wife who was about to have her second child. It shocked her when, at the end of October, Dr Barry died: "the physician was taken and the patient *left* – and of course deeply affected and shaken." Once more, she was faced with the transitory nature of life and with the thought that her own was trickling away:

"How we drag our weary wills after God's will . . . reluctantly sadly heavily." Her new doctor, Dr Scully, tried to be encouraging but she told Miss Mitford "I am a useless, helpless person – scarcely worth taking care of . . ." She was assured again, "What they call the tubercular disease is supposed not to have taken place in me." When she asked to be told, absolutely truthfully, whether it was possible she would ever recover properly she was told, "yes, it was". She promptly burst into tears, at which Dr Scully said in despair there was no reasoning with her. Sleep was her refuge, "Opium – opium – night after night! – and some nights . . . even opium won't do."[3] She was sure she was dying and began to write in terms of "if I live out a few months longer". Her father held her up to Sette as "a brilliant example of humble submission and pious resignation". She was depressed and wished even more than usual she was back in London where Queen Victoria's approaching wedding day (1st February 1840) was causing such excitement. She lay in bed writing verses on this (published in *The Athenaeum*) and was pleased when Miss Mitford thought the Queen might read them.

It was in this depressed state that Elizabeth heard that her brother Sam, aged twenty-eight, had died of fever in Jamaica. The injustice as well as the horror of it overwhelmed her. Sam had been young, six years younger than she was, full of health and with his whole life before him. She became delirious when told, passing from fainting to sleeping (as she described it). Her father came to her at once and stayed a whole month. He wrote to Sette, "What a Creature she is, I reverence her for the beauty of her character, so happy a specimen of christian submission and devotional feeling never was surpassed." When Elizabeth was conscious, her mind was full of Sam the wit, Sam the dandy ("enchanting with his gadding tongue, black silk stock and couleur de rose garters" as she once described him), Sam the good, who was always "so amiable in every way." Even with all the "christian submission" her father talked of, she could only tolerate Sam's death by reminding herself that love never dies. Sam was in another world, not dead, a world upon whose very threshold she had stood for so long. Mercifully, she knew nothing of the more distressing details of Sam's death. According to the fiercely puritanical, self-righteous Hope Waddell, the Scots Presbyterian minister who worked as a missionary on the Barrett estates, Sam had succumbed to those evil influences his father so feared for his sons. He had taken to native women and only the ministrations of the zealous missionary were supposed to have saved his soul.[4]

Torquay was now "dreadful dreadful" and Elizabeth wanted either to leave it at once or to be left alone to die. She was "crushed trodden down" and instead of being comforted by the family faces found them oppressive. In her own agony she could not appreciate that of others. Henrietta had been as close to Sam as she herself was to Bro. She had seen her brother only for the brief two weeks he spent in Torquay on his last leave from Jamaica and wrote to him she had been "very angry" that this was all she was able to see of him. But Elizabeth's grief was so all-consuming that Henrietta's was hardly noticed by Mr Barrett. He was solely concerned about the effect of Sam's death on his beloved eldest daughter. He wrote to Sette only of Elizabeth: "how to leave my beloved Ba I know not, I fear the very mention of it for she is indeed lamentably weak and yet it is absolutely necessary I should go; I really know not how to act." It was a rare admission of helplessness. But Sam's death, terrible as it was, proved to be only a dress rehearsal for a tragedy so complete that Elizabeth wondered how she could ever have imagined she had suffered pain before.

Sam died in February 1840. Throughout the spring and summer nothing interested Elizabeth. But Bro, her main support, had a new interest. In a letter to George in June, Elizabeth makes the only reference at that time to a romance of Bro's, jokingly telling George that Bro had "discarded his green eye blind and indeed ventures to show his whole face out of doors by twilight instead of waiting for the very pitch black". He was thirty-three, an age at which his father had been married for thirteen years and had sired eight children, but Bro had no means of marrying without his father's financial assistance. This was not forthcoming. The extraordinary thing about Mr Barrett with his fierce pride in the importance of family was not that he would not let his children marry but that he took no steps to force at least one son to marry and continue the family line. But by then Mr Barrett's whole attitude to marriage had become extremely puzzling. During their adolescence, Elizabeth and Henrietta had laughed affectionately and even proudly because they knew their father would not even consider a prince good enough for them. But by the time they were grown up they were aware that their father's views were not quite as charmingly prejudiced in their favour as they had thought. Mr Barrett's own marriage had been happy but, when it ended with his wife's death, his ideas on the institution of marriage became greatly affected by his fervently religious outlook. He found in the Bible the evidence he wanted – in this case, to confirm that a father had authority over his children in all respects – and ignored any that conflicted with his opinion. He saw it as his plain duty to keep his children from sin and he suspected sin in every rumour of attachment which reached him. As far as he was concerned, no adult child of his ever came to him with a chaste, respectable and irreproachably correct suitor. He judged Henrietta as flighty, Bro as undependable and both of them as lacking the economic means to consider marriage. He never at any time issued an edict saying his children could under no circumstances marry but he pointed out whenever any of them showed signs of wishing to do so that what they had in mind was impossible for very good reasons which he delighted in listing. He foiled their attempts but there was always the suggestion that if a marriage of unimpeachable rectitude had been broached, he might have approved. In fairness to him, it is true to say that few Victorian fathers would have approved the matches which his children proposed.

The details of Bro's romance are obscure to this day. At the time, Elizabeth said nothing more than she said to George. (It was much later in her life that she made veiled references to having wanted to give her money to Bro to enable him to marry.) Whatever the truth, Bro and she were not as close as they had been. On July 11th, when Bro went sailing with three others, Elizabeth parted from him with, in her own description, "a pettish word". Mr Barrett, in a letter to George, described what was presumed to have happened next. Bro and friends left at noon on the 11th, in fair weather, and at the time he was writing, almost midnight on the 13th, "they have not been heard of, further than that on Saturday afternoon about ½ 3 o'clock a Gentleman in his Yacht about 4 miles to the East of Teignmouth saw a boat exactly corresponding to the one they went in . . . he observed it go down; He set sail immediately to the spot which he says he reached in 4 or 5 minutes but nothing whatever could he see." Mr Barrett went on to report that what had puzzled this observer was that the boat could not have keeled over because "he saw the point of her mast above the water last". What puzzled Mr Barrett himself was why, since they could all swim, the observer had not found them treading water when he got there so quickly? There was a chance it had not been Bro's boat at all, or that yet another yacht unseen by this observer had picked up survivors or even that they had been strong enough to swim ashore. In the middle of his own intense confusion and distress – "billow upon billow pass over me" – Mr Barrett's one thought was for Elizabeth.

She lay, waiting, for three weeks. Her sisters constantly pointed out that the sea was calm, that it was unlikely anything had happened in spite of the very brief squall on the 11th. Her father described to George how she was "scarcely conscious" and told him "her mind wanders, but if I can once get her to fix it on her *lord* all will be well". Henrietta wept, Arabel wept (though her father was pleased to see she also prayed) but Elizabeth did not. By August 1st the bodies had still not been found but most people had given up hope. Mr Barrett, in a letter to Sette, showed himself, in the middle of his own anguish, fully aware of his daughter's greater agony. "I confess," he wrote ". . . it is wonder to me that she lives, for her love for him we mourn was truely great and in addition their friendship was uninterrupted and it began in infancy and has gone on growing with their growth. He was always the adytum of all her secrets and plans . . ." He confided in Sette that he simply could not believe Bro was dead; he found himself practising how he would break the news of Bro's reappearance to "our suffering one". But Bro did not reappear. His body, that of one of his friends and the boatman's were all washed up in Babbacombe Bay on August 4th. They were buried in Torre churchyard two days later. Mr Barrett, in spite of his desperate need to return to London, stayed at Elizabeth's side till December, watching over and suffering with her.

Between July and October 1840, Elizabeth wrote no letters. Months later, she recorded that all reading and writing stopped because she felt "bound, more than I ever remember having felt, in chains, heavy and cold enough to be iron – and which have indeed entered into the soul". Dreams took over her mind, "nothing but broken hideous shadows and ghastly lights to mark them". In October, she at last took up her pen again when "in a trembling hand" she wrote to Miss Mitford, gathering the tattered threads of her life together again. Miss Mitford empathised completely with her friend's anguish but could not help feeling that she needed, if not anything as insulting as distraction, an outlet for her distress, some tangible comfort no human could offer her. In her own case this was provided by her dogs. With the right amount of diffidence, she offered Elizabeth her spaniel's new puppy, Flush. The offer was declined, on the grounds that Flush was too valuable. But Miss Mitford persisted and Elizabeth weakened. She had always loved pets. At Hope End she had tamed a squirrel and kept it in a cage and there had been pet rabbits, a goldfinch, a hen and a Shetland pony called Moses. Since moving to Wimpole Street, Stormie and Henry had acquired big dogs –

a bloodhound and an Alpine Mastiff – and Occy a small one, a terrier called Myrtle which Elizabeth declared "that ugliest dog of all Christendom". She herself had her doves. Finally, she was unable to resist the temptation any longer. Flush was gratefully accepted and arrived in January 1841, aged six months. Letters to Miss Mitford now became one third about Flush. Even when perfectly aware that she was being faintly ridiculous Elizabeth could not restrain herself: all the demonstrative love of which she was capable gushed out over Flush. When she was younger, Occy had satisfied this side of her nature but, since he had grown too old to cuddle and kiss, only Mary Hunter and her niece Ibbit, Aunt Jane Hedley's middle daughter, had allowed it occasional expression. To those who mistakenly imagined that to be intellectual was to be austere, it was always a revelation to see Elizabeth with any animal or child. To see her with the adored Flush was barely credible, so extravagant was her adoration.

Those around her were naturally delighted with the therapeutic effects of this golden cocker spaniel. The entire household was more than ready to pander to Flush in such a good cause, exacting and sometimes silly though his whims often were. Flush would not touch unbuttered bread so the butter was spread thickly upon it until such time as muffins were preferred; Flush spurned mutton so beef was ordered; Flush disliked being on his own so a companion was provided at all times. "Voices to the north and south cry 'Flush is spoilt!'" wrote Elizabeth, relishing the truth of this accusation. It thrilled her to see Flush returning her love: he had no time for anyone but her and, at a pinch, her maid Crow. Dr Scully warned her that the animal must not be allowed to sleep on her bed and that, if she were going to handle him as much, then he must be regularly bathed. Elizabeth, although dismissive about the necessity of such extreme measures, submitted. Flush was bathed every day so that he would be fit to leap through the bed curtains into a place beside her in the morning. There he stayed most of the day, unless he was moved to a shawl beside the fire. He did what no one else had managed to do for six months: he made her smile and even laugh.

But, for all the pleasure he gave her, it was not the arrival of Flush any more than the tender ministrations of her family which pulled Elizabeth out of the pit of misery into which she had been pushed by Bro's death. It was work. There was no studying of Hebrew as there had been after her mother's death. This time, she was incapable of beginning the process of regeneration herself but when an approach was made to her she had just enough mental energy to grasp the helping hand. Once she had done so, she was on her way to a complete escape. The hand extended was a stranger's, that of Richard Henry (or Hengist) Horne, editor, critic, poet and traveller. In August 1839, Elizabeth had written to Horne at Miss Mitford's instigation to ask him to contribute to her friend's album. Her letter went through an intermediary, an old governess of hers called Mrs Orme, who was known to be a friend of Horne's. Horne wrote a dashing reply agreeing to contribute and began to correspond regularly, obviously alerted by Mrs Orme to Elizabeth's situation. In the dull Torquay days his letters were enthusiastically received and looked for. Horne told her he would send "anything *amusable*" that might pass through his hands and thoughts. His generosity and thoughtfulness raised him high in Elizabeth's estimation: he was "a very very kind person" she told Miss Mitford (who promptly wondered if he were married and was told by Elizabeth "he *deserves* to be and well married"). Throughout the summer of 1840 Horne's letters became increasingly valued by her. He was much livelier than any other male correspondent she had had and best of all told her secrets, "*very highly connected literary* secrets". She, in return, promised him she could be "secret beyond womanity, if you are frank beyond discretion". It was the kind of witty challenge Horne found irresistible.

Horne was born in 1803, making him almost exactly the same age as Elizabeth herself. His career had been excitingly varied and strange – he had been a midshipman in the Mexican navy, he had lived with Indians, been shipwrecked, broken two ribs swimming Niagara Falls and survived a mutiny. He returned to England in 1836, where he began his literary career by writing in *The Monthly Repository* about his many adventures and then branched out into dramas. Everything was developing most satisfactorily in their epistolary relationship when Bro was drowned and it came to a full stop. But in the first letter of any length that Elizabeth wrote to Miss Mitford afterwards she mentioned Horne and a few weeks later, when she was stronger, she complained she had not heard from him. It was May 1841 before Horne wrote to her but his letter was worth having waited for: he suggested that the two of them should collaborate on a drama.

Elizabeth was immediately taken with the idea, though collaboration ran counter to everything she had said about her own character. Her pride had always been in working on her own and of work being an intensely private affair. But now she wrote quite feverishly to Miss

Mitford about the project, telling her that the hero of the proposed drama was to suffer "persecution from the hauntings of his soul". She could hardly wait to begin and was full of ideas. She wanted "real situations" and "men and women talking aloud to each other". She intended to explore real emotions: "there will be joy and grief – a child and a bridal!" What flattered her most, and showed her success in 1838 had not gone to her head, was that Horne thought her worthy of collaboration at all. He had apparently made a similar suggestion before, or so Elizabeth told Miss Mitford, but she had not taken him seriously because it was so like "a show with a giant and a dwarf together". She was perceptive enough, of course, to realise that Horne was making the offer "half out of kindness and the wish to amuse my mind, and perhaps *whole*" but it was a sign of her desperation that she was not disposed to reject him because of his likely motive. She suggested the title, *Psyche Apocalypté*, and the subject and "we were agreed in a minute". She sent him a preliminary sketch which he broke up into acts for them each to work on independently. What pleased her most was the feeling she soon had that "the weak sides of Mr Horne and myself bend the same way – to the *mystic* . . . the only excuse for such a partnership". He wrote to her, too, she told Miss Mitford, "as if I were well" which was what she most wanted.

The surge of creative power she felt for the first time since Bro's death, coupled with some recovery of physical strength during the summer, made Elizabeth face up to the fact that "the worst – what people call the worst" was not going to happen. She was not going to die. Even more, she no longer wished to die though she had difficulty admitting it. "Once I wished *not* to live," she confided in Boyd, now in London and to whom she still wrote occasionally, "but the faculty of life seems to have sprung up in me again, from under the crushing foot of heavy grief." It surprised her, as she reflected "the poetical part . . . is growing in me as freshly and strongly as if watered every day". This being so, her thoughts once more dared to contemplate the future and she began to long once more to be back in London. But Mr Barrett, who had been so reluctant to let Elizabeth go to Torquay, was now reluctant to let her come home. She had gone to the south coast because Dr Chambers had given him a categorical assurance that London, with its fog, might prove fatal to her. Since he could see for himself that she was little better, he could not understand how London could now suddenly be safe. He could appreciate that it was better for his daughter's mental health to move her away from the scene of Bro's drowning but he could not believe that, for her physical health, London was the answer. Bringing his whole family together again under one roof was of no importance compared to Elizabeth's complete recovery and so he began trying to find somewhere healthier than Wimpole Street to which she could be taken. To her alarm, he talked instead of moving her to Clifton near Bristol as an interim step. The thought appalled her but she vowed to Miss Mitford that "if his wish remains fixed on Clifton, then even to Clifton I must go . . . I came here, you see, not indeed against his desire but against the bias of his desire. . . ." She never intended to go against that bias again. It seemed to her that to do so was to tempt disaster. Her "poor Papa's *biases*" were "sacred" from now on and she "would not stir them with a breath". It was both a deeply superstitious and a remorseful response which did not bear logical examination for a minute; she saw cause and effect where she wanted to see them, overloading herself with a complicated and unnecessary guilt. She was making a primitive bargain with fate, or what she chose to call fate, and also rewarding her father for the depth of his lavishly bestowed love. Ironically, her father did not want her gift. At precisely this moment he most uncharacteristically told her, "Decide". She told Miss Mitford she had refused to do so. The decision was referred to Dr Scully who, to Elizabeth's immense relief, came down against Clifton: "he wd. rather . . . that I went straight to London and shut myself up in a large airy room and took counsel and guidance with Dr Chambers." Only the journey was daunting.

Once the return to London had been agreed on, Elizabeth settled down to endure the rest of her stay in Torquay as stoically as possible. It was not easy. The sea, once the "dear dear sea", was hateful, the noise of it torture, the sight of it even at its calmest and most sparkling, horrible. It amazed her that Henrietta could still go out for walks along the sea-front; the only way Elizabeth could endure Torquay was to shut herself away. Her contempt for her sister was apparent. "She goes out a good deal," Elizabeth wrote. "I wonder she can *bear it* much less like it," and, "Henrietta goes out indefatigably . . . when she falls back on *only us* we are found hard and dry." She failed to realise that she *was* both hard and dry in her lack of sensitivity towards her sister's quite different way of handling her own grief: there was something about the dogged ordinariness of Henrietta's routine which enraged her. Arabel, now with her too, annoyed her less because her activities were more virtuous. She had become involved in a nearby school and even organised a tea party for poor children which met with Elizabeth's approval (she complained to George that Henrietta had refused to support Arabel's charitable gesture and that she was cross with her).

George was Elizabeth's main Wimpole Street correspondent at that time. Ever since he had begun practising law Elizabeth had not only admired him but had realised that he was a potential ally in anything to do with persuading their father. Well before Sam and Bro's deaths he alone of the brothers had an occupation unrelated to his father's concerns, and had pursued it with a diligence satisfactory even to the exacting Mr Barrett. Elizabeth marvelled at how this brother sat up "night after night". His high moral standards fascinated her. He thought, for example, that it would be improper to marry on less than £3,000 a year and so was waiting till he earned that "as a preliminary to falling in love" as Elizabeth told Miss Mitford. She thought this absurd but nevertheless recognised George's worth, "so good, so upright, so persevering . . ." It was to George that she began to apply to persuade their father to organise her transport to London. More and more she was coming to depend on him and felt that they had a great deal to give each other. The rest of her brothers were missed by her, too, but in a different way: she did not see any of them as useful to her. Stormie worried her deeply. After Sam's death, he returned home and had hardly stirred from it since. Elizabeth confided in Miss Mitford that "*he never goes out at all*" and she was sure she could help him if she could only get to his side. She made her brother sound agoraphobic – as on occasion indeed she made herself and her father sound – but Stormie's problem was more an acute form of the social difficulties she and her father experienced. It was not going out that any of them feared – on the contrary, all three of them, in their various ways, liked to attend theatres, art galleries and church meetings where large numbers of people were present – but having to engage in social intercourse. It was individual encounters with strangers they dreaded, not crowded gatherings. For Stormie to have to make small talk was agony: even an exchange of pleasantries paralysed him. Elizabeth understood precisely and so, to her relief, did her father. He was intensely irritated by this exaggerated manifestation of his own shyness in this son but he never forced him to overcome it.

Of the other brothers, Henry was still rebellious, full of "military or naval fancies" and to Elizabeth's annoyance still causing their father unnecessary worry by refusing "to make up his mind to some occupation which is not insurmountably objectionable to Papa". Alfred was still at

London University, and was improving his artistic skills. But it was Sette and Occy, aged eighteen and sixteen, whom Elizabeth missed most of all. Sette amused her with his professed ambition to be "historical and logical and oratorical all at once" and she missed his "gossipings" and "secret tellings" as she did Occy's droll observations and day dreaming. "What are you thinking of Occy?" she had been in the habit of asking and would smile at the answer (likely to be Mr Pickwick, for whom he had a passion). Weather predictions were his speciality and she longed to go over the state of the wind and what it portended.

She missed them all individually but it was the collective family life she longed for most. To be in a back room in Wimpole Street was *never* to be alone as she was in Torquay. The comings and goings of eight people as well as of her father, the noises and silences that punctuated the life in a day of the house, the following of all the varied rhythms, the association at one remove with scores of friends and acquaintances, this was food even the weakest invalid could feed on. Lying on her sofa, Flush gently biting her hand, she tried to stifle her frustration by absorbing herself in *Bells and Pomegranates*, the series of pamphlets Robert Browning had begun to publish. The first was *Pippa Passes*, which she read in July 1841, at the height of her anxiety about returning to London. She was at first puzzled by it, telling Miss Mitford it outdid "Mr Browning's ordinary measure of mystery", but on her third reading the "full glory" of it struck her.[5] All that worried her was a certain "coarseness": she could not see the need for the mention of nipples, the reference to prostitutes sitting on men's knees, or any of the unmistakable sexual metaphors. But, on the other hand, the poem had "genius" and she was scornful when critics failed to acknowledge this. She acclaimed the power of Browning's poetry, telling Miss Mitford he had "a strong and deep individuality" and that the obscurity of it hardly mattered when it was "so worthwhile to get out our dictionaries".

There was a recovered vitality in all her letters by August 1841 – she was once more witty and incisive and clearly absorbed in her project with Horne – but her father did not seem to acknowledge that she was ready to come home. "My patience has dreadful chilblains from standing so long on a monument," she complained to Miss Mitford. She went so far as to confess she was "a little vexed" with her father but had "not climbed so high in ingratitude as to *complain* of the delay, the least bit!" That would be breaking her resolution. But when Dr Scully suddenly said that no journey could be taken any later than 10th September she began to panic. It was the 4th of August. Her brothers wrote encouragingly that they heard rumours she was to be brought home soon but she had enough experience of rumours about Barrett plans to place no faith in them; they were "flattering apocryphal voices". Then on 25th August she told Miss Mitford, "we are going, I believe. The carriage, the patent carriage, was to set out yesterday . . ." But had it? And would it arrive before the mysteriously significant 10th September? Dr Scully began to lose his confidence that she was after all fit for the journey, even in a specially designed carriage more like a litter. She told him, "If I suffer, it is my own fault," but that was no comfort to the doctor who would bear the responsibility. On 25th August, the carriage arrived. "Oh my dearest Miss Mitford," she wrote, "We are going!" Suddenly, she was nervous: "There is much to bear, much to dread." There would be "days and days on the road, if not longer". The slightest sign of a collapse and she would have to stop. Eventually, on 1st September, she set off, with Arabel, Crow and Flush. They travelled twenty-five miles a day, with Elizabeth lying prone, and arrived in London on 11th September "just after post time". She was home at last, after the three most wretched and miserable years of her life. She vowed never to leave home again.

Chapter Seven

I WAS a real joy to see her brothers again, especially Sette and Occy who were almost unrecognisable – " 'little brothers' . . . I looked for them in vain! Not a brother to be seen out of a tail coat . . ." After two weeks she vowed to Miss Mitford, "I am sure I am in fairyland all at once . . . everybody smiling as if grief were not in the world." She was so happy she hardly cared that she was also so weak it was difficult for her to stand alone. Her determination to get better was strong; she would have no more doctors. She would rest, keep warm and try to eat sensibly, but her night-time opium was essential to give her sleep. She urged Miss Mitford to try her prescription: "The muriate of morphine is what I take – what I call my elixir, and I take it in combination with aether and something else."[1] Taking this magic draught produced "a sort of ubiquitous influence upon all parts of my system – quiets my mind, calms my pulse . . . spirits away any strange headache – gives me an appetite – relieves my chest – to say nothing of the bestowment of those sudden pleasant feelings belonging by right to better health . . ." It was a glowing advertisement but Miss Mitford tried it and found it did not do as much for her.

But dependent though she was on her nightly dose of opium Elizabeth was in other respects weaning herself off her other invalid props. The almost daily cataloguing of her own symptoms stopped and she did indeed try to adopt a more healthy way of life. It helped that her spirits were lifted not only by her family but by the renewal of Kenyon's visits. He came to see her within a week of her return, full of fascinating gossip, slipping easily and quickly into his old habits. Through him she was once more in touch with the literati, once more brought books the day they were published, once more invited to glittering occasions. She was too weak to go, of course, but she encouraged her sisters to accept Kenyon's invitations and felt, through them, that she had been present. She was not confined to her room but she liked it so much that she rarely left it for long. It was, to her, a pleasant place to be. In the window she now had a flourishing window box filled with "scarlet runners, nasturtiums, convolvuluses and ivy". Here she held court, constantly aware of the domestic tenderness by which she was surrounded. By the spring of 1842, its healing properties had made her feel better, but she confided in Miss Mitford that, though she was making progress, she felt a fundamental change had taken place within her. A whole phase of her life had ended and "my castle building is at an end!" She could "scarcely recognise" her old self. "I am *content* . . . at least," she wrote, but real happiness was beyond contemplation. "My only individual hopes now are prospective actions and duties," she concluded. Most of these were towards her family, especially her father, and her work which was making as big a contribution as ever towards her psychological recovery. This was also assisted by the general stimulus of being back in London even if she was confined to Wimpole Street. Current events had always had the power to take her out of herself, to startle her out of depression, and none were more startling than the attempts on Queen Victoria's life made that summer. On 30th May 1842 shots were fired at the Queen on Constitution Hill and again, on the way to church, on 3rd July. Elizabeth was enthralled, describing breathlessly to Miss Mitford how "a boy – having the appearance of an errand boy – and the pistol loaded with tobacco pipes – and a stander by snatching it out of his hands while he was preparing the gunpowder in the park!" She was "very angry" at these attacks – "What is this strange popular mania for Queen shooting?" – and her indignation in a curious way made her feel better. It was precisely the kind of distraction she needed because she was not as immersed in work as she liked to be.

The drama she was working on with Horne had languished because of his other commitments but fortunately at this point Elizabeth was offered another form of literary work which had not come her way before: reviewing. She was widely read, had an analytical mind and was interested in all branches of literature: she was an obvious candidate to be a critic. Charles Dilke, who had taken over as editor of *The Athenaeum*, wrote to her "very courteously, to ask me to send him some prose papers in the form of reviews . . . to which I have said a kind of yea . . ." She did rather more than that by putting up the idea of "a series of sketches of the Greek poets of the early Christian centuries with translations". Dilke accepted, though nervously asking her to keep away from too much theology. She plunged at once into a re-reading of all those Greek poets she had read first with Mr Boyd. "I am really half afraid that it's conceited of me to let myself be lifted up to this 'Bad eminence of criticism'," she told Miss Mitford, but was clearly excited by the challenge. She prepared four papers, which appeared in February and March 1842, and then began a survey of English poets. Her days, from being empty, were suddenly crowded; she wrote of "writing to the clock" and of being "busy upon busy". She took her work extremely seriously, anxious to check every quotation, and fearful that she was not doing the poets justice. It "pulled" at her more than she had anticipated and she told Miss Mitford the sense of responsibility sat heavily upon her. This attitude made her a conscientious and honest critic but at the same time it made her style a little too leaden: she proved the sort of critic who is dependable but hardly inspirational, offering facts rather than insight. Miss Mitford at least wondered if it was worth all Elizabeth's labour: her friend seemed, on her own admission, to be wearing herself out on what was in her opinion hack journalism. She cautioned her not to waste her talent. Elizabeth told her not to worry, she had not forgotten her real calling. Her critical pieces were sharpening her poetical intellect all the time and she had "plenty of short mss. half-written and half blotted". She was tempted by the thought of another volume of her own poems but was waiting until she had some single substantial piece around which to group the ballads and lyrics she had completed since 1838 (and which continued to appear in magazines). Kenyon thought she should consider a classical subject, her father a religious one and she herself was tempted by Napoleon. She was confident that, given time, a theme would choose itself.

Her days were full of literary work but also of Flush. He worried her at first by seeming to hate London. He was terrified outside the house by the noise of the traffic and inside it by the noise of Catiline and Resolute, Stormie and Henry's massive hounds. He barked his own protest and annoyed Mr Barrett but fortunately he seemed to realise that his fate hung in the balance and suddenly settled down. At first, he refused to leave Elizabeth but, after a great deal of fuss, condescended at last to accompany Arabel on her many walks through Regent's Park and to Hampstead Heath. Elizabeth was offended if people implied that Flush led an unhealthy, unnatural life, retorting that he was given plenty of exercise. He also had plenty of treats which were definitely not healthy. Mr Barrett started bringing him cakes and even Treppy, who lived nearby, succumbed to Flush's charms and slipped him goodies – all the more surprising since she was known to detest dogs. The hot city weather was a trial for Flush: in 1842 it was a burning summer, so hot that even the heat-loving Mr Barrett was discomforted. It amused Elizabeth to watch him pretending he did not find the heatwave unbearable. She said his "ideal of a temperature is taken from an oven" but one blistering day he did go so far as to complain "'*the tea* was too hot' ... Those were the precise terms of his complaint! Not a sigh against the sun ... only against the tea because it was boiling. I said simply 'That is a triumph.'" No mention was made of escaping to the country or – unmentionable word – the sea. Outings to Strawberry Hill with Kenyon were the limit of the family's excursions and Elizabeth (who stayed at home) was glad of it: the family *ought* to stay together, all safe at home. When her father went off in July to look at an estate in Wales she was "anxious, *pre*-sentimental ... disquieted without a reason ..." She could not relax until his return. If anyone suggested she too should go for a holiday, she was violent in her protestations that she was perfectly all right; no one must try to part her from her "new found consolations". She was "well, wonderfully well" where she was. She had walked unaided round the house and by August was thinking about going out, though in a wheelchair at first.

There was no doubt that in the two years since Bro's death Elizabeth had made great strides. Absolute despair, and the longing for death that had accompanied it, had given way to a pitiful resignation which she had imagined was the furthest she could go. But by the end of that mercifully good summer of 1842 she herself knew that she was moving by barely perceptible degrees towards some state more positive than the humble submission to God's will which her father so admired in her. She might not dare to build castles in the air but nevertheless her horizons were once more lifting. She felt this subtle change and was afraid: it was much easier to bow her head and suffer. All the time she repeated to herself, as though reciting a refrain in one of her own poems, that she must not be "too happy". There were warnings everywhere that this would be fatal and she heeded them. The slightest accident could upset her equilibrium for weeks, as when Sette, fencing with his tutor on the roof of the house, while not wearing a mask, slipped and was struck near the eye. A surgeon had to be sent for, Sette nearly fainted and for a while there was panic which penetrated eventually even into Elizabeth's sanctum. But the wound was superficial and Sette suffered only a black eye and a small cut. This did little to reassure Elizabeth who was far too preoccupied with imagining what might have happened to rejoice over what had not. She wrote to a friend, "one half a quarter of an inch higher and the stroke wd. have been . . . instantaneously mortal". What made the situation worse was that her father was away at the time and Sette "might have died – died on the spot!" This death would only have fitted into what she saw as the pattern: other people's loved ones died after months of preparation but Barretts were doomed to be snatched without warning. She never felt safe: just as she thought a measure of serenity had been granted to her this was exposed as an illusion. All around, her contemporaries forged ahead, improving their reputations while she stood still and felt in any case that she had hardly started.

The rest of 1842 and all of 1843 were dominated by the completion of her new collection of poems. She wanted to write some impressive new ones as well as to include those she had been sending to magazines and saw all of them together making one "five shilling book". To balance her slighter pieces she had been working on a "Vision of Poets", which was "allegorical and mystical". Its "six or seven hundred lines" she thought more suitable than her other new poem, "The Dead Pan", to be the centre-piece of her volume. But she was without a publisher. Moxon, who published all the best poets, had told George, now her intermediary, that although he had great respect for Miss Barrett's genius, he had little faith in her commercial value and could not afford to publish her. George, unlike Bro on that previous occasion, did not attempt to sweeten the news, telling her that Moxon had been "unhesitating and decided". Elizabeth took the rebuff well. She decided not to approach any other publisher at the moment but to wait a year, write some more new poems and try again. The only drawback was that in her head she was already contemplating "a poem of more importance" and she would have liked her volume of shorter pieces out of the way. It was a great consolation, hard on the heels of Moxon's rejection, to receive a letter from Cornelius Mathews, a New York editor, who in asking her to send him some poems assured her he was her "trustee for the further extension of [her] reputation in America!" She was delighted and amused to find she had one to further; it was the beginning of her love of Americans who were "kind and courteous" and valued her more than certain people in her own country who seemed to think some other poets superior.[2]

Elizabeth watched her contemporaries keenly and in a few cases jealously. Poets of the calibre of Browning aroused no envy because she

1. Coxhoe Hall, near Durham, where Elizabeth Barrett Browning was born

2. Edward Moulton-Barrett,
Elizabeth's father,
as a young man

3. Mary Graham-Clarke,
Elizabeth's mother,
before her marriage

4. Hope End: view from the Lower Pond

5. Elizabeth aged 12

6. A sketch of Hope End mansion, believed to be by
Elizabeth's sister, Henrietta

7. George, Arabella ('Arabel'), Samuel and
Charles ('Stormie') Moulton-Barrett

8. Edward ('Bro'), Elizabeth's
favourite brother

9. Elizabeth aged 14 (until recently this was thought to have been painted much later, when Elizabeth was in her 20s)

10. Edward Moulton-Barrett,
Elizabeth's father

11. Mary Moulton-Barrett,
Elizabeth's mother

12. Elizabeth aged 17: a water-colour by her mother

13. Fortfield Terrace, Sidmouth, where the Moulton-Barretts
moved in 1832 (second from left)

14. Tor Bay and Beacon Terrace, where Elizabeth lived in Torquay

15. No.50 Wimpole Street as it would have been in the 1840s; it is no longer standing

16. Arabella ('Arabel') Moulton-Barrett

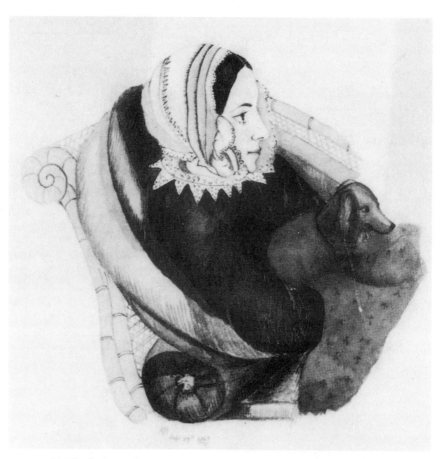

17. Elizabeth, aged 34, with Flush: a water-colour by her brother Alfred

18. Surtees Cook

19. Henrietta Moulton-Barrett

thought him a genius. His *Dramatic Lyrics*, published at the end of 1842, had roused in her an ecstasy of admiration: he had "the glory of lightning". Kenyon, to whom she had enthused, tried to arrange an introduction but she had turned him down emphatically. She could not bear the excitement of such a visit, though she did not deny her fascination with Browning (whom she and Miss Mitford often discussed, pooling their gossip). But, as well as the unbearable tension such a thrilling visit would have produced, there was also another kind of tension which explained her refusal. She wrote to Miss Mitford that her father would "certainly open his eyes and set me down among the *inclined*-to-be 'good for nothing poetesses'". She added she could just see his face if she had Browning (and also Horne, who was eager to pay court) "up stairs in my bedroom". It was not to be thought of. "This winter I must be quiet," she wrote, as though she were ever anything else. She could not, she felt, emulate Browning but she could at least put poets like Caroline Norton in their place. Mrs Norton was obviously a source of extreme irritation to her. She had published four volumes of poetry by 1842 and all of it had been both praised and bought. She was much talked of (mainly for her beauty and her personal life) and Hartley Coleridge had placed her first in a list of ten British poetesses in a review in *The Quarterly Review*. Elizabeth found this difficult to take. It was not that she minded Coleridge putting her second in his list but that she thought most of Mrs Norton's work "feeble". It was nonsense, and a mockery of Elizabeth's hero, to refer to Mrs Norton, as Coleridge had done, as "the Byron of Modern Poetesses". Elizabeth conceded, grudgingly, that some of her rival's poetry had "true pathos" but rated it all as minor. Seeing the *Quarterly* praise Mrs Norton made her even more restless than she already was. By April 1843 she was confessing to Miss Mitford, "it is my tendency . . . to aspire beyond myself – which is not a bad tendency – except that it makes one discontented and restless."

She worked hard, seeking diversion only through her novels. She was "charmed for the better" by Frederika Bremer's *Neighbours*, translated from the Swedish by Mary Howitt. Elizabeth thought it far better than any of Jane Austen, mostly because she identified with Serena, the heroine, a very un-Austen creation. Serena's problem is that she loves her grandparents, who have brought her up, far too much to leave them for her prospective husband – she is extremely doubtful about the merits of the institution of marriage and the author applauds. Elizabeth, who thought Serena's spirit of self-sacrifice uplifting, was pained that neither

Miss Mitford nor Mr Kenyon agreed. In vain she urged upon them "the serenity, the sweetness, the undertone of Christian music . . ." There were none of these qualities in another novel which absorbed Elizabeth. *Leila* by George Sand had a much more stirring subject – "passion". Elizabeth had first read George Sand in 1839, and her curiosity had grown ever since. She thought this author "wonderful . . . in eloquence and passion". But the amount and kind of passion in *Leila* made her "blush in my solitude to the ends of my fingers – blush three blushes in one . . . for *Her* who cd. be so shameless – for her sex, whose purity is so disgraced – and for myself in particular who could hold such a book for five minutes in one hand while a coal fire burnt within reach of the other". Yet the book was never dropped into the fire. The novel was written in a series of monologues from one character to another and it was Leila's address to the poet she loves which caused all the blushing: "Oh, I remember the burning nights I passed pressed against a man's flanks in close embrace . . ." Leila says she knows she "summoned pleasure at the price of eternal damnation" yet she takes that pleasure and is tormented by the way "gross pleasure mingles with the most sublime impulses of intelligence". Elizabeth called *Leila* "a serpent book both for language, colour and soul-slime" but she could not deny its power and significance. The central theme of the novel is that everyone, but especially women, have warring instincts and that the struggle to control them is a violent one for those with strong passions. Elizabeth was aware that she, like Leila, had difficulty resigning herself to reality. She had had none of Leila's experiences, nor lived a life that flouted convention like George Sand, but that had not made her immune to feelings of passion in the broadest sense. Her passion went into her poetry, masked in all kinds of ways.

There were other painful conclusions to be drawn about herself from the last novel which influenced her that winter. This was Balzac's *Le Père Goriot*. There were no burning nights or heaving flanks within its chaste pages but it captured Elizabeth's imagination no less. The widower Goriot is fleeced by his two selfish daughters of all he possesses. When he lies dying neither daughter will come, though he cries out, "I want my daughters! It is I who made them, they are mine!" His final bitter words are "Don't let your daughters marry if you love them." Yet Goriot is no tyrant – quite the reverse. He has elevated fatherhood to an exalted plane and what has made him happy is giving life to his children. Elizabeth judged *Le Père Goriot* "a very painful book" and thought about it a great deal. Her father, like Goriot, adored his children and for him, as for Goriot, they had taken the place of his wife. Like Goriot, her father could not contemplate marriage for any of them: he feared marriage for them because of his love for them. Elizabeth did not need Balzac to explain Goriot to her; she understood him only too well. Increasingly, she was beginning to think that love of such intensity, love that was so all-consuming, was dangerous (though she had not yet begun to wonder if this sort of love *was* love at all). She saw her father as the victim of his own system, suffering even more than his children from the stranglehold he had put upon them. They could not move but neither could he. Her father would never end up like Goriot but with nine children he could not expect to keep them all in his embrace. Elizabeth knew *she* would always remain faithful – she had not the slightest desire to leave her father – but she suspected Henrietta of feeling differently. Henrietta had a tendency to dine "without a chaperone" and Elizabeth feared the consequences. She wrote to George that, although not a prude, she thought her sister "should be particular in regard to her associates". If Papa discovered that Henrietta had been at Mrs Whithead's alone he would be furious and Elizabeth went so far as to ask George, in her best pompous imitation of Mr Barrett, to use his authority and "put an absolute end to it". She also had misgivings about Henry, who was breaking out. That very summer, given money for his twenty-fourth birthday, he had announced he was going to Dover to see some friends. "What nonsense," his father said and forbade it. Next morning, Henry vanished with his carpet bag. Elizabeth held her breath: "At breakfast people waited in awe for the enquiry 'Where is Henry?'" It did not come, Mr Barrett simply assuming Henry was in bed. Elizabeth prayed Henry would re-appear "before an actual explosion". She found it impossible to believe that the memory of her father thundering "What nonsense" had not echoed in Henry's ears and made him turn back at Canterbury. There was no sympathy expressed by her for him; her sympathy went to her father.

It would have been much easier, as Elizabeth knew, for her brothers and sisters to obey their father's strictures about visiting if they had lived in a more hospitable environment. Mr Barrett had no wish to deny his children amusements: it was more that he saw no reason for them to look outside the family for them. *He* found his large family made him self-sufficient: why did not they? He hated strangers and being what he called "imposed upon". He worried about whether guests would be happy and worst of all whether he had it in his power to amuse them sufficiently. Elizabeth, though exasperated, saw this trait of his as endearing at the time and went to some trouble to explain to Miss Mitford that what her father suffered from, just as she herself did, was only a complicated sort of shyness. He appeared to have a total lack of confidence in his own ability to be a host to anyone outside the family. He felt intimidated. He claimed, for example, that Kenyon would be bored. "It would be impossible," commented Elizabeth sarcastically to Miss Mitford, "for anyone to persuade him that Mr Kenyon could dine anywhere out of a draught of epigrams, with a lion's hide for a tablecloth . . ." She was equally "vexed" when he would not ask Horne, who had been so kind to her, to dinner. Instead, grimly determined to do what must be done, Mr Barrett went to see Horne to thank him but, as Elizabeth remarked, "you see the never asking him to dinner makes the calling worse than nugatory". It was all due, she insisted, to that "shyness" she had tried to explain, especially of anyone considered intellectual. Her father's shyness was of the most unfortunate variety. It made him seem gruff instead of attractively diffident. People put his unbending manner down either to ill temper or to hostility. He put up a tremendous fight against Miss Mitford being invited to stay – the usual fuss, with transparent excuses about the lack of room, the lack of suitable entertainment for her – but, when Elizabeth insisted, he succumbed quickly to Miss Mitford's charm and had no difficulty whatsoever with the dreaded entertaining. Her visits became pleasures for him as well as for his daughter but it was no good Elizabeth's claiming he would enjoy the company of other strangers – she was told Miss Mitford was an exception. The same stubbornness stopped him enjoying other social pleasures too. He had always wanted to belong to the Reform Club and yet he consistently refused to allow anyone to put him up for membership because, as Elizabeth told George, he had "the most transcendental fear of being blackballed". When, in March 1842, someone put him up without his knowledge and did not tell him until he had been safely elected, he was, Elizabeth wrote, "thrilled by the honour because it was 'uncourted, unsought . . .'"

It upset Elizabeth frequently that hardly anyone, even within his family, knew just how thoughtful and tender her father could be. When Miss Mitford's father died, in December 1842, Mr Barrett's sympathy touched Elizabeth. She had not, she wrote to Miss Mitford, asked him to pray for her friend but "he did it out of his own mind and quite from his heart . . . and I kissed him twice instead of once afterwards because it touched me." She had some interesting comments, in view of the way in which she was to present them later, about these prayer sessions. "Papa is my chaplain," she told Miss Mitford ". . . prays with me every night . . . not out of a book but simply and warmly at once – with one of my hands held in his and nobody besides him and me in the room. That is dear in him – is it not? And he with his elastic spirit and merry laugh! One might as little expect such an act from the youngest of my brothers (at first sight!) as from him."[3] She remembered that when she was ill at Torquay and her mind wandered she heard her father praying and, though she could not make out what he was saying, she had felt "a sort of vague satisfaction in seeing him kneel down there". There was no suggestion whatsoever that it was her father who imposed this ritual on her – quite the reverse – nor was there the faintest hint that it was a duty and not a pleasure. She was proud, too, of the evidence that her father was solicitous for the welfare of others. During Dr Mitford's illness, he had asked after him every day and had encouraged the sending of gifts – oysters, grapes, chocolate from Jamaica, anything that might tempt an invalid. At that particular stage in her life, she was closer to him than she had been since she was a child. The life she led, and the spirit in which she led it, met with his entire approval. She was doing all the things he had urged on her so many times with little response – eating sensibly, trying to exercise, discouraging all visitors except Kenyon and Miss Mitford, not getting over-excited about anything and not being too intense about her work. He was gratified to see her so apparently content. There were few challenges to his authority and, when they did arise, he was disposed to be indulgent. The loss of Flush in the autumn of 1843 illustrated beautifully how far Mr Barrett was prepared to allow his daughter to go in contesting his will so long as she took care to save his face.

Flush, as everyone had predicted, was stolen by dog snatchers on 13th September 1843. He was out walking with Crow in Mortimer Street, just round the corner from Wimpole Street, when he disappeared with a parting yelp. Poor Crow, in floods of tears, did not even see who had snatched him. She had to return home and confess the dreadful news. Elizabeth sobbed so hard she made herself ill: her imagination tortured her as she felt what her little dog must be feeling. All available brothers were sent out in different directions in search of Flush, handbills offering a reward were printed and posted everywhere in the vicinity; but by the end of twenty-four agonising hours there was no news. Then, as

Elizabeth reported breathlessly to Miss Mitford, "the organised dog-banditti" (known as The Fancy), who made four thousand pounds a year from their evil trade, claimed responsibility. The drama was unbearable. First of all the leader of The Fancy, one Taylor, said Flush would never be seen again because his owner had had the temerity to post bills; then they were told Taylor would "see what he could do"; then Taylor swaggered into Wimpole Street saying Flush would be released upon payment of five guineas. And at that point Mr Barrett intervened.

The family was at dinner. Alfred stood in the hall bargaining with the disreputable but entirely self-possessed Taylor. He realised that he had no money himself and so would have to ask his father for the necessary cash at some point. But Mr Barrett, who like everyone else had been listening, got up from the table as soon as he heard the terms, strode into the hall and confronting Taylor told him he was "a rascal" and would get no more than two guineas. Elizabeth, straining to hear from the open door of her upstairs room, heard him add that unless Taylor complied with these new terms he would be given "into the charge of the police; and that as to the dog, it and him might go!" The Barretts quailed but Taylor was not in the least put out. He just smiled and said, as Alfred showed him the door, that the dog would never be seen again. Mr Barrett told them all not to mention the scene to their sister but of course she had overheard and was already planning her strategy. It would be pointless to plead with her father: in such a mood he was implacable. She must go behind his back. "My despair," she wrote to Miss Mitford, "overcame my sense of obedience." But she could not manage alone: she needed at least one co-operative brother. Luckily, Henry was the only one at home next day. Knowing he had sufficient spark of rebellion in him to dare to act as her intermediary, Elizabeth gave him five guineas (three of her own on top of her father's two) and sent him off to find Taylor. This Henry did (though he had to pay the insolent Taylor yet another half guinea for his "extra trouble"). Flush was delivered home safely. But the most interesting outcome was Mr Barrett's reaction. He was not, of course, fooled for an instant. He was "delighted to come home and find Flush", Elizabeth wrote but he cross-examined Henrietta as to how much had been paid. Henrietta managed to keep her wits about her, replying, "two sovereigns, I believe – but really I know very little about it", which, as Elizabeth told Miss Mitford, was true. Mr Barrett had said drily, "Ah! Two sovereigns and I dare say three besides." There was no explosion of wrath, no inquisition into the details, no interrogation of Elizabeth herself. As far as Mr Barrett was concerned, his authority had not been publicly flouted. The notion that he had in any way lost a battle was not entertained by anyone. But he had. Elizabeth had in this small but significant way brought herself directly and knowingly to disobey her father and to involve another family member in that disobedience. She was amazed at the power of love: only love of Flush had given her courage.

She was by then besotted with Flush, to the increasing irritation of the rest of the family. They had discovered that she was so convinced of her dog's intelligence that she was teaching him to read. Her brothers were beside themselves – "laughed the tears into their eyes" – and pronounced her completely mad. She told Flush, "Kiss A, Flush – and now Kiss B." Witnessing this, they almost doubted her sanity. Then there were the arithmetic lessons. She held up a piece of cake, counted to three, and Flush had to take it on three and not sooner. What she wanted was for Flush to be competent enough to play dominoes (she had read of a gentleman and his dog doing so and had felt "jealous . . . I can't help it"). In her eyes, Flush could do no wrong, but to her brothers, he was a nuisance. Once Henry's dog Catiline attacked and injured Flush so badly that he could only walk on three legs and was "in very low spirits". Elizabeth was furious and told Henry he should look after his brute of a dog better. Henry, supported by his brothers, rounded on her and said it was Flush who had caused all the trouble and had driven Catiline to defend himself. Elizabeth retorted that the next time a dog was stolen she hoped it would be Catiline.

It was during rows like this that Elizabeth temporarily doubted the wisdom of her own wish to keep the entire family in Wimpole Street. She yearned sometimes to escape just for a while. By the summer of 1843 her health had sufficiently improved to permit her to take regular wheelchair outings with Crow but dreams of more exotic journeys than to Regent's Park began to creep into her correspondence. She felt guilty about having them: to dream of travelling was to betray her vow. "If I were strong and free," she wrote to Miss Mitford ". . . I should be running myself all over the world – I should be in Paris . . . I should be in Italy . . . I should be longest in Germany – I should be in the Alps and Pyrenees – I might be peradventure in the eternal mist of Niagara."[4] Another time, when Miss Mitford was astonished people ever went abroad, Elizabeth retorted she was astonished they stayed at home: "who, with strength and opportunity, should pass into the world of spirits without a glance at the Jungfrau . . ." It distressed her most that she had never been to Italy – "Am I never never to see Italy with my eyes?" – and she wrote that it made her "sigh like a furnace" to think of it. She joked about how she would behave if she could travel: "smoke, take a master's degree in mysticism". Her brothers' travelling opportunities made her envious. In August 1843 Stormie and George went on a modified Grand Tour and Elizabeth, though pleased for them, was envious. The instant contentment which had filled her just to be home in London had worn off. It was a good, not a bad, sign. The past no longer dominated the present and the future was not excluded from her thoughts. By the beginning of 1844, the year her most important volume of poems to date was published, she had acknowledged to herself that this future could not be denied, that hopes, dreams, ambitions and aspirations had all risen once more to the surface.

This change was reflected in her poetry. There was still an overwhelming pre-occupation with death in most of the poems she was writing, but the timid optimism pervading them was new, as was the recognition, uncertain and hesitating, that the world was not necessarily a dark and dismal place best left as soon as possible. There was, too, an interest in the present and its concerns. Elizabeth followed developments in the arts in London with her old keen interest. The arts, like so much else, were undergoing a period of rapid change in the new Victorian England. The young Queen had been ruling since 1837 and the effects of having a happily married woman on the throne were noticeable: the arts were less licentious in tone, much more solidly respectable. They were also broader based to take into account the tastes of the ever-expanding reading public. By the 1840s an enormous number of new magazines had been launched in London. Elizabeth loved magazines – she was quick to sample *Punch* when it appeared in 1841 – and informed herself through them. She did not go to the theatre but read all reviews closely so that she was well aware of Macready's fame as an actor not to mention that of the Kembles. She did not go to concerts but knew that contemporary British composers counted for little and that audiences wanted to hear Mendelssohn above all. She rarely visited art galleries but was familiar with the work of Sir Edwin Landseer, William Etty and J. M. W. Turner.

And, where art was concerned, Arabel was a useful informant. It was Arabel who visited Benjamin Haydon in his studio (suitably chaperoned by Sette) and described it to Elizabeth. She admired Haydon's portrait of Wordsworth on Helvellyn and said how her sister would love to see it if only she had been able. (Haydon promptly sent the picture round to Wimpole Street in a cab.) This talented artist became another correspondent of Elizabeth's in the spring of 1842 (the introduction was through Miss Mitford) and for the next two years amused and entertained her. The same age as Mr Barrett, Haydon's cross in life was that he felt he was a marked man whose progress in his career had been deliberately halted by the Court, the Royal Academy or Sir Robert Peel. Haydon quickly became very fond of his sympathetic "invisible friend" whose love of gossip as well as intellectual discussion matched his own. Without realising it, he fuelled several of Elizabeth's prejudices, in particular, her rivalry with Caroline Norton, based not only on her slight envy but on her mistaken assumption that Mrs Norton was the wicked lady she was painted. Haydon told her many indiscreet tit-bits about Mrs Norton, with whom he had at one time been infatuated. Haydon also had the distinction of having breakfasted with Keats and of having been present in Paris during Napoleon's entry as well as at all kinds of other events quite outside the scope of Elizabeth's limited experience. Like Horne, Haydon was in and of the contemporary world and as such an exciting person to her.

But in her room in Wimpole Street Elizabeth did not feel as cut off from the real world as some people thought her. She followed not only artistic and literary concerns but also politics. It helped, of course, that her father and brothers were there to talk of the Queen's battle with her new minister, Sir Robert Peel (whom Elizabeth liked no more than Victoria at first did), or what O'Connell was going to do about Ireland, but even without their encouragement she was interested in all that happened and prided herself on being well informed. Miss Mitford was treated often to her outspoken views on O'Connell in particular. Early in their correspondence it had emerged that Miss Mitford hero-worshipped Daniel O'Connell, applauding his attempts to "liberate" Ireland from the union with England, whereas Elizabeth had strong reservations (unlike Stormie who adored him). That summer of 1843, as O'Connell organised enormous rallies to gain support for his cause, Miss Mitford outraged Elizabeth by comparing him to Napoleon. "After all," Elizabeth argued, "what is he doing or about to do in Ireland?" She thought he was "playing at ninepins with the souls of men" and "amusing the world by causing the Irish nation to stand balanced on one toe on the single air-hung rope". She said he made her feel "giddy to look on". But she loved to do just that: look on and pontificate. Her passion for current affairs continued: and so did her interest in new inventions. In December 1843 she wrote to Miss Mitford about "that wonderful invention of the day, called the Daguerreotype". This early form of photography completely fascinated her – "think of a man sitting down in the sun and leaving his facsimile . . ." Her brothers sneered at it and thought portraits still infinitely preferable but she was instantly drawn to this exciting development and its possibilities. Confined to a back room in Wimpole Street though she generally was, Elizabeth was firmly in touch with the contemporary world and in spite of her circumstances had a remarkable degree of knowledge about it.

She was beginning to find these interests creeping into her poetry – current events, particularly broad social questions like the employment of children in factories, stirred her to write, to take up a position. She had always thought there was *no* subject a poet should not touch and now she began to test her conviction. To write about what was happening in the world made her feel more alive than she had done for years – she could not help looking ahead to 1844 as a year of promise. Her poems were almost certain to be published, her health almost certain to improve, her circle of friends (even if they were only paper ones) almost certain to widen. She felt in control of her life, she was "strong now to what I once was". In her first letter of 1844 to Miss Mitford she sounded happy and even talked of being "lucky". In her second, she spoke of being "resolved to look at the brightest side as long as there is any life left". Life already held more prospects than death, though these prospects she saw only in work terms. She wrote to Haydon that "all my earthly futurity as an individual lies in poetry. In other respects the game is up . . . But poetry . . . lingers . . . it is like a *will to be written*." The urge she felt to write was her life force, restored to her when she had believed it to be taken from her.

Chapter Eight

T HE year from which Elizabeth hoped so much began with a bitter
blow. Crow, her personal maid for the last five years, gave notice.
Her mistress cried "till I was faint with crying" and would not be
consoled. It was not simply that Crow was everything to her, but that she
dreaded having to train a new maid. Only a few weeks before Crow
broke the news, Elizabeth had been telling Miss Mitford, who was
having problems with her own maid, how much her servant meant to
her. "I am attached to my own maid," she had written, "by quite as
continual moment-by-moment series of attentions from her to me as you
can be to yours – and from my illness which at one time made attention
all day and night a necessity of my existence, she has been as closely
drawn to me personally as yours can be to you." What was most
valuable about Crow was her particular personality: she had laid to rest
that quite unjustified childhood nightmare of Elizabeth's about there
being no one to look after her. Elizabeth liked to be "managed" and
what she called "Crow's imperative" suited her very well. Crow was
firm, strong (she was capable of lifting and carrying her mistress), kind,
and above all immensely cheerful. As well as being Elizabeth's servant
she was her loving, compassionate protector and admirer. The thought
of her leaving made Elizabeth feel instantly helpless and vulnerable.

But as well as being genuinely grief-stricken, Elizabeth was also
"vexed". The truth was that Crow had had to confess the reason for
leaving: she had secretly married the butler, William Treherne, son of a
Hope End tenant farmer who had first worked for the Barretts in the
stables, risen to be the driver of their carriage and then to being head of
the servant household in Wimpole Street. Furthermore, Crow was
pregnant. Knowing that instant dismissal would result for both of them
once the news was out, the couple had made plans to open a baker's shop
in Camden Town. Instead of being sympathetic and delighted, Elizabeth
felt she had been tricked. She maintained to Miss Mitford that "I do not

blame her for leaving me" but at the same time told her friend that Crow "should not have married so – it was imprudent and might have led to inferences most painful and prejudicial to her". Although Elizabeth did not know it, those inferences would have been correct. Crow broke the news in the third week of March 1844, confessing that she had been married some time, since 30th December of the previous year. She did not confess that on her marriage she was already three months' pregnant. As Elizabeth was writing serenely to Miss Mitford on 16th January, "I know what it wd. be to lose my faith in her," Crow was wondering how long she could conceal her condition. Throughout February, as Elizabeth discussed the pregnancy of Miss Mitford's maid and pontificated about chastity, Crow was terrified of being exposed. Elizabeth wrote to Miss Mitford that *she* would not keep a pregnant, unmarried maid because of the deceit which she had practised. Like her father, she regarded deceit as the most heinous of crimes. Melodramatically, she declared, "Nay, – if she administered to me like an angel . . . if I were solitary by my own hearthstone . . . helpless on my sofa . . . not all these circumstances . . . cd. induce me to retain in my service . . . an individual *I could not trust*." Fortunately, until June when Crow's baby was born and simple arithmetic revealed all, Elizabeth was spared the extent of Crow's so-called untrustworthiness.

But what also "vexed" her was that, in her opinion, William Treherne was not good enough for Crow: she had thrown herself away, been blinded by the young man's admittedly handsome appearance. Treherne was "honest" and "good in a common way" but not "*remarkable*" for his personality as Crow was. His "mind and heart" were definitely not "so finely tuned". Elizabeth concluded disdainfully that his looks had "triumphed . . . over her love for myself". It was extraordinary that she was prepared to admit the full extent of her own self-interest without any sense of shame, especially since she had so often emphasised that servants were human and had a right to human dignity. The Barretts as a family had indeed a good record with servants. Minny Robinson, once Arabel's nurse and now housekeeper, had been with the family twenty-six years and there were at least three others, including Treherne himself, whose history stretched back to Hope End days. The servants were treated well, thanks to a tradition laid down by Mary Barrett to which her daughters responded. It had always shocked Elizabeth when people taught their children "not to talk to servants! . . . It is an atrocity both in morals and instincts." She had boasted to Miss Mitford that she had "a fine madness for turning servants into friends". Now her definition of friendship was revealed as strictly limited. She also liked supplementing their limited education. Crow, for example, had been given Miss Mitford's *Our Village* to read and Elizabeth was proud of her "delight in it". She fostered good literary taste in her maid; some of her happiest hours were spent reading selected texts to Crow with Flush on her lap. In turn, Crow had her own influence. In matters of etiquette Crow was the instructor: she knew what was appropriate (whereas Elizabeth said she "could not care less"). Once, when Elizabeth wanted to send Miss Mitford a poker and a pair of tongs as a moving-in present Crow indignantly objected "because it would be thought *odd*". Elizabeth liked to be odd but gave way, bowing to Crow's superior knowledge in this sphere. The delicate balance between friendship and familiarity was carefully maintained until Crow told her news and all Elizabeth's pious words were seen as hollow. Why had Crow not trusted her? Why had she not confided in her as a friend? Why had she not been honourable and left before getting married? It never seemed to occur to her – she, who talked so airily of not minding poverty if it fell to her – that the answers were economic ones. The average wage of a butler in 1844 was £40 a year, of a lady's maid £16. Between them, Treherne and Crow had roughly £1 a week out of which to save for their perilous future. This being the case, every week they could cling to their Wimpole Street places was vital. To stay as long as feasible they were prepared to go through the frustration of living and sleeping in the same house, married and yet separate. The strain of such a life was one the highly imaginative Elizabeth ought easily to have imagined – the furtive meetings, the constant pretence in front of others. It was one thing for Elizabeth to admire George Sand for living according to her convictions, for extolling passion in her novels, but quite another to empathise with her unfortunate maid. Her attitude to Crow simply revealed that far from being a woman of advanced ideas she was disappointingly hidebound by convention and in this case totally selfish. Put to the test – and she had not been so severely tested before – Elizabeth's compassion failed her.

But she gave Crow a handsome sum of money as a wedding present and, the first shock over, Elizabeth's sense of justice and real affection for Crow helped her to come to terms with the situation. Treherne left as soon as the truth of his marriage was known, but Crow stayed on until April (with the whole family concealing her condition from Mr Barrett). The actual date of her departure was kept a secret from Elizabeth by her sisters until she had gone. Even then, Crow did not entirely desert her but trudged, seven months' pregnant, from the other end of Camden Town to minister to Elizabeth's needs, thereby making the break easier. Every time she left to go home to the bakery, Elizabeth cried and Crow cried, telling her mistress, "it was as great a deprivation to her as it could be to me".[1] Elizabeth reported to Miss Mitford, slightly sceptical in tone, that Treherne's bakery was flourishing. She also said Crow had told her that her husband was "very attentive" towards her and "very fond" (though Elizabeth could not resist slanting this good news by sticking an "apparently" in front of it). She referred to her maid as "poor" Crow at all times. She was also selfish enough to complain that when "poor" Crow had her baby "*then* will come the full loss to *me*".

Crow's willingness to make the break as easy as possible, at great cost to herself, meant that the new maid was introduced into Elizabeth's life as gradually as possible. Her name was Elizabeth Wilson. Elizabeth told Miss Mitford at the beginning of April, a week after Crow's revelation, that Henrietta had interviewed and engaged "a young woman whom I have not yet had the heart to see". She had been brought down from Northumberland by a Barrett cousin and was said to be "gentle-voiced and of a bright and kind countenance".[2] Wilson started her duties properly at the beginning of May. Naturally, she had a gigantic inferiority complex about Crow. In her first week, Elizabeth had mistaken her for Crow and Wilson had been obliged to say sadly, "Ah no! I am afraid it is nobody equal to Mrs Crow." Such humility touched Elizabeth so much that she confided in Miss Mitford that she was sure she would learn to like Wilson in time. She did, in a remarkably short time, too. Her first impression had been that the new maid was both too soft and too lacking in vitality whereas Crow, though gentle, had exercised great authority. She had adopted a "sort of half-nursing" attitude frequently issuing commands like "you must NOT have the window open . . ." Now, as Elizabeth complained to Miss Mitford, if she opened a window it stayed open without Wilson daring to remark on it. This did not please her. At the age of thirty-eight her attitude was childish; she loathed her new liberty because of the responsibility it brought: "I may take double morphine draughts if I like! I may go to bed as late as I please – and talk as long." Then there was Wilson's personality with which to contend. Watching Wilson tip-toe around, hesitating over every decision and treating her like glass depressed Elizabeth. She was, she admitted to Miss Mitford, ashamed of herself – "how querulous! how childish!" – but she could not help pining for Crow's boisterous confidence. Yet within a month Wilson was discovered to have no serious drawbacks. Elizabeth wrote that it touched her "to see how she exerts herself to be talkative and cheerful" once she had learned this was what her mistress liked. It made a difference that Crow was no longer coming occasionally to Wimpole Street (she had gone to her mother's at Caistor where she had a daughter, Mary Elizabeth, on 5th June). Now that comparisons could no longer be made, the situation was easier for Wilson. Within another month, Wilson had become "interesting", if quiet, and letters to Miss Mitford were scattered with "Wilson says" and "Wilson thinks". By July, Wilson's welfare was of such concern to Elizabeth that she would not allow her out of the house in case the pain she had in her face was made worse by the damp weather. And, best of all, Elizabeth had discovered her new maid's most unusual quality for someone of her station in life: she was discreet.

The change of maids was not the only annoyance which 1844 brought. Elizabeth was also irritated, though to a much lesser degree, to find herself bracketed together with Caroline Norton in her friend Horne's critical résumé of contemporary literature, *A New Spirit of the Age*, published that spring.[3] Elizabeth was taken aback to find "Mrs Norton and I are fastened up in a gold cage together". Only recently, she had written revealingly to Horne that she thought the latest high opinion of Mrs Norton, expressed in *The Quarterly*, was absurd but that "you know how prejudices work and I confess to you a little disinclination . . . which may vibrate in spite of me . . .". She thought it insensitive of Horne, knowing how she felt about Mrs Norton, to mention them together. There was one general, descriptive sentence she found particularly offensive: "one is all womanhood; the other all wings." Hardly less annoying was Horne's blatant flattery of her – she found it "detestable". She wrote to Miss Mitford that she was "disappointed moreover on the point of his personal view of my poetry . . . I had an impression . . . that he had thought better of it" (Horne had praised her for her "great inventiveness" but said she lacked an "equal power of construction"). The pages of hyperbole and an overwritten passage about her life as an invalid also offended her. Such a résumé in so important a book made it all the more imperative that she should bring out her new volume and show the world that she was most decidedly *not* to be bracketed with Mrs Norton.

That spring, Elizabeth finished "A Drama of Exile". She had begun it in "a glow of pleasure", starting with the idea of Eve's anguish at being turned out of the Garden of Eden, but once finished, she immediately had doubts. Was this, her most ambitious work yet, worth anything? The more she read it, the less sure she was. She worked herself into such a panic of doubt that she almost put her manuscript into the fire but Kenyon, who was visiting the day she came nearest to doing so, took it from her, read it and pronounced it "more sustained and full of power" than anything she had written before. Greatly heartened, she went ahead with plans for the new volume. But Moxon, who now agreed to publish it, persuaded her to bring out a two-volume edition (instead of the "five shilling" volume she had had in mind). He was prepared to print 1,500 copies and halve the profits with her. At the same time, her American publishers were willing to bring out their own edition, either simultaneously or soon after.[4] This proof that her work was valued on both sides of the Atlantic excited her and made her impatient for publication day. Her poems were ready in March but Moxon was not. Elizabeth wrote to Thomas Westwood (an aspiring poet she had added to her list of correspondents) that "I hear Mr Moxon says: I suppose Miss Barrett is not in a hurry about her publication, and *I* say, I suppose Mr Moxon is not in a hurry about *the* publication."[5] She admitted she might be partly to blame because she had kept the proofs longer than agreed (and made many small alterations) but thought Moxon guilty of delay too. By the end of July she was sure he was prevaricating and was ready to be angry. Her anger turned to consternation when Moxon suddenly informed her that the two volumes were unequal in length and needed to be balanced. Elizabeth wrote to Boyd that she had seventy-two pages to make up on Volume Two and that Moxon was so cross he "wished to tear me to pieces". She felt like tearing herself to pieces. Moxon's solution was that they should just shuffle the order of the poems about: "tear away several poems from the end of the second volume and tie them onto the end of the first!" Elizabeth was outraged at the suggestion. She was a perfectionist who had spent days organising the order of her poems for best effect and meaning. The only alternative was to finish "Lady Geraldine's Courtship", a poem she had begun too late to include. She had written two hundred lines and now proceeded to compose another one hundred and forty-two in a day. She told Boyd she seemed to be in a dream all day. She was exhausted but, as she wrote to Miss Mitford, she now had nothing to do but "be idle and think wickedness . . ."

The two-volume edition appeared in the middle of August 1844, not the best time (then as now) to be published. Elizabeth showed herself sensibly aware of this, telling Mrs Martin it was "the dead time of year, when the very critics were thinking more of holiday innocence than of their carnivorous instincts". This did not upset her. It would not hurt her poems "ultimately" because "the regular critics will come back to it". Sending copies out gave her great pleasure but also caused her some modest hesitation. Should she, for example, send a copy to Carlyle, whom she did not know, and to Wordsworth, whom she had met but with whom she could hardly claim friendship? It made her nervous. Each book she posted needed "a great gasp of courage". But she was not in the least nervous about reviews. On the contrary, she hungered for them, the more the better whatever they said. She was desperate not for praise or fame (though not averse to either), so much as for the thrill of seeing what people made of her. The prospect of slashing attacks actually attracted her more than the chance of compliments: flattery which she despised would be lurking in those.

One of the first reviews was in *John Bull* and she wrote with glee to Miss Mitford that it "is said to cut me into gashes". Her father was furious with her for sending for *John Bull* at once, so eager was she "to know the head and front of the violence done to me . . ." She longed to be judged by impartial critics because she was convinced that friends "show only the sunny sides of their thoughts" and that their reactions could not therefore be of any consequence. As to sales, she had resolved not to enquire; she had no illusions about her book "going off like a pistol shot". Her view was that "poetry, if worth anything, will make its own way and if *not* worth anything will fail and die . . . and I do not *wish* the general law to be reversed on my account. It is a righteous law . . ."

The reviews, when they did come in, pleased her on the whole. The most gratifying aspect of them was their length. Reviews were, in those days, extremely long anyway but hers were exceptionally so and were a sign that her work was at last being taken seriously. *The Athenaeum* said sufficient to separate her forever from Mrs Norton: it defined her position as a woman poet as being in quite a different class from other poetesses. *Blackwood's* devoted a whole article to her and Elizabeth was not prevented from being pleased by "some hard criticism" which was mixed "with the liberal sympathy", announcing that "some of it I deserve, even in my own eyes; and all of it I am willing to be patient under".[6] John Forster praised her in *The Examiner*, and *The Atlas* agreed. The only disturbing part of reading the reviews was that the shorter poems, particularly the ballads, were yet again getting the most attention. "A Drama of Exile" was hardly mentioned. It occurred to her that the shorter poems were easier to write about and required less review space, but even so she was surprised that critics ignored her ambitious "Drama" and concentrated almost exclusively on the ballads. They called them "sweet", "full of feeling", and "beautiful", without in the least appearing to understand them. These "sweet" ballads were in fact about something quite sinister: the terrible dangers of love for a woman and the worthlessness of man's love for her. Underneath the attractive veneer her ballads were full of violent messages if only they had been heard. In "The Romaunt of the Page", for example, Elizabeth struck out against what men have made of so-called love, and the heroines of "The Rime of the Duchess May", "Bertha in the Lane" and "The Lay of the Brown Rosary" all die after the futility of earthly love, *man's* love, has been exposed to them.

But if the ballads were too subtle for critics fully to understand (and have remained so until recently) they nonetheless received a great deal of attention. The lyric poems suffered comparative neglect though they were infinitely better, and so did the sonnets. The general consensus of opinion about everything she offered was still that her strange rhymes spoiled her work. The critics did not like her by now well-known fondness for double rhymes, half-rhymes and what might be called trick-of-sight rhymes. Her friend Horne was anxious to explain why, taking most of his examples from "The Dead Pan". He himself could, if with difficulty, accept the rhyming of "rolls on" with "the sun", and even "flowing" with "slow in" but he thought rhyming "iron" with "inspiring" and "panther" with "saunter" going too far. He did not like this rhyming of first syllables only, "leaving the last to a question of euphonious quantity".[7] But Elizabeth was not prepared to allow this criticism as valid. She insisted that she was "speculative for freedom sake" rather than deliberately awkward and, when told that some people thought her double-rhymes in particular were "negligences", she was insulted. She explained to Boyd her "theory about double rhymes", writing, "Now, of double rhymes in use, which are perfect rhymes, you are aware how few there are, and yet you are also aware of what an admirable effect, in making a rhythm various and vigorous, double rhyming is in English poetry. Therefore, I have used a certain licence . . ."[8] She maintained stoutly that "the spirit of the English language was on her side", starting with Chaucer, and would not concede that sometimes this "spirit" carried her too far. (Readers of "The Lost Bower", for example, could be forgiven for balking at the rhyming of "hazels" with "dazzles".)

In spite of protests about her rhyming schemes the whole experience of having her new volumes out and so widely received was exhilarating. For weeks and weeks she corresponded happily with people who were anxious to give her their opinion and she greatly enjoyed defending her idiosyncrasies. What pleased her most was that so many people re-marked on the progress she had made. Those who harked back to "The Seraphim" volume annoyed her, except for Boyd whose preference for that type of poetry she was willing to allow. It was to Boyd that she wrote, with some exasperation, "It seems to me that I have more *reach*, whether in thought or language . . . All the life and strength which are in me seem to have passed into my poetry." Equally annoying, and a great surprise to her, was the discovery, as the letters came in, that a great many people appeared to take their opinions from reviews and actually imagined she would not notice. She curled her lip in scorn at such feebleness – ". . . the manner in which the most intelligent are content to take up or rather make up their opinions from periodical literature is to me extraordinary and repulsive; and the general want of sensibility to poetry and imaginative literature is to me extraordinary and repulsive."[9] When someone of the calibre of Harriet Martineau (the journalist and political economist whose controversial *Illustrations of Political Economy*, 1832–4, Elizabeth had greatly admired) wrote to her, she was thrilled not by the congratulations – Miss Martineau also had strong complaints – but by the evidence of "close reading". She wrote to Mrs Martin that "my hands shook as they broke the seal" of Miss Martineau's letter and that when she had read it what pleased her most was the writer's opinion that the "predominant impression" was one of "originality" and "immense advances".

She was currently very interested in Miss Martineau for reasons quite other than her critical views. This redoubtable lady was supposed to have been cured of cancer by mesmerism. All matters even remotely to do with the supernatural had always intrigued Elizabeth: "there never was a more foolishly weakly superstitious being than I am," she had written in her diary with feeling. She was, she said, "credulous nat-urally" and "ready . . . to . . . believe in a spirit world". At Hope End once, when the farm workers were frightened by what they declared were ghosts, Elizabeth did not for one minute join in the ridicule. She had never seen a ghost but constantly expected to. She listened "with interest to every goblin story" and in spite of her father's derision and strong disapproval could never stifle her natural leanings. When her artist pen-friend Haydon attempted to expose mesmerism as a fraud (though he too was inclined to believe in the supernatural) she would not be convinced by his personal experiences of cheating. Curiously, it was one of her growing new bonds with Henrietta, who once went to dine at a house where one of the Queen's doctors enthralled the company with his account of witnessing the amputation of a limb while the patient was in a magnetic sleep. Harriet Martineau's evidence impressed her. "It is wonderful!" wrote Elizabeth ". . . What a sensation in favour of the mysterious agency . . . Who will dare to doubt any more the existence of the agency?" She could not sleep for excitement when she heard that Miss Martineau's maid was mesmerising her twice a day and as a consequence she was recovering instead of dying. It made Elizabeth feel "astonished" and also "fearful". She thought it a terrible thing to put oneself under the will of another: "to submit myself body and soul to another will . . . is revolting." But, revolted or not, she was deeply attracted to this "proof" that there were supernatural forces and began collecting cases of "cures". To her delight, Wilson was equally interested and contributed her own examples gathered in the servants' quarters. It was, Elizabeth convinced herself, merely an extension of her own "natural leaning towards mysticism".

A corrective to this enthusiasm for mesmerism was provided by an important new friend – Anna Jameson. Mrs Jameson, the daughter of an artist who had specialised in Court miniatures, was an interesting woman with a growing reputation as an art and literary critic and writer. By the time she made Elizabeth's acquaintance, she had published eleven books of which the most original were *Characteristics of Women* (1832), an analysis of Shakespeare's heroines, and *Memoirs of the Loves of Poets*, a series of biographical sketches of women celebrated in ancient and modern poetry. Her art books and travel books were less celebrated but far more lucrative, which was important to her since she had to earn her own living. Every bit as precocious as a child as Elizabeth herself – she learnt Persian at seven and was fluent in French, Italian and Spanish by ten – she had been a governess from a young age until she married (disastrously). Travelling abroad with the families for whom she worked had given her the idea for a series of cultured travel books which eventually she made her speciality. Elizabeth had mentioned to Miss Mitford how much she had enjoyed one of these, *Pictures of the Social Life in Germany*, published in 1840. She admired its excellent "artistic taste" as well as its informative side. But what really enthralled her about Mrs Jameson was the wonderfully inaccurate gossip she had heard from Kenyon about her marriage. According to Kenyon (and half London), Mr Jameson had at first been rejected by his wife and was so outraged that he vowed to win her and then avenge himself by deserting her at the door of the church. Elizabeth, demonstrating her love of gossip, the more exaggerated the better, improved even on this when telling Miss Mitford that "two steps from the altar he broke upon the echo of his own oath to love . . ." She had him crying out, "I have overcome – I am avenged – Farewell for ever!" It was like the plot of one of Elizabeth's favourite novels. She clung to the story even after discovering that, far from leaving his bride two steps from the altar, Mr Jameson had lived with her for several years and had been joined by her in Canada where he took up a government post. Elizabeth felt the essence of the tale was true (which, very broadly speaking indeed, it was). Her first chance to fit face to fancy had come in 1842 when Kenyon had invited her on an outing which included Mrs Jameson in the party – but she was too weak to go. There was far more justification now for the care she took of her health than there had ever been before. Her system had taken, within the last four years, very severe physical as well as emotional blows. A blood vessel had indeed burst in one lung in 1838 and heart irregularities had been thought sufficiently serious to treat with digitalis. The treatment, of rest and increased doses of opium – because her regular dose no longer enabled her to sleep – had been disastrous. There was no need for her to nurse her weakness – she undoubtedly was weak and the frequent mentions of "congestion in the chest" indicated not only weakness but a permanent bronchial condition. Her muscles were feeble through in-activity, her lungs further harmed through breathing the close air of her room, her general strength debilitated by her inability to eat anything but slop food or drink anything but strong black coffee (which she loved). She was not malingering but nevertheless the way in which she lived was making her weaker still.

An outing with Kenyon was unquestionably beyond her limited resources but she had a by now highly developed and useful talent for living vicariously. She commissioned her sisters to go and meet Mrs Jameson for her and afterwards wrote to Miss Mitford, with great satisfaction, "I . . . have her now in her whole anatomy." But still she resisted all Kenyon's attempts to arrange a private meeting. When her 1844 poems came out, Kenyon reported that Mrs Jameson loved them and was going to write and say so. Elizabeth waited. At the end of a week, when no letter had appeared, she prompted Kenyon to remind Mrs Jameson because "I should very much like to have a full sincere letter from her". From what she had read of Mrs Jameson she had concluded she had the "very genius of criticism" and longed to benefit from it. No letter arrived. Instead, to her consternation, Kenyon told her Mrs Jameson had not written because she was thinking of dropping in, not realising that 50 Wimpole Street was an address where both father and eldest daughter found such appallingly casual visiting abhorrent. To Elizabeth's relief, she did in fact write after all, though the letter was disappointingly general and short. That, she imagined, would be that. But then in November Mrs Jameson was visiting a friend at 51 Wimpole Street and dropped a note into No. 50 saying where she was. Elizabeth replied, with a prevarication worthy of her father, that if only the note had come at 5 pm instead of 6 pm she would have asked Mrs Jameson to step in but, regretfully, it was not now possible.

Elizabeth did not know Mrs Jameson's persistence. A week later, she returned to No. 51 to stay and dropped in another note saying she could call "at any hour". There was no escape, unless illness was pleaded, and Elizabeth did not like to tempt fate. She was driven into a corner, just as she liked to be when there was something she really wanted to do but could not face it. As usual, the physical manifestations of her acute nervousness were alarming. Her "heart almost broke itself into pieces with bumping" but she saw she was obliged to fix an hour for receiving Mrs Jameson. Not to see Mrs Jameson would be "too ungrateful". It would also have been ridiculous and masochistic since she had for years longed to meet her. As usual, she enjoyed the visit when it took place. As usual, once it was over, she found it hard to remember why she had resisted. But Mrs Jameson had been a surprise. Although "cordial and kind" Elizabeth told Miss Mitford her new friend was also "a little deficient in that impulse and spontaneity which help to make up the charm in a certain quarter known to me". In other words, Miss Mitford need not be jealous; she was still the favourite. But it was ironic that Elizabeth should have an impression of reserve because reserve of any kind ran counter to Mrs Jameson's nature. She wrote in her own Commonplace Book that "the fear of not being loved where I had

attached myself" was her strongest characteristic and that she consequently exaggerated her demonstrative enthusiasm. With Elizabeth,
Mrs Jameson initially showed restraint. Their main topic of conversation had been Harriet Martineau and mesmerism. Mrs Jameson spoke of
"the awfulness . . . and of the difficulty of knowing where to stop in
one's degrees of belief". She also added "if there is anything in it there is
so much it becomes awful to contemplate". Elizabeth was disappointed
that her new friend had none of her own readiness to believe – quite the
reverse. Mrs Jameson's mind was sharp and incisive and she queried all
received ideas. She instructed Elizabeth to keep her mind open. Mrs
Jameson's strength of mind chilled Elizabeth, even though she admired
it. Also, she found Mrs Jameson's way of talking strange: "She does *not*
seem to *me* to speak in sentences. It strikes ME still that she wants . . .
what the French call *abandon*." But Mrs Jameson nevertheless was a
valuable addition to Elizabeth's extremely limited number of regular
visitors. She was a stimulating contact rather than a confidante like Miss
Mitford. The trouble was that Elizabeth had difficulty at first in seeing
past Mrs Jameson's appearance. With some delicacy, she described her
to Mrs Martin as having "an indecision of exterior", by which she meant
"very pale red hair . . . no eyebrows . . . thin lips with no colour at all".
(Carlyle, totally lacking in any such delicacy, described her as "a little,
hard, brown, red-haired, freckled, fierce-eyed, square-mouthed
woman.")

It was noticeable, that autumn, how much Elizabeth's health began to
improve. She was now walking about the house and survived a visit her
father made to Cornwall without being more than slightly depressed,
though she missed his presence, which she described as "cheering and
soothing". Henrietta missed it rather less. She took the opportunity to
have "a little polka (which did not bring the house down on its knees)"
as Elizabeth indulgently remarked. One of the guests with whom
Henrietta enjoyed dancing the polka was a cousin called Surtees Cook
who was becoming increasingly smitten with this pretty, lively second
Barrett daughter. Elizabeth managed, too, to let Stormie and Henry go
off on a trip to Egypt without too much distress. When they came to say
goodbye to her she came as near to being philosophical about their
departure as she was ever to be. She could see with her own eyes their
excitement, particularly Stormie's. He "sang for joy" she told Miss
Mitford, a most unusual reaction. Elizabeth commented that shutting
Stormie up in a ship's cabin was hardly going to solve his problems but

on the other hand she saw the value of travel. "He can rough it excellently," she told Miss Mitford, "but he cannot struggle against carpet difficulties". Remove Stormie from the agony of social intercourse and, as a stranger, unobserved, he thrived (as he had done the year before on his trip with George). This time Stormie and Henry were going on one of Mr Barrett's ships which took coal to Alexandria and brought back wool. Elizabeth reported that her father was providing for "the boys" (now twenty-nine and twenty-six years old) lavishly, arranging for "hermetically sealed cream and Champagne" for them. No wonder they were wild with delight and "smiled on" even when Elizabeth allowed herself a few tears. For one mad moment she thought of going with them as far as Malta – "flying an English winter in the act" – but then she remembered that this would break the family further and "I swore I never would again".[10] She was pleased to find envy did not make her depressed: "I am more cheerful than I expected," she told Mrs Martin and added that, thinking about the risks her brothers might encounter, "*I am surprised to feel* so little anxiety". It showed that all her battles with herself were not useless, that she could overcome her morbid thoughts if she struggled hard enough. "I have not striven in vain," she concluded with pride.

The same kind of victory over excessive, exaggerated fear had been won when Flush was stolen a second time in October, soon after Stormie and Henry left, and again safely recovered. This time he had been out walking with Arabel. As she stood at the door of No. 50 Wimpole Street, waiting for it to be opened, not for the moment expecting danger on the very threshold of her home, a man walked past with a dog which had been, Elizabeth told Miss Mitford, "properly prepared . . . for the work of attraction". Flush dashed down the street after the decoy, with Arabel following in vain; he had disappeared by the time she turned the corner. Elizabeth, though upset, was controlled. She sent off Alfred at once to contact Taylor who was known to operate from Shoreditch. He found Taylor easily enough but returned with the news that the price had gone up: the ransom was seven guineas. There could be no question of asking Mr Barrett for the money. On the contrary, Elizabeth gave strict instructions to everyone not to mention Flush's disappearance. She was even prepared to flout her own rules about trust and truth by herself dissembling. She knew that her father would realise that Flush was not about, and would need only to take one look at her own countenance to guess what had happened, so she stayed in her room and "took advantage of a headache" to bar her door to him. She did not see him for a whole day. Naturally, he was concerned and anxious. The next day, she could not refuse to see him without causing real alarm. She let him in and "talked fast away his observation of Flush's empty place". The fast talking could only be lies. Her father's only comment was "What a bad headache you must have had." But he did not press Elizabeth for the truth, nor when Flush re-appeared did he ask any other member of the household to divulge it.

Surtees Cook was slowly beginning to appreciate just how complex these Barrett games were and how very complicated their inventor. It confused him that Mr Barrett seemed to enjoy family parties so much, but would then suddenly forbid entertainments that were only a similar kind of fun. For example, Surtees wrote in his diary that he had never had a happier evening in his life than on 30th November when he dined at Wimpole Street in the company of Henrietta, Arabel, Sette and Mr Barrett. They ate, drank, sang songs and talked. Mr Barrett said they could get up a play if they wanted. Surtees suggested *The Rivals* which gave him a good part and the perfect excuse for rehearsals with Henrietta. One day as they rehearsed Mr Barrett walked in and immediately banned the play. Surtees could not understand either his volte-face or the lack of any explanation. On Christmas Eve, again in the Barrett house at a dinner party, Suntees got his own back. Someone suggested charades, Mr Barrett graciously agreed, and Surtees promptly acted one he had written himself: MAT-RYE-MONEY. He recorded that even though the audience included Mr Barrett his effort was wildly applauded.[11] Hardly less odd to Surtees was the behaviour of Henrietta's elder sister. He came and went frequently to Wimpole Street but never once met Elizabeth. She did not appear at family meals, nor in the drawing room, and Henrietta never took him to be introduced. She remained at all times, when he was visiting, in her sanctum. It was natural that Surtees should find this strange: Henrietta obviously talked about him all the time. Why did her sister not wish to meet him? It is Elizabeth's attitude which was extraordinary. She, too, was deeply curious and was very close to Henrietta to whom Surtees was so important. The whole family, even her father, had met him and accepted him. It is inconceivable that Henrietta did not wish her sister to meet her suitor; much more likely that Elizabeth was nervous about becoming in any way involved in an affair of the heart. It was the dreaded Barrett fear of involvement: Elizabeth knew that if Henrietta decided to marry

Surtees then she would ask for her help in dealing with their father. It was politic for Elizabeth to keep her distance but of all the times she refused to be introduced to a stranger this was quite the most peculiar.

By that Christmas of 1844, Elizabeth had a faint feeling of anti-climax. Her new poems were long since out, they had been widely reviewed and her feeling of elation had passed. The two volumes had sold reasonably well, her reputation had undoubtedly risen, she had derived a great deal of pleasure from her success, but now she was left with that feeling so common to writers after publication: what next? What was to happen now? What difference had this longed for event really made to her life? Again and again she had written to friends that these latest poems already felt outdated, that they simply amounted to a stage on a longer journey. Her best work, she had no doubt, was yet to come. But in spite of such innate confidence there was a return of that restlessness which periodically plagued her and which had been allayed during the long wait for the publication of the 1844 poems. She had had a specific goal towards which to work. Now she had none. Her ambition was more raging than ever, spurred on rather than satisfied by her success, but there was no corresponding sense of a precise direction. What she wanted to do, she told Kenyon in October 1844, was to "write a poem of a like class" to "Lady Geraldine's Courtship". But upon which subject? She had only the vaguest ideas, she told Miss Mitford in December, of "a few characters – and a simple story – and plenty of room for passion and thought – *that* is what I want and I am not likely to find it easily".[12] The only clue she had as to the way she should go was provided by the attention attracted by one of her ballads. "Lady Geraldine's Courtship", the ballad completed hurriedly to balance Volume One, had turned out to be most people's favourite. Elizabeth, who was surprised, concluded that its popularity was due to the simple fact that it had a story and "people care for a story". Furthermore, the ballad dealt with "the conventions of vulgar life" which she interpreted as meaning that people liked poems about "this real everyday life of our age". The poem deals with class and its importance (or lack of it) for people who love each other. Lady Geraldine marries her low-born poet and proclaims, "I shall not blush in knowing that/Men call him lowly born." She wants her "low-born" poet for himself and his art and has the courage of her convictions. It was the only ballad in which Elizabeth allowed herself to be optimistic about love – Lady Geraldine holds all the cards, her lover none. It is he who weeps and even faints, overcome by the hopelessness of his love. Instead of thinking this absurd, people responded to it. Elizabeth could hardly be blamed for thinking this significant. It gave her courage to develop similarly unconventional themes.

But "Lady Geraldine's Courtship" had an even greater significance. In the poem, Bertram, her lover, reads to Lady Geraldine some modern poetry, among it passages from Wordsworth, Tennyson and Browning. It was a deliberate selection of Elizabeth's, her way of paying tribute to some of those "next to the Gods". There is not the slightest doubt that she knew all three poets would hear of her reference, even if they did not first read it for themselves, and that she expected they would register the compliment. Wordsworth was the only one of the three to whom she sent a copy but she knew the London literary circle was small and that someone would draw Tennyson's and Browning's attention to her graceful mention of them. The reference to Browning was not only the longest (four lines instead of the two words spared for each of the others) but also the most unusual. Wordsworth was a giant, to whom everyone paid tribute and Tennyson, though not yet at his peak, was already garlanded with praise. Browning was not. His name was known only to a discerning literary coterie; the wider reading public were unfamiliar with it. Elizabeth knew perfectly well that this being so her reference to Browning would be as striking as it was unexpected. She knew that Browning was away when her volumes came out in August 1844 – he had sailed for Naples – but that Kenyon had given his sister Sarianna a copy. It all happened as anyone could have forecast, especially Elizabeth: Browning read her poem, was flattered as undoubtedly he was meant to be and responded as most people would. On 10th January 1845 he sat down to thank Miss Barrett.

Chapter Nine

ELIZABETH had never met any young man remotely like Robert Browning. She was used to saying, with suspicious emphasis, that she disliked *all* young men and it was true that when Sam and Bro had wanted to tease her in Hope End days about imaginary beaux, all they had been able to come up with were the names of elderly intellectuals. In her youth, no young man was ever worth praising either in her diary or in her letters: they served only to annoy. And yet, because she was surrounded by brothers of very different tastes and personalities, Elizabeth was not in the unfortunate position of so many Victorian, invalid spinsters who were virtually unacquainted with the male sex and consequently both in awe of it and frightened by it. She was neither afraid of young men nor did she think them heroes. She knew enough to know that in most respects they were like young women, except in their position of power. Familiarity with eight of the male species had made her feel sophisticated on the subject of young men but of course her knowledge was regrettably limited. Since her experience came from her brothers she lacked the kind of awareness that comes from regarding men not just as people but as sexual beings.

Any attraction, sexual or otherwise, that she had ever felt was towards older men. This attraction took the form of admiration either of intellectual power or strength of personality. This was where the distinction between young men and older men lay in Elizabeth's opinion – in the various powers they had. Her brothers were not feeble or stupid. Bro, Stormie, George and Septimus were all clever and certainly possessed of considerable intellectual powers; Alfred and Octavius had distinct artistic talent; Henry at least showed plenty of spirit with his flashes of defiance. But, compared with Sir Uvedale Price or Hugh Boyd, their learning paled into insignificance and, compared with their own father, their strength of character was puny. They stood at all times in his shadow, in awe of him even when it was an awe based on love and respect and not on fear. So young men, throughout Elizabeth's life so far, were inferior to older men, except in fiction. In the novels to which she was addicted, and from which she thought she learned so much, young men inspired passion. The idea that any young man of her acquaintance could inspire her passion was ludicrous. As a witness to her brothers' capacity for rousing passion in others or feeling it themselves she was driven to mockery. Which young man could really know anything about passion? None, except the young poet Robert Browning.

Right from her very first reference to him in 1835, ten years before he wrote to her, Elizabeth had made it plain that what attracted her to the poetry of Browning was its passion – passion in its broadest, deepest sense. As she had told Miss Mitford, people who thought that because she was virtually a recluse she could know nothing of passion were greatly mistaken. She knew about it, instinctively. Passion was not an emotion with only a sexual connotation, but one embracing a spiritual feeling. She felt its existence within herself often and had no outlet for it but in her poetry. Passion was the name she gave to that stirring of ambition within her, to that restlessness that made her hunger for change, to that overpowering frustration of spirit which made her want to burst out of the confines of her life. Passion was a life force she recognised. She did not dream of falling in love and exploring sexual passion, but of finding a true poet whose *poetic* passion could match her own.

She suspected from the moment she read *Paracelsus* that Robert Browning was this poet. Everything she knew of him was taken from his poetry, or from what she read into it. The few details she knew of Browning the man were accumulated slowly and by 1845 did not amount to much. Through Kenyon, Miss Mitford and Mrs Jameson, she had learned that he lived at home with his parents, to whom he seemed as devoted as she was to her father, and with his sisters (she did not know he had only one); that he was "learned in Greek"; that he worked only at poetry; that he had travelled on the Continent; that he was often seen around London at parties; that he was fond of skulls and spiders; and that he suffered from headaches which sometimes incapacitated him. As far as his reputation went, Elizabeth knew that *Paracelsus*, published in 1835 when he was twenty-three, had made his name but that the subsequent publication of *Sordello* – which was thought obscure – in 1840 had badly damaged it. Between the two publications he had turned to drama and built another reputation. Everything Elizabeth knew about his social background came from Kenyon. Browning's family, strangely enough, also had West Indian connections. Kenyon himself had been, briefly, at the same school as the young poet's father and knew that the older Browning had rejected the way of life offered to him in Jamaica in order to return home, much to his family's fury. Browning senior had become a Bank of England clerk and was far from wealthy. Even so, he was content to support his son's poetry. The Brownings lived in New Cross, in what was then a rapidly growing pleasant suburb south of the City of London. This was the sum total of Elizabeth's information.

In essence, it was correct. Robert Browning had never worked (as Miss Mitford contemptuously pointed out), even though his family were hardly rich enough to support him without strain. His parents were quite happy that his talent should be fostered and had not the slightest desire that he should aspire to worldly goods. They adored their son and he adored them. The unit of four mutually admiring people (Robert's sister Sarianna was two years his junior) provided a remarkably soothing and settled atmosphere for any poet. It had not, by 1845, been threatened by any outside forces: neither Sarianna nor Robert had shown any signs of wanting to leave the happy home. Robert, at the age of thirty-two, had had no serious relationship with any woman. Indeed, his knowledge of women, considering the much greater opportunities available to him, was very nearly as limited as Elizabeth's of men outside her family. Like Elizabeth, youth did not seem to prove attractive to him: he liked older women. Apart from his half-aunt Jemima (a year older than he) his only youthful flirtations had been with two women nine and seven years older than himself. These were the Flower sisters, Eliza and Sarah, daughters of family friends living nearby. Robert was their "poet boy" and their role, as they saw it, was to be his patrons. He loved both of them, but especially Eliza, until in adolescence he began to have arguments about religion which affected their relationship. After the Flowers became less important to him there was only one other acknowledged recipient of his admiration and that was Euphrasia Fanny Haworth, eleven years older than he was. He first met her at the actor-manager Macready's home when he was writing a play for him and was inspired to make an obvious reference to her in the ill-fated *Sordello*. She had already paid him the compliment of writing verses (printed in *New Monthly Magazine* in September 1836) praising *Paracelsus*. They had written to each other frequently and met at other people's houses and public functions but the relationship had gone no further. Robert's real friendships were with men, just as Elizabeth's were with women, although unlike her female friends his male friends were his own age (the two closest were Alfred Domett[1] and Amédée de Ripert-Monclar)[2]. Elizabeth assumed him to be both a fashionable young literary man-about-town and a man of worldly experience but neither image was as true as it seemed. Robert's home life was far more important to him than any socialising and his worldliness had not extended to affairs of the heart. He had given up all thoughts of ever finding any woman to love deeply: women were a surface distraction from his real purpose in life which was the writing of poetry. When he wrote to Elizabeth it was as one poet to another, one poet grateful for another poet's approbation. He wrote out of a sense of duty. It would have been most churlish not to acknowledge the compliment paid to him.

His first letter was written on 10th January 1845. It did not read like a letter of obligation, with its extravagant use of flattering phrase, but it was in fact very much in Robert's general style of letter-writing. In 1837, he had written to Fanny Haworth in much the same breathless, impetuous, enthusiastic way when he thanked her for her verses. It is true that he did not say he loved Fanny as well as her verses, as he did to Elizabeth, but he had come near it with his gushing "I cannot say or sing the pleasure your way of writing gives me" and his invitation to her to help him think of "a subject of the most wild and passionate love" to write about.[3] It was not Robert's custom to write stiff, stilted notes even to ladies he did not know. But to Elizabeth, who had no way of knowing this, his letter was startlingly unusual. She had received dozens of admiring letters about her work by then but none so open and passionate in expression. Robert wrote of his "flush of delight", his love of her poems "with all my heart" (twice), his "true thankful joy" that she had written them.[4] He made no mention whatsoever of her reference to him in "Lady Geraldine's Courtship". It was a graceful, flowing, eloquent letter full of the kind of spontaneous vitality Elizabeth so prized in people ("few things are more provoking to me than impassiveness" she once confided to Miss Mitford). She was excited to receive it and did not try to hide her excitement, telling Mrs Martin it had thrown her into "ecstasies" (she was later ashamed of having done so). There was no trace of ecstasy in her own reply. On the contrary, hers was a practised letter, composed, a trifle over-earnest and even pompous. She wrote of Robert's praise being "the quintessence of sympathy" to her and of her "high respect" for his power in his art. She was his "devout admirer and student". The most significant passage in this letter was the central part in which Elizabeth took Robert up on a passing reference he had made to having thought at first of offering her advice "as a fellow-craftsman should". She seized upon his offer (which he told her he had rejected) and urged him to "*tell* me of such faults as rise to the surface and strike you as important". She told him he would "confer a lasting obligation" on her if he did. Even "a sentence or two of general observation" would do and she asked for it wittily "in the humble low voice which is so excellent a thing in women – particularly when they go a-begging". As with Price, as with Boyd, what she wanted above all else was a teacher. Her letter invited criticism of work he had already praised, neatly turning the compliment inside out.

This clearly surprised Robert. He did not know how to interpret such a response. He thought at first he had offended Elizabeth and hastened to reassure her that far from spotting faults he had simply noticed "where the brush has dipped twice in a lustrous colour". Again he praised her poetry, said it was "infinitely more" to him than his could possibly be to her and assured her that she was doing in poetry what he wanted to and had not yet managed: "You speak out, *you*." Her voice was, for him, above all original and personal. He could not have said anything more pleasing to Elizabeth. But in assuming she did not really want criticism Robert was of course mistaken. She had, in turn, begged Price, Boyd, Kenyon, Miss Mitford, Mrs Jameson, Horne and a host of less intimate correspondents to tell her the truth. Because she thought Robert a genius himself his "truth" would be more welcome than anyone's and she was determined to have it. His purpose was to criticise and teach. Firmly, she let Robert know this, telling him in her next two letters that she knew he was a master of "abstract thought" and of "human passion in the most passionate sense" and that this being so he had much he could teach her. Stepping delicately, Robert responded as she hoped. He mentioned which poems of hers he liked best – "Bertha in the Lane", "A Drama of Exile", "The Romaunt of the Page", "The Rime of the Duchess May" – and agreed that, if she really wanted him to, he could "pencil . . . and annotate and dissertate upon that I love most and least".

It was done. Three letters from him, three letters to him, all in the space of three weeks, and the basis of this new friendship between Elizabeth Barrett and Robert Browning had been most satisfactorily and speedily laid – satisfactorily from her point of view, that is. She had at last the correspondent she had been looking for all her life, a true kindred spirit who was a poet after her own heart, able to understand not just what she was trying to do but how she was trying to do it. They were to write to each other about their work, to comment on each other's efforts and to encourage each other to greater things. But Elizabeth wanted more than that, just as she had wanted, and failed to receive, more from Boyd. She told Robert in her fourth letter "teach me yourself, you". She urged him to show "no constraint or ceremony" but to tell her *everything* because she wanted to know him by "refracted lights as well as direct ones". The contract, as Elizabeth called it, signed and sealed – that they would be "articled" as correspondents to discuss their work – it was she who expanded its terms. From her fourth letter onwards she began visibly to relax, to drop the rather mannered style of her first letters, so foreign to her real nature, and to open out to reveal her inner self. Unhappily, there is no diary available to put what she said in her letters to the test, but she began quickly to give them a diary flavour. She was witty and curious and tremendously eager to entertain her new pen-friend. She took him to task for saying he hated letter-writing, declaring it was "as good a social measure" as any other and that she derived great fun and profit from it. There was no need, she assured him, to have any letter manners (not that Robert had shown any signs of having any). He, of course, thought that the letters were the prelude to a meeting and therefore was from the first impatient with them whereas she knew otherwise: the letters were the relationship in themselves. She loved them, not trying to conceal the tremendous pleasure they gave her. Within a very short time she was sure the two of them had "great sympathies in common" and sought to discover what these were. Strings of questions followed: did Robert think an artist was reflected in his work, how important was praise to him, which books had he read, what were his writing hours, which poets did he admire most? On and on she went, reflecting that it was all perhaps "too much indeed, past all bearing I suspect".

Fortunately, Robert did not think so. He replied to this particular piece of self-consciousness with one of the longest letters he had ever written in his life, in which he wrote that he already sensed Elizabeth was "different" and not to be classified with anyone he had known before ". . . for reasons I know, for other reasons I don't exactly know . . ." He would, he told her, rather hear from her than anyone else. All that worried him was that she did not really know him: she was judging him by his poetry and he was most emphatically *not* his poetry in the way that she was hers. If they were to go on writing she would have to get to know what he was really like. It was a warning which only intrigued her more. Was Robert's poetry a mask? If so, as he seemed to assert, what lay behind it? His confidence in himself, mask or not, impressed her. He did not boast but talked of his faith in his own powers, if only he could learn to use them, with total assurance. The severely adverse criticism he had received after *Sordello* did not appear to trouble him. He even wrote, ". . . for *me* . . . the not being listened to by one human creature would, I hope, in nowise affect me". Elizabeth's admiration increased with each letter she received as Robert expounded his views on poetry and art in general and showed himself in the process as quick and learned with the apt quotation as she was. By the end of another month they were both confiding plans for work. Elizabeth told Robert she was planning a long prose poem, Robert told her he was finishing one more play, then giving up drama altogether; she was pleased, believing that writing for the commercial theatre wasted his talent. By March 1845 and Elizabeth's thirty-ninth (but unmentioned) birthday, personal details were creeping into letters. Elizabeth was the more painfully honest and self-revealing. She told Robert how she had lived "only inwardly" and that there were few women in the world "who have not seen more, heard more, known more of society" than she had. She told him she had grown up in the country "with no social opportunities" (not mentioning those available she had scorned or refused to try). She described her youth as "lonely", with the life of her family only buzzing gently around "like the bees about the grass" (not mentioning her earlier boisterous participation in games and outings, nor the degree to which her solitude had been self-imposed). She made herself sound, without actually saying so, like an only child with the vaguest reference to "one" of whom she could not speak. She wrote that when she had almost died a few years before she had been filled with bitterness because she had never had the chance really to live. The consequences of her art, she pointed out, had been grievous: she was "a *blind poet*". And yet, she told him she had, in her poetry, lived "down all the fibres of being, passionately and joyfully". Her purpose in this confession was not to ask for pity but to bring home to Robert the enormous difference between their experience. If he was concerned to emphasise that she did not know him, she wished to stress that at least in his case there was something to know, whereas she had nothing to offer.

All this time, during the three months in which these confidences had been exchanged, Robert had thought he would soon meet Elizabeth. It was a natural assumption. He knew Kenyon visited her and had no idea how deep rooted was Elizabeth's aversion to other visitors. He did not know that Horne, to whom she was so indebted, had eventually been offered one meeting and that, on being unable to keep his appointment, had not been given another. He did not know that Haydon, who had promised that if she did not allow him to visit after three months he would come and reproach her through the keyhole, had nevertheless been denied entry. Robert assumed at first that Elizabeth's reluctance to meet him was because of her invalid status. She told him she would be stronger and feel better in the spring but, when there was no denying spring had arrived and still she fobbed him off with excuses, he realised her reluctance had nothing to do with the weather and very probably nothing to do with her health. This puzzled him until he sensed her fear. It was fear which made her defer the meeting; he saw the fear in her letters that he would not like her, that he would find she lacked in person the attraction she had on paper, that rather than binding them closer a meeting would end their relationship entirely. She would not risk it: better to keep herself on paper. Once he understood this fear, he set about trying to dispel it. Behind it, he sensed her anxiety that he was simply curious, that he wanted to see her to satisfy some vulgar urge, like wanting to see a freak. He convinced her that idle curiosity did not come into his desire to meet her – "often as I see Mr Kenyon have I ever dreamed of asking but the merest conventional questions?" – and that he was hurt she could for one moment think so. He was equally hurt, he told her, that she could imagine he would change towards her once he had met her. Did she not know him better than that? With a nicely judged expression of injured pride he told her in May that he could only conclude, sorrowfully, that she was "mistrustful" of him.

This brought Elizabeth to her senses. She saw that the more fuss she went on making about a meeting, the more significant such a meeting would appear, confessing, "I have made what is vulgarly called 'a piece of work' about little". She asked his forgiveness. She could not bear to seem mistrustful, so told him "if you care to come and see me you can come". But she warned him he would be disappointed and begged him to have no illusions. "There is nothing to see in me; nor to hear in me . . . ." If he still thought her worth visiting he could suggest when. She stipulated only that it should be in the afternoon, after two and before six o'clock. There was an attempt to cover herself with a remark about perhaps having to cancel any arrangement made because of "an unforeseen obstacle". Robert replied immediately, fixing his visit for Tuesday 20th May at 2 pm. He assured her it did not matter if she had to cancel this appointment because, since his time was of no importance, he would simply "come again and again and again" until he finally saw her. The message was clear: evasion would not work. She read it correctly and braced herself, replying the same day, "I will be ready on Tuesday, I hope." Yet still she could not resist clutching at straws, telling him not to come if a headache, from which he had told her he was suffering, had not cleared. She ended gloomily, "Well! We are friends till Tuesday – and after, perhaps."

Life that spring of 1845 was certainly dominated for Elizabeth by her growing friendship with Robert but it did not block out everything else that was happening. She was well aware that Henrietta was in love with Surtees Cook and watched with interest as well as some anxiety the development of this relationship. She had still not met Surtees (though by now she realised Henrietta's romance was serious), but since Henrietta talked so much about him she had formed quite a detailed picture of him. She knew that he was younger than her sister (by four years) and that, although his widowed mother was extremely well connected, he was only a poor lieutenant in the army. This did not stop Surtees hoping that his pursuit of Henrietta would come to something. As well as attending Barrett family dinners he also came frequently for lunch, when Mr Barrett was not there, and with Alfred as chaperone took Henrietta skating, escorted her to chapel and went walking with her in Regent's Park. That March, he had managed to evade the obliging Alfred long enough to put both his hands round Henrietta's waist and kiss her. Recording this in his diary he also added gloomily that Henrietta had told him there was no hope, however much they loved each other: her father would never consent to a marriage. Even thinking about it made Surtees weep. His only consolation was to lose himself in the novel he was writing, inaptly entitled *Johnny Cheerful*, which he hoped would make his fame and fortune. Henrietta was proud of his literary endeavours and said she would give it to her sister to criticise when he had finished it.

Elizabeth was meanwhile busy trying to decide whether or not to write a poem against the iniquitous Corn Laws for the Corn Law League. Anyone with any feeling for the poor had been outraged since the passing of these Corn Laws in 1815, at the end of the Napoleonic Wars.

The point of them was to protect landlords and farmers from the low price of corn, resulting from the importation of foreign corn now that trade with Europe was re-established. The laws kept the price of home-grown corn artificially high and as a consequence bread was expensive. There was always opposition to the Corn Laws but in 1839 this became organised with the foundation of the Anti-Corn Law League. Their campaign was fought on moral grounds that appealed to Elizabeth: the Corn Laws were unchristian. She followed the course of the agitation closely – "my sympathies go strongly with the body" she told Miss Mitford – and like all members and supporters of the League she was hopeful that in 1841 when Robert Peel became Prime Minister the Corn Laws would be repealed (Peel adjusted but did not repeal them). Mr Barrett was not as convinced as his daughter that the Corn Laws should be entirely abolished: Elizabeth commented she was "leagues before the rest of my house in essential radicalism".

Elizabeth eventually decided she would like to contribute a poem as requested but her brothers came out vociferously against it. She had, she wrote to Miss Mitford, "a regular quarrel" with them about it and became very upset when they roared with laughter at the very idea of any of her verses doing any good or mattering a jot: "a woman's verses! – oh think of the impertinence of it," commented Elizabeth savagely.[5] More influential than her brothers' derision was her father's disapproval. He decided he did not want her to do it and she "would not vex Papa for the world". The Reverend George Hunter, who had come to live in London the year before, visited her while she was pondering and was equally violent about the possibility of involving herself in "political" work. She was annoyed. Just as Robert Browning was writing with such respect for her opinions and abilities, all the men around her were telling her what to do as though she had neither mind nor will of her own. She resented Hunter's overbearing attitude in particular, complaining to Miss Mitford that it amounted to a kind of "masculine rampancy" which she hated. Hunter even objected to her name being mentioned in a magazine in the same sentence as George Sand whom he called "that abandoned woman". It made Elizabeth desperately want to stand up to them all but she felt the lack of any support to stiffen her resolution. On the very day she received a letter from Robert begging her to "tell me of your present doings and projects", and assuring her of his passionate interest in everything to do with her, she herself was writing to Miss Mitford that "there is at my side a vacancy and silence which strikes on me sometimes as freshly as ever, and sometimes as despairingly". She was looking for what Robert was offering. A modicum of restored health – she was leading a much more active and normal if still restricted life – and her small success with the 1844 poems had given her an energy which had no direction. She was tired of her books, her way of life, her own emotional isolation. Questions like the Corn Law poem – she did not do it – made her long for a like-minded companion at her side who would encourage her. She was "so low and weary and tired of this life" but it was the weariness of frustration, of never seeming to do what she wanted to do, and not of resignation.

In April, when Robert pointed out that spring was well and truly here, she had lain on her sofa and read a novel which seemed to epitomise everything that was wrong in her life. It was Stendhal's *Le Rouge et le Noir*. She thought it "so dark and deep . . . very striking and powerful and full of deep significance . . . a first class book . . . a book to read at all risks." It had, she confessed to Miss Mitford, "ridden me like an incubus for several days". The novel is full of the dissatisfaction women feel with men and of their desire for real passion. "The boredom of married life," Stendhal announces, "is . . . the death of love." His compassion for the way women were treated in society is matched only by his contempt for the men who made the rules. Stendhal made her see how much she had to learn, how pathetically colourless her own life was.

Robert Browning, when he called on Elizabeth that Tuesday in May 1845, was unaware of her state of mind. Miss Mitford was privy to her most intimate thoughts but Robert had not been, not yet. So far as he knew, both from common knowledge and what she herself had told him, she was "weak" because of her ill health and nothing else. Her illness led him to expect a pitiful, wasted creature but he did not find the idea of this repugnant. In his family, there were several members who carried on what had become a tradition of the Rosicrucians – Christians in the hermetic mould who believed that to give succour to the sick was their life's purpose – and his most successful work to date, *Paracelsus*, had been about such a healer. Whereas other men often found sickness repulsive, Robert, partly through upbringing and partly through a strange natural inclination, did not. He found it intriguing if not positively attractive. He was also fascinated by the details of her illness, shrouded as they were in rumour. He truly thought she was a cripple, unable to walk after a childhood riding accident which had injured her spine. The cruelty of such a fate disturbed him. He was rarely ill himself, except for headaches, and led a particularly vigorous outdoor life, riding and walking with tremendous energy. Elizabeth's poetry – its occasional wildness and passion – was hard to equate with the image of a pale and wan invalid lying on a sofa. So Robert approached No. 50 Wimpole Street unable to suppress a touch of that curiosity which he had denied motivated him. Luckily, it did not make him nervous. Robert was never socially nervous. On the contrary, he exuded confidence, never lacking things to talk about in that voice of his which was so loud it often irritated people. Catherine Bromley in her diary ten years before had commented that "Robert talks immensely, and how self conscious: to me distressingly so", but Sarah Flower had admired his "great power of conversation" in which the young man displayed "thorough originality".[6] It never crossed Robert's mind to think of things to say: there was too much to say, always. He had no need to rehearse how he would address Elizabeth Barrett, nor to wonder what he would talk about. He was quite sure of himself.

Elizabeth, of course, felt quite differently. She lay on her sofa in her back room as if waiting for the executioner. Two o'clock was the quietest time of day in the house: Mr Barrett who had no objection to "Ba's poet" visiting was in the City, George at work in the Inns of Court, the other brothers almost always out at that hour. Henrietta and Arabel were sometimes out visiting, leaving only Wilson to see to Elizabeth's needs. The blinds, showing a castle (her father said they made the room look like a confectioner's shop), were half-pulled against the afternoon sun and the ivy Kenyon had given her to plant in her window box partially concealed the remaining window. It was a gloomy atmosphere which reflected her mood. She felt miserable. She fretted about her thin, reedy voice which under pressure might fade away to nothing and about her appearance – her pallor was shocking, her eyes "two dark caves", and her thinness alarming. She was dressed in black silk (since Bro's death she had worn only black, velvet in the winter, silk in the summer). It made her look, she was well aware, like a ghost. Her hair, still glossy and comfortingly thick, hung around her face. She had no hopes at all that her visitor would find her pretty, but then she scorned such vanity. This was to be a meeting of minds, not flesh. Yet it was the flesh that let her down. She had trembled at the thought of meeting Miss Mitford, her heart had thudded at meeting Mrs Jameson but neither symptom of alarm compared with the violent agitation which possessed her as Robert Browning's foot was at last heard on the stair.

The moment Robert entered the room her panic subsided, as it always did, and by the time he left, after an hour, had been replaced by an exhilaration she had rarely felt. Reporting the meeting to Miss Mitford, Elizabeth was careful, but she had already become instinctively careful now that she had something worth confiding. She wanted to protect herself and so did not write too much about Robert in her letters. In her first to Miss Mitford after his visit she did not even mention it and in her second pretended she could not remember whether she had done so or not. All she gave her former confidante were a few scraps – casual, fragmented comments – and the news that she had liked her first new male visitor in years very much. She said he was younger-looking than she had expected (he had just become thirty-three on 7th May) and that he had "natural and not ungraceful manners". The best thing about him had been that he was "full of his art". His appearance and bearing had been a surprise to her: they no more fitted in with his poetry than she did with hers. Robert was small (five foot six inches) with a large head, a strong torso and short legs. All his movements were quick; he walked with great energy and had a general boisterous air. His manner was confident and self-assured, so much so that many people considered him brash. He had a disconcertingly bold, direct gaze (he was short-sighted in one eye and long-sighted in the other which in fact gave him some trouble with his vision). His hair was as dark and luxuriant as Elizabeth's own. His clothes were always immaculate, setting off his slim figure to perfection: "a neat, dainty little fellow," said Carlyle, who was a friend of his. When he opened his mouth listeners were always amazed by the loudness of his voice (and often of his opinions). He was not the common idea of a poet: he was not shy, retiring, soulful, diffident or gentle in bearing. Elizabeth gave Miss Mitford no inkling of how she had responded to her visitor. She had felt an instant rapport with Robert. It was a rapport he had felt too and unfortunately he allowed it to carry him away. He moved much too fast after what he had felt, correctly, was a successful visit. The moment he reached home he wrote an elated but polite note, hoping he had neither stayed too long nor talked too loudly, and saying he was "proud and happy" in their friendship. That was acceptable and even expected. Elizabeth wrote back saying he could come again next Tuesday but made a rather significant remark about him not possibly being able to appreciate her "mental position". She was right: he did not. Misinterpreting it, Robert made a grave error of judgement. To Elizabeth's distress, he replied this time with a passionate love letter in which he appears (though we only know from her anguished reply because his letter was destroyed) to have asked her to marry him at once. She told him it made her "recoil by instinct" to get such a letter. At one blow he had destroyed the whole delicate balance of their relationship; it was irrelevant whether what he had said was sincere or the result of "intemperate fancies" as she suspected. It was "unbecoming" and humiliating for him to address her as a lover when he was her friend and teacher. The absurdity of it made her cringe. She felt mocked. She told him she had destroyed his letter and now made it a condition that if ever he referred to it again, or referred even to her reply to it, "*I will not see you again.*" There were, all the same, "grateful tears" in her eyes but they had not blinded her. He could come next Tuesday if he so wished but he must come as a critic, ready to help her improve her poetry. That was his role.

This reaction was naturally a shock to Robert who knew nothing of Elizabeth's terror of mockery. She was her own harshest judge, proud of knowing herself through and through, proud that she was immune to flattery, fierce in her realistic appraisal of her own worth. She suspected everyone, always had done, of not telling her the truth. When she told Robert his letter had caused her "pain" this was a precise statement of feeling: she suffered real pain whenever she imagined people thought she did not know herself. Horne's description of her in *A New Spirit of the Age* had caused her similar pain: she could not bear his unctuous words. Now it seemed to that her Robert was playing with her. She was an invalid, a virtual recluse, wasted through illness, exhausted through grief and he had been in her company only one hour. In such circumstances to be treated as a female so desirable she could not be resisted was simply grotesque. What kind of man could have imagined she would be taken in? It made her not only recoil but doubt him. Why had his sensitivity as a poet not made him aware of how she would feel? She could only excuse him by trying to regard what he had written as "a misprint between you and the printer". It occurred to her belatedly that Robert might be so offended by her reaction that he would not want to continue their relationship. This so distressed her that she pleaded with him "to spare me the sadness of having to break through an intercourse just as it is promising pleasure to me; to me who have so many sadnesses and so few pleasures."

Robert could hardly fail to realise that he had "bungled notably", as he put it, but he was determined not to do so again. He felt that to ignore, as she wished, what he preferred to call a misunderstanding would only make matters worse. So he wrote Elizabeth an admirably strong, open letter in which he sought to explain without in any way excusing his apparent rashness. He pointed out that, if she claimed he had not understood her, he could claim he had actually told her she did not understand him. What had happened was only evidence of this. He described himself as a deeply secretive person, with "huge layers of ice and pits of black cold water" lying beneath the surface of his character, someone who had never even attempted to communicate his inner being to another soul. Compared to his real feelings his letter, far from being rash or intemperate, had been "the blandest utterance ever mild gentleman gave birth to". He asked her forgiveness, while subtly implying he had done nothing he need ask it for and that he had nothing of which to be ashamed. He promised to be more "considerate" in the future but she was not to think he had been in any way "attitudinising" nor to despise him. There was in him – she was welcome to check with Kenyon – a strong vein of common sense which had only temporarily deserted him and would not do so again; he would be "now and henceforth on my good behaviour". He kept his word. That upsetting tone of tortuous embarrassment rapidly disappeared from both their letters and they spent several weeks exchanging jocular notes full of anecdotes. But Robert had learned a great deal about Elizabeth and gained from it. He knew, now, how mistrustful she was, and how sure she needed to be of people before they could become close.

The way to Elizabeth's heart, as Robert discovered that summer, was of course through her work. She was in the process of reworking her translation of *Prometheus* with which she had never been satisfied and he helped her. She told him she had "never thought of meaning to inflict such work" on him but that his assistance was undeniably "of the greatest value" and she was very grateful. Robert's skill at rendering a tricky Greek phrase into euphonious English impressed her deeply – there was nothing she revered more than scholarship – and so did his familiarity with the other versions of Aeschylus. He seemed to have read everything. Not since the days of her "tutorials" with Boyd had she enjoyed herself so much and, unlike Boyd, Robert was only too willing to stray from Greek and discuss literature in general. They discussed Shakespeare and Marlowe, Tennyson and Shelley, George Sand and dozens of other writers both dead and contemporary. Then there was Robert's current work in which she was soon proud to be involved. He was preparing the penultimate issue of *Bells and Pomegranates* and Elizabeth told him she would be honoured if "you would let me see anything you may have in a readable state by you". She particularly wanted to see the long poem about which Robert had told her, his "Flight of the Duchess". Robert was charmed. "I will bring all I dare, in as great quantities as I can," he replied, though he confessed he was worried that the state of his manuscript – the handwriting, the blots, the crossings out – would mean she could not read it. Elizabeth laughed at the idea. She could read anything and declared "really I rather like blots". Robert duly fed her parts of "The Duchess" as he wrote it and she told him it was brilliant, one of his most striking poems, and would soon be "the world's Duchess". This poem appealed to Elizabeth in every possible way since it was in praise of passion, of true love, and opposed to the sanctity of man-made marriage vows. Yet, in spite of her admiration, her critical faculties were not silenced: she saw ways of improving the poem and suggested a long list of changes, many of which Robert accepted and worked on. He was as excited, he told her, to have this kind of working partnership as she was and had lacked it just as much. He likened his work to building and said she helped him with the scaffolding.

Elizabeth now had the perfect correspondent, better by far than Price, or Boyd, or Horne, or Haydon and better also than her dear Miss Mitford. It was noticeable that almost immediately after Robert's first visit, when the pattern of three or four letters between weekly visits became established, Elizabeth's letters to Miss Mitford became less frequent. She had turned to Miss Mitford for advice, for discussion on literary topics, for gossip and for a general warmth of character but now found that Robert could give her all these as well as something else besides which sprang from his being a poet himself. It was a combination Horne had seemed to offer her but she had never felt such understanding, such an effortless sense of ease, as she did with Robert. By midsummer's day she reported to Miss Mitford that she had been "growing and growing just like the trees – it is miraculous, the feeling of sprouting life in me and out of me – and now I begin to sleep and to look altogether like another person". Happiness was having its own effect: she was resolved to "get on" while the summer lasted and try to capitalise on her new energy. At last she accepted Kenyon's invitation to use his house, as a break from her room, and began to make regular visits instead of occasional forays to Regent's Park. By the middle of July she was getting out of her carriage or chair and walking, though she said scathingly she did so "as well as a child of two year's old". She forced herself to drink milk for strength and made sure she emerged to sit in the sun whenever it was out. The difference in her appearance was widely commented on: "people cry out, to see me growing back again into my self and able to walk . . ." What made her health and happiness all the more noticeable was that Henrietta was wilting under the strain of her affair with Surtees. After a summer of carefully contrived outings with him she had organised a party with Surtees as chief guest and her father had been furious. Surtees was appalled to find himself reflecting in his diary that he entertained murderous thoughts towards Mr Barrett.

Robert, on his weekly visits, noted Elizabeth's improved health with the greatest satisfaction. He had not urged upon her anything that others had not at some time or another done but the difference was that it was he whom she chose to obey. Robert encouraged her to take exercise, to eat sensibly, to get as much fresh air as possible, so she did, which must have been extremely galling for those around her, such as her father, who had been urging all these things for years. The only thing Robert could not get her to do was give up opium: she insisted she had to have it. By now, she had been taking it for twenty-four years. She no longer took it only to help her sleep at night but also mentions taking it when she felt "irritable" to "steady the action of the heart". She believed opium did "positive good" to the lungs and subdued her cough. She wrote to Mrs Martin in the autumn of 1845 that she took forty drops of laudanum a day, but without knowing the strength of the alcohol with which the grains of opium were mixed it is still impossible to estimate this dosage correctly. Some of the apathy, depression and lassitude complained of would correspond to the known pattern of opium addiction but, on the other hand, the more serious side effects (such as hallucinations) were absent. Elizabeth's memory remained impressively sharp yet weakness of memory almost always betrays the true addict. Nor did she have a permanent headache. But there is no doubt that she depended on opium, whatever the level or effects of her addiction. She liked opium, thought it did her good and had not the slightest desire to give it up. It annoyed her that Robert made such a fuss about it – "that you should care so much about the opium!" But she was more than willing to consider another bit of advice which he began to repeat around August, which was the absolute necessity of her escaping another English winter by going abroad. Again, this was not new advice: Kenyon had been urging it for years and Mrs Jameson too. But Elizabeth's answer, though she was sorely tempted and would have liked nothing better, had always been the same: she could not and would not break up her father's home again, as she had done when Dr Chambers insisted on her going to Torquay. She had to explain the reasons for her reluctance to Robert which inevitably meant touching on the untouchable and by doing so admitting him to another level of feeling. On 25th August she wrote him a highly emotional letter describing Bro's death, something she had never committed to paper before. She exposed her suffering to Robert and at the same time the curious nature of her love for her father. Until this letter, Elizabeth's references to her father had been brief and unflattering. Mr Barrett was given lines such as "declares angrily" and was shown as the person consistently holding her back from doing what she wanted to do. Suddenly, Robert was presented with another Mr Barrett – "kind and patient and forbearing" – who loved his children "through and through" and of whom it could be said "there never was . . . a truer affection . . . no, nor a worthier heart . . . a heart loyaller and purer and more compelling to gratitude and reverence than his . . ." It was all extremely confusing for Robert. He showed commendable restraint, merely thanking her for "this admission to participate, in my degree, in these feelings". By then he knew Elizabeth better, knew her horror, after she had confided some intimate piece of information, that it might be treated as though it were commonplace.

But the explanation for the vow did not make Robert give up. He set himself to making her see that her vow was based on a false feeling of guilt from which she should free herself. She clearly thought that her father, in not reproaching her for Bro's death, was being wonderfully generous but Robert tried to make her see instead that, as it had not been her fault, this generosity was an illusion. It was, in any case, all in the past. She had a duty to be as well as possible, for the sake of her father, if she liked. She would not be abroad forever but only for a few months and when she returned he would rejoice at the improvement in her. Firmly, Robert told her, "all seems to rest with yourself". She could not expect other people to speak for her, though in fact Kenyon had already done so. He had suggested Malta as a wintering place for Elizabeth to Mr Barrett (and thought he had met with no response though Surtees Cook recorded in his diary that on 20th August 1845 Mr Barrett had been heard telling Aunt Jane Hedley that when Ba was in Malta *he* was going to Jamaica).

Elizabeth did not know why she needed so much courage to ask her father to arrange for her to go abroad. Her feelings of nervousness were not entirely explained by the memory of the last time this had happened and she had gone to Torquay. On that occasion, Dr Chambers had ordered her to go. He had been prepared to confront her father and deliver an ultimatum. And Mr Barrett had had before him the clear evidence of his own eyes: Elizabeth's collapse, in the spring of 1838, had been dramatic. But now, in the late summer of 1845, it was a different situation. Elizabeth was visibly better than she had been for years. Her chest was clear. No doctor had issued a decree. There was more to Elizabeth's desire to go abroad than the benefit to her health, and her father knew it. He could be forgiven for being suspicious. The truth was that Elizabeth knew she would be leaving her father in more ways than the purely physical this time and she knew that since he was acutely sensitive to anything to do with her he would recognise this. She saw "a growing gravity" in his eyes and sensed "perhaps displeasure deeper within him" even though "his *manner* is most affectionate to me". Long ago, in her twenties, she had warned Boyd that where she was concerned her father was "a Lavatar" (a person who can judge mind and character from facial and physical features). She felt she needed strong medical backing to face him and so called in Dr Chambers whom she had been proud not to have needed for months. He supported her, but only so far as to say that a winter abroad would be of *probable* benefit, and suggested Pisa or Madeira instead of Malta. She was excited beyond measure at the prospect of sitting "perhaps out of doors every day in the Italian sun . . ."

But on 17th September everything collapsed. She wrote to Robert, "it is all over with Pisa . . . I cannot tell you how it has happened – *only do not blame me*". She was not even sure of her own feelings, let alone her father's or the sequence of events. All she knew but found difficult to articulate was that a tremendous struggle of wills was taking place, a struggle complicated by the fact that neither she nor her father spoke plainly. She found it impossible to tell him that she was in love with Robert Browning and that she wished to change her life in more ways than merely wintering abroad. And her father, in so brutally resisting the innocuous sounding idea of escaping to the sun, was challenging her to tell him the whole truth. He remembered perfectly well how, in the last three winters, when Mr Kenyon and Mrs Jameson had mooted the wintering-abroad plan she had sided with him, proclaiming she was "just as well off" in her own warm room and that it was not worth the upheaval. Suddenly, the upheaval was worthwhile. Why? Elizabeth found it too terrifying to think of answering this unspoken but implied question. If she said she loved Robert, her father would be devastated. He had come to believe her above such feelings. She was afraid not just of him but for him and fear made her cowardly. The blame, whatever she said, was hers, however dreadful her position and however unfair it was that she had conspired to trap herself within it.

In other accounts, she wrote that she had tried to stand her ground but had not been able to. Her head had ached and she was exhausted. Her father had not delivered his final verdict but she knew it would be "no". George had pleaded for her but this had only angered her father more: he had begun to complain of the "undutifulness and rebellion" of everyone in the house. The atmosphere was dreadful. Finally, he played his old card in telling her she could do as she liked, "for his part he had washed his hands of me altogether". George, to her surprise, pointed out that as things stood she might as well go since, once gone, "the irritation will exhaust and smooth itself away". For another agonising month she contemplated departure. Plans were made, ships almost booked and then on 13th October she wrote to Robert, "*I do not go to Italy*". Her conclusion at the end of the whole upsetting episode was that her father did not, after all, love her as much as she had always thought, nor, more significantly, as much as she was beginning to believe Robert did.

Chapter Ten

THE failure of her plan to winter abroad did not bring about the collapse of Elizabeth's health and spirits as had been expected. On the contrary, once the decision not to go against her father's wishes had been made, she was immensely cheerful and philosophical. Nor did this unusual buoyancy come from bowing her head to fate, an attitude in which she was well practised. Only her sisters suspected the real cause: she was in love and furthermore knew herself to be loved. Next to such rapture, going abroad was unimportant.

For a whole month before Mr Barrett won, or appeared to win, his battle to stop Elizabeth wintering in Pisa, she and Robert had been "dearest" to each other. There was more in this form of address than there had ever been in Haydon's "My dearest Dream" or "My Sweet Unseen" and Elizabeth knew the difference: Robert had again declared his love for her and this time he had not been told he was suffering from "intemperate fancies". He told her, in August, that he loved her from his soul and quite independently of whether she loved him. Knowing Elizabeth's likely reaction, he promised not to refer to his feelings when next he met her. Elizabeth responded swiftly, not rejecting him but saying she was compelled through her condition to hold back from "the fullest expression" of how she felt about him. She was not worthy of his love, she was a jinx, made everything she touched turn to evil and had a duty to prevent him sacrificing himself.

It was tedious and exasperating for Robert to be told this again and again but he acted with the wisdom which had come from learning to understand her character. Patiently, he stressed that she would be doing him the honour. He was poor stuff, she was a prize. Bit by bit he struggled to erode that huge mountain of pessimism which oppressed her. He would not allow his love to be pushed away into a dark corner, to be hidden in case it vanished, but displayed it repeatedly so that she would become familiar with it and learn to trust it. Gradually, she did indeed become less alarmed by what she termed his "extravagancies" (which had at first made her write "I am frightened, I tremble!") and learned that she must let him say what he wished to say and rejoice in his fervent protestations of love. But she would not let him dwell on the future. His letters were full of "I acquiesce" and "I submit" when it came to her wish that he should behave as she directed. They were to be secretive, tell no one, preserve the convention that his weekly visits were on a par with Kenyon's. Unless he complied, she warned him, her father would find out and all would be lost.

Robert had still not met this terrifying father. Everything he knew of him came through Elizabeth's words and those words were calculated to make him hostile to Mr Barrett. It was extraordinary how Elizabeth managed to present her father to Miss Mitford as an endearing eccentric but to Robert as a cold, unfeeling monster. It was partly, of course, that she needed reasons to keep Robert away from her father whereas she had nothing to fear in bringing Miss Mitford close. But it was also because she was by now seeing her father differently. The more she loved Robert the more she questioned the nature of love. Robert was giving her a vision of love which contrasted sharply with her father's. To love and be loved by Robert was to feel free, happy, at ease with the world; to love and be loved by her father was suddenly to feel anxious, constrained and afraid of offending. While she was enduring this confusion – caused by her re-assessment of what love meant – she wanted each of these men whom she loved in very different ways to be kept in quite separate compartments in her life. She was obliged to make her father appear intimidating to prevent Robert from confronting him and forcing her into a choice she was not ready to make. She had no faith whatsoever in Robert's ability to charm and win her father over. The battle had to be fought and won or fought and lost or run away from entirely by her. It is very easy to understand her decision, in the light of what is known about Mr Barrett, and even easier to agree that she was right but nevertheless there is always the lingering suspicion that in preventing Robert from approaching her father, as he wished to do, she was severely underestimating him. So she told Robert of her father's nightly visits to pray, described to Miss Mitford with such gratitude and charm, as though these were unpleasant sessions imposed upon her by the force of his will. Most unfair of all, despite scores of references she had made to Miss Mitford about how she hated her father being away, she made it sound to Robert as though it was this father who kept her a prisoner. She had to a very great extent created her own prison and it was one, moreover, in which she had wanted the warder on constant duty. When, after the failure of the Pisa plan, she realised she had represented her father as an ogre to Robert she tried, too late, to change the image. "*Don't* think too hardly of Papa," she pleaded with Robert. "You have his wrong side . . . his side of peculiar wrongness . . . to you just now. When you have walked round him you will have other thoughts of him." But Robert was never given any chance to do any walking around: Elizabeth kept him as far from meeting her father as ever.

It was undoubtedly hard for her. She knew she had created the situation in which she now found herself and that her father could not be blamed for thinking she wanted only to stay in her room, reading and writing, and wished nothing else from life except her family around her. He had come to believe her implicitly. Henrietta might cause him concern but Elizabeth never. He saw in her everything that was good in women and, if he kept her on a pedestal, she had climbed up there herself. Elizabeth knew this. Her problem was how to climb down, saying she had after all discovered in herself the appetites and desires of a normal woman. She did not know how to do this. Her father, to whom she wished to speak of carnal love, believed her to care, as he did, only for the love of God. In the terms of their existing relationship the truth amounted to blasphemy. Elizabeth was well able to empathise with what would be her father's horror at the idea of his pure, saintly, middle-aged invalid daughter declaring she passionately loved a younger, virile, penniless poet. Proud though Robert's love made her, she was also humiliated by the vulnerable position in which it placed her. She was aware, too, of how scornful she had always been of marriage, how cynical about the possibility of love within it. It would have been difficult in her twenties for her to say she had changed her mind but on the verge of forty it was doubly hard. Her only resource was to keep her feelings secret and hope some miracle would occur which would solve her dilemma, which was a real one. Even in a normal family of the period the sudden love affair of a daughter of Elizabeth's age, and in her state of health, would have been difficult to accept. The entirely natural questions would be whether such a daughter was deluded, desperately trying to escape her spinster state six months before her fortieth birthday and whether her suitor was out to take advantage and if so why and for what particular gain? No father would clap his hands for joy and hasten such a pair to the altar. To Mr Barrett, his eldest daughter was in addition unbelievably precious. He had guarded her as she had wished him to, loved and admired her without stinting. It will not do to brand him as a tyrant and leave it at that. But equally it will not do to exonerate him from all charges of tyranny. Just as she was striving to pretend nothing had happened, so was he; but he was the parent, the older, wiser, more worldly person who had been in love himself even though a long time ago. Memory was there to come to his aid but he would not unlock and use it, partly because he simply could not believe what his instinct told him was true and partly because the habit of repression was so ingrained. He was as trapped as Elizabeth and both were to be pitied.

Robert had no pity for Mr Barrett. His own father, as he frequently told Elizabeth, would no more dream of dictating to him what he should do than he would dream of dictating to his father. There was between them a mutual respect and love which made such a thing impossible. His family was quite different from the Barretts. Both his parents were indulgent and, to complete the perfection, his sister Sarianna wished only to help him. At least, in this respect, Elizabeth had no cause for envy or shame. She introduced Henrietta and Arabel to Robert who saw them so frequently they became, if not friends, then well liked acquaintances and allies. Of her brothers, Robert knew only George whom he met at someone's house. To Elizabeth's delight, they liked each other in spite of their very different temperaments and interests. She did not meet any of his family though he longed for her to do so. It would have been relatively easy to arrange for Sarianna at least to visit, but Elizabeth was adamant: the risk was too great. Robert did not exactly see what this risk was but he obeyed Elizabeth's wish, his idea of Mr Barrett growing wilder and wilder. He judged that the time had not yet come to force her to give up her role as the blindly submissive daughter. She needed to conserve her energies and be ready to use them once spring came.

The winter of 1845 to 1846 was spent writing increasingly tender letters to each other in which they exchanged the tremulous endearments of lovers who have lost all trace of self-consciousness. A great deal of the content was self-congratulatory, full of how wise they had been not to love before when this was waiting for them, and even more was nostalgic. Each loved to reminisce about crucial visits or letters that were in fact only a few months in the past but seemed to belong to another lifetime. Then there was the sheer wonder of their love to exclaim about. "I never thought that anyone whom *I* could love would stoop to love *me*," Elizabeth wrote, marvelling, and Robert replied astonished that she had felt for him the same love. He showered her now with kisses: "I do kiss your feet, kiss every letter in your name." He was, he warned her, "supremely passionate" but she needed no warning: it was his passion to which she had responded from the beginning. She had her own images to describe to him how he met her need. In January, she told him she loved him from "the deepest part" of her nature, that there was at her centre "a black gaping hole" he filled. She was beginning not just to match but to surpass Robert's declarations, telling him "no man was ever before to any woman what you are to me". By the time the anniversary of their first letters had passed they were both swept away by thoughts of their love for each other and had little time for the trading of literary opinions or discussions on their own work (although they did discuss interesting new developments such as Dickens' new newspaper, the *Daily News*, about which Elizabeth was patronising and Robert critical). Only occasionally did Elizabeth's old doubt re-assert itself – what if she ruined his life, what if he discovered after all that she was unworthy of him? – and now Robert had little difficulty dealing with it. She believed, at last, that he did love her and that he knew her.

But inevitably this idyllic interlude came to an end. The approach of spring made Robert restless. Just as Elizabeth was triumphantly telling him how happy she was, he was beginning to feel distinctly unhappy. Waiting was destroying him. He pointed out to her how well she was: "that is not my dream you know but what all see". The winter was over, the time for action had come. What she must do was agree to plan "a new life", one that included him. The future, contrary to what she appeared to think, was not something which would take care of itself. It must be fought for and she as well as he must be prepared to fight. They must decide what to do and do it because "this living without you is too tormenting now". He had warned her "*not* to receive me *standing* – I should not remain master of myself" and now wrote, "I claim your promise's fulfillment – say, at the summer's end". She replied there were problems she could still see no way round. The major obstacle was her father's anger which she did not think herself capable of withstanding in any confrontation. To impress upon him what she meant she described a scene that had taken place years ago when Henrietta had asked permission to marry a certain young gentleman (before the advent of Surtees) and Mr Barrett had been furious. "Oh the dreadful scenes! . . . I hear how her knees were made to ring on the floor now! She was carried out of the room in strong hysterics." Though only a witness, she had fainted herself. "I belong to that pitiful order of weak women," she wrote to Robert, "who cannot command their bodies with their souls at every moment and who sink down in hysterical disorder when they ought to act and resist". But Robert was not to interpret this as meaning she would give up his love if challenged. She would not, not ever. (Henrietta, she added with that touch of arrogance she often displayed towards her sister, had not of course *really* been in love.) All she meant was that, because of her proven physical weakness, any open contest was to be avoided. But, if this was to be the case, she offered no other solution. It was curious to Robert that she did not seem as obsessed by the future as he was. On the contrary, she had never thought less about the future (bearing in mind that she had tried for years not to think about it at all). The present was quite brilliant and exciting enough for her. She was savouring her happiness, relishing every aspect of it. The prospect of an even greater happiness in the future made her feel greedy.

So Robert had to make do with her vague if firm promise that she would not fail him and that when summer came they "would see". Elizabeth repeatedly reminded him he would have to take charge but every time he tried to do so she stopped him. He began to suffer terrible headaches, worse and more frequent than he had ever had. He complained about them incessantly. For Elizabeth, who had never felt better, it was a new experience to be the stronger one giving out medical advice. She enjoyed it. She urged Robert to take a short break somewhere warm for his health but, when he refused to leave her, urged walks and riding and a vigorous open-air life. Robert was quite willing to follow this obvious suggestion since it was to his liking anyway but he spurned her other recommendations. He did not want to smoke, did not want to drink the black coffee she swore cured her headaches, did not want to drink wine regularly, did not want to sit with his feet in a mustard bath and most definitely did not want to take opium. What he wanted was an end to all this prevarication: he wanted Elizabeth to marry him at once and go to live with him somewhere warm enough to benefit her health permanently.

Every time Robert burst out – and he did – that he could not go on like this, existing on one weekly meeting of an hour and otherwise on inadequate letters, Elizabeth produced another horror story about her father to scare him. She had told Robert at the end of January that her father would rather see her "dead at his foot" than married. There was no disputing this: "I see, I know." She then, as usual, defended her father's abhorrent behaviour. There was, she now told Robert, "a fountain within the rock" which she had heard. Her father was courageous and strong and had "high qualities" (not enumerated). She loved him and was proud of him. She sketched her relationship rapidly for Robert – her illness, his concern, his tenderness – but ended with a rather strange statement that she had "proved a little my affection for him by coming to London at the risk of my life rather than diminish the comfort of his home by keeping a part of his family away from him". This was a gross distortion of the truth as it appeared at the time in her letters. She had longed to come to London for her own sake. Giving her father his complete family back was by no means her main aim. The prospect of being sent to Clifton at one stage had made her frantic, not because she would not be with her family but because she would not be in London. But Robert, as ever, saw Mr Barrett through her representations; it was useless for Elizabeth to end this kind of account with the words "you would esteem him, you would like him I think". How was he to be given the opportunity to do either? Any suggestion that he should meet Mr Barrett was met with such hysterical vehement refusal that he had to drop it. No meetings were possible, Elizabeth told him, and for good measure added that visitors were not invited to the house, unless they had a family connection; not even George's eminently respectable friends. There was no attempt, as there had been, when explaining this to Miss Mitford, to describe her father's attitude as his "peculiar brand of shyness". Shyness was never mentioned to Robert. Nor was there any mention of Mr Barrett as the life and soul of the dinner parties Surtees described in his diary (where non-family guests were included, too, giving the lie to Elizabeth's protestations that only family were ever invited). It occurred to Robert that, whatever Elizabeth's reasons for not introducing him to her father, it was actually rather odd that Mr Barrett had not asked to meet him on his own initiative. In a similar position, Robert felt he would have wanted to meet someone who was such a regular visitor of *his* daughter's. Here again Elizabeth lost an opportunity to present her father sympathetically, telling Robert that her father never thought of thanking anyone for their obvious kindness to her. He had not even had Kenyon to dinner to thank him; but there was no mention of her father being intimidated by thoughts of Kenyon's supposed intellectual brilliance as there had been to Miss Mitford. Elizabeth always ended any recitation of her father's unreasonableness with the warning "let *that* be the last word".

Robert was obliged to let it be. It was, he commented, like fighting a particularly menacing shadow with whom one could never come to grips. Meanwhile, spring had arrived, but on cue it went back on itself with a March that was wet and cold. Elizabeth's fortieth birthday passed entirely without comment, though she wrote Robert a long letter that day. She continued to tell him "the whole rests with you" without specifying what this whole was to be. Any suggestion from Robert that it meant facing her father and asking his blessing on her marriage was greeted with terror: no, no, that was not the way. What, then, was the way? She put no alternative to Robert, merely continued to stall. Robert's forbearance was exemplary. April was warm and sunny, his impatience even greater, Elizabeth's procrastination worse. She talked of windows being open, metaphorically as well as actually, and of leaning out of them. Robert was exasperated: if windows were open why did they not both jump out of them? Elizabeth replied that they might crash to the ground, causing Robert to reflect, a little bitterly, that she always beat him on paper, managing to turn "my own illustrations into obscurations". He wrote, "I *do* hate, *hate* having to write and not kiss my answer on your mouth". How much longer would he have to endure this awful letter-writing: "love, shall I have very, very long to be hating to write, yet write?" Elizabeth evaded a direct answer. It was all like her own "especial fairy tale" she told Robert and quite frankly she was far from tired of it yet. The postman's knock was the equivalent, she said, to the fairy's wand. Robert found talk of fairies irritating; he wanted above all else to be practical and "soon, very soon, end all this".

The only promise he could get from Elizabeth was that she would act that summer. She agreed they could not go through another winter apart. Her greatest concession was to calm Robert by showing herself willing to discuss where and how they would live after the break was made. She preferred this game to concentrating on the break itself and how it was to be made, because she still had no idea. Robert enjoyed the act of writing a little more as he extolled the virtues of mosquito netting for beds and he loved it when Elizabeth indulged him by saying she had bought a new bonnet to keep off the Italian sun. Spring turned into a brilliant summer – the average temperature in June 1846 in London was 84° Fahrenheit in the sun – and Elizabeth's health improved even further (though once she had said such heat enervated her). Running through her letters there was now a thread of anxiety about what the world would think of the marriage she was coming to believe would happen. It would think her "bad" and Robert "mad". She speculated which of her friends would be shocked (Miss Mitford) and which approving (Mrs Jameson). Robert was scornful that she gave the subject two minutes' consideration but she could not help being on the defensive. She also made a great performance of telling Robert how she despised lavish wedding ceremonies and certainly would have no regrets about trousseaux and white dresses and all the nonsense about to be indulged in by her Hedley cousin Arabella.

Another running topic that hot summer was how little each could live on. Both of them vied with each other as they boasted how frugal were their needs, without either having any kind of realistic appraisal of expenses. Robert, who had never supported anyone by his earnings in his life (as Miss Mitford had not been slow to point out), was vociferous in his assurances that if need be he would have no trouble earning a decent income. Part of him, he told Elizabeth, wanted to earn fifty thousand pounds and build a fine house just to show he could do it even though he despised such ambitions. After some weeks of this kind of encouraging speculation he pressed Elizabeth harder: "May I count by months, by weeks?" He reminded her yet again of how good her health was: she was walking unaided in Regent's Park, going out to post letters by herself, travelling as far as Hampstead to pick dog roses in the lanes, stealing flowers for him in the Botanical Gardens and staying out so late that she saw the gas being lit in the shops. She was eating, sleeping, putting on weight and getting some colour into her pale cheeks. Psychologically too she was tougher, able to withstand the kind of emotional shocks that normally prostrated her. At the end of June, for example, the horrible suicide of Haydon – he shot himself then finished the job off with a razor – appalled but did not destroy her, even though just before his death Haydon had given into her keeping twenty-five folio volumes of his journals and some pictures which made her feel she had some responsibility towards him.[1] She was affected enough to cancel a visit to Boyd but wrote to Robert that, although the news had "chilled the blood" in her veins, writing to him about it had made her feel "better and lighter" and her grief was lessened. Her comment was "we are so selfish on this earth that nothing grieves us very long". In her love for him she realised she had become totally selfish. He was her own "dearest beloved" beside whom no one and nothing else mattered. It was natural that, given this amazing proof of her single-mindedness, Robert should cry, "Why wait!"

But then there began a series of letters quite different from any that had been written in the previous eighteen months: they began to argue. Early on in their correspondence Robert had smugly wondered where the lovers' quarrels were: they never quarrelled. Later, a few differences had surfaced, about abstract topics like the rights and wrongs of duelling, but still they never seriously disagreed about anything. It was one of their joys, both marvelling at how many opinions, tastes and judgements they shared. Elizabeth was deeply gratified to discover that Robert showed no signs of behaving towards her as she was tired of seeing so many men behave towards women. He neither flaunted any superiority nor relegated her to an inferior category just because she was a woman. She told him that she was pleased not to see in him any "of the common rampant man-vices which tread down a woman's peace – and which begin the work often long before marriage. Oh, I understand perfectly how as soon as ever a common man is sure of a woman's attention he takes up the tone of might and right . . . and he *will* have it so . . . and he *won't* have it so!" This, she maintained, was the root cause of lovers' quarrels: "the growth of power on one side . . . and the struggle against it . . . on the other". But it would not be "possible for *me* to quarrel with *you* now or ever" because there was no power struggle between them. Ironically, as she wrote these words at the beginning of July 1846, Elizabeth was in the process of a quarrel she had denied could ever be possible.

It hinged at first on whom to tell and whom not to tell about their marriage. Robert could not believe that Elizabeth expected him to keep it secret from his parents: "Why should I wound them to the very soul and forever?" he thundered in a rare display of righteous indignation. It was unthinkable. His parents could not be treated like that. Hastily Elizabeth replied she had only meant they should not be made a party to the marriage. Robert hardly saw the difference, but conceded the point when Elizabeth explained she wanted to protect his parents from being involved in what the world and certainly her father would consider underhand behaviour. He wrote that he had expressed himself with too much warmth and that, if she wished, his parents need not be present (but they must be told). They argued the same point, though much less fiercely, over Kenyon. Robert wanted to tell Kenyon before the marriage. Not only was he an old friend of them both but he had been the person through whose action they had been brought together and he might also be useful as an intermediary with Mr Barrett. Elizabeth shuddered at the idea. In her opinion, it was as necessary to protect Kenyon from the charge of conspiracy as it was to protect anyone else. Furthermore, she did not quite trust his reaction. He had a way of looking at her through his spectacles that made her think he had guessed but his stare was accompanied by an expression which made her hesitate over believing in his absolute loyalty and approval. What she wanted was complete secrecy. Robert, exhausted, was defeated.

But these quarrels were mere minor disagreements (though more significant than Elizabeth at least cared to admit) compared to a more fundamental difference of opinion which began to emerge from them. This was about money. Here was a real quarrel. Protected though both had been from the harsher realities of living, they nevertheless appreciated that they would need money to leave London. Robert had travelled in Europe, he knew the cost of boats and hotels and carriages, and Elizabeth was a Barrett, brought up to know the virtue of economy. She had run her own household in Torquay and not all the facts of day-to-day expense were mysteries to her. She might find the whole subject of money "hateful" but she could be practical when she chose. She told Robert that she had a small income of her own, thanks to the investment of her Grandmother Moulton's money, and that they could live abroad frugally on this. Robert loathed the idea. He did not want to live on his wife's money. Cleverly, Elizabeth argued that in this case her money merely compensated for the fact that, since she was an invalid with an invalid's expensive extra requirements, she would be a liability to him. Reluctantly, Robert was obliged to accept the truth of this. He had no money of his own. Even he could not expect his long suffering parents to support a sick wife as well as himself. But he was adamant about one thing: there must be a proper marriage settlement in which Elizabeth's money was made over to her sisters in the event of her death. Elizabeth objected to this. She wanted Robert to have her money in such an event because she would have ruined his life. Backwards and forwards they argued, each discovering just how strong and determined the other could be when roused. Neither wanted the other to give way without being genuinely convinced. Elizabeth was even more insistent than Robert who continually pulled back from an open rift. He could not help thinking that if their arguments had all taken place face to face there would be no problem. The trouble was "all this missing of instant understanding" which came "from our letters and being divided".

They were still divided on the subject of money as the summer showed signs of coming to an end. Robert had decided to borrow money from his parents, a hundred pounds, to use for initial expenses. Elizabeth was full of ideas about how to contribute some hard cash herself through contributing some poems to *Blackwood's*. She was sure, she said, she could make a hundred a year. It worried her that, because she was so afraid to take any brother into her confidence, she could not have access to her own income easily. Her father still handled her finances for her (at her request). The amounts she was used to receiving were spent on clothes and most of all on drugs. But she was indignant when Robert suggested he could raise more money by selling his copyrights. "That," she wrote, "would have been travelling at the price of blood and I should never agree to it." Once they were safely married and abroad, of course, she would get her own money and thought the best plan would be "to place our money somewhere on the railroads".

It did not escape Robert's notice that all this delicious future planning was evading the more important issue of *when* exactly they would marry and how it would be managed. In mid-August he declared he could wait no longer. He had just paid his eighty-second visit and though his soul "revolted" at the notion of a scene every bit as much as Elizabeth's he had come to the conclusion that there would have to be one. Every time he arrived at 50 Wimpole Street he expected to find that all was discovered and the door barred to him. Only the week before, a sudden storm had detained him and he had stayed twice the usual length of time till the rain stopped. Elizabeth reported that her father had thundered, "It appears Ba that *that man* has spent the whole day with you." Robert was tired of all this: it was an impossible situation in which he was made to feel deceitful. He was beginning to think he had made a great mistake in allowing it to continue. As a gentleman, he should make a stand, and should approach Mr Barrett in a direct, decent way. But every time he brought himself to the point of insisting, Elizabeth passionately pleaded with him not to be so foolish and warned him that diplomacy would not work. What she made Robert see was that if it came to a choice between him and her father and if that choice was made in front of them both, then her father would win. Once any ultimatum had been issued she doubted her ability to survive it, not because she loved her father more but because in his presence she felt her will ebbing. It was her own physical cowardice she feared, a cowardice arising from witnessing her father's anguish and fury. Logic had no part to play and neither did right. She was not a rational being when confronted by her father. Any scene would prove a contest in which love was ranged against love, hurt against hurt, pain against pain. She would see she was taking from her beloved father the only emotional sustenance he had, that she was smashing the ideal he had admired for so long. She would not deny Robert, ever, no matter what her father said, but she would collapse. Short of Robert kidnapping her she would never be able to get out of the house. (Just such a fantasy had occurred to Robert: he imagined himself rescuing Mr Barrett from robbers and having Elizabeth's hand bestowed on him in gratitude.)

But at last Elizabeth made her decision: they would marry first, secretly, so that she could be quite sure of belonging to him, and then they would leave, equally secretly. Only after both deeds were done would anyone be told. She could face anything then. But when Mrs Jameson teased her on a visit about an elopement being the only escape for her, Elizabeth was shocked and saw for the first time what she really might have to endure. She was upset and wrote to Robert, "dearest, nobody will use such a word surely . . . we shall be in such an obvious exercise of Right by Daylight – surely nobody will use such a word."[2] She saw how, if they did, her father would suffer doubly. Public disgrace would make his pain even greater: the mere notion of a Barrett eloping would be unspeakably offensive to him. Naively, Elizabeth assumed that, if she married before she left her father's house, nobody could say she had eloped. Everything must be planned with the greatest care to protect her father where possible. The fine details mattered and she devoted all her energies to getting them right during what Robert called "the critical weeks". They agreed to marry and leave at the end of September. Once the decision was taken, time seemed unbelievably short. With the planning of this secret marriage of her own filling her thoughts, Elizabeth wrote to Miss Mitford, "A year for marriages is it? Well – it seems so – and some marry unfortunately (or fortunately) *without* trousseaus . . ." Watching the feverish preparations that month of August for her cousin Arabella Hedley's wedding, Elizabeth commented, ". . . there does enter into the motives of most marriages a good deal of that hankering after the temporary distinction, emotion and pleasure of being for a while a chief person . . ." The only way she could imagine how it felt was to think of bridal glory as being "like seeing one's name in print for the first time perhaps". But the expense struck her as absurd. Arabella had "six dress pocket handkerchiefs, at four guineas each . . . forty guineas of lace trimming on the bridal dress". The wedding breakfast for forty would cost, Elizabeth reckoned, "some thousand pounds in the livery and paraphernalia of it". She was proud of scorning such a show.

As she went ahead with her own modest arrangements Elizabeth seemed stimulated by the drama of it, while Robert became increasingly nervous. She wrote to him with relish, "There are nets on all sides of us . . . the hunters are upon us," but would continue with a matter-of-fact discussion on which books to take in the same letter. Robert could concentrate on nothing. When Elizabeth told him Stormie had asked Arabel if his sister and Browning were engaged, he was plunged into despair; surely they should take her brothers, or some of them, into their confidence. Elizabeth was adamant: neither brothers nor sisters should be told (though she knew her sisters were aware of everything except the arrangements for her wedding and flight). After she had gone, she wanted them all to be able in truth to protest total innocence as a protective device against the terrible wrath of their father. But Robert's nerve was failing him. He was reduced to suggesting the sort of strategy usually proposed by Elizabeth: to deflect suspicion he would not come so often. Now that the time for action was so near the strain was telling, and seeing her and being in Wimpole Street with her was hard to endure. For once, he felt safer apart from her.

It was Elizabeth, not Robert, who broke the vow to tell nobody whatsoever. She told Boyd. In one of her now rare letters to him she remarked, "A prophet said to me (by the way) a week since that God intended me compensation even in the world and that the latter time would be better for me than the beginning."[3] The average person would, as Elizabeth said, see little particular significance in such a general remark but Boyd "like a prisoner in a dungeon sounds every stone around him and discerns a hollowness . . . patiently pricks out the mortar with a pin". That was in July. On the next of her infrequent visits to him in St John's Wood, where Arabel often visited him, he subjected her to ruthless cross-questioning as to what she had meant: what compensation, why would the end be better than the beginning? To Elizabeth's amusement, he hazarded a guess that she was about to become a nun. In August, he guessed again and was "precisely right". She had tried to evade a direct answer but when a lie became inevitable told him the truth. Boyd was overjoyed; Elizabeth had picked the right confidante. Instead of being grave and moralising he encouraged her "with ever such exhortation" to stick to her resolution. Boyd had never liked Mr Barrett, however much Mr Barrett had come round at one time to him, and thought Elizabeth right to resist his desire to keep his family to himself. They had an enjoyable session during which an animated Boyd trotted out endless quotations from numerous philosophers to convince Elizabeth she was acting in accordance with the very best authorities. It delighted him that he had guessed ("Was I not acute?") and that nobody else knew. Justifying her decision, Elizabeth told Robert there was nothing to fear from her poor, blind old friend to whom she had given such innocent pleasure.

It had made a refreshing change to tell someone, when she spent the rest of her time evading long, hard stares from her brothers, especially Stormie and George. She felt they were deliberately not challenging her for the same reason that she was not confiding in them: they wanted protection. They were Barretts, playing the Barrett game of see-no-evil, speak-no-evil, hear-no-evil, all terrified of becoming involved in a secret kept from their father. She told Robert she was watched "on all sides" but no one said anything. Kenyon was another watcher (Elizabeth was glad when his spectacles broke), and the Hedleys, in town for the wedding of Arabella, watched, too. But most feared of all, of course, was her father. He walked round her room, admiring her flowers (from Robert) and clearly searching for that old closeness between them. It had gone. She watched him furtively, hiding her letters from Robert, willing him to go. She knew he sensed her agitation as he prowled about, making harmless pleasantries. She could not meet his eyes, could not endure the most perfunctory embrace. The quieter he seemed, the greater her panic. Any small act of kindness or consideration on his part was anathema to her: she wrote to Robert that she could not stand his affection now. The nearer the time came for what in his eyes would be the ultimate betrayal, the more she needed him to be at his implacable worst, as cold as possible.

The Hedleys were less dangerous but more irritating. The house was full of them blundering about in their usual good-hearted, boisterous way, forever making heavy jokes about beaux and attachments. They knew about Elizabeth's poet and indulged in banter which would have been harmless if it had not come unwittingly so near the mark. In Elizabeth's room, with her father present, Aunt Jane enthused about how well her niece looked, how she glowed, and asked Mr Barrett repeatedly to agree with her. Elizabeth trembled with embarrassment and apprehension. Her father commented eventually that on the contrary he thought she looked "mumpish" (his word for sullen). The moment passed but Elizabeth decided she could not risk further comment being invited and spoke to her Aunt Jane. Aunt Jane took the hint. She observed, "Ah, Ba, you have arranged your plans more than you would have us believe. But you are right not to tell us – indeed, I would rather not hear." But, though Aunt Jane did not draw attention to Elizabeth again, she kept up her insistence that she ought to be thinking yet again about wintering abroad. She should go to Italy, Aunt Jane said in front of Mr Barrett who, surprisingly, did not explode. Elizabeth maintained that his composure sprang from his confidence that she would no more live "beyond these four walls" than she would "journey to Lapland". Robert reflected how funny it would be if Mr Barrett were actually phlegmatic for another reason: because he was himself arranging for her to winter abroad.

On 31st August Robert burst out that it was insane to wait another month: "if the cold plunge *must* be taken, all this shivering delay on the bank is hurtful as well as fruitless". Elizabeth felt it was unfair of him to stampede her but said she would comply with his wish so long as she had a week's notice. She wanted him to fix the actual date. Unfortunately, Robert was unable to fix anything because he fell ill. He was feverish and had the worst headache ever. By the time he had recovered enough to start looking at boat and train timetables prior to naming the day, another calamity overtook them: Flush was once more stolen and Elizabeth incapable of action. She and Arabel had had him with them while shopping (a sign of how complete her recovery was) and he had disappeared between shop and carriage. Henry was sent to negotiate with The Fancy while Elizabeth poured out her grief on Robert. To her dismay, his reaction was, she judged, callous. He wanted her to get on with more important things like planning their escape – as if, compared to the loss of Flush, such a thing were important. He even made offensive remarks about Flush's courage, joking "did all that barking . . . spend itself on such enemies as Mr Kenyon and myself leaving only blandness and waggings of the tail for the man with the bag?" Most inexcusable of all, he spoke of darling Flush in the past tense as "our friend and follower that was to be at Pisa". Clearly, Robert had no idea what Flush meant to her. Soon he was expressing sentiments which sounded exactly like her father's about how it was wrong to pay ransoms to dog-snatchers. Furious, she wrote back that she could not take any risks or adopt any high moral stance. She wanted Flush back and could not "bargain or haggle". But she was not given a chance to do either because Taylor came to the house to state his demands and was confronted once more by Mr Barrett who would not allow Henry to hand over any money at all. Taylor left, nonchalant as ever. Elizabeth expected Henry to go after him for her but he refused to disobey such a very direct order from his father. She accused him contemptuously of being "lukewarm" and said she would find Taylor herself.

The whole household was aghast as she made her preparations. Henry told her that she would be "robbed and murdered". That evening, on 7th September, five days after Flush had been stolen, Elizabeth got into a cab with her frightened but loyal maid Wilson and drove through what she described as "obscure streets" to the district of Shoreditch where she knew Taylor lived. The cabman stopped at a pub and asked the way. When they arrived at the address given, "two or three men" came out and invited Elizabeth to come in and wait for Taylor who was not at home. Wilson, "in an aside of terror", begged her mistress to do no such thing. They stayed in the cab, now surrounded by a "gang of benevolent men and boys who 'lived but to oblige us'". Eventually, Mrs Taylor was produced. She was "an immense feminine bandit" who graciously promised to inform her dear husband when he returned that a lady had called and was waiting for her dog. Feeling she had done rather well, Elizabeth returned home quite triumphant from her adventure. Taylor soon followed and Elizabeth sent down the six guineas he demanded. At that moment, Alfred arrived home and, though not normally of an aggressive nature, chose to call Taylor "a swindler and a liar and a thief". Taylor swore at him and said Flush would never be seen again. Elizabeth raged at Alfred, saying he had ruined everything, and she would have to return to Shoreditch. It was now almost dark and her brothers and sisters gathered round telling her she was "quite mad and obstinate and wilful". Arabel wished aloud Mr Browning was there to "manage me a little". In the end, Sette said he would go on condition Elizabeth went to rest in her room. He brought Flush back at eight o'clock after paying yet more guineas (the final total was twenty).

Robert, told of all this as it was progressing, said he would never have paid the ransom. Elizabeth accused him of making principles more important than life and put to him the question of what he would have done if it had been she who had been captured and not a dog. Would his splendid-sounding "abstract principles of justice" have held? Robert replied at great length, setting out his whole theory about the necessity of resisting known evil wherever and whenever it arose. If she had been held to ransom he informed her that he would have paid it but then shot the bandits even if he had to follow them for fifty years to do so. That ended the matter on a satisfactorily elevated note. They returned to their plans. The weather was hot, thundery and oppressive and so was the atmosphere in Wimpole Street. On 10th September, Mr Barrett delivered an edict: the whole household would move out of London while the house was papered and painted. "Now!" wrote Elizabeth dramatically to Robert. "What *can* be done?"

Chapter Eleven

R OBERT'S reaction was instant and decisive. "We must be *married directly* and go to Italy," he wrote. "I will go for a licence today and we can be married on Saturday." He was aware that this would seem abrupt, and that it broke his promise to give Elizabeth at least a week's notice, but he thought he was justified. Nevertheless, his fear that she might panic brought from him a warning. "Your words first and last," he added, "have been that you could not fail me – you will not . . . see the *tone* I take, the way I write to *you* . . . Now *your* part must begin." If she failed to play this part and allowed herself to be taken off to the country somewhere, then "our marriage will be impossible for another year – the misery!" His last sentence was a kind of test: "It seems as if I should insult you if I spoke a word to confirm you, to beseech you, to relieve you from your promise, if you claim it."

Elizabeth replied swiftly, "I shall not fail you – I do not. I will not. I will act by your decision and I wish you to decide." But she pointed out that it was he who was in a panic, for which there was no need – George had only been sent to *look* for a house – but she agreed it would be as well to take the first step and marry at once. It was all, she wrote, like a dream which might "break on a sudden". Robert visited her the next day, the 11th, when the rest of the family were on a picnic at Richmond. Together, they planned their wedding day, Robert feverish but authoritative in his excitement, Elizabeth tremulous and in a daze. But she had it all planned: she would go out as though on a visit to Boyd whom she had begun to visit more regularly, telling Arabel that she and Wilson were taking a cab to Hampstead and that, if she and Henrietta would follow, they could bring her home. Meanwhile, she would have gone straight to the church and then on to Boyd's. It was all quite simple. Robert left, the ring in his pocket, with last words of encouragement.

That night, as Elizabeth prepared for bed, she took Wilson into her confidence and asked her help. From the beginning of the planning to go to Italy, Elizabeth had told Robert she would find it hard to manage without her maid and he had been swift to agree that if Wilson could be persuaded then she must come. She had already been vital to them: it was Wilson who was privy to all Elizabeth's secrets, Wilson who knew the importance of collecting and posting certain letters, Wilson who knew how to deflect other visitors when a certain person was with her mistress. Without Wilson, Elizabeth would have needed the assistance of either Henrietta or Arabel to leave the house and she was determined to involve neither. To her relief but not her surprise Wilson was "very kind, very affectionate". She would stand by her. If they were found out then of course Wilson faced instant dismissal and no hope of a reference from Mr Barrett. Her loyalty was not without risks.

Naturally, Elizabeth could not sleep. The enormity of the step she was about to take overwhelmed her. It was not what she was going to do so much as how she was going to do it which made her afraid; she could hardly bear to subject her own behaviour to the kind of analysis she usually gave it. She would not have said that in such an important matter she could ever go behind her father's back and she was doing it, moreover, knowing full well the consequences for him as well as her. What she was doing was right – she had no last-minute bridal fears – but the way in which she was doing it was wrong. And in committing this wrong she was committing other wrongs. Robert's parents and sister should not be shut out of his wedding. Only once in her life had she been to a wedding, Annie Boyd's (she had recently evaded her cousin Arabella's where Henrietta was bridesmaid), and the memory of that unsatisfactory occasion gave her courage. There had been little feeling, then, of two people in love. At her lonely wedding, love would fill the empty church. She had no need of pomp and circumstance, of flowers and frills, of congratulations and smiles from a big congregation. She had Robert and that was enough.

Wilson had her up and dressed by ten o'clock. Together, they quietly left the house an hour later, as though going for a walk. It was a sunny September morning. The two diminutive women walked up Wimpole Street to turn into Devonshire Street, a mere two hundred yards away. But Elizabeth could not manage even that short distance. On the corner, she staggered and clutched Wilson's arm. The resolute Wilson, seeing her mistress was about to faint, coaxed and encouraged her to a chemist's shop where she purchased some smelling salts. Revived, Elizabeth managed to walk as far as the fly-stand in Marylebone Street, another five hundred yards. It was hardly worth getting into a cab – St Marylebone Parish Church was literally two minutes walk away by then – but in Elizabeth's condition it was necessary. Robert and his cousin James Silverthorne were waiting outside the portico of the church, on the steps. A verger watched Elizabeth being helped into the church where the vicar waited. There was no choir, no singing. The silence was eerie as they repeated their vows. Elizabeth stood before the altar in the silent, dark church, thinking of "the many, many women who have stood where I stood and to the same end, not one of them all perhaps, not one perhaps, since that building was a church, has had reasons strong as mine for an absolute trust and devotion towards the man she married – not one!" The service, restricted as it was, was over in minutes. Husband and wife at last, Robert and Elizabeth left the church at half past eleven on the morning of Saturday 12th September, 1846. They parted at once. The same verger who had watched them go in stood in the doorway, his mouth wide open in mute surprise as the bride got into one cab and the bridegroom into another and they went their separate ways.

Elizabeth went straight to Boyd's house, as planned, sending Wilson on home as soon as she arrived there. Boyd's doctor was with him so she had a few minutes alone to regain her composure. A fierce pride and joy struggled to overcome the deep exhaustion she felt and an ever deeper dread of what was now to come. Boyd, sensing her weakness, made her eat some bread and butter and sip some wine. Henrietta and Arabel arrived later with "grave faces". Arabel, forgetting that Elizabeth was visiting Boyd, had been alarmed to find both her and Wilson gone and had thought – "What nonsense . . . what fancies you have to be sure," Elizabeth broke in. To convince her sisters everything was quite normal she brightly suggested a drive along the Heath road. All the way there and all the way back to Wimpole Street Elizabeth chattered vivaciously. As the cab passed St Marylebone Church there was, she wrote to Robert later, "a cloud before my face". The effort of will needed to enter her home, to act as though nothing had changed, drained her. Only Wilson knew the truth even if her sisters suspected it; Wilson was the only person before whom she could drop this ghastly pretence. Robert was only too aware of how much was owed to this quiet servant girl and in his first letter after they were married asked Elizabeth to "thank Wilson for me".

That letter, written an hour after his marriage with all the strength and love of which Robert was capable, reassured Elizabeth that she had not been dreaming. Robert told her she had given him the "highest, completest proof of love that ever one human being gave to another". He urged her to try now to be composed above all else, fearing she would collapse entirely after such an ordeal. But Elizabeth knew she would not. She felt she had been launched on a new path down which nothing and no one could prevent her walking. She had a new duty overriding all others: to her husband. He could, if need be, legally claim her as his own and the relief of knowing this calmed her. Yet there were still difficult days to get through with no fixed end in sight. George was rumoured to have found a house and on top of the excitement this generated there were visitors from Herefordshire disrupting the routine further. In one way all this was excellent camouflage but in another the cause of extra strain. Elizabeth was afraid to retreat to her room, in case it caused comment now that she was used to appearing in the drawing room, but her head seemed to be splitting in two. In the middle of all the talking and laughing, church bells rang out and one visitor asked which church it was. Henrietta, standing behind Elizabeth's chair, said, "Marylebone Church Bells". Elizabeth could not trust herself to remain any longer. She went to her room but even here did not escape what she imagined was persecution. Kenyon arrived and was admitted. His first words were, "When did you last see Browning?" Knowing she blushed as she spoke Elizabeth tried to answer evasively, "He was here on Friday." It was the truth but also a lie. Realising she could not stand up to any cross-examination she began to talk rapidly of other things. Kenyon hardly listened. Instead, he stared hard at her. Elizabeth reported to Robert that she was sure he "saw something". Before he left he asked her when she would next see Browning. It was a relief to be able to say she did not know. (Robert had already said he refused to visit his own wife and ask for "Miss Barrett" so this was perfectly true.) Kenyon gone, Elizabeth wrote to Robert of how she had hated taking off her wedding ring and concealing it. Without it, she felt once more in a dream which might at any moment yet turn into a nightmare.

Robert felt wonderful. The morning after his wedding he wrote, "Dearest, I woke this morning *quite well* – quite free from the sensation in the head. I have not woke *so*, for two years perhaps – what have you been doing to me?" He was full of energy and threw himself enthusiastically into preparations for their journey – newspaper advertisements, cards, passports, tickets, nothing was too much trouble. But he had the strangest ideas. Elizabeth, so fond of boasting to Crow once upon a time that she cared nothing for social etiquette, now showed herself very bothered indeed by Robert's lack of it. He wished to put "At Home" on their cards or else "In Italy for a year". Elizabeth remonstrated, "you must not think of putting At Home anywhere or any other thing in place of it . . . Put simply the names." Anything else would be "quite wrong". Then there was the wording of the notice to go in *The Times*. Robert wanted to put the date on but Elizabeth told him there should definitely be no date and told him off for needing her to put him straight. He was, she complained, "acting throughout too much the woman's part" and making nonsense of her vow to obey him. In spite of sounding sharp and alert, she was feeling faint and dizzy but fortunately this did not prevent her from spotting Robert's more stupid mistakes. He had misread timetables, failing to realise there were two railroad companies each with different schedules, and had only the haziest notion of which Channel crossing would be best. He had the greatest difficulty absorbing Elizabeth's perfectly clear strictures on when she could travel, which depended on leaving the house not earlier than ten in the morning or later than five in the evening. She was constantly reminding him that, if she were discovered, "I shall be *killed* – it will be so infinitely worse than you can have any idea".

As the time approached to leave, the burden she was placing on her sisters troubled Elizabeth more and more. She worried particularly about the effect of her departure on Henrietta's future plans. For the last two years she had drawn closer to this sister than she had ever been because she too was in love. Elizabeth might consider Henrietta's love for Surtees could never be compared to her love for Robert but she sympathised with her and knew that by her own marriage and flight she would make her sister's plight infinitely worse. Henrietta's chances of following suit, should Surtees find some more money to make marriage feasible, were slim indeed and she had been loved and courted by Surtees longer than Elizabeth by Robert. Since December 1845 Henrietta had been the proud possessor, in secret, of a pretty watch given to her by Surtees when he was promoted to captain. It was in lieu of an engagement ring without any wedding in sight. Unlike Robert, Surtees, as a distant relative, had often been invited to share family evenings, but with this useful privilege had gone the more doubtful one of being obliged to listen to Mr Barrett in full spate against undutiful marriages. Any marriage between him and Henrietta would be undutiful because in spite of his promotion he was still poor and, unlike Elizabeth, Henrietta had not a penny of her own. When she came to writing the letter to her sister which she was to leave behind Elizabeth was overcome with guilt and emotion. What would be poor Henrietta's fate after this?

But compared to other letters she had to write Elizabeth found those to her sisters easy if painful. She knew they both loved her and understood what had driven her to such subterfuge. But there were others of whose love she was not completely confident and whose real understanding she doubted. It was hard to write to Miss Mitford who would feel she had not been treated as a confidante of long standing. It was harder still to write to Bummy and Treppy, both of whom had known her since she was born and would feel slighted. Her hand trembled as she wrote these necessary letters, each one needing a different style, but what she had to say was firm enough. She described Robert's wooing of her, the growth of their mutual love, the misery of having to act as they were acting; she was fluent, while confessing she wrote in "a sort of *stupour*". Stupor or not, she was efficient until she came to the two most vital letters. The first was to George, the brother she was leaving to present the news to her father. Here, her powers of explanation and justification almost broke down. Her letter to him was impassioned, pleading with George to love her: "love me George while you are reading it – love me . . ." She wanted him to fight for her, she appealed to his legal mind to put her case to their father as best he could (and as he had done during the Pisa affair). In case he should think Robert had chosen this way, she was at pains to claim "the whole responsibility of his omission of the usual application to my father". She also swore "everyone in the house is absolutely ignorant and innocent of all participation in this act of my own". In the envelope containing the letter to George she enclosed another to her father, inviting George to read it first, "breaking gently the news of its contents" before giving it to him.[1]

She had first started writing this crucial letter to her father the day after she was married. She had had to abandon that attempt. Three days later, she tried again but told Robert, "I am paralysed when I think of having to write such words as . . . Papa I am married; I hope you will not be too displeased." It was grotesque, she could not do it. On September 17th she started again: "I began to write a letter to papa . . . and could do nothing but cry." But it had to be written and time was now forcing her hand. George had found a house, and the move was fixed for the following Monday. She and Robert would leave on the Saturday when the confusion during the necessary packing would be at its height. Again and again she tried to write to her father until the words "dear Papa, dear Papa" beat in her head. He *was* dear. The thought of his fury and anguish – she desperately hoped more fury than anguish – appalled her and made him dearer still. It was useless for Robert to say he was prepared to submit to any conditions to placate her father; he would be so far beyond being placated that the idea was ludicrous. She was the only person in the world who understood him and at one blow she would rob him of this sympathy. Never, at any moment, did she delude herself into thinking that what she was doing was less terrible than she knew it was.

Robert, meanwhile, was urging her to pack but not to pack too much. Elizabeth had no intention of taking too much: she was proud of her unfeminine ability to travel light. She and Wilson had between them only "a light box and a carpet box", both of which Wilson managed to get out of the house and despatched by cab to the railroad office in Robert's name. In the light box, Elizabeth had packed Robert's letters which she could not bear to leave behind and also another secret packet most precious to her. This contained the manuscript of the forty-three sonnets she had written to him during their courtship. Taken together, they told the story of her love for him – the first realisation, the doubts, the growing strength, the joy, the glory, the triumph. They were a part of herself she could not leave behind. Robert knew nothing of them: they were a stowaway, to be revealed to him at a later date. Until then, they could stay tucked under her dresses next to her diamond necklace and the fur-lined boots she had bought for all the walking she intended to do in the winter at Pisa.

On Friday 18th September Robert sent her his final instructions. She was to meet him at Hodgson's, the bookshop on the corner of Marylebone High Street, between half past three and four on the following afternoon. He would already have taken his luggage to join hers at Vauxhall Station. The train they were to take left at five o'clock. The boat they would board left the Royal Pier, Southampton, at eight. It was imperative that she, Wilson and Flush should arrive at Hodgson's precisely when stated because the timing left no room for manoeuvre. "One struggle more," he pleaded and then they would be safe. She was unable to keep out of her reply the agony she was experiencing – "It is dreadful . . . dreadful" – and quite unable to match his elation. Without Wilson she could not have moved. Wilson, the north country girl who had never been abroad, who spoke not a word of any foreign language, who was leaving her own family whom she had not visited for months and a secure job, Wilson had been "perfect to me". Elizabeth told Robert she had been amazed at her maid's resourcefulness: "And *I* . . . calling her 'timid' and afraid of her timidity!" As she prepared to spend her last night ever in Wimpole Street, Elizabeth was suddenly aware that her debt to Wilson was incalculable and her gratitude matched it. Once she was in Robert's hands all would be well but until then, she was in Wilson's.

Wilson and Elizabeth, carrying Flush, left 50 Wimpole Street just before dinner time on the afternoon of Saturday 19th September, while the family were gathered in the dining room. So great was Elizabeth's nervousness that she forgot to fasten round her neck the chain and locket, containing Arabel's picture, which she had put out to wear. Left behind in her room, it lay with its sapphires glinting, ready to attract the attention of her sisters when they came to look for her later. It was still her habit to dine alone most evenings and then receive visitors; she knew she would not be missed for a couple of hours at least. The letters announcing her departure had already been posted, timed to arrive by the last delivery that day. Worry about the accuracy of her estimate heightened considerably the tension of leaving: she knew from two years of waiting for Robert's letters how the post, with its four collections and four deliveries a day, could go wrong, but she had been unable to bring herself simply to leave the letters behind. The risk was too great. They might be found as she left and precipitate that confrontation she so dreaded.

Robert was waiting, as arranged, at Hodgson's. He had been worrying about the weather, realising neither of them had made provision for rain so torrential that Elizabeth's exit would be bound to cause comment. But it was, he noted later, "a delicious day". Elizabeth and Wilson walked along a sunny Wimpole Street and turning the corner were soon in sight of Robert. Elizabeth looked near to fainting but once in a cab with Robert she revived. From then onwards, his was the greater anxiety. Elizabeth was shut off from him, once more "in a stupour", her head full of images of what would be happening in Wimpole Street. The present passed her by in a mist. But Robert was supremely concerned with the moment: the burden of carrying out their plan sat heavily upon him. He watched Elizabeth carefully, terrified that the rigours of travel would be too much for her. She was unused to the violent noise of railway stations (though Kenyon had taken her to see one of the first trains as a curiosity) and had never had to cope with crowds. He was profoundly relieved to have the calm, unflappable, experienced Wilson with him. She would know how to look after her mistress as he certainly did not. He had no rapport with her – Wilson had merely shown him in and out of Elizabeth's room – nor did he know if she approved of him. Her loyalty was to her mistress alone and he had yet to win her over.

They caught the train without difficulty and were at Southampton in time for the Le Havre ferry. This was the part Robert had dreaded. He had not doubted that the first part of their journey would prove easy enough for his wife but the Channel crossing was an endurance test for anyone. He had wanted to spend a night in Southampton to prepare her for the rigours ahead but she had been against this. She wanted to be out of the country as soon as possible. So they were to cross the Channel at night which, in Robert's mind, doubled the danger. He was afraid that lack of sleep and violent sickness might so incapacitate Elizabeth that she would be seriously ill. It haunted him to think of this and worse: the possibility of her death, a death for which he would hold himself responsible, was constantly before him. Elizabeth had only crossed the Channel as a healthy child and had little memory of what an ordeal it was, but Robert had recent experience and was appalled at the prospect for her. What he failed to understand until he witnessed it was the extent to which Elizabeth was a stoic. The crossing was "a miserable thing in all ways", as she later described it to Arabel, but she endured it without complaint and, more important, without any obvious ill effects. She and Wilson, who had never been at sea in her life and was twice as frightened as her mistress, lay down, loosened their stays and prayed. At Le Havre, Robert insisted on some rest. All three of them, and Flush, were "exhausted either by sea or sorrow". Elizabeth took some coffee then rested at an inn until nine that evening when they left by diligence for Rouen, en route for Paris. Robert managed to get them a coupé to themselves and Elizabeth pronounced it "as comfortable and easy as any carriage I have been in for years". The night-ride thrilled her, with the horses "now five ... now seven ... all looking wild and loosely harnessed ... manes leaping as they galloped and the white reins dripping down over their heads ... such a fantastic scene it was in the moonlight!"[2] By Rouen, excitement had made her feverish. Robert carried her to their room through a crowd of curious onlookers. It was, Elizabeth later wrote to Arabel, like a dream, that image she had been using for weeks. Everything that happened to her was a dream, a nightmare, a vision and she was permanently in a daze, a stupor, a fever, obsessed with the terror of reality breaking through in the end.

To a certain extent this happened when she reached Paris, where there was time to take stock of her new life. This was quite literally what it was: a new life. Few people have been able to say, at forty, that their life became "new"; fewer still have been able to pinpoint the exact moment at which it became so. Elizabeth could. The complete reversal of her life, of her expectations and prospects as well as her day-to-day routine, had been dramatic and sudden. In Paris, her head stopped whirling, her heart stopped pounding, and her vision cleared. She was alive, well, if exhausted, and both married to and living with the man she loved. But it felt, in those first two days in Paris, not as if they had finished with subterfuge but as though they were still in hiding. Robert would hardly let his wife move: he waited on her hand and foot, deeply impressing Wilson, and would not let her venture forth to see the city. He was worried that the hotel they were in was not quiet enough and that she would not get enough peace, but Elizabeth had finished with peace and quiet for the time being. She craved not only to see Paris but for Paris to see her, for some recognition of her new status. Knowing that Mrs Jameson had expected to be travelling through Paris, with her seventeen-year-old niece Gerardine, at about this time, Elizabeth urged Robert to send a note to the Hôtel de la Ville de Paris where she had said she would stay. It was a note of succinct drama: "Come and see your friend and my wife EBB – Robert Browning."

Mrs Jameson was for the first time in her talkative life rendered speechless. She rushed to the Brownings' hotel wide-eyed, arms outstretched and embraced them both. When she found words it was to admire and congratulate and marvel. For both of them this reaction was of the greatest importance: it was the first test of "the world and its opinion". Mrs Jameson's unfeigned delight and repeated assertion that they had done the right thing was the reception they needed. (Privately, Mrs Jameson implied that she doubted whether Elizabeth would survive the shock and that Robert was an innocent who had no idea how to cope.)[3] What they also needed was the help their friend now gave them. She moved them to her own much quieter hotel and took them under her very capable wing. But she could not help wondering how these two unworldly poets would survive now that their romantic courtship and escape from England was over, little realising that as far as they were concerned it had just begun. For the first time they could be together not just all day but all night – no more partings, no more anguished farewells, no more counting the hours till they met again. Elizabeth wrote to Arabel, "I am seeing near in him all that I seemed to see afar . . . thinking with one thought, feeling with one heart." It was, she wrote, "like riding an enchanted horse". Robert she began to stress (and never stopped) was *perfect*. He was so good, so tender, so true. They were able at last to behave like the lovers they were, to "sit through the dusky evenings watching the stars rise over the high Paris houses and talking childish things . . ." Every day Elizabeth felt stronger and could no longer be restrained from going out. They went to the Louvre where she was thrilled to stand before "the divine Raphaels" (the visit she had made with her mother as a child brought back no unhappy memories). They walked along the Seine and even dined at a restaurant, the first time Elizabeth had ever done so in her life.

Paris lived up to its reputation for honeymoons. Elizabeth was entirely happy now that she had Robert, body as well as soul. A kind of touching pride, even triumph, rises from her letters to Arabel: there was no need, even if it had not been much too indelicate to contemplate, for her to tell her sister that "in *all*" aspects Robert was "perfect". Her happiness spoke for itself. All that marred it was the underlying tinge of fear whenever she allowed herself to think of Wimpole Street (and she made superhuman efforts not to do so). She had left a poste restante address in Orleans for her family and friends, knowing that this was on their route to Italy and the most likely place for letters to have time to reach her. She and Robert would not reach Orleans for another two weeks but already in Paris she was confessing, "oh my letters, how you frighten me at this distance!" She never wanted to leave Paris, never wanted to receive these dreaded letters, and yet at the same time she was desperate to know the contents of some of them. She had no illusions about what her father would write, if he wrote at all, but she passionately needed the support and absolution of her family. She had discovered already that this family was as loved by her as Robert was but in a different way: there was room for love of family and love of Robert. Neither superseded nor cancelled out the other, both were necessary to nourish and inspire her emotionally. And as well as receiving such family love she was conscious of wishing to give it. "My heart goes out to you," she wrote to Arabel. Now that she had left Wimpole Street, the strange life there seemed even more unendurable for those left behind. How would they survive the catastrophe she had brought down upon them all? A wavering postscript told it all: "Do you think, Arabel, that dearest Papa will forgive me at last? Answer."

Before the answer could be obtained she and Robert had to proceed to Italy, where they planned to stay six months. Mrs Jameson undertook to travel with them (though she was worried at the effect that travelling with lovers would have on the impressionable Gerardine). This made everything not only easier for them but considerably less expensive. She found she could not resist piloting them through France: she could not behave like "a brute or a stone" when they were in such obvious need of her. But her genuine affection for Robert and Elizabeth was mixed with a relish for the drama in which she was now a participant. Her sense of this and of her own importance became quite inflated as they travelled on together. She became convinced she was saving Elizabeth's life and that Robert could not have managed without her. They, for their part, were simply relieved to have trains and diligences and steamers organised for them as they went through France on a winding, delightful route. Robert was a brilliant travelling companion even if the planning honours went to Mrs Jameson. He was full of little bits of information, endlessly resourceful at discovering how to add to their comfort and popular with fellow travellers. Elizabeth became quite animated and even adventurous herself, the old tomboy in her re-emerging enough to frighten Robert on occasions. There suddenly seemed nothing she might not do as she visibly gained strength during their leisurely journey through so many places she had given up hope of ever seeing. Her old life was clearly finished with forever.

But not quite. As they neared Orleans Elizabeth became quiet. She told Robert she was approaching her "death warrant". The light went out of her as they entered the city, her suffering was painful. Robert was sent to see if there were any letters. He brought back a large packet. She held it in her hands for a moment and wondered: the weight of grief or joy? Robert wished to stay with her, to support her whatever the letters said, but she insisted her ordeal must be private. He was sent away "for ten minutes" so that she could "meet the agony" alone. All the letters took immense courage to open but especially, of course, her father's. The mere sight of his handwriting was enough to make her heart flutter. She scarcely dared to read it; a glimpse was all she was able to endure but it was enough. It was as she had anticipated: the tone was "hard and unsparing", the verdict that she was disinherited and cast out of his affection forever. She turned with relief to George's letter, and was shocked to find it hardly less brutal than her father's. George was furious with her and violently attacked her behaviour. He said both she and Robert were without honour and that, far from interceding with his father on her behalf, he wanted nothing more to do with her. At first, Elizabeth was incredulous – it was George who had encouraged her to go to Pisa – and then she realised what had really hurt George. She had exposed him and the whole family to the ridicule and contempt of everyone in their world and his affection for her was not great enough to stand the slur. In the matter of Pisa, his father had been consulted; in the matter of her marriage and flight he had not. The crucial difference was the deceit practised, which he could not forgive and neither could his brothers. All the Barrett men – even shy, gentle Stormie, even rebellious Henry – were in agreement: they had been insulted and seen their father insulted and could not forget it. The Barrett pride was damaged.

But the Barrett women were different. The love of Henrietta and Arabel went far beyond any hurt pride. Elizabeth's intense distress at her brothers' attitude was soothed by the loving, encouraging, joyous letters from her sisters. She had always known they were "the best, the most affectionate sisters in the world" and now she had proof. They were thrilled beyond measure at what she had done; there was not a word of reproach, not a hint of bitterness, not a trace of self-pity in what they wrote. They identified totally with her and what she had suffered from the overbearing masculine pride rampant in their family; they were glad to see it hurt. Elizabeth was immensely comforted and touched and found similar consolation in Kenyon's letter. It was to both Robert and her and said that they had done the right thing. "I sympathise in all you have both been thinking and feeling," Kenyon wrote and added, "if the thing had been asked of me I should have advised it." Miss Mitford, too, rose to the occasion, writing to say how glad she was and that, if asked, she would have gone to stand by her at the church (but she told one friend of hers that she thought Elizabeth was committing a sort of "sentimental suicide").

The ordeal, so long dreaded, was over. Elizabeth's sisters and her friends had not failed her. She was surprised and disappointed to find that all her brothers had done so, but she showed great firmness in not letting this destroy her new happiness. If necessary, she would trade the love of all five of them for Robert. Her father had reacted as she had expected. She prayed instead that "God may turn those salt matters sweet again". The break with her old life was now complete. Like many a nineteenth-century woman she had had to fight for her freedom, freedom from being regarded as having no will or rights of her own. Her biggest triumph had been over herself. She did not intend to waste her new liberty and happiness: she knew it was up to her to make of it all she could.

PART TWO

1846–1861

Chapter Twelve

O N the morning of 12th October 1846, Elizabeth went up onto the deck of *L'Océan*, the French steamer which had brought her and her companions from Marseilles to Genoa, to catch her first sight of Italy. The sea was rough, the coast far off, but as she huddled there in a thick cloak she glimpsed at last the mountains gleaming in the sun. For a while excitement banished her exhaustion but she admitted, once they had reached Pisa and were settled in an apartment found by Mrs Jameson, that she was very tired, "so tired, so tired".

But tiredness did not prevent her from taking up her pen and writing letters at once, chief of them to Henrietta and Arabel. This was a new kind of correspondence for her, to most intimate correspondents, and with an entirely different subject matter to any she had had before. For the first time she had actions to describe as well as thoughts and ideas. She wrote in a different style to her sisters – breathless, slightly jumbled – hardly pausing to see that she was making sense in her haste to communicate with them. Every detail of her travelling adventures was passed on to them; she wanted to share with them the beauty of the cathedral windows at Bourges, stained "with all the sunsets of time", and the thrill of standing beside the pool at Vaucluse where "the fountain in its dark prison of rock flashes and roars and testifies to the memory of Petrarch". Everything she had seen she wanted them to see through her eyes, eyes that saw only what was wonderful. It took Mrs Jameson's steely gaze to state the facts of the journey behind them: the weather had often been awful, either raining or suffocatingly hot; the roads at times so bad that Elizabeth had been painfully bruised by the jolting carriage; and the sea voyage made in a ship that rolled violently in the near-storm conditions. To Elizabeth it had all been "glorious".

Robert realised that a period of complete rest was necessary and, once installed in their apartment near the leaning tower – "three excellent bedrooms and a sitting room matted and carpeted" – he saw to it that

Elizabeth was given it. His precautions were elaborate. No visitors were allowed, no demands whatsoever were to be made upon her. She was cut off from the outside world even more completely than she had been in Wimpole Street. But of course it was a very different seclusion. Their daily routine began with breakfast – coffee, eggs, hot rolls – as they sat close together laughing and talking. Then Wilson would dress Elizabeth, while Robert exiled himself to another room to get dressed himself before he rejoined her for more laughter and talk. Dinner was at two, and since neither they nor Wilson had the remotest idea of how to cook, they had their meal sent in from a trattoria. Elizabeth loved not knowing what they would get; whatever it was she found delicious and distinctly preferable to the mutton and beef dinners in Wimpole Street. Neither she nor Robert much liked meat, except for "chicken with plenty of cayenne", but they both loved puddings. They ate a lot of fruit too. Elizabeth went into ecstasies over the oranges "hanging on a stalk with the green leaves still moist with the morning's dew". They drank chianti. Robert had great faith in its restorative powers and made Elizabeth drink such a big tumbler of the wine (they had no wine glasses which Wilson found rather scandalous) that her head swam. She slept after dinner while Robert walked and then in the evening he roasted chestnuts over a fire and peeled grapes for her and they ended the day as it had begun, laughing and talking. Flush was equally happy since there were no dog-stealers in Pisa and he could wander where he liked (and Elizabeth wrote gravely to Miss Mitford that he learned to speak Italian in no time). Wilson was the only one not initially enthusiastic about Italy. Upon her fell the burden of shopping for the things not supplied by the trattoria and, since she spoke no Italian and was as shy as her mistress in new situations, it was all something of an ordeal. Whereas Elizabeth had Robert, she had no one and inevitably missed Minny Robinson and the other Wimpole Street servants.

After a month, Elizabeth was recovered enough to be permitted some exercise and fresh air by Robert but by then it was November and colder. She insisted, nevertheless, that the climate was "miraculous". The cold was "only a healthy cooling of the air". There were no east winds, no frost and the sun still shone. The air, she wrote, "seems to float its balmy softness into you" and when the balmy softness produced snow even the extreme cold that went with it was labelled "different". The air, she now maintained, might be cold but it was "not *metallic* as in England". She had "to struggle a little against the old languor" because of the cold, but it was not the same struggle as in England. Nobody dared to say it sounded exactly the same. But once the snow had gone, after Christmas, the weather was warmer and she was able to make the kind of outings which would have been quite impossible for her in a London winter. She walked by the Arno with Robert and went to the seaside and to the foot of the mountains and into the pinewoods. Her health improved notice-ably with the fresh air and exercise but Robert did not relax his vigilance for one moment: "he is so afraid of my suffering." The least sign of "the old uneasiness in the throat" and he kept her inside. Again and again she repeated to herself, "I shall not be ill", as a sort of creed. Being ill was something she had finished with. She wrote to Henrietta, "If I were to be ill after all, I feel I should deserve to be stoned for having married." Mind was given every help by her to triumph over matter and she agreed only reluctantly to take extra care. This seclusion was in any case no hardship because, as she told Henrietta, it gave them both the chance to "*learn one another better* by it".[1]

   In fact, it was not Elizabeth who fell ill first; it was Wilson. Wilson had never felt quite well since their arrival in Pisa. She had a pain in her stomach and had felt bilious since the sea passage from Marseilles. She doctored herself with a variety of remedies (eight shillings' worth of pills plus a concoction of herbs and cream of tartar). But one night in January, while undressing her mistress, she collapsed, moaning with pain and shivering uncontrollably. Elizabeth was terrified and ran bare-footed for Robert, urging him to go at once for Dr Cook, the resident English doctor. Robert was more concerned with his wife's bare feet but at last went for the doctor. When he came and examined Wilson, Dr Cook pronounced it a case of an inflamed stomach which had been irritated by "improper remedies". Robert, who had suspected as much, was relieved it was nothing worse, sorry for Wilson's pain, but a little annoyed with her for (in his exaggerated opinion) imperilling his wife's own health. Elizabeth scorned the ridiculous idea that crossing their apartment in bare feet imperilled her health and was most sympathetic to Wilson. She insisted that Wilson stay in bed for ten days and she took pleasure in attempting to look after her, even trying her hand at "cooking" for Wilson's sake. Since the suffering maid could not be expected to eat the spicy trattoria meals, Elizabeth made toast for her. She described her attempt to her sisters, knowing it would amuse them highly, especially when she added that Robert had advised her sarcastically not to burn it entirely. She was determined not to hire a replacement for Wilson, though their landlady helped out, but of course the main challenge was not so much caring for Wilson as caring for herself. At the age of forty she had never dressed herself or done her own hair. Her struggles to do both she mocked to Miss Mitford, telling her, "I have acquired a heap of practical philosophy and have learnt how it is possible (in certain conditions of the human frame) to comb out and twist up one's own hair . . ." But it was all part of her new life to try to be more self-reliant and in keeping with a pattern she liked to think of as Bohemian.

Unfortunately, just as the embarrassed and miserable Wilson recovered, Elizabeth herself began to experience unpleasant pains of a kind she had never known before. They came on in the night, somewhere in the region of her stomach, and yet did not feel like stomach pains. She took a few sips of brandy and they passed off. Wilson, in charge again, was more concerned than the sufferer herself because she suspected the cause of the mysterious pains: she thought her mistress was pregnant and threatening miscarriage. Elizabeth would have none of this. From everything she afterwards wrote to her sisters it was obvious that she had no idea she was pregnant and thought Wilson was being foolish. Either menstruation was sufficiently irregular for her not to think a long gap significant, or so slight she thought it was normal (perfectly possible early in many pregnancies). In any case, she later wrote "I had treated myself improperly for a condition of which I was unaware."[2] Robert, told what Wilson suspected, panicked and wanted to go for Dr Cook at once. Elizabeth refused to let him. She said she was sure Wilson was mistaken. The pains had in any case stopped: there was nothing for which to call a doctor. To put Robert's mind at rest she wrote to Mr Jago, her last London medical adviser, putting to him an absurd hypothesis about a lady without certain symptoms . . . as soon as she had posted it she realised how ridiculous she had been. But she dreaded being made to look foolish and a false pregnancy would certainly do that. She was almost forty-one, a very late age indeed in Victorian times (in any times) for a woman to have a first baby. Robert, who had been bold enough always to envisage children, fussed and worried but, as ever in such situations, Elizabeth's will was the stronger. She obstinately refused to call a doctor and, by trying to overcome this stubbornness, he saw he only upset her, which was another threat to her health.

Six weeks later, the pains returned. This time she was in such pain she had to agree to send for Dr Cook. He came, finding her weak, her pulse racing and the room far too hot. After examining her he vindicated Wilson: Elizabeth was indisputably pregnant. Robert was plunged into a state bordering on terror. His wife was too frail to bear a child, too delicate to survive the ordeal. The next day, 21st March, the pains were almost continuous. Elizabeth did not scream, surprising the doctor but not Wilson who knew how physically brave she could be. Her bravery was put to a severe test the next morning when she had a miscarriage "of *five months* date"[3] (she was so astonished at how advanced her pregnancy had been that every time she mentioned it later in a letter she underlined this). It meant the baby must have been conceived as soon as they reached Pisa and that all through the winter, when she ought to have been conserving her energies, she had on the contrary never been more energetic.

After it was all over, her pride in having been pregnant at all far outweighed her sadness at losing the baby. Robert, on the other hand, was wretched. The whole experience had been torture for him. While Elizabeth suffered acutely he had sat outside her door sick with fear at what would be the outcome of the drama. He was terrified that she would die as a result of his passion. For the first time in their short married life, they were separated. Robert's was the lot of the average Victorian husband, doomed to exclusion while doctor and maid went backwards and forwards. A five months' miscarriage is a messy business: Robert could not escape being aware of how much blood his wife had lost and it made him so afraid for her life that when he was allowed in to see her he expected to find her in a coma. To see her smile and hold out her hand was too much for him; he flung himself onto the bed beside her "in a passion of tears, sobbing like a child". The doctor and Wilson were astonished and moved, neither ever having seen a man behave like this before. It was clear that this grief was for his wife, not the lost child (whose sex at five months would have been visible but was never mentioned). Dr Cook was unable to convince this distraught husband that his wife was now out of danger. Robert did not see how she could be. He himself neither ate nor slept for the next few days as he watched over her. He read to her, talked gently to her, bathed her forehead, cut up her food, gave her drinks. Wilson was finally brought to admit that this was the world's most devoted and loving husband.[4]

The miscarriage had no depressive effect on Elizabeth. After only a week she felt particularly cheerful and buoyant. She got up (against Robert's wish) and walked about (even more against his wish) and felt that in some curious way the miscarriage had actually done her good. She wrote to Henrietta that she now had so little feeling of congestion in her chest that she almost felt she no longer had a chest. She was not troubled much either by guilt or remorse, even though Dr Cook had told her quite plainly that if he had been called in earlier she need not have lost the baby. She acknowledged the probable truth of this but it did not distress her. Nothing could spoil her happiness, not even that kind of small tragedy. Her marriage was "perfect", Robert was "perfect" and since they were "happy, happy, happy" she had no right to complain about such blows of fate. Her sisters were treated to extravagant descriptions of this idyllic happiness until she grew exhausted writing them. Sometimes, she went a little too far in her fervent protestations, telling Henrietta and Arabel that they could not expect such happiness because she knew Robert was unique: "Why, where are such men in the world?" It was "the wonder of my life" that she had been chosen by such a paragon and even when, as her sisters realised, she was half-mocking herself for their entertainment it was obvious she meant it. Robert was reported to be equally rapturous. It was he who kept the weekly then monthly anniversary of their wedding day, notching up the score with the greatest pride. They never, Elizabeth boasted to her sisters, quarrelled. She was witty about why not: Robert knew *she* was always right. These boasts were so innocent and joyful that they could provoke neither disgust nor distaste: "I am as happy as any one ever was in the world . . ." she wrote to Arabel, ". . . if we ever quarrel you may expect it to snow stars."[5] To Miss Mitford she wrote that there had not been "a shadow . . . nor a *word*" between her and Robert though she had observed "all married people confess to '*words*' ". She wanted everyone back home to be left in no doubt that her flight had been worth it: she was the happiest and luckiest woman alive.

She knew that, because of her happiness, the opinion of other people was immaterial but all the same every letter from England that winter was of great importance to her as she received the judgement of friends and relatives on her marriage. Many of them took time to decide. She was surprised to find that people she thought her champion often sided with her father in spite of being fully conversant with the situation as it had been. One such was Bummy, closer to her than anyone at various crucial stages in her life. Bummy was unsympathetic. She wrote to Elizabeth that she had been "wicked" not to ask her father's permission and that she thought less of her for subjecting him to such disgrace. Her conduct, Bummy wrote, would be bound to bring her unhappiness. Aunt Jane was kinder, though she too thought her brother-in-law should have been told, whatever the consequences. But sometimes a letter brought a different kind of surprise and she discovered an unexpected ally. Mrs Martin, who was not influenced by family loyalty, sent Elizabeth her unsolicited approval and there were congratulations in plenty from literary people. But the letters Elizabeth really craved, from her father and brothers, did not come. She did not expect one from her father – she was prepared for even the smallest measure of forgiveness to take years – but she went on looking for signs of relenting from her brothers. In February 1847, she had written to Arabel that George had *seemed* to offer an olive branch but on closer inspection she did not find it was any such thing. He had suggested an amnesty that did not include Robert. Elizabeth was contemptuous: "good heavens," she wrote to Arabel, "how little they know me if they imagine it to be possible to thrust me into the position, the possibility of which they assume!"[6] (Presumably, George's amnesty was agreeable to at least some of her other brothers since she referred to the plural.) To make her attitude clearer she added, "if they do not love me enough to accept *mine* with *me*, why, they must cast me off". Her brothers deserved no concessions but her father did. For him, with Robert's agreement, she would be willing to accept any terms he chose to dictate, short of leaving Robert. But Mr Barrett made no terms. He wanted no contact. Her sisters informed her that in spite of this she must not imagine him shut up in a room, grieving and desolate. On the contrary, he was inviting people for supper every night and was the most animated of hosts. Elizabeth was surprised by this uncharacteristic behaviour, even though she realised it read like conscious defiance, but considered it a good sign. She went on writing to him regularly, choosing to believe that as her letters were not returned he might be secretly reading them. She thought about her father every day but the misery she felt at his treatment of her did not overwhelm her. She did not allow the weight of his displeasure to become oppressive. If she fell ill, as she had told Henrietta, she deserved to be stoned; if she spoiled her new found bliss by dwelling on her father then equally she deserved punishment. Her attitude was commendably sensible, if dangerous: she was blocking out grief and pain rather than dealing with it.

But then her whole philosophy of life had undergone a radical revision. The woman who had written to Miss Mitford, "Pleasure upon pleasure is sure at last, if piled high enough, to reach a melancholy . . .

the senses fall asleep in superfluous enjoyments,"[7] had changed her mind. Pleasure, she had discovered, did not eventually breed melancholy nor prove soporific. The more pleasure she took, the sharper her senses seemed and the greater her appreciation of life. Death no longer had "a pleading tongue". For the first time in the whole of her adult life she was not disposed to think of it at all. Once, her highest aim had been "to be tranquil". Now, she spurned such feebleness. She did not always imagine the worst and was re-thinking her former conviction that earthly happiness was not worth pursuing, that it should not be an end in itself. She wrote repeatedly to family and friends of how happiness had changed her; her letters were full of confidence. (They were full of laughter too, with the verb "to laugh" used in all its variations for the first time in her correspondence.) She had always thought "happiness requires . . . teaching . . . and more than Sanscrit".[8] Robert had taught it to her and she had proved a quick pupil. Almost everything she had believed about marriage he had shown her to be untrue; almost every-thing she had hoped about love he had shown to be absolutely true. Miss Mitford had once angered her by saying someone they knew was too old to fall in love ("you desecrate the physiology of love . . . by confining the sentiment to youth," Elizabeth had retorted). Now she knew that what she had instinctively felt was a fact: she and Robert were not young and yet their love, of both soul and flesh, could not be greater. The love of man could, after all, be mentioned alongside the love of God. She realised in herself the power of such love, how it could transform a whole outlook on life. When Robert told her every day in Pisa that he loved her more and more she wrote to Henrietta that she could see it was true. Such tangible evidence confounded once and for all her former belief that there was nothing but affliction in store for her.

Elizabeth, in recognising and proclaiming this change, wondered what effect it would have on her work. All her poetry had been born out of suffering. Now that she was happy, would it flow differently? She had not ceased to be a poet in becoming a wife but she was aware that, for the moment at least, she lacked the need to turn to poetry for sustenance and as a means of expression. That endless self-analysis, that constant raking over of the past which had provided the ground upon which she worked had stopped. The last work she had done was before her marriage. During Robert's courtship of her she had written her sonnets (still unrevealed to anyone) and a few poems she had left behind which had appeared in *Blackwood's* for October 1846, the month after she left

London. These had already reflected the beginnings of new pre-occupations (though still containing the old). Two of these poems, "A Woman's Shortcomings" and "A Man's Requirements" would now be labelled feminist; it was no wonder she worried that her father would think the inadvertent timing of their publication "impudent". The woman in the first poem seeks a "truer loving" than any she can see around her and resolves never to love any man until she feels he can love her until death. Love, the poem says, is useless unless it can be eternal: "Unless you can swear 'for life, for death'/Oh fear to call it loving!" The second poem continues this theme and is more explicit. The woman in it begs to be loved "in full being" and "for the house and grave". In return, she promises sarcastically she will love the man "half-a-year/As a man is able". In yet another of these *Blackwood's* poems, "Change upon Change", a woman reflects bitterly that, while she does not change, the man does, just like the seasons. Women are constant, value love, and are content to wait for true love and refuse anything less. Men, on the other hand, are cruel and fickle, confuse attraction with love, passion with real feeling, and never understand the enduring nature of love or what it means.

These were the last poems Elizabeth wrote before her marriage but at a stage when she was already sure of Robert and his love for her. Robert, clearly, could hardly be the inspiration for the sentiments expressed in them: he was the exception that proved the rule and inspired instead the sonnets. It was her experience, before Robert, of male bearing and behaviour witnessed within and without her family that drove her to write these poems. After them, she married, went to Pisa and wrote no poetry for several months. Robert settled down to prepare a new edition of his last volume but wrote nothing entirely new either. Yet part of their planned future together had always been the work they would both do. They had discussed endlessly during their courtship how the pattern of their days would be arranged round the writing of poetry better than they had ever written before. It was more important to Elizabeth that Robert should write, and in due course receive the acclaim he deserved, than that she should herself. She was unconcerned that the only poem she wrote herself at Pisa was "The Runaway Slave at Pilgrim's Point" which she had begun as long ago as December 1845 especially for the Americans (it was not printed until 1848).[9] She thought it "ferocious" and was proud of its theme which she saw as anti-slavery but which reads more like anti-men and is in the tradition of her pre-marriage

Blackwood's poems. A slave girl falls in love with another slave in the sugar-cane fields but he is killed. She is raped by a white man and bears his child, which she strangles with her shawl. She is then flogged and dies, her faith in God unshaken by the behaviour of white men. The poem is melodramatic, sometimes unintentionally ludicrous, but the passion of the slave girl and the anger at her fate are real enough and redeem the poem's bathos. Completed at a time when she felt herself almost transfigured by love of and for Robert, it seemed that the happier Elizabeth became with her man, the more furious she became at how most men abused women. Women were victims, men perpetrators of crimes in the name of love. Robert's perfection appeared from now on only to emphasise the grossness of the male race in general. She seemed determined, from her position of strength, to become the champion of all those women less fortunate than herself.

Elizabeth's miscarriage made Robert disinclined to push her in any way: he encouraged her to rest and read. Obtaining novels was a problem. Rather to Robert's bewilderment, Elizabeth's hunger for contemporary novels was hardly assuaged at all by marriage. In Pisa she quickly became exasperated by what fiction was on offer from the limited sources available. Robert at first did not take her seriously. What he had failed to appreciate was that novel-reading was not primarily a matter of withdrawal from the world for Elizabeth so much as a means of communicating with it. Robert was not disposed to try too hard to find novels until he saw how eager Elizabeth was and then, with a good deal of grumbling (he was watching the bills closely), he joined an Italian lending library. This made Elizabeth only marginally happier: Italian contemporary fiction, she wrote to Miss Mitford, was heavy and dull and subjected to such rigorous censorship that it was almost devoid of interest. Fond of saying she could even "read a book upon a walking stick" if it were written eloquently, she now found Italian novels so lacking in "style and language" that their content was immaterial. She could not read them. Robert could find nothing wrong with them, protesting they were perfectly readable, but Elizabeth wrote a malicious account of him saying this and yawning as he did so. Goaded by her, he then switched libraries to one where French novels were sometimes available. This proved hardly more successful. The French novels on offer were not new (Elizabeth liked them hot off the press) and furthermore were expurgated; it drove her mad to find her beloved Balzac ruined. She had heard there was a new Dumas, she wrote to Miss

Mitford, and she supposed it would come her way sometime. Sometime could not come soon enough and perhaps never in Pisa.

As the spring arrived it emerged that there were other things wrong with Pisa, too. It had never in any case been their intention to stay there long but their intentions, as Mrs Jameson had discovered back in October before she continued her own well-planned tour, were vague in the extreme. When Pisa was reached, the ease of obtaining rooms and Elizabeth's exhaustion had over-ridden all other considerations. They had rented their apartment until 17th April 1847 but by February, even before Elizabeth's miscarriage, they were regretting being bound for so long. Pisa, from being "oh so beautiful and so full of repose yet not desolate", had become a city where "there never was a deeper dullness". Part of the trouble was that they had proved not quite so self-sufficient as they had imagined themselves. In England, with the pardonable arrogance of all lovers who have not yet been able to live together, they had been sure all they wanted in the way of company was each other's: they would need no other entertainment or stimulation. But as the months passed, they found that, though very far from being in the least tired of each other, they did after all need a little more liveliness and a few amenities lacking in Pisa. Elizabeth tended to pick on practical defects to complain about (the walks were too flat and limited to satisfy Robert) but knew really that it was the lack of congenial society that, for Robert's sake, worried her most. She was always afraid Robert would become bored, particularly as she had (Robert alleged) a highly exaggerated view of his past social life in London. She was determined not to be the invalid wife who kept her energetic husband chained to her sick bed. Once she had recovered from her miscarriage, they picked up again the discussions they had been having all winter about where to go next. Florence, so conveniently near, was the obvious choice but Robert had his doubts. Florence was labelled "English ridden", overcrowded and full of contaminated water supplies. But it was larger than Pisa with many more attractions and Dr Cook thought Elizabeth would do well there. They decided to go to Florence, and then in September move to Venice.

Another point in favour of Florence was its cheapness. To their chagrin, the Brownings had discovered that, while they congratulated themselves on how little everything cost in Pisa, they were secretly laughed at for throwing their money about like millionaires on lodgings, food and everything else. In a burst of indignation (and she hardly ever allowed any criticism of Italy to come from her pen) Elizabeth told Henrietta "cheating is systematized in Italy to a frightful extent". She learned that for the rent they had paid they could have had a better place and kept both a carriage and a man servant. Wilson, more understandably, had also been exploited: coffee, tea and other staple commodities had cost her twice the price everyone else paid *and* she had been given short measures. In Florence, Elizabeth vowed things would be different because they would "take our experience with us". And so, prepared not to be so gullible, they set off for Florence on 20th April.

They left Pisa without reluctance, except for Elizabeth's regret that she had not climbed the leaning tower or been in more than two churches. The journey was rough but mercifully short. No matter how much she suffered physically, Elizabeth loved to travel: the actual process of being displaced pleased her. As she lay across Robert's knee (to cushion her frail body against the jolting of the carriage) she had a distorted view of the scenery through which they were passing. It charmed and surprised her to glimpse the "vine-festooned plains and breaks of valley and hill . . . and sweeps of river". Everything was so much more beautiful than she had imagined. All she saw of Florence as they rattled across the city was one flash of the "dear yellow Arno" and then the carriage had stopped and Robert was carrying her to a room in the Hôtel du Nord. In spite of her pleading, he would not let her go out. His anxiety about the effect of any travel on his wife was so great that it was useless for Dr Cook to tell him it was quite safe; he did not believe it could be. But for Elizabeth to arrive and see nothing was very annoying. She wrote to her sisters that it was also ridiculous: she had only to walk from one room to another for Robert to follow at her heels, very like Flush, asking if she was well. But she was aware that, however boring, hers was the easier role. Robert was running round Florence trying to rent a suitable apartment, a job to which he was constitutionally unsuited. He hated the search, hated the haggling over prices. But he quickly found rooms in the via delle Belle Donne, just off the piazza Santa Maria Novella, not the best of Florentine addresses but it would do for the moment. Feeling very knowing and wise, he took only a three-month lease.

It was not until they had moved into these rooms (where Elizabeth was again kept in) that the advantages of Florence over Pisa were revealed. It was pleasant to have better furniture, especially a proper spring sofa, and much more convenient to have a bell pull to summon Wilson instead of having to go and fetch her. It was luxurious to have wine glasses and linen and all those accoutrements of civilised living about which Elizabeth claimed she cared nothing but which she clearly relished (though not as much as Wilson who had been offended by the makeshift nature of their Pisan living arrangements and now declared this was "something like"). They even had a charwoman which gave Wilson time for more congenial occupations. One of these was dressmaking. Florence required elegance, and Robert was fussy. If he saw a hole in Elizabeth's gloves he would point this out rather as her father had done and with the same expectation that she would see to it at once. Elizabeth liked to please him in this respect, seeing nothing overbearing about so trivial a point. Robert greatly influenced not just the condition but the style and colour of her clothes. He liked strong colours, could not bear "fainting away" pinks or blues, and was very particular about hats. Bonnets he disliked, preferring "little front caps". And he liked Elizabeth's hair to be done in an "old Grecian plait behind" which Wilson found hard to do and grumbled about. Ribbons were banned – "he *hates* ribbon" – as were all trimmings because "he prefers everything as simple and quiet as possible". Her sisters at this time sent some material for a new dress – which, considering they had virtually no money of their own, was most generous, as Elizabeth fully appreciated – and fortunately it was dark green, Robert's favourite colour for her. Wilson made it up beautifully, following a fashionable new pattern, and Elizabeth was pronounced very smart and fit to go anywhere.

But Robert would not allow her to go out yet. She longed for him to show her the wonders of Florence but he would not let her move from her new sofa. Luckily, Mrs Jameson and her niece arrived on 23rd April to distract her. If she had wished to contrive the scene for maximum effect Elizabeth could not have arranged it better: there she was, reclining on the sofa looking pretty in her new dress and cap, while Robert played "Light of Love" on the piano for her. No wonder Mrs Jameson cried "upon my word here's domestic harmony!" as she walked in, all ready, with a bottle of wine, to celebrate Shakespeare's birthday. They all had coffee and supper together and toasted the bard, and then they talked for hours. Elizabeth was extremely conscious that this was entertaining and was as proud as any "little woman" over it. The pleasure of providing hospitality in her own home was an entirely new one for her and she loved the informality of the occasion – no fuss, no preparation, no chance to become nervous. She promptly invited Mrs Jameson and Gerardine to stay with them (they could easily rent another bedroom). She felt she had excelled as a hostess and wrote to Henrietta, "Think of our doing hospitality for a week!" She knew her sister, in charge at Wimpole Street, would barely be able to credit it and sought her praise: "wasn't that rather magnificent of us!" Wimpole Street was very much in her mind as she presided over dinner. She found Robert had one defect: he could not carve as carving was done at home. Mrs Jameson was indulgent and "good natured" about Elizabeth's own lack of expertise when it came to serving the food but her eyes were taking in every detail. The Brownings, when she had left them in Pisa, had been still on their extended honeymoon. Now, it was six months of ordinary married life later. She was eager to examine the idyllic couple's romance and see if it was still intact. Back in London, she knew that she would be bombarded from all sides for news of the Brownings whose flight had caused such a sensation (and a good deal of sniggering as well as amazement and admiration). Mrs Jameson saw only one change: Robert was even more solicitous than before. She could carry back to England the authoritative verdict that the Brownings' marriage was an outstanding success.

It was obvious that Robert and Elizabeth would be unable, after all, to visit London themselves that summer. Her miscarriage had made all thought of such an arduous journey "foolish and imprudent". Then there was the expense of it, no small consideration now that the hundred pounds Robert had borrowed from his parents was finished and so was the small sum Elizabeth had managed to contribute. She had an income from her shares in her Uncle Sam's ship, the *David Lyon* (usually around £200 a year but it varied), which had not yet reached her and they both expected Moxon to send money earned from their poetry (estimated to be about £70). But at that point, in April 1847, their financial position was genuinely precarious and to go to England would be unwise. Elizabeth was not too disappointed. She would have liked to see her sisters and for Robert to see his family but otherwise nothing about England attracted her. Already, she was beginning to compare it unfavourably with Italy where the climate, the food, the prices and even the manners were better. When she thought of England it was only of "those beloved faces". Increasingly, they haunted her. Robert noticed that, no matter how carefree the contents, any letter from Elizabeth's sisters left her in a sad reverie. She missed those sisters more than she had ever expected to do, even though Robert was not only the perfect lover and husband but the true "partner of my soul". She had no female friend except Wilson who was a friend but still a servant; their relationship was no substitute for the easy intimacy Elizabeth had enjoyed with her sisters. "I love my family," she wrote to her sisters with touching simplicity, and she needed the constant reassurance that they loved her. Their letters were neither frequent nor long enough and never satisfied her. She was merciless in her demands upon them, ordering both of them to write at least once a week. If they failed to, she upbraided them bitterly for their laziness and reminded them that exiles, like lovers, were dependent on letters and that to withhold them was cruel. Robert, she told them jealously, got three to her every one: it was not good enough, not fair. She thought neither sister took enough care over addressing letters so precious to her. She was terrified they would get lost. Henrietta especially was scolded for sloppy handwriting: "Write the BROWNING very plain," she instructed her. She was always "waiting and groaning" for their letters and if she found one had been kept at the post office because the address was indecipherable she was furious: "Henrietta, you must write the directions as clearly as possible and not in a running hand."

But the good news was that her family correspondence was increasing. George capitulated first. By the time she was settled in Florence, Elizabeth had received a note saying she was forgiven. That was all, but it was a start. Then Stormie wrote from Jamaica, where he had been sent by his father. This was particularly pleasing because Elizabeth had found Stormie's attitude even harder to understand than George's; she had thought Stormie, with his disposition, would empathise easily with her and care less than George for honour. Another delight, quite un-expected, was a letter from Henry that summer, Henry, always famous for not writing to anyone and never close to her. It seemed to Elizabeth that when she did return to England there was every hope that all her family would have come round – all, that is, except her father. He had not weakened at all. Her name was not to be mentioned before him. On 28th May, his sixty-second birthday, Elizabeth lay all day on her sofa thinking about him. Robert, sensitive to her mood, suggested drinking Mr Barrett's health as some small gesture of affection, but Elizabeth could not bear to. She prayed instead and reflected that "no one in the world has more tenderly loved him than the one he has cast off. *Has* loved him? *Does* still love him, as God knows well." Instead of becom-ing reconciled to his treatment of her, she was resenting it more. The happier she was with Robert, the greater the emphasis she laid on her unhappiness over her father. She so dreaded more pain for him that, when Henrietta wrote saying she was preparing her trousseau and proposed to marry Surtees soon, she found it hard to support her sister wholeheartedly: such a second act of disobedience would increase her father's suffering and she could not bear it. Her attitude to her sister's own prolonged suffering was a little callous.

Robert was preoccupied with having a marriage settlement at last drawn up, signed and witnessed, which he hoped would ease Mr Barrett's mind. He had been emphatic that this must be done so that no one, particularly no Barrett, could ever allege he had married Elizabeth for her money. If no settlement was made then, under the law of England as it stood until 1886, everything Elizabeth owned had become Robert's the moment he married her. Robert wanted none of this. He might have written "you are mine" and "I possess you" to Elizabeth after he married her but he did not want her goods to be made legally his. Kenyon had been entrusted to see to the legal niceties and in May a box of deeds arrived in Florence. Three weeks later, two friends of Kenyon's passing through the city witnessed the signatures of both Brownings and took the documents back to Kenyon. Both Robert and Elizabeth claimed not to have read this vital settlement. Both trusted Kenyon to have made sure that, in the event of Elizabeth's death, whatever she possessed would go either to any children she had or to her sisters. It upset Elizabeth to think that Robert was not to have the little she could give, but he was adamant. Kenyon consoled her by pointing out she could make a will superseding the marriage settlement and choose to leave everything to Robert. This she resolved to do. Meanwhile, Robert's action went a good way towards killing unpleasant innuendos. Elizabeth had always known he was a man of scrupulous honour, especially over money, but others needed proof. Her father, she hoped, now had it; but Mr Barrett was unimpressed. It was Elizabeth's own behaviour to which he objected, not Robert's.

Robert opened champagne to celebrate. Elizabeth helped to drink it merely to celebrate the end of the whole distasteful legal business. The signing of that marriage settlement nevertheless was important: it signified the end of another stage in their life. All that remained was for them to find a more permanent home and then they could begin work, the drama, upheaval and excitement of marriage, flight and honeymoon over.

Chapter Thirteen

IT was a little mortifying for both Robert and Elizabeth to face up to the fact that they were not nearly so well suited to a Bohemian or a gypsy life as they had liked to imagine. The truth was that it was not good for either of them to be constantly on the move, never knowing where they would go next. Elizabeth, that summer of 1847, was very well, reporting to Henrietta that she often found herself "running unawares". Her mental health was no longer of any concern. Not only was she in good spirits but that dark side of her personality seemed to have disappeared; with Robert at her side she was not afraid to meet new people and although she was still quiet in company it was a different kind of silence. She was not struck dumb through nervousness or social embarrassment but merely observing and listening, especially to her voluble husband. Because she was happy she felt well and the connection was not lost on her, even if she was unable to decide which way round it should be made: did her mental health dictate or follow from her physical well-being? She knew only that in the warmer climate of Italy her lungs seemed clear and that under the new régime imposed by Robert she ate and drank properly and took exercise and was stronger every day.

But nevertheless she needed the stability of a permanent base, and so, for different reasons, did Robert. Whereas Elizabeth benefited psychologically from change, Robert lost. A great deal of his energy was being frittered away searching for rooms and worrying over terms: the cares of a husband whose wife needed more than an ordinary measure of protection sat heavily upon him. In such circumstances neither of them was going to be able to work. This made the finding and renting of the Casa Guidi, which was to be their first real home, the most important event of the year.

The lease on their first lodgings ran out in July and the rooms were in any case, by mid-summer, uncomfortably hot. Most English visitors moved to the mountains or the sea in June but, though they talked endlessly of doing so, the Brownings did not manage to arrange any escape except for one excursion. This was to the Benedictine monastery at Vallombrosa outside Florence. Women were not allowed there but Elizabeth decided, stubbornly, that this was the only place for her. It was, she acknowledged to Arabel, quite perverse of her. Robert, anxious as ever to please, secured a letter from the Archbishop of Florence to the Abbot granting Elizabeth and Wilson a special dispensation to stay. On 14th July they all rose at three in the morning and at dawn began the thirteen-mile drive to Pelago where Elizabeth and Wilson were transferred from a carriage to old wine baskets and Robert to a horse. The baskets were pulled for five hours up the mountain to the monastery by two white bullocks while Robert rode alongside. Elizabeth was in "an ecstasy of admiration": this was the kind of adventure for which she had left Wimpole Street. But her excitement faded when they were met by a frigid reception at the monastery where the Abbot was unimpressed by the Archbishop's letter. He, so long as he was Abbot, would keep "unclean" women out. Elizabeth and Wilson were lodged in a guest house outside the monastery walls and given three days to leave. Elizabeth called the monks "idiots" and expected Robert to work miracles. He failed. Obliged to leave, Elizabeth first made a point of putting her tiny foot just inside the door of the monastery and stamping on the ground, hoping, as she wrote to Fanny Dowglass, she was "profaning it forever".

Returning to Florence in three days instead of the anticipated two months, the Brownings faced a crisis. The lease on their existing rooms expired in less than a week. Robert, "white with exhaustion", trailed round the burning hot city looking for somewhere else. He found an apartment in the Casa Guidi at literally the last minute. He rented six furnished rooms, plus kitchen, on the *piano nobile* of the Casa Guidi, near the piazza San Felice, for three months, 20th July to 19th October. The cost was a guinea a week, which included admission to the Boboli Gardens (except, annoyingly, for Flush who was banned). The move was an instant success. The building had once been a palace and had huge, high-ceilinged rooms which were relatively cool and airy as the temperature soared. Elizabeth was much more comfortable, though still spending most of her days clad only in a thin white dressing gown because it was so hot. Robert did not object, though normally he disliked such slovenliness as much as Mr Barrett did. Elizabeth was as eager to point out to her sisters that Italian heat was not the same as English heat as she had been to make the distinction between the two kinds of cold. "Wilson and I agree," she wrote on 2nd August as the thermometer in the evening stood at 86° Fahrenheit, "that the meaning of heat in Italy is a different thing from what it is in England – the air is so much lighter and more elastic . . ." But light and elastic though it was, it was also enervating. The summer slipped by with Elizabeth lolling on her sofa, desperate for the evening when she could take the air by walking with Robert on their terrace. This so-called terrace was a mere strip of balcony and the walks no more than twenty paces. It was overshadowed by the side of the San Felice church opposite so there were no views of any kind. The location of the Case Guidi was far from perfect – it offered none of the many visual delights available in other parts of Florence – but Elizabeth loved it.

She discovered on 12th September that the street in which she lived was on a processional route and that the inadequate balcony had its uses. This was the day the Florentines celebrated the recent granting to them, by their Grand Duke, of a civic guard. Elizabeth wrote one of her longest and most enthralling letters describing the procession to Henrietta. She was sure there were four thousand extra people in Florence that day, flooding in from all the surrounding Tuscan states. There was class after class – peasants, nobles, priests, magistrates and tradesmen – all resplendent in vividly coloured garments and bearing richly embroidered flags. Every window was crowded with cheering spectators, all waving white handkerchiefs and throwing flowers which floated like clouds. The air was full of happy noise – music, clapping, singing, cheering. Sitting on her balcony, spell-bound, Elizabeth noticed how well behaved the crowds were: nobody was pushing or shoving, nobody's temper was giving way under the strain of the heat. She noticed too how elegantly dressed women mixed easily with ordinary people. She waved a handkerchief till her wrist ached and was driven inside only by the need to rest. At night, she and Robert walked by the Arno, illuminated and glittering under the stars. Now that she was among them, she was even more struck by the innate courtesy of the crowds, among whom there was neither drunkenness nor fighting. Little children and frail old people were perfectly safe and so, she found, was she. It made her decide that English crowds wanted "educating into gladness" (though she had no experience of English crowds on such joyous occasions). She and Robert walked slowly home, reminiscing about their wedding day and the year of bliss that had followed. "There has never been a cloud, nor a breath,"

Elizabeth told Henrietta. Thinking back, she again paid tribute to Wilson: "If it had not been for Wilson, on the real day, it wd. have been worse with me than it was. I assure you she only knew *the night before* and had her own share of suffering . . ."[1] That day, they gave her a present to mark her devotion, a turquoise brooch they had chosen together "as a memorial". Wilson responded by baking knead cakes (a kind of scone popular in the north-east of England) and selecting a particularly fine water-melon to serve with them.

But her wedding anniversary was also significant in another respect: it marked the beginning of another love affair for Elizabeth. There had been faint intimations already that she was beginning to feel something a little stronger than affection for the country in which she had found so much happiness but it was on this day, while watching the procession, that a great burst of emotion broke from her for Italy. The Italians from then onwards were "our" Italians, the Grand Duke "our" Grand Duke, the whole country dear to her in every way. The celebrations that day seemed to intoxicate her, the idea of liberty being given to thrill her. She became an avowed champion of the cause of liberty throughout the whole country and identified with it so completely she could think of nothing else. The ruling Austrians were "hateful and loathesome" to be occupying a country not theirs, Metternich had "fangs" sunk into it and the rest of the world were cowards for not forcing him to remove them. The violence of her partisan view was sudden and extreme. She was not entirely uneducated politically – from her childhood, after all, she had been eager to discuss political affairs with her father and brothers – but now she seemed to become totally absorbed in politics just at a time in her life when domestic happiness was so complete it seemed odd that she had any interest in anything outside. It was not Robert who gave her such a personal, subjective vision because he did not have it himself. She took from him an understanding of the facts of the political situation but then she transformed them into something else. There was such an exaggerated element of personal identification with Italy that it does not seem too fanciful to suggest that she saw the country as the victim of an oppressor just as she had been the victim of her father's oppression (and still was). It was the same kind of emotional response that she made towards women who were exploited. The only way she knew how to fight for them was by writing poetry. Inspired by what she had seen and felt on her anniversary, she began to write a poem in defence and praise of Italian liberty, her first overtly political poetry.

This poem, begun in the autumn of 1847, was eventually entitled "Casa Guidi Windows". It amounted to an eye-witness account of all Elizabeth had seen and heard and understood of what was happening all around her in Florence. She was well aware that she might get things wrong but stated in her preface that if she did so it would be because she had made her own mistakes and not because she had accepted facile opinions of the day. It was unfortunate (and unfair) that this first part of "Casa Guidi Windows" was carelessly read (and still is). Elizabeth was accused of being taken in by the Pope, Pius IX, and by the Grand Duke Leopold. But she makes it plain she does *not* trust the Pope and that she has strong reservations about the Grand Duke. What she did say was that she had high hopes of both of them but never at any time in her poem does she acclaim either as heroes who cannot fail. All she wanted to do was to mirror the excitement of the times, capture the mood and atmosphere. "Casa Guidi Windows" was reportage in which she saw herself becoming politically engaged, nailing her colours to the mast. She was fulfilling her own aim that poetry should be a form of action. Her function was to write, just as it was the function of soldiers to fight. "And I, a singer also, from my youth/Prefer to sing with those who are awake," she proclaimed. She had never sung better, nor been wider awake.

But she did not begin writing straight after her anniversary. First, there was another dreaded move to face. They were both happy in Florence and had once more rejected the idea of wintering elsewhere but their lease ran out on 20th October and, when Robert applied to renew it, he was told the winter rent was double the summer's. Poor Robert haggled valiantly but could not get the rent down far enough to make it feasible. Out he went, once more scouring the city for lodgings. All the best places were too expensive or else passed on from tenant to tenant in a network of contacts to which as yet he had no access. Elizabeth grew to dread his return from each day's hunting. He could neither eat nor sleep and appeared quite demented at the prospect of being soon homeless. She was not as sympathetic as she ought to have been because his passion for living strictly within their budget exasperated her. To her, it was silly to leave the Casa Guidi for the sake of a few shillings. But 20th October came and they left. There was a dreadful ten-day interlude in the via Maggio, in rooms which turned out to be so sunless Elizabeth said she could not endure it, before they moved into a "little baby house" opposite the Grand Duke's palace in the piazza Pitti. They had to pay "heaps of guineas" to get it and since they had broken their lease on the previous rooms they had to pay for that too, wrecking Robert's careful calculations completely. He did not reproach his wife, even though he had argued against the disastrous via Maggio rooms: as Elizabeth wrote remorsefully to Miss Mitford, "Any other man a little lower than the angels would have stamped and sworn a little . . ." But Robert had made a resolution: he would not go through this again. Next time, he would take either a very long lease or find somewhere permanent.

They passed a satisfactory winter in the "baby house" but Elizabeth was faintly uneasy. She was writing "Casa Guidi Windows" but Robert was writing nothing still. Not only was he not producing any new work, he had no desire to do so. Happiness, she commented to Miss Mitford, seemed not to agree with literary activity. She wondered whether, if they had their own home, the atmosphere would become more conducive to work, or whether, alternatively, carrying out some of their ever-vague plans to travel on to Rome or Venice would prove stimulating. Her own writing was interrupted by another kind of productivity: she was once more pregnant. In February 1848 she wrote to her sisters and Miss Mitford that Robert and Wilson had been sure for months that she was pregnant but that since she continued to menstruate ("I have had my usual health *as regularly as possible*") she had thought them mistaken. But now she was beginning to suspect she was indeed expecting a child, particularly as she had been sick. Robert, she reported, would not let her "say yes or no too loudly". He also wanted her to give up her opium mixture completely. For two years now Elizabeth had been decreasing the amount of opium she took. Before she left England, when she was feeling so well in the summer of 1846, she had finally succumbed to Robert's plea that she should give up the drug but her medical adviser at the time, Mr Jago, had told her, she reported to Robert, that this would have to be done "very slowly and gradually". She was at pains to assure Robert she did not take much anyway and that she had "never *increased* upon the prescribed quantity . . . prescribed in the first instance – no!" but, without a knowledge of the amount or date of that "first" prescription, her protestations have little meaning. But by February 1848 she had certainly reduced her opium intake to the lowest level it had ever been in her adult life and was taking it only at night, to make her sleep, as she had done as an adolescent.

She longed for a baby but at the same time confessed "it strikes me often that I have no right to ask for more filling of this cup which has the 'golden beads' swelling to the brim of it already". Robert was unconcerned about the arrival of any baby: he was interested only in her safety, announcing that he could not love any child as he loved her. He watched over her with his usual solicitude, fretting in case the influenza prevalent in the city should reach her. Wilson thought her mistress had never looked so well in her life as she approached her forty-second birthday (not mentioned in any correspondence when March 6th came round, though Henrietta's thirty-ninth on the 4th was remembered). But the day after this birthday Elizabeth began a letter to her sister with the unhappy words, "I have been ill again . . ." She had had another miscarriage. The disappointment was much more marked than before. Knowing she was pregnant this time, she had had time to dream and now, her dream shattered, there was a sense of despair because she knew "the habit of miscarriages is hard to break". Resolutely, she reminded herself that she was already blessed enough. Robert, far from letting her think of herself as a failure, was overjoyed that she had survived the ordeal. "How can I find words to tell you of all the dear and untiring tenderness of my husband?" she wrote to Henrietta. "Instead of loving me less, it is surely more and more that he loves me." She felt guilty about her opium, though, which Robert had yet again begged her to give up completely. (Dr Harding, the English doctor called in, unfortunately said he doubted if it was to blame.) He also had another theory: the day of the miscarriage she had written an enormous number of long letters and he was sure the intensity with which she wrote them and the sheer exhaustion induced by the act of so much writing had contributed to the disaster.[2] She grew so excited as she wrote and he had observed her face grew flushed and her body tense. Whatever the cause, the miscarriage had happened and was over. The layette Elizabeth had been working on, even though she loathed needlework, was put away in a drawer. She firmly suppressed morbid thoughts about whether it would ever be taken out again.

There was excitement in plenty that spring to distract her. Every morning, when Robert went to collect the mail and to read the newspapers in the reading room, it was a standing joke that Elizabeth would say, "Bring me back news of a revolution!" As she wrote to Henrietta in April "generally he brings me back news of *two*!" Throughout the whole of Europe in 1848 social coherence, as well as governments, was breaking down, ending the thirty years of relative peace which had followed the Vienna Peace Treaties of 1815. Nineteenth-century liberalism (with which Elizabeth was in perfect sympathy) was on the rise. In each country where authoritarian rulers were threatened there were attempts at appeasement and some acknowledgement that the appalling conditions of the poor (made so much worse by the Industrial Revolution) should be ameliorated. In February 1848 the King of France abdicated and a provisional government was established there. Elections (by direct male suffrage) were held in April for a constituent Assembly. As Elizabeth lay recovering from her miscarriage she was convinced (wrongly) that liberal reform had triumphed in France. Next to ignite was Germany, where demonstrations led to the King of Prussia granting a constitution and promising a re-organisation of the confederation of states. Meanwhile, Emperor Ferdinand of Austria had confirmed Hungary as a separate state, driven to this by similar pressures. It was no wonder that Elizabeth was excited: the whole of Europe seemed in turmoil.

In the Italian states the situation was more complicated because, ever since 1815, foreign rule had been imposed upon them as well as authoritarian government. Lombardy and Venetia were under direct Austrian rule; Naples and Sicily had a puppet ruler under Austrian control; Parma, Modena and Tuscany had rulers friendly to Austria. Only Piedmont (which included Savoy, Nice, Genoa and Sardinia) was a true Italian state. No state had a parliament and any movement towards unity was hampered by poor communications and natural geographical barriers. Hatred of Austria was almost the only common bond. But in January 1848 rebel forces in Sicily forced the King to accept a constitution. In February, as Elizabeth had witnessed, the Grand Duke of Tuscany granted a constitution. In March, Piedmont gained its constitution, as did the Papal States, while in Venice the Austrians were expelled and an independent Republic proclaimed. At the end of March, the King of Piedmont attacked Austrian troops in Lombardy. The excitement in the Casa Guidi was tremendous.

Elizabeth realised how worried her family would be as this news filtered through and reassured them that "suppose the *worst* and most improbable, that the Austrians march straight on us! Well, *we* are not going to fight you may be certain. We shall be as safe as you are." But she promised that, in the "nearly impossible case of any bombardment" they would leave in time. It was not something she thought would be necessary, despising as she did those craven English who had already started to desert Florence at the first hint of approaching trouble. They were not true lovers of Italy as she was, nor were they republicans as she was. In several letters she took the opportunity to expound her political beliefs. Years before, she had said, "I do like a nation to be free", and had gone on to define a free nation as one in which "the people should . . . influence the government". Now she expanded this to include her definition of a republic as being "for every born man in it to have room for his faculties – which is perfectly different from swamping individuality in a mob".[3] To Kenyon, she wrote that some people thought that she and Robert were communists but that they certainly were not, "farther than to admit the wisdom of voluntary association in matters of material life among the poorer classes". Her ideal was for "the government [to] educate the people absolutely and *then* give room for the individual to develop himself into life freely".[4] Far from being communist, "nothing can be more hateful to me than this communist idea of quenching individualities in the mass". She admired what was happening in France (or what she thought was happening) and only wished Italy would follow suit. All groups of revolutionaries, out to overthrow absolutism and establish republics on egalitarian lines, met with her approval. Defiantly, she told Kenyon she wished England had more Chartists and that she certainly did not think her old country a paragon of political virtues as others did. Property there ought to be "better divided" and "heredity privilege abolished". England had nothing to be proud of because it respected the ruts "while everywhere else they are mending the roads". What she really wanted to see, she told Miss Mitford, was "liberty and civilisation married together lawfully". Elizabeth was found of these fine-sounding political generalisations which tended to reveal how emotional her opinions were. This is not to argue that she was ignorant of facts, nor that reason played no part in her reckonings, but that she did not always properly connect cause and effect. She tended to see effects and assume both cause and cure. She read of hungry crowds rioting and immediately concluded this was caused only by individual greed, the greed of the rich, instead of by a much more complicated general economic situation. When she was young and her father and Bro "tallied politics" during the 1832 Reform Bill period she had grown bored and impatient when they began to speak "very technically and deeply". She confessed she did not even understand her father sufficiently to précis his words. Her political understanding, except in relation to Italian affairs where she too learned to talk "technically and deeply", never developed beyond the standard liberal viewpoint of her times. This meant she was for justice, freedom and prosperity for "the people" with only the most vague idea of both who "the people" were and what the realisation of this objective would entail. What *was* laudable about her politics was her passion to become involved, not to stand aside. Her concern was never in doubt, nor her feelings of responsibility.

In Italy she thought "liberty and civilisation" about to be joined when, just before her miscarriage in early March, Grand Duke Leopold granted Tuscany "an excellent constitution". If there was one thing Elizabeth loved to see it was a person in a position of absolute power giving it away to others or at least inviting them to share in it: this she greatly preferred to revolutionaries seizing it. The Grand Duke appeared to have given freely and she was full of admiration. There was a great fiesta and the whole of Florence was illuminated. Elizabeth was entranced by the sight of the Pitti Palace opposite them "drawn out in fire". They looked at it all evening as they ate their sandwiches ("think of having sandwiches at that time of night"). Afterwards, she undressed and let her hair down and was sitting combing it over her shoulders when Robert shouted for her to come to the window quickly. She was just in time to see the Grand Duke's carriage "in the midst of a milky way of waxen torchlights". On all sides exuberant crowds cheered and sang and Elizabeth was over-come when she heard that the Grand Duke had walked among them to the Opera. She was sure "her" Florence was going to be an example to the rest of Europe though she was aware that, in spite of the new constitution, "the heart of the people boils". The English, who were "flying helter-skelter" she told Miss Mitford, were "dreadful cowards".

This cowardice did the Brownings a favour: it emptied Florence just as the lease on the piazza Pitti house ran out. The usual summer exodus from the city began earlier and landlords unexpectedly had property on their hands. Robert, by this time more *au fait* with the situation, was poised to take advantage of it. He knew that yet again plans to go to England must be abandoned – Elizabeth was still weak after her second miscarriage, though she was up and out driving and seemed well – but he was determined, as Elizabeth described it, to "stop throwing money into the Arno". He had decided to take a long lease on some unfurnished property, thereby cutting costs dramatically. He began searching for an apartment, feeling a great deal more hopeful and in control than he had ever done before. His confidence was justified. He discovered almost at once that their previous rooms in the Casa Guidi were to let, unfurnished this time, at twenty-five guineas if they took them for a year. Furthermore, this long lease allowed subletting. Once he'd done some rapid sums, Robert was elated: it was an economic miracle. When he judged Elizabeth was well enough, they could go to England and in their absence let their apartment for, he reckoned, ten pounds a month which would pay their travelling expenses and give them the wonderful security of having a home to come back to. He promptly signed the lease and felt himself to be the best business manager in the world. "Such prudence was never known before among poets," commented Elizabeth mockingly to Mrs Martin. But she was delighted. Robert's endless fuss over money had begun to do more than mildly irritate her. She complained to Henrietta that Robert carried things too far: "Oh what a fuss . . . because the remittance . . . did not come on the right day – a fortnight before we wanted it." She was bored with Robert's constant calculations, his endless speculation that "if something happened and something else followed and something else didn't happen and some-thing else didn't follow why we should be 'embarrassed' – how dreadful to be sure!"[5] When he had been explaining this to her she had asked him tartly to put her pillow straight and pass over the novel she was reading. He told her off for "insouciance" and said her cavalier attitude to money was nothing to be proud of. But now Robert was happy and she was only too ready to acknowledge his financial acumen.

On 9th May 1848 the Brownings moved back into the Casa Guidi unaware that they would not leave it again for thirteen years except for long holidays. They now had a proper home and almost instantly reaped the benefits. Furnishing and decorating it proved far more fun and much less tiring than they had thought and revealed unexpected qualities about both of them. Robert might hate searching for rooms but he discovered that he loved searching for furniture and Elizabeth might boast she knew nothing of housekeeping and cared less but she found she actually liked thinking of colour schemes and choosing fabrics. Robert, of the two, was "far more particular". They slept on a hired bed until, to Elizabeth's amusement, he had found one sufficiently "ducal" to buy (the framework was £1.10s, the mattress with springs and including pillows £6). He had a passion for chests of drawers, buying six, and Elizabeth had one for sofas, of which she had eight. A carpet for the enormous drawing room floor was a problem until Robert found a second-hand one for £8 and also a chandelier for the same room for £2. Lucky buys included a magnificent mirror for £5 and a beautifully carved wooden bookcase for £6 both from the house of the French

Chargé d'Affaires who was going home. Within a month, they had all the essentials. They would not need curtains till the autumn, which gave Elizabeth plenty of time to order white muslin from England at vast expense and arrange for heavier outer curtains to be made, of crimson velvet, in Florence. She had decided red and green were to be the colours used, green for the walls and red for the soft furnishings.

The Casa Guidi was not the easiest place to make look comfortable and cheerful. The narrow hall with its stained glass partition, is dark and austere and, inside, the rooms are of a daunting size. The drawing room, twenty by twenty-three foot, seems even bigger because of the tremendous height of the ceiling. The dining room next to it is only slightly smaller and the main bedroom, though not so broad, is equally huge. All three rooms, now as then, need a great deal of furniture to make them seem less barrack-like, especially when the two people using them were so very small. The other rooms, to be used mainly by Wilson, are by contrast exceptionally cramped and small. Wilson's bedroom was tiny but not as absurdly small as the little slot allocated as a kitchen. It is divided into two levels with the upper loft, just big enough for a cook to sleep in, reached by more of a ladder than a staircase. There was also a dressing room for Robert, twice the size of Wilson's bedroom (so much for her employers' much vaunted republican sentiments), a little sitting room (also bigger than her room) and a studio. There was, of course, no garden. There was an internal courtyard for the whole building with a well in it but, compared to the many beautiful courtyards full of trees elsewhere in Florence, it was a bleak place. Their narrow terrace had plants on it, which left even less space to edge along, but gave them little more greenery than Elizabeth had had in her overflowing Wimpole Street window box. She saw none of the imperfections of the Casa Guidi. "I love this house," she declared, and felt instinctively she could be happy there. The huge rooms, far from inhibiting her, seemed to make her feel free. The grey stone wall of the church opposite, which blocked her view and was as dreary as the brick she had seen in Wimpole Street, did not depress her but made her feel secure. She felt temperamentally comfortable in the cool and gloomy apartment.

She was reminded surprisingly often of Wimpole Street, especially when Punch played in the street underneath her window. She wrote to Henrietta that whenever she heard "Punch talking under the windows" she found herself "unawares . . . in London". It did not seem to be an unpleasant feeling: her thoughts of her own "prison" were affectionate ones, mainly because of the people still in it. Not only did she think of them all the time, she also fantasised their arrival in Florence. She once described to Henrietta how Robert had come in beaming and saying he had been kissed by someone since he saw her last. His teasing had the most extraordinary effect: she was seized with "the most absurd, supernaturally absurd idea in the world; for actually it came into my head that you and Arabel were in Florence – Arabel at any rate!"[6] Robert was disconcerted to see her "gasp for breath", and even when he had explained that it was only Father Prout, an old friend of his, she took time to recover. She worried terribly about the health of everyone in Wimpole Street, especially her father's. If he were reported, in her sisters' letters, to have a cold or to be suffering from his old asthma complaint she was frantic for regular bulletins. "I see you in my dreams, all of you," she wrote to Henrietta adding, "if there is any difference in my love for you it is through increase and not diminution." Sometimes she was given "dreadful frights" over letters with black seals. One letter came for her with "a black edge an inch deep and a black seal, sealed, as struck me in a moment, with Papa's well known griffin seal!" She went as white as the envelope, and Robert, realising what she was thinking, snatched the letter and took the unprecedented step of opening and reading it himself. It was from a total stranger requesting permission to use some of her poems in an anthology. Robert read up to half way then threw it into the fire. Elizabeth sobbed with relief: "I thought, you see, vague thoughts about Jamaica" (where Stormie was). It was a reminder that the morbid streak was still there, even though her life was happy, and she had thought to have conquered it entirely.

She knew her image of Arabel appearing in Florence was silly but she felt aggrieved that none of her brothers made the effort to come, particularly George who had the means and liberty to do so. He travelled, he could easily include Florence in his itinerary. It upset her to realise that none of her family had yet been received into the home of which she was so proud nor met Robert now that he was her husband. Her friends were little better than her family. Kenyon came to Italy but did not visit them; he went to Rome, to Venice, but for some reason which was to her inexcusable not Florence. It took Robert's common-sense to restrain her from becoming paranoid on this score. The trouble was that the new friends they were making still failed to fill the gap, interesting though they were. They were people like the sculptor Hiram Powers, whom Elizabeth thought "a charming, simple, straightforward, genial American"; Miss Boyle, niece of the Earl of Cork, "a very vivacious little person" who amused Elizabeth with her "sparkling talk"; Mr Ware, an American Unitarian minister and novelist who was "an earnest simple man" towards whom Elizabeth felt protective; and Mme de Fauveau, a French aristocrat and sculptress who was rated "a most interesting woman". All these people took coffee or tea at the Casa Guidi but although Elizabeth quite enjoyed their company she had, as usual, contradictory feelings about them. On the one hand, she wanted just to be shut up with Robert "like two owls in a hole" or "two toads under a tree-stump", but, on the other hand, she recognised the need for some stimulation of the right sort, the sort so far unavailable in Florence. She could neither love nor be intimate with the few women she knew: what were Mme de Fauveau and Miss Boyle compared to Henrietta and Arabel or even Miss Mitford?

It was ironic that Wilson fared better. She was now proficient in Italian after teaching herself from a book lent to her. Elizabeth admired her determination and described to Henrietta how her maid could communicate very well and was making her own way. It helped that she now worked with a second maid they had hired, who was Italian, and with an Italian cook called Alessandro. He was a mixed blessing. Elizabeth said he was "excellent", and he certainly managed the heroic feat of producing splendid dinners from the miserable cubby hole termed a kitchen at the Casa Guidi, but Wilson detested him. According to her, he never stopped boasting of his Continental experience, prefixing everything he said to her with "I have been to Paris – I have been to London – I have been to Germany". She was "tired of it". Even harder to endure were his lectures on England's moral decline. These infuriated Wilson but, when she tried to put Alessandro straight, her head swam with the effort of controlling her rage. But she thought better of certain other Italian men upon whom she practised her Italian. Elizabeth had observed ever since their arrival in Florence that her maid was bound to marry one of the Grand Duke's bodyguard because they were such magnificent specimens of manhood – six foot tall and resplendent in gorgeous uniforms. In the summer of 1848 she learned that her jesting prophecy had come true: a "Mr Righi" of the ducal guard had proposed to Wilson. Elizabeth was "confounded" but pleased that Wilson, unlike Crow, had taken her into her confidence. She could see many difficulties ahead, mainly religious ones, but Wilson was sensible and, since she saw the problems, had resolved to wait six months before committing herself. Mr Righi (as the Brownings always called him), in any case, was not, as a ducal bodyguard, allowed to be married any more than was a Barrett butler. He was willing to leave the Duke's service, however, and since he had a good education (even Latin) he anticipated being able to get another job easily. Robert thought Wilson's suitor "very good and superior" but Elizabeth, always deeply suspicious about what she called "externals", was less enthusiastic. She "earnestly hoped" Wilson would be happy.

But, as well as her gentleman friend, Wilson also had the kind of female companionship Elizabeth missed. There were many English maids in Florence and in no time at all Wilson knew a number with whom she enjoyed all kinds of outings. Rather to Elizabeth's amazement she went into the Grand Duke's reception rooms, with the maid of a Mrs Loftus, and also on a jaunt to a splendid villa where she visited the maid of the Princess of Parma. Elizabeth, who had not at the time been in sight of one of these impressive villas on the hillsides outside the city, was intensely curious about what it had been like. It was clear that Wilson had made an active social life for herself and that, even though she missed her family and the servant household in Wimpole Street, she had to a great extent found substitutes. She liked having letters from England, too – her mother and sisters and Minny Robinson all wrote to her – but had no unbearable longing to see those who had written them. Her lot in Italy was infinitely preferable to what it had been in England. This was a relief for Elizabeth. When Wilson was ill in Pisa she had offered to send her home and her maid had declined the offer; now that she was happy Elizabeth felt instrumental in the achieving of her happiness and better prospects. At twenty-eight, it looked as though Wilson would make a better marriage than any she could have made in England.

Elizabeth was glad, because she was once more pregnant, that she was not to be robbed of her maid too suddenly. Robert wanted to keep Elizabeth on her back wrapped in cotton wool for nine months but, failing that, earnestly begged her to do two things: keep calm at all times and give up all opium mixtures. Elizabeth agreed. This time, if she miscarried, which she was well aware was more than likely, she did not want to feel it had in any way been her own fault. In these circumstances, it was surprising that she went on holiday at the end of July when she was in the earliest and most risky period of pregnancy but the heat in Florence was excessive and it is always possible that yet again she did not believe she was pregnant. Robert certainly cannot have known or he would never have trusted her to an arduous carriage trip. They went by diligence to Arezzo, travelling by night for coolness, and from there to Fano, where they intended "to get into some kind of nest". They had now been nearly two years in Italy and Elizabeth was extremely conscious of how little she had seen of the country – most of the trips they had envisaged had never taken place. She passionately wanted to explore and visit as many areas as possible and to take in as many literary shrines as Robert could find for her. But Fano was a disappointment. It was hot and dull with none of the reviving sea breezes they had been promised. They went on, after three days, to Ancona, "a striking sea-city, holding up against the brown rock and elbowing out the purple tides – beautiful to look upon". At last, Elizabeth felt she was really seeing Italy and was content. They stayed a week, living on "fish and cold water". In this out-of-the-way place, Elizabeth was allowed to wear only a white dressing gown, "sans stays, sans shoes, sans everything", she told Miss Mitford, painting a picture of herself as thoroughly abandoned, lying with her hair dishevelled and loose. Eventually, they moved on to Pesaro and Rimini where they halted briefly before making for Ravenna which, apart from its churches, was not a success ("keep me from Ravenna!" said Elizabeth after one whiff from the marshes). A mile out of the city they visited Dante's tomb at dawn but were annoyed to be barred because they lacked written permission to go in, and had to continue straight on over the Apennines and back to Florence. The scenery all the way was spectacular: Elizabeth was thrilled by the "chestnut forests dropping by their own weight into the deep ravines" and by the spectacular rocks "clean and clawed by the living torrents". The discomfort of bouncing along rough roads in a carriage was not thought worth mentioning.

What was appreciated at the end of such a journey was having a home to which to return. Elizabeth wrote, "I took possession of my own chair and put up my feet on the cushions and was charmed." The arduous travelling had miraculously done her no harm: she was three months pregnant by mid-August and feeling very well. Robert, on the other hand, was ill. Hardly were they home than he became feverish and Elizabeth was made frantically aware of how fragile her happiness was. Robert's being ill was far worse than being ill herself. She stopped writing letters entirely to concentrate on nursing him, only to discover she had little idea how to do so. It was her turn to be distraught because *he* would not see a doctor in spite of his fever and ulcerated throat. His hands burned when she touched them and his eyes were frighteningly languid. He would neither eat nor drink and she was in despair until they were fortuitously visited by the ubiquitous Father Prout. "Father Prout" was the pseudonym of a Jesuit priest who had been dismissed from the order in 1830. His real name was Mohony and he was the Rome correspondent at that time of the *Daily News*. Prout, a flamboyant personality, took one look at Robert and boomed that he could cure him in a minute. He sent Alessandro for eggs and port wine and before the astonished and apprehensive company whisked it all up and made Robert drink it. He told Elizabeth she was a baby for being so worried and promised that Robert would sleep and feel better the next day. By the time Prout called again (to take the credit) Robert's fever had abated and he was brighter. Elizabeth thanked their friend profusely and said she would always be grateful. But by the time Prout had called every day for a week and Robert was long since recovered, her gratitude had been severely tested. She found Prout domineering and disliked some of his more unpleasant personal habits (such as spitting). He became, Elizabeth told Henrietta, "our man of the mountain, whom Sinbad carried on his back". His ebullient personality was an intrusion but he appeared genuinely to think that they loved to have him and remarked that, although he was obliged to go to Rome for a while, he would hurry back for their sake. Elizabeth could not think what to do. Their precious evenings were now "ground to powder, smoked to ashes". Each time Prout at last departed, after average sessions of three hours, there was "a general burst of indignation" from them both and a "throwing open of doors to get rid of smoke and malice". What irritated Elizabeth most was that neither she nor Robert had much in common with Prout to whom they felt beholden nevertheless. His was not the kind of company she wanted in their home.

That first winter in the Casa Guidi she wanted no company at all. She was willing herself to keep this third baby and obeying all Robert's commands. The hardest was the one about giving up all opium. She found this very, very difficult and needed all Robert's help. It is, however, unlikely she ever succeeded in giving it up completely.[7] Her only activity, apart from reading and writing letters, was supervising preparations for her confinement. White muslin had arrived from England and the curtains were made. The bed had white drapes and Robert had found the perfect chest of drawers to go beside it (walnut wood inlaid with ivory). The bedroom was now "something splendid" and a pleasure to rest in. While she dutifully rested, Elizabeth gazed at the portrait of her father which had just arrived, swathed in cambric and flannel, in a box full of her things from England. She wrote to Henrietta, "I tremble to look at the dear face again," but still she wanted to have it in front of her when she opened her eyes each morning and before she closed them at night. To have it in such a position was a disquieting choice but, since her bedroom was a place into which no visitor came, it was also the most private. As she lay there, quite serene, Elizabeth could hear overhead the crying of the baby just born to the new tenants, Mr and Mrs David Ogilvy. They had moved in, with their two-year-old daughter Louisa, while the Brownings were on holiday, and their son Alexander was born in September. Elizabeth had already met the couple through a mutual acquaintance and was glad to have a neighbour with young children. She had hopes of a friendship blossoming between herself and the pretty, lively Mrs Ogilvy who also wrote poetry. If her own baby survived, they would have children almost the same age. Mrs Ogilvy embroidered some baby caps for her and was most supportive. Elizabeth sewed some baby clothes too, to join those sent by her sisters, and boasted that in spite of her hatred of needlework she did it so well that she had decided it was her vocation after all: she would forget the poetry. Wilson sewed all the time in a fever of preparations. Looking at the cradle Wilson had lined, Elizabeth was full of "fatal presentiments" but had enough sense to know these were common to most expectant mothers. She worried most that her baby might be deformed because she had fallen, although only from a chair and before the baby had begun to move. She felt well, looked well, was even eating well. There was every reason, at the beginning of 1849, to think that one of her dearest wishes would be granted.

It was only one of these wishes. Bearing a child was not of unique importance to Elizabeth. She had other desires, the most important of them being the hope for some measure of reconciliation with her father. She wrote to Miss Mitford that the smile of her father would be dearer to her than that of any child of hers, though of course these were in a sense empty words because she had not then had a child and did not know what she was talking about. The continuing pain of her father's treatment of her was still a small price to pay for Robert's love but she felt, by 1849, that the price had been exacted long enough. Another strong desire within her was that Robert should start writing poetry again. At

Ancona, he had written one poem but this had not been followed by the great blossoming of his genius as she wished and hoped. She herself had written something more original and substantial (the first part of "Casa Guidi Windows") than he had. Unlike Elizabeth, Robert was always looking for excuses not to write (though once he began, his application could match hers). This was puzzling to his wife, though she well understood that inspiration did not arrive to order. But she was under-estimating how difficult it was for Robert to adapt to his new circum-stances: the change in his life style was very nearly as great as that in her own. At home in New Cross his writing had had complete pre-eminence. He was not responsible for anything in the running of the Browning household and had parents and sister ministering to his every need, anxious only that he should have ideal conditions in which to write. But now he was permanently distracted by the cares of looking after a delicate wife – cares which through his devotion he made more onerous than they needed to be – and simply did not feel like writing poetry. He himself was unworried, confident that when he was ready he would resume work. What Elizabeth dreaded was the thought that marriage to her had finished Robert as a poet, but he had no such fears.

As she drew near the time for her baby to be born, she measured the stillness of her bedroom against the turbulence reported outside. What-ever happened, they could not move now. Circumstances as well as loyalty would keep them in Florence, witnesses to revolution or in-vasion. In February, the Grand Duke was deposed. Elsewhere in Italy, Mazzini was advocating republicanism (but Elizabeth did not trust either him or his brand of republicanism). The Pope fled, Garibaldi marshalled an army, Mazzini arrived in Rome and became a dictator: every day there was dramatic news. To calm herself, Elizabeth took up a novel, newly arrived from England though, to her annoyance, not new. It was *Jane Eyre*, which she was mortified not yet to have read, but which she found not nearly as good as people had said.

By the end of February, she knew she had successfully carried her baby to full term. Now it remained only to survive the birth. Dr Harding announced the obvious to a terrified Robert: this would be "a critical case".

Chapter Fourteen

IN spite of her doctor's apprehension, and the far greater anxiety of Robert and Wilson, Elizabeth found that as the approximate date of her confinement drew near those "fatal presentiments" of hers grew less rather than more formidable. She wrote to Miss Mitford that she had "no misgivings" except the usual feeling that someone as happy as herself could not reasonably be expected to receive more blessings. But she took the precaution of writing what she called "last messages" to her family, including her father and estranged brothers. As she put it to Mrs Martin "with certain hazards before me, my heart turned to them naturally". Yet she was not afraid of the physical pain involved in those hazards: pain was something she knew she could endure, especially when it had both a known cause and cure. She was proud to have gone to full term and proudest of all that she had very nearly done with all opium (though as late as 30th January she was referring only to having "steadily diminished" it).

Wilson was much more obviously excited than she was and like her mistress anticipated a girl. The lining she had made for the open-work wicker cradle was pink and so was the pillow. Elizabeth solemnly and unnecessarily informed Henrietta that pink was the colour for a girl. There was no doubt that she believed she would have a girl, although she never at that time said she wanted one. It was simply that, because she was frail and slight, she somehow thought herself more likely to have an equally frail and slight daughter. The last letter she wrote before the birth was to Henrietta, on 4th March, her sister's fortieth birthday. She wished her well and remarked that she knew her sister cared "less than I do" about her age. But there was an obvious poignancy about Henrietta's fortieth birthday which could not be ignored – she was still not married to Surtees. Two days later, on 6th March, Elizabeth's own birthday, her forty-third, passed, as it almost always did, unmarked.

At five o'clock on the morning of 8th March Elizabeth went into labour. For most of the day, Robert sat with her while Dr Harding and a nurse came and went and Wilson hovered in permanent attendance. Robert was astonished at how well Elizabeth bore the pain, writing later to her sisters that "she never once cried out or shed a tear, acute as the pains were".[1] By evening, when the labour was well advanced, Robert was excluded. He waited next door, separated from the bedroom by thick wooden doors. From within there was an eerie silence, no groans, no screams. Dr Harding emerged occasionally to say that everything was proceeding normally and there was no cause for undue concern. Elizabeth, he said, was bearing up better than any woman he had ever attended. But for Robert no amount of reassurance was enough. It had always seemed to him that his wife was too small and weak to be able to deliver a child without damaging herself: like most people, he wrongly associated physique with childbearing ability. By midnight, when still the silence beyond the doors continued and he thought of the hours and hours his wife had suffered, he was beginning to dread the next bulletin and was mentally preparing himself for Dr Harding's grave face. Then, at a quarter past two on the morning of Friday 9th March, Robert heard the strangest sound: the strong, lusty cry of a baby. Even then, his heart did not leap; it was his wife's safety he was concerned with, not his child's. Until he saw her for himself, his anxiety remained undiminished by the news that he had a healthy son. He had to wait a long time – seven hours – before he was allowed into the bedroom. At last, he believed the truth: his wife had not only survived the ordeal but had presented him with a superbly healthy child. Until Robert himself told her that their son was healthy Elizabeth could not bring herself to believe it. She wrote revealingly afterwards that, if her baby had been "a puny, sickly infant", it would have been "a matter of course" to blame this on her and especially on the opium she took. She described how "one of the great London physicians" had "predicted evil" because she took opium when pregnant and how the knowledge of this had haunted her. When her baby cried and the doctor pronounced him perfect she wrote that her relief was "an unspeakable rapture".

Elizabeth was immensely proud of her achievement. What thrilled her most was to have performed a natural function, "the highest natural function of a woman" as she had once described it, perfectly. She wrote to Miss Mitford that "everything was right as could be" and that she had heard Dr Harding tell the nurse "that in all his practice he had never seen the functions of nature more healthfully performed". Since she had gone all her adult life labelled unhealthy, this was music to Elizabeth's ears. And if it had not been for Dr Harding's unaccountable caution, she would have gone on to perform another natural function perfectly by breastfeeding her son as her London adviser, Mr Jago, had encouraged her to believe she would be able to. But she did not feel she could challenge Dr Harding's verdict and was not disposed in any case to make a fuss over what was, by comparison with giving birth, a trifle. The wet nurse employed was such an obviously robust woman, with huge breasts dripping milk, that Elizabeth felt embarrassed to have imagined she could compete. Signora Bondi, as well as being "stout and rosy", had "no nerves at all" and would, Elizabeth thought, be very good for her baby even if she did not know so much as the names of the months and was illiterate.

One curious aspect of Elizabeth's attitude to motherhood emerged very quickly: she had no faith in her own ability to fulfil her new role, in spite of giving birth without difficulty. Just as she had once said she was not good enough for Robert, she now pronounced herself not good enough for her baby. She was not possessive with her son. On the contrary, she relished seeing him in other people's arms, especially Robert's, telling Mrs Martin later on, "I do like men who are not ashamed to be beside a cradle." She maintained that her son preferred to be in his father's arms; it was as though she were deliberately distancing herself from this new, overwhelming form of love which had taken her by surprise. Before their son was born, Robert had consistently said that beside his wife a child was nothing to him, but he announced within a day of the birth that he would give his life for him. Only Flush spoiled the atmosphere of radiant joy in the Casa Guidi. Understandably, he was jealous. The sight of everyone cooing over a bundle in a white shawl drove him first to frantic barking and then to outraged sulks. "For a whole fortnight," Elizabeth wrote to Miss Mitford, "he fell into a deep melancholy and was proof against all attentions lavished on him." After that, he accepted the inevitable to the extent of what Elizabeth called "patronising the cradle".

But the state of euphoria ended very soon when news came that Robert's adored mother had died on 18th March, without ever understanding that she had a grandson. Sarianna, Robert's sister, had been courageously shielding her brother from the truth about their mother's health, knowing as she did of Elizabeth's imminent confinement and the impossibility of his leaving her. She wrote in February that her mother was ill and in early March that she was no better but, until she heard Elizabeth was safely delivered, she concealed the gravity of the situation. A week after receiving the news of Robert's son, she had to write following her congratulations with a note telling him his mother was dead. Elizabeth was grateful for the self-restraint she had shown, writing to thank her sister-in-law and express her appreciation of what it had involved. The effect on Robert was devastating. Elizabeth was acutely sympathetic to his degree of sorrow. She grieved not just for but with him, feeling again how she had felt when her own mother died so suddenly and without any farewell. (There was guilt mixed with her distress: it was because of her that Robert had not seen his mother for three years, because of her that he had had to leave his mother.) She emphasised to Sarianna that she had experienced this particular kind of grief and tried to explain the philosophy she was urging on Robert: "to live rightly we must turn our faces forward and press forward and not look back morbidly for the footsteps in the dust of those beloved ones who travelled with us but yesterday. They themselves are not behind but before . . ." She urged Robert to go at once to his bereaved father but he said that to return home would destroy him. The only shred of comfort Elizabeth was able to offer him was to name their son Robert Wiedemann and call him Weidemann, Robert's mother's maiden name.

Elizabeth recovered quickly from childbirth but Robert remained overcome by his mother's death for most of the summer. "I wish," Elizabeth wrote to Sarianna, "I could get him to go somewhere or do something." He was, she added, "very much depressed". Fortunately, Pen – as their son came to be known – was a great comfort.[2] Robert was visibly soothed when he cradled the baby in his arms. He watched him being bathed every day and was eager to help care for him, though Signora Bondi and Wilson between them left little to do. He agreed with Elizabeth that this was the most wonderful baby ever to be born. In letters to her sisters she boasted of her baby's beauty and brilliance, though never without an ever present tinge of satire which showed she was well aware of how ridiculous she often sounded. Pushed to be more precise about her son's staggering beauty she told Henrietta he was like "Raffael's" baby in an engraving of Virgin and Child which used to hang in her room in Wimpole Street: "baby's arms and legs perfectly justify the engraving, I assure you . . . he is so rosy and round." Miss Mitford was told he was "a lovely, fat, strong child with double chins and rosy cheeks and a great wide chest". People openly marvelled that such a fine specimen could have come from Elizabeth's body and instead of being hurt or irritated she reported triumphantly that she too was almost sceptical of him being hers. When Arabel teased her by writing that she was not to carry the baby around by its head, Elizabeth retorted the insult was "gratuitous" but was not offended. She knew perfectly well her sisters would think such an intellectual as herself hopeless with babies: it was an image she had created and fostered long ago as a protective device. She now happily demolished it and regaled her sisters with every particular of babylore in which she was becoming proficient.

Robert did not object. He walked Pen up and down, in every way a model father, but he was too upset to find in him the sheer happiness that he wanted. However hard he tried, he could not share his wife's exuberance. One of Elizabeth's great advantages, faced with the depth of Robert's acute depression, was her similarity to him. Her love for her parents was as great as his: it needed no effort to understand Robert's extreme misery because she had experienced it herself. When her own mother had died she had gone so far as to wonder if happiness of any kind would ever be possible again. She did not for one moment think Robert exaggerated his grief or that it was an insult to her that this grief over a parent's death completely overshadowed their life. By June, she had acknowledged that, far from recovering, Robert was even more depressed. He did not eat, nor did he sleep, and his appearance was witness to both. The heat was extreme but no plans had been made to move out of Florence. Robert had neither the will nor the energy to organise any exodus. For once, it was up to Elizabeth to initiate action and she rose to the occasion. It was she who insisted the baby could be left with his wet nurse and the devoted Wilson while they both went together to hunt for a suitable summer residence. She told Miss Mitford that she had to use subterfuge to get Robert to agree: she swore that for the sake of her own health and her baby's they must leave the inferno that was now Florence for the next three months. Robert, as she well knew, would do anything for her sake. At her insistence, the two of them went off on a quick reconnaissance of Carrara, Spezia, Seravazza and Bagni di Lucca, all within a fifty-mile radius of Florence. Leaving her three-month-old baby was hard, but Elizabeth was resolute: Robert's health and happiness must come first and Pen was in capable hands. She greatly enjoyed the exploratory trip, writing enthusiastic descriptions to her various correspondents. The olive forests around Carrara had charmed her and so had the "white marble mountains" beyond and the vistas of vines which "swing such portcullises of massive green from one tree to another". It was her conviction that nature's beauty could beat Robert which made her agree at first that the fashionable Bagni di Lucca was not the place for them but, when all the seaside places they visited proved too expensive (and also too hot), she persuaded Robert that they might look at it. Bagni di Lucca proved irresistible. The highest of the three villages, which together formed the resort, was empty of visitors and seemed totally secluded. Prompted by Elizabeth, Robert made an offer to rent an apartment for four months. The offer was accepted and they returned in haste to collect their baby, its nurse, Wilson, Alessandro and Flush.

Elizabeth felt a sudden dreadful surge of anxiety, as they approached the Casa Guidi. She wrote afterwards to her neighbour Mrs Ogilvy, who was already installed at Bagni di Lucca for the hot season, that she had not been able to help saying to Robert, "If we should find anything gone wrong . . ." she would never forgive herself. Robert, to her distress, did nothing to allay her fears because, still in a depressed state, he was for once prey to the same morbid fancies as herself. It was a great relief when the porter of the Casa Guidi building put them out of their misery: all was well. There was Pen, "looking fatter and rosier than ever and rounding his blue eyes with a sort of wild wonder at the sudden storm of kisses". Re-united, the little family and its entourage prepared to leave Florence, but first Pen was christened, in a simple ceremony without godparents, in the French Lutheran Church. Then they boarded a train, leaving behind a city of which even Elizabeth had begun to despair. Florence was now occupied by the Austrians who were ostensibly "protecting" the re-instated Grand Duke whose constitution, so freely granted, had proved a mockery. Elizabeth wrote to Mrs Martin that, although she could never lose sympathy with the people, she could not help a "certain political latitudinarianism from creeping over me". The more she became properly acquainted with the political complexities of Italian affairs the more jaundiced her views on "the people" became – the rose-coloured republican spectacles were slipping a little. What had happened had been so "ignoble . . . a revolution made by boys and vivas and unmade by boys and vivas". She felt less emotional and more hard-headed and was glad to leave, especially as a new law had just been passed against dogs: "all dogs found in the street to be killed straightway lest they shd. interfere with the movements of the Austrian horse!" The sooner Flush was removed the better.

They all arrived at the Bagni di Lucca on 30th June. They travelled part of the way by train and Elizabeth had been full of righteous indignation because she found that two of the children with whom they were obliged to share a carriage had whooping cough. They whooped all the way and she thought it "most wrong and cruel for people to expose others to such dangers". Mercifully, her baby escaped the dreaded cough and almost as soon as they arrived Robert began to look better. Elizabeth wisely encouraged him to go off on his own to "lose himself in the forests", calculating that, if nothing else, the exercise would remedy his lack of appetite and insomnia. The house they lived in lay "at the heart of a hundred mountains, sung to continually by a rushing mountain stream". Robert could walk from it straight into the woods and cover ten or twenty miles without meeting anyone. Sometimes, Elizabeth accompanied him, astonishing herself as well as Robert with her new energy. She was stronger than she had ever been as an adult, able to walk long distances and to climb all but the steepest hills without tiring. If Robert judged any stretch too hard for her he would sweep her up into his arms and carry her, though she swore he was more likely to harm himself than she was likely to do herself an injury. Side by side, mostly silent, they walked in the chestnut forests, listening to the waterfalls, admiring the golden mist which transfigured the mountains, both exhilarated by the air "sheathed in Italian sunshine". The only people they ever met were "a monk girt with a rope" or "a barefoot peasant". The beauty, the solitude, the purity of the air and the harmony between them restored Robert to his former self. Elizabeth had never been so happy. One day in particular epitomised this happiness. It was 17th September, five days after their third wedding anniversary, when Pen had been carried in to congratulate them "with a rose in his fist stretching out for me to take; and then he took another to Robert (that was dear Wilson's contrivance)". They set off, the entire household complete with Flush, at half past eight, on an excursion to Prato Fiorito. The women rode on donkeys and the men on mountain ponies with the baby alternately with Wilson and his nurse. Their three local guides took them up a faint track, not wide enough "for the wheel of even a wheelbarrow", with ravines lying below on either side ("frightful they were"). The scenery was "magnificent" and when they finally reached the top it was to see "a great world of inumerable mountains, the faint sea beyond them, and not a sign of cultivation". They all sat on the grass and had a picnic – "cold chicken and ham and tart" – and the baby rolled around on a shawl Elizabeth had spread out. Going down afterwards was "wild work" and Elizabeth was obliged to get off and walk when the descent became so steep she feared she would go over the head of the donkey. They reached home at 6 pm, exhausted but exultant. "Wasn't it daring of us to take baby?" Elizabeth wrote to Arabel, knowing full well what the scandalised response would be.

She was entirely happy in this mountain village but, although he looked and sounded and felt better, she sensed a basic change in Robert. The death of his mother had brought him to the kind of crisis of faith to which Elizabeth was accustomed. He needed, she felt, to draw strength from a re-affirmation of love so that he could be reminded that love was eternal, that it flowed on in various guises, and that his love for his mother had not been pointless but part of a richer whole. She chose this time to present to him the sonnets she had written during their courtship. If any absolute proof of Elizabeth's sensitivity was needed the occasion upon which she gave Robert these sonnets would provide it. She had kept them secret for three years after their marriage without once hinting at their existence. Clearly, since she had them with her at Lucca without knowing she would at last reveal them, she took them everywhere, like a talisman of her love. She wrote to Arabel afterwards, "I felt shy about them altogether" and gave as her reason that she had once heard Robert "express himself strongly against 'personal' poetry." She needed him to say "something on the other side", which apparently he now did, to release her from her sense of inhibition. According to Robert, she said to him, "Do you know I once wrote some sonnets about *you*?" and then, "there they are, if you care to see them". And there indeed they were, forty-three sonnets tracing the whole course of their love, marking her hesitation, her doubt, her disbelief before she moved on to rejoice in the glory and wonder of their reciprocated love. Elizabeth, writing to Arabel, did not convey Robert's astonishment and pride; she said merely, "he was much touched and pleased". But he wrote to his sister that during this summer he had come to know his wife as he had never known her before and that he had been mistaken in thinking there was nothing left to know. The depth of her love finally healed the inner as well as the outer man. To be loved *so* defied death, all death.

In October, as the mountain air sharpened and the mists became less golden and more sinister, the Brownings returned to the Casa Guidi determined to make this a winter during which they would both write poetry. Elizabeth, as usual, was more anxious that Robert should write than that she should herself and felt instinctively that the ordeal through which he had just passed had prepared him. Robert began work on a new long double poem to be called "Christmas Eve and Easter Day", with Elizabeth strongly influencing his choice of theme. She urged him to speak out in his own voice, without using dramatic devices, and to say what was in his heart. She wanted him to explore and express his doubts, fears and hopes, especially religious ones, in his poetry. She, for her part, began to revise her 1844 poems to which she would add the sonnets and her new translation of *Prometheus Bound* to make a new volume. But she did not write any new poems: she saw Robert, that winter, as the truly creative one.

That autumn, Elizabeth was blooming and engrossed in her baby (though never to the exclusion of Robert). Her letters, once full of Flush's antics, were now full of Pen's. At six months she reported he had to be restrained from walking and that his grip and attempts to stand up were prodigious. Already, she was putting into effect theories about the upbringing of children which she had held since Sette and Occy were born. She had always thought it nonsense, for example, that at a set age boys should be suddenly shorn of their curls and put into supposedly "masculine" attire. In one of her earliest poems, "To A Boy", which was one of the shorter pieces attached to her 1833 translation of *Prometheus Bound*, written when Sette was eleven and Occy nine, she had mourned the golden hair "long and free", now brutally cut despite her "bootless prayer/That they should pause awhile . . ." But she had no desire to make her son girlish, nor was she trying to pretend he was a girl because she wanted one (as people have alleged ever since). Some hundred years ahead of her time, she was rejecting accepted concepts of what was feminine and what was masculine. She also had other unconventional ideas on the upbringing of children, such as her belief in freedom of movement. She liked her baby to have total liberty to roll around: she was always putting him on the floor or the ground and delighted in his uninhibited acrobatics. Robert found them a little too boisterous. Once, when the baby rolled too hard and banged his head, he remonstrated with the words "really Ba I can't trust you". Elizabeth laughed in his face and retorted that babies' heads were not made of Venetian glass. They differed, too, over what language should be used with their son. Elizabeth spoke Italian to him, because she thought it far too confusing for the child to have to learn two languages at first. Robert disagreed. His son was an Englishman and he wanted him to be able to speak the tongue of his fathers from the beginning. Such discussions were daily affairs in the Casa Guidi, with Pen's upbringing and education of supreme importance.

It still grieved Elizabeth that none of their families had yet seen this wonderful child. Reports of a cholera epidemic in London in the autumn of that year, 1849, terrified her into suspecting it might be too late soon. Elizabeth wrote to Henrietta that it was no good telling her not to be frightened about them catching cholera: "I am frightened, must be frightened, can't help being frightened." When, early in 1850, her father had an asthma attack every letter from home made her heart race. She was furious with Henrietta for innocently remarking that such illnesses must be expected since their father was getting old (he was sixty-five) and dashed off a list of people she knew who were older than Mr Barrett and whose health and minds were "brilliant". But the distance between Florence and London depressed her and made her long to be in Paris. It was not that she was unhappy in Florence – on the contrary – but that the ties of family pulled harder than ever now that she had a child of her own. Underneath her emotional reasons for wanting to move to Paris, to be near London, were more practical ones. In Florence there was not enough social and intellectual stimulation of the right kind. It was a paradoxical situation: on the one hand, she and Robert were so happy they wanted no interruptions but, on the other, they relished and benefited from certain interruptions. A visit that autumn from Margaret Fuller, the American writer with controversial views on women's rights, now married to an Italian, was greatly relished. In Paris, the opportunities for such encounters would be many.

But there could be no thought of moving anywhere during the winter – and what a winter. This was one of the rare occasions when Elizabeth admitted that Italy had let her down: "Arno frozen, snow in the streets, icicles in certain situations . . . not for five and twenty years has there been such a frost." But she could not go out in any case because she was once more pregnant and being very careful indeed. Her own fertility pleased and astonished her: she was now forty-three and yet had conceived only seven months after the birth of Pen, making a total of four pregnancies in three years. This time, she wanted a daughter. Unhappily, at the end of November she began to bleed and, though Dr Harding said this was not necessarily a sign of miscarrying, she was less optimistic. By Christmas, she was proved right. The miscarriage caused her "vexation and disappointment certainly" but she got over it rapidly, announcing that her little boy "does for us very well". She adored him more every day and Robert had to ask her to try not to be so "offensively maternal". She spoiled her son shamelessly, and acknowledged she did, but even then queried what so called "spoiling" meant. She would admit only that Pen lacked discipline, and she commented to Miss Mitford that the root of this lay in her fear and Robert's of being the unpopular one: "Robert and I contend who shall NOT cross him in any of his wishes." Yet, so far as she could judge, this did Pen little harm. He had a "sweet sunshiney temper", and was a delight to play with. Elizabeth wrote to Henrietta once that "Robert spent the whole of last Sunday morning between breakfast and church time in learning to spin a top". She herself stood and watched him desperately trying to get it to work, saying he considered it his "religious duty" to make it do so. The sheer fun they had buying toys and then playing with them speaks for itself.

Otherwise, their life was quiet. Margaret Fuller's visit was almost the only social excitement of that 1849–1850 winter and gave Elizabeth material for letters over a long period. She was, as usual, flattered that such an eminent person should seek her out and eager to show she appreciated Mme d'Ossoli's (as she now was) compliment. She knew her work and admired her for it but kept her real opinions to herself. Mme d'Ossoli's classic work had appeared in 1845, *Woman in the 19th Century and Kindred Papers relating to the Sphere, Condition and Duties of Woman*. Elizabeth had read this and other works (on art as well as women's rights) and, though impressed, told Mrs Ogilvy, "*Don't read her writings* because they are quite below and unworthy of her."[3] The reason Mme d'Ossoli was in Florence was that she and her husband had just fled from Rome where the Republic they supported had just been overthrown.[4] She was writing a history of this event: something that intrigued Elizabeth far more than any tract on women's rights. But what thrilled her most about becoming friends with Mme d'Ossoli – several other visits followed the first – was that, apart from being "one of the out and out REDS", she had actually met George Sand in Paris. There could be no greater accolade. More and more, Elizabeth day dreamed about Paris and the possibility of genuflecting before the great George Sand. Robert cautiously agreed that perhaps they could *try* Paris after their long delayed return visit to London. No sooner was this decided than, as Elizabeth described it to Arabel, their plans were "caught in a net": she was pregnant yet again. Her disappointment was particularly keen because, although balanced by her delight in being given another chance to bear a daughter, she had good reasons for wanting to be in London that particular summer. Henrietta had finally married Surtees Cook on 6th April at St James's, Westminster. Mr Barrett's permission had been asked and refused. None of Henrietta's brothers attended the wedding in order not to antagonise their father unnecessarily, though they considered that Henrietta and Surtees had acted honourably, and made their support known. Elizabeth grieved for her father. She was concerned, too, for Arabel, now thirty-six, the only unmarried daughter left sisterless in gloomy Wimpole Street. Henrietta had only angered her father more by requesting his permission to marry: he said she was a hypocrite since she had already made up her mind to marry Surtees, a man without sufficient means and whose religious beliefs were unacceptable.[5] Elizabeth was contemptuous when she heard this – "I cannot under the circumstances think an objection of the kind tenable by a third person . . ." – but relieved that a letter from Henrietta asking her advice did not arrive till it was too late. She thought "no advice *ought* to be given on any subject of the kind". Her own letter back to her sister was full of joy – "You will be very happy Henrietta and all fear is stilled when I think of you" – but it also carried a warning. Elizabeth staked her claim to Arabel "if any cause should dislodge her from her present home without providing her with another of her own . . ." To make it perfectly clear, she wrote, "Arabel belongs to me," and told Henrietta "that is a fixed thing" rather in the tone her father used to write "there is no appeal".

All through June, Elizabeth was as careful as possible in an attempt to keep the baby she well knew might represent her last chance to have a daughter. She lay thinking of Henrietta much of the time. The sisters she missed were the only ones who could provide her with what she called that "slip-slop" of female gossip, the sole closeness and pleasure which Robert could not quite give her. What exacerbated this feeling was the departure for Naples of her neighbour Mrs Ogilvy with whom she had grown to enjoy at least a faint shadow of the real thing. The more Elizabeth thought of her married sister, the more ridiculous she thought it that the Surtees Cooks did not come to live in Florence. She began to exert pressure on her sister to be "sensible" and come, and was impatient with Henrietta's apologetic reply that she did not think she *could* live outside England. Such patriotism was "sublime" indeed, commented Elizabeth at her most sarcastic, especially when England had "the worst climate in the world". In a cross mood, she told her sister she supposed she knew best but really it was hard to understand how anyone could wilfully deprive themselves of the chance to "quadruple their income" and free themselves of those necessary "small stringent economies". It was ironic that, as she boasted to Henrietta of the cheapness of Florence, Robert was once more in a panic about money. Money that should have arrived – from the *David Lyon* shares – had not. He did not know if they could even afford to rent a summer place to get out of Florence during the hottest months. In July 1850, when the thermometer stood at 86° Fahrenheit in the evening, it was clear that something would have to be done. For the first time in their married life, Robert left Elizabeth, three months' pregnant, to go and inspect a likely villa in nearby Siena. He was away for only twenty-four hours but all day she felt, as she wrote to Mrs Ogilvy, as though she had lost her heart. She sat up until midnight, "perfectly miserable", then fell asleep only to be woken at three in the morning by Robert's return. Rather than stay a night away from her he had hitched a lift back from Siena with two priests. But his journey had been fruitless: Siena was "far from desirable".

It turned out to be fortunate that Robert had thought so, because on 25th July Elizabeth had her most serious miscarriage of all and without medical assistance (hard to come by in a remote villa) she would have died. She bled so heavily and profusely that Dr Harding resorted to packing her body in ice to stop the haemorrhaging. For two days, Robert sat at her side, the sight of her "poor, white face" tearing at his heart. He held her hand and talked constantly to keep up her courage. He had no need to do so. She wrote afterwards that she knew how near to dying she was and that she determined that if will power could keep her alive, it would. Other times, near death, she had prayed for it to come; now, she fought it off because, as she put it, she had "a Robert and a Penini". On the third day, the bleeding began to stop and exhaustion became the main danger. She was literally drained of strength. For ten more days her condition was critical but afterwards she began to recover rapidly. Dr Harding, immensely relieved, told Robert he had never seen "such an excessive case". Just as Elizabeth was out of danger, Pen fell ill with sunstroke one August day. His head was hot and heavy, his eyes "glassy, staring", and he lay "half in a stupor" which in a hyperactive young child was very alarming. Elizabeth was distraught and feared the worst, but Pen recovered. Dr Harding nevertheless said he should be removed from Florence and Robert decided they would have to go to Siena after all. On August 31st they left by train, with Elizabeth in a "miserably helpless state" and Pen looking little better. Robert had to carry her to the train from the carriage and she saw the pitying expressions of the other passengers who clearly thought she would never survive the journey. She wrote to Mrs Ogilvy that, when she looked in the mirror before she left, she saw "a perfectly white and black face, the eyes being obliterated by large blots of blackness . . ."

Two weeks later, she was able to walk a mile. It seemed to Elizabeth herself a miracle. All other illnesses left her prostrate for months but she had a remarkable facility for recovering from miscarriages (and her one confinement) with ease. It did not, she admitted, make sense but she was grateful. What deepened her gratitude was the news which Robert had delayed breaking to her until now: Mme d'Ossoli, her husband and their child had all been drowned when their ship was wrecked in a storm. "Oh Great God, how terrible are Thy judgements!" wrote Elizabeth to Mrs Ogilvy. She lay recovering from her own latest brush with death in the villa Poggio dei Venti. This charming small house was two miles from Siena with a large garden in which Pen could run wild. It was not a romantic place, like Bagni di Lucca, but it was "verdant and various and exquisitely undulating" and the green lanes reminded her of England. Pen, now aged seventeen months, who had arrived looking like "a wax doll with the rouge left off", was back to his rosy-cheeked self. He adored the animals – a yellow dog, a horse, a pig – and ran everywhere till he was exhausted. It had not been easy, in the Casa Guidi, to cope with Pen's love of the terrace (which they had had to rope in). Here in Siena there need be no restrictions. Seeing her baby so well and strong convinced Elizabeth that this was the time to wean him, something she dreaded not just because it was likely to be difficult but because it marked the passing of a stage. She had defended protracted breast-feeding on the (excellent) grounds that it prevented gastric upsets but she knew it had to stop sometime. It was already an odd contradiction to see Pen racing round the garden then climbing on Signora Bondi's knee to suck her milk. So bitter aloes were smeared on the robust wet nurse's nipples and the puzzled, irritable Pen tried to work out what had happened. Elizabeth noted, with sympathy and amusement, his attempt to get his nurse to move seats, obviously hoping there was something wrong with her location rather than lactation. But finally he gave her up and switched to his new passion, grapes and prosciutto.

They returned to Florence in the first week in October. Elizabeth spent the next months writing a second part to "Casa Guidi Windows", expressing in it her disillusionment with the way in which things had turned out since she wrote the first part in such triumph. But in her letters she talked more of Pen than politics, fascinated by his emergence as a person from the chrysalis of babyhood. "A most curious child he is," she told Mrs Ogilvy, especially in his methods of communicating. Spurning speech – "he won't talk a bit" – he used gestures and touch to indicate both what he wanted and how he was feeling. It was easy to deduce that he wanted his shoe put on when he stuck out his foot but harder to interpret what an ear-splitting scream in the street meant. Sometimes he not only screamed but fell down on his knees and folded his arms across his chest which actually meant he had heard music coming from a church and wanted to be taken in. As Robert remarked drily it was "as well to have the eye teeth and Puseyistical crisis over together". Elizabeth thought this kind of extravagant behaviour a sign of great imagination in their son, but Robert was less convinced, remarking, "I hope that child is not mad, Ba." Mad or not, both parents were convinced of his many talents. At the age of one, he could sing the nursery rhyme, "Margery Daw", even if he would not try to talk; before he was two he could hold and use a pencil; and from birth (or so his mother swore) any kind of music sent him into ecstasies. When he was two, he acquired the habit of sitting on his father's knee, while Robert played the piano, and then trying to imitate him. But what struck them most forcibly were the signs of independence he displayed: "he wants nobody's sympathy," wrote Elizabeth approvingly. He clung to neither of them. They shared their little routines with him – he shared their coffee, taking a spoonful in turn from each parent – but also created his own. It was strange, Elizabeth thought, watching such a young child being solemnly "busy". As he trotted about on his own self-imposed tasks Elizabeth observed the change in his physique now that Signora Bondi was no longer fuelling him. His true shape showed. "He looks like a small Puck," Elizabeth wrote (and sometimes behaved like one by "upsetting water jugs" or "pulling brooms to pieces" not to mention "cutting up frocks with scissors"). Frequently, she described him as a fairy or an elf and told Sarianna she would "fancy he must have begun from a mustard seed". Robert measured him weekly, convinced he would be tall (he never was) but Elizabeth cared nothing for height; his loving nature was more important. "If someone pricks a finger with a needle he begins to cry," she wrote with satisfaction not embarrassment. Henrietta, whose first son was born on 23rd January 1851, was given a lecture on how love for a child grows as the child grows and changes.

By the beginning of 1851, Elizabeth was strong again. She took her longest walk ever, to San Miniato from the Casa Guidi and then down the avenue from the Poggio Imperiale. This year *must* be the year, she vowed, that they should go to England. Robert agreed. He renewed their lease on the Casa Guidi but arranged to sublet it at the same time. They had arranged to vacate the place on 3rd May and, as the day drew nearer, Elizabeth's excitement grew. She longed passionately to see her sisters. But there were also other reasons for wanting to be in London: she was anxious to see how she stood critically since her 1850 new volume had appeared. It had come out the previous November and contained, as well as "Sonnets from the Portuguese" (the title selected to fool people into thinking the poems were not personal), "*all* my poems worth a straw though many I should like to burn as stubble and cant". All but nine of the 1844 poems were there, as well as all those which had appeared in magazines in the interim. Her old poems were heavily revised and made a good many concessions to those who had thought her rhymes impossible and her language archaic. The result was sharper and cleaner. The contemporary critics failed to notice this. She was still attacked for obscurity, strange images, faulty rhymes and affectation. *The Spectator* gave the unkindest cut of all in doubting if Mrs Browning had made much progress. It was the one criticism Elizabeth hated but she took it well, admitting the basic truth that apart from the sonnets there was little there that was entirely original. What *was* original was "Casa Guidi Windows" both parts of which appeared only in May 1851, as she prepared to travel. She had high hopes of this poem.

She had heard, of course, that she had been suggested the year before as the new Poet Laureate and had been amused rather than flattered. This was lucky because, although it has been taken extremely seriously ever since, it was not a serious suggestion. The recommendation was made anonymously in a literary news column in *The Athenaeum* (in fact written by Chorley). Immediately after Wordsworth's death, in its issue of 27th April, *The Athenaeum* began a campaign mocking the office of Poet Laureate and advocating its abolition. It said it was "an offensive title" and a form of "intellectual servitude" which no self-respecting poet would accept. It was in this deeply unflattering context that Elizabeth's name was now mentioned. In the next issue after it was suggested, *The Athenaeum* emphasised the post was "so meaningless" that "any poet – or indeed no poet – would do as well as any other". The campaign continued over several issues and their final word on the subject was that if the ludicrous post were kept and Elizabeth were appointed, this would "in a manner recompense two poets by a single act". In fact Tennyson became the next Poet Laureate.

As she prepared to leave Florence, Elizabeth had mixed feelings about going back to London. The joy of being re-united with her beloved sisters was balanced by her dread that her father would continue to ignore her, a sorrow less easy to face when she would be round the corner from him. Robert, more than Elizabeth, feared the return to England. Much as he yearned for his father and sister, he dreaded going home and seeing his mother's things without her presence. There was also his wife's health to consider. In Florence, she was as safe as he could make her; in London, she could hardly be protected from both emotional and physical strain. In many ways he wished never to leave the Casa Guidi. But the visit home had been their object for so long, it simply had to be made.

Chapter Fifteen

THE Brownings, Wilson and Flush left the Casa Guidi at six o'clock on the morning of 3rd May 1851, in the rain. The Ogilvys, long since back from Naples, shared their carriage and were to accompany them as far as Venice via Bologna, Parma, Modena and Mantua. The three women and Pen had the comfort of being inside the coach while Robert and Mr Ogilvy travelled on the outside. Each night at the inns where they stayed Robert took a single room to himself while Elizabeth and Wilson slept together with the baby beside them. It was, Elizabeth explained to her sisters, much more convenient to have Wilson handy at dressing time and to have all their overnight things in one carpet bag. While Wilson attended to the two-year-old Pen and engaged in the exhausting task of getting him to settle down for the night, Elizabeth became quite adept in other ways. Once, at a very cold inn near Bologna, she was triumphant because she managed to lay and light a fire. They were all glad to reach Mantua where the railroad began, and from then on the journey was easy. They swept "along the glittering snow Alps as in a vision – then shot into the heart of Venice".

Elizabeth was stunned by the beauty of Venice. It was the first time in her life that any place had exceeded her expectations. She wrote to Arabel that from everything she had read she had visualised "floating sea pavements, marble palaces with sea weed on their marble steps and black gondolas sweeping through sunlit and moonlit silence".[1] She had imagined a ghostly, eerie city at which one gazed and shivered and then recoiled from so beautiful but so melancholy a sight. The reality was so violently different that it sent her into "a sort of rapture". What she had not envisaged was the sheer exuberance of Venice, the vitality, the glowing colours and the effect of the glittering water everywhere. From the windows of the apartment they had rented on the Grand Canal Elizabeth looked down on the life below and never grew tired of it. "I can't describe what the scene is," she wrote to Arabel, "the mixture of intricate beauty and open glory . . . the mystery of the rippling streets and soundless gondolas." She liked Venice better than Florence or even Paris and knew within hours of arriving that she would be happy to live there forever. Unfortunately, neither Robert nor Wilson felt the same way. Robert soon became "uncomfortable and nervous" and could neither eat nor sleep, while Wilson was sick and complained of a continual headache. Elizabeth was impatient with both of them: she liked "these soft, relaxing climates" and so did Pen.

In spite of his indisposition, Robert gallantly led "a truly Venetian life" with his eager wife. They went in a gondola to the Lido, to a festa at Chioggia and even to the opera and to a play. They took Pen with them to "a day theatre", rather against Robert's wishes, paying eighteen pence to have a whole box to themselves. The play was a heroic verse melodrama in five acts but, as Elizabeth wrote to Mrs Ogilvy (who had left Venice by then), it was only in the fifth that Pen showed signs of being "a little tired". He started to sing a song of his own composition which had a complicated melody but only two words ("Mama" and "Papa"). He also did a little shouting to the audience and a lot of clapping in the wrong places. When an actor was very convincingly put in chains, Pen started to scream and Robert removed him saying that "it was quite wrong to expose a young child to the shows of grief before he could possibly discern the meaning of the imitation of Art". Reluctantly, Elizabeth agreed that experience had proved him right and was obliged to cancel another theatrical outing for Pen. She realised Robert was becoming increasingly irritated with her determination to treat their two-year-old son as an adult. They had already had "words" – just as she had once said married people were supposed to – over how she dressed Pen. Robert thought it time that he looked more like a boy. People were always admiring his son as the prettiest of little girls and he did not like it. Elizabeth jeered at him and swept aside his objections, once more repeating that it was absurd to declare some clothes for children masculine and others feminine. She argued "if you put him into a coat and waistcoat forthwith he only would look like a small angel travestied". As far as she was concerned, children of two were neither boys nor girls but "neuter".

But it was not only Robert who disapproved of her treatment of Pen; Wilson did so too. It was not so much the fancy clothes Wilson objected to as the hours Pen kept and the unsuitable nature of some of his activities. Elizabeth might say, indulgently, how Pen enjoyed a late dinner but it was Wilson who had to calm the overstimulated gourmet afterwards. The child had trouble sleeping in any case and would often wake up very agitated when she had finally managed to get him to sleep. She prophesied "nervous collapse" which Elizabeth dismissed as non-sense and put down to Wilson's general sulkiness. The previous year Wilson had been let down by her intended, Mr Righi. Elizabeth had told Henrietta that Wilson had been "very sensible" and was "quite over" the shock, but the truth was she remained depressed. Elizabeth observed with alarm that her maid grew thinner and thinner as she herself thrived. Robert was all for leaving sooner than intended because, quite apart from Wilson's condition and his own feelings of malaise, Venice was too expensive. He commented that they would soon be reduced to bread and cheese. Elizabeth was unperturbed. As far as she was concerned, bread alone would do.

They left Venice for Milan on 13th June. They went by Padua, where Elizabeth insisted on making a literary pilgrimage to Arquà to see Petrarch's house. Once more, Wilson was left with Pen while his parents struggled in the burning heat to reach their destination on foot after their coach driver had told them the last mile was too steep for his horses. Elizabeth was exhausted but reckoned it worth the gruelling climb to see Petrarch's "little, little room . . . the homely look of that room". She and Robert were both moved to tears just by the sight of it. A sixteen-hour coach ride followed from Padua to Verona and so to Milan. Pen enjoyed it hugely: "think of that child!" wrote Elizabeth fondly. Wilson, a trifle grimly, waited for the reaction after sixteen hours of bouncing and shrieking in a coach. In Milan they stayed two days to rest before continuing to Switzerland. Only Elizabeth did not rest; instead, she climbed the two hundred and fifty steps to the top of the cathedral. This more than anything she had ever done demonstrated how strong she now was: at Pisa, five years before, she had been quite unable to contemplate climbing the leaning tower. Whenever Robert attempted to veto some expedition as too arduous on this trip she brushed his anxieties aside. When they reached Lugano, she was so eager to include Lake Maggiore on their itinerary that she once more left Pen with Wilson and went off with Robert to visit it.

Her own theory about her renewed energy was that having a child had somehow mysteriously cleared her whole system but there were more prosaic explanations. The last five years had been spent in what was on the whole a mild, sunny climate of the type greatly beneficial to anyone with incipient bronchial troubles. During them she had been eating and exercising very nearly as well as a normal healthy person and she had greatly reduced her dependence on opium. And yet, in spite of climbing so many steps and both feeling and appearing well, Elizabeth's new found good health was not stable. She was only strong by comparison with her former state of health and Robert understood how fragile her recovery was. He correctly saw it as dependent on certain conditions: Elizabeth was well *if* the climate was mild, *if* she ate, rested and exercised as directed and *if* emotional distress was avoided. She was cured not of her tendency to bronchitis and other lung infections but of depression, unhealthy living habits and the conviction that she never could be well.

As they set off to go through the St Gotthard Pass, Robert was worried. They had arrived at Lucerne with only ten francs and his relief at finding the *David Lyon* income awaiting them was spoiled by discovering that this time it was a mere £50. He told Elizabeth they could not possibly continue on the extended sightseeing tour they had planned but must push on with all haste to Paris and hope to find that a little money from their poetry had come in. Disappointed and a little resentful, Elizabeth had to agree. Robert was firm, announcing there was no room for argument. The passage through the Alps so thrilled her ("to the soul") that she found herself uncharacteristically floundering for words. It had snowed heavily that winter and even now, in July, the banks of snow towered above them as they passed along the narrow road cut through it. Elizabeth had the temerity to sit on the outside of the coach some of the way, wrapped in a double shawl so that only her eyes showed. She thanked God for having allowed her to see a sight so "terrible, wonderful" and was proud that Pen appreciated the privilege too. All the way the child had exclaimed and pointed and clapped and sighed and rolled his eyes: Elizabeth saw it as proof of his incredibly developed aesthetic sense. Robert and Wilson thought it mere affectation and alleged he was only imitating his mother. Elizabeth did not deign to argue. They went direct from Strasbourg to Paris, stopping only for quarter of an hour for breakfast and half an hour for dinner during the whole twenty-four hours. Even Elizabeth wondered whether this was too much for a two-year-old but Pen loved it: "poor little babe slept at night and laughed in the day and came into Paris as fresh in spirits as if just alighted from the morning star, screaming out with delight at the shops!"

Robert, on the other hand, was certainly not feeling "fresh in spirits".

Paris depressed him. It rained the first two days and he had booked them into a poor hotel. Elizabeth declared she felt as if she had "dropped into a new brilliant world" but Robert felt he had dropped into problems. There was no money waiting in Paris and he was unsure for how long they could manage. Elizabeth was exasperated: the money from their poetry and from Kenyon (who had been paying them an annual allowance of £100 since their marriage, out of pure generosity, but who tended to forget that it was due) would come, so what did it matter when it came? Robert simply could not get her to understand his horror of anticipating income. But she was much more understanding about the other weight he carried, the dread of visiting his now motherless home. At one point, he did not know if he could put himself through this ordeal at all and since his father and sister were willing to come to Paris it was not strictly necessary that he should. Elizabeth passionately wanted to see her sisters but bravely suggested they cancel their visit to London altogether and she would cling on to the (faint) hope that both her sisters could come to her. In one way, it gave her the alibi she was seeking: she dreaded London herself since it symbolised pain and trouble.

It was the realisation of how cruelly disappointed Arabel would be that persuaded Robert to brave London after all. Henrietta might manage a visit to Paris but Arabel could see no possibility of doing so. They decided to go for a short time to London and, though the decision was "full of pain", Robert felt it was the right one. Elizabeth wrote to Kenyon that he could expect them at the end of July but that she would have "no heart to go out of a very dark corner". England was "dear" but also "a place of bitterness". She felt more for Italy and even France. Paris pleased her immensely. It was, she wrote, a country city, full of greenery, and yet so civilised, full of "brilliant life". She felt near enough to London to hope that in time everyone she wanted to see would eventually come to Paris. Almost immediately after their arrival her Uncle Hedley, passing through on his way to his house in Tours, came to visit them. The transformation he saw in his niece astonished him and, as for her child, he was "fabulous". There were also others, even more interesting to Elizabeth, who passed through Paris. Tennyson, for example, the new Poet Laureate, arrived hard on the heels of the Brownings and, hearing of their presence, invited them to dinner. When the summons came, Elizabeth had just returned to their hotel where she had collapsed with fatigue after a tiring visit to the Louvre. But, confronted with Tennyson's invitation, she was revived in an instant, ("resurrected"), and swept aside Robert's reminder that on her own admission she was too exhausted to stir from the room again. The mere thought of meeting the great man whose *In Memoriam* she had just read and admired was enough to re-vitalise her completely. Robert, who did not share her "organ of veneration", as she put it, was obliged to take her. The dinner was a great success. Tennyson, who sensed a communion of spirit between the Brownings, was charmed by them. Told of their impending visit to London, he at once offered them the use of his house at Twickenham. Elizabeth, thinking mainly of the autograph, was thrilled by the letter he wrote for them to present to his two servants still in residence. Robert was "touched to the heart" by Tennyson's offer. It warmed him towards London, reminding him of all the friends there whom he had missed without realising it. His wife did not know half of them and he longed to introduce her.

But Elizabeth had asked Arabel to look for "a mousehole" somewhere near home, as cheap as possible, and she had found one: three small cramped rooms round the corner from Wimpole Street at 26 Devonshire Street. A visit that was destined from the first to be traumatic was made worse by the location of these lodgings. Elizabeth felt as though the clock had been put back and she had never escaped. July that year was cool and wet. Everything seemed dark, cramped, dirty. Elizabeth was immediately affected by her surroundings. She blamed the weather for the cough she quickly developed, forgetting she had been coughing in Florence before they had left but had dismissed it as nothing. Robert, before his visit to his home at New Cross, was himself on the edge of breakdown. Once they were settled in their mousehole, he went off alone to his old home. Though emotional, the visit was not as terrible as he had feared and his pain was partially balanced by the joy of being reunited with his father and sister. Elizabeth was glad when he returned but still felt, she wrote to Mrs Ogilvy, as if she were "hanging on the sharp edge of some strange whirling planet – and how it cuts!" She felt oppressed by the weather, by her cough and by "the moral influences" around her.[2]

By this she meant her father. His presence in nearby Wimpole Street – a few hundred yards away – agitated her. It was not that she was afraid of him so much as acutely sensitive, now that she was so physically close, to the pain he was both suffering and inflicting. To say she was bowed down under "moral influences" was precisely right. All the old dilemmas, pushed below the surface of her happy new life, returned to torment her which she found emotionally exhausting, even though she was as confident as ever that she had made the right choice. She assured Mrs Martin that "so far from regretting my marriage, it has made the happiness and honour of my life and every unkindness received from my own house makes me press nearer to the tenderest and noblest of human hearts . . . I neither regret my marriage nor the manner of it because the manner of it was the necessity of the act."[3] But, though she meant every word of this, she found it hard, living so near her old home and yet not welcome in it, to keep her mind from "bitter thoughts". She had for a long time hoped that the fact that her letters had not been returned to her *might* mean they had at least been secretly read by her father. Once in London, Robert wrote to Mr Barrett "a manly true straight forward letter" (Elizabeth said) begging for a reconciliation. Elizabeth thought his appeal was irresistible, telling Mrs Martin it was "so touching" she could not "believe in the probability of it being read in vain". She wrote too, asking yet again, after five long years of punishment and consequent suffering, for forgiveness. Mr Barrett did not reply to her but he replied to Robert in a letter since lost. It was, said Elizabeth, "violent and unsparing", but a more sickening shock to her was the return of all the letters she had sent her father from Italy.[4] They were unopened. Some of them, after the death of Robert's mother, were sealed with black wax and could well have announced, as she pointed out bitterly to Mrs Martin, the death of her child. But this piece of cruelty revealed to her an aspect of her father she had not recognised: he was implacable. She began to doubt whether he had ever loved her, as she understood the word. She now had a child herself and knew that however severe the trial, there were no circumstances in which she would cut Pen off. It would be like cutting her heart out. She began to wonder if pride was more important to her father than love. She could not identify with this. It left her confused and intensely distressed to see the extremes to which he was prepared to go. She had understood very well what his pain and misery would be like, she had known very well what she was doing to him, but what she had not known was that his love for her was not strong enough to grant her, in time, some small measure of forgiveness when he had exacted any due he cared to name.

But at least her brothers did not prove so obdurate. Elizabeth had always been more angry than upset that they had not stood by her, but she had missed them nevertheless, especially George upon whom she had mistakenly relied. He had written her the occasional note since his first furious reaction to her marriage but she could not claim they were reconciled. Robert now made it his job to win George over and compensate a little for his failure with Mr Barrett. Robert's letter, which followed George to Wales where he was on holiday, was answered instantly. His reply was "kind" and said he would be with them that evening. He was as good as his word and they were once more "good friends". Elizabeth told all this to Mrs Martin and said she had "seen in his eyes that I was still something more to him than a stone to throw away". She realised Henrietta's experience had influenced this most just of all her brothers: Henrietta had behaved with absolute honour and had still been brutally cast off. George had stood by her and was now prepared to let bygones be bygones in Elizabeth's case. The rest of her brothers also came to pay their respects and show they felt five years a long enough sentence of banishment. Occy, twenty-two when she had last seen him and young for his age, had grown so broad she hardly recognised him and she could not get used to his "whiskers" which highly amused her. She was comforted by these emotional reunions but also a little hurt that afterwards her brothers did not call as often as she would have liked, now that she was living so near.

To be with Arabel was naturally an undiluted delight. Elizabeth was relieved to find her sister looking well; in fact, she was quite surprised to find everyone looking "rather better than worse for these five long years". She saw Arabel every day and even visited her in Wimpole Street while her father was in the City. This was an undeniably masochistic choice, for there was no need for her to go to Wimpole Street at all since Arabel was perfectly willing and able to come the short distance to her lodgings and always expected to do so. But 50 Wimpole Street had a fatal and terrible attraction for Elizabeth. It made her shiver to go in there but, on the other hand, the house drew her like a magnet. Once inside, she saw it with eyes made objective by her long absence. She found it dark and stuffy and not nearly as comfortable or imposing as she had remembered. She thought it could do with "a good clean" now that she looked at it with new, housewifely enthusiasm and that it had a decidedly old-bachelor air. It was distressing to think of Arabel cooped up in that heavily masculine environment but she had to admit that her sister seemed remarkably content and not the sad waif of her imagination. She did not see Henrietta immediately but there was a deliriously happy reunion when she managed to come up from Somerset, where she and Surtees lived, bringing her nine-month-old son Altham with her. Elizabeth could not get over her nephew's "gigantic" size, especially when compared to the fragile two-year-old Pen, and she saw at once how Henrietta sparkled with the joy her marriage had brought her. The three sisters talked and talked and talked: at last, that "slip-slop" of gossip about babies and people, matters mundane and domestic, all incomprehensibly trivial to any listener outside the magic circle (including Robert). When Henrietta had to return to Somerset Elizabeth wrote to her, "I shall live a long time on thoughts of having seen your beaming face," and told her that "the perfume of you will last to me for hours and days and weeks and months".

Robert was equally happy, enjoying his own form of "slip-slop" gossip. He was much more pleased than he had imagined he would be to find himself once more part of the London literary circle and decided he had underestimated its worth. To Elizabeth, the entertainments provided for them were "a great dazzling heap of things strange and new" but to Robert they were simply a return to a way of life he had once known (though he had often denied the extent to which he had participated in it when trying to persuade his wife he was quite happy in Pisa). Kenyon invited them to dinner and there Elizabeth met for the first time Robert's old friend Carlyle and a gathering of important critics. She had sworn she would go only to Kenyon's and nowhere else but could not resist John Forster's invitation to a dinner at Thames Ditton which turned out to be a splendid affair where she met another collection of famous names. It was equally impossible to refuse Carlyle's invitation to dine in Chelsea or Fanny Kemble's, delivered in person, to see her act in *Hamlet*. People also visited them in Devonshire Street, though, as ever, only for tea: Elizabeth's pleasure at "doing hospitality" to the extent of providing proper meals was very short lived indeed. She was particularly gratified that Horne came, "miles upon miles just to drink tea", and so at last she met him. And of course Miss Mitford came and was rapturously received. All this was exciting but overwhelming. Elizabeth wrote to Mrs Ogilvy that she had not yet managed to finish a cup of tea because she was always just half way through it when someone called. It was "kindness on all sides" and, though tired, she was amazed to find she enjoyed such an active social life. It was the familiar paradox at work: she liked peace and quiet and it was best for her physical health but on the other hand her mind and spirits craved stimulation. Robert, however, frankly loved a good social life – though he was not as uncritical a worshipper of the famous as Elizabeth could be – and it never tired him. He was far more likely to be tired when inactive and bored.

All this "whirling about" (which was how Elizabeth thought of it) came to an abrupt end for her after a month in London when Wilson went home to see her mother who lived near Sheffield. Elizabeth had always realised that of course her maid must go home but she had been under the rather extraordinary impression that Wilson would take Pen with her. It was a shock when Wilson made it plain she intended to do no such thing. Ever since they had arrived in London the child had been unsettled and fractious. He hardly slept, hardly left Wilson's side and was twice as demanding as usual (which was very demanding indeed). So Wilson for once put her foot down and said she wanted two weeks' holiday on her own with her mother. Elizabeth had not the slightest desire to deprive Wilson of this but nevertheless she was plainly aggrieved and this crept into her correspondence. She had been magnanimously prepared to let her darling child go with his nurse to be shown off to her family and now her kindness was thrown in her face. What she simply could not understand was that Wilson chose to leave Pen behind. The minute her maid had gone, Elizabeth rapidly acquired an appreciation of her choice. The tyranny of a two-year-old, from which she had always been protected, now broke upon her. She wrote to Mrs Martin that Pen was "in a state of deplorable grief" from the moment Wilson, or Lily as he called her (though her name was Elizabeth), left him. He would not let his mother out of his sight, obviously thinking she would be the next to desert him. "I hold him in my arms at night," Elizabeth wrote, "dress and wash him in the morning, walk out with him, and am not allowed to read or write above three minutes at a time." It was a catalogue of the life of many a mother of a two-year-old, but to Elizabeth it was a revelation. On the one hand it made her proud to be a "proper" mother but on the other she was appalled at how it affected her as a writer. Three minutes a day to write was an absurdity; her very life had always depended on having uninterrupted hours. She was breathless with relief when Pen made a friend of a little girl in the same house and played in the passage with her. This extended the three minutes' freedom to five though she commented gloomily "even that is doubtful". Arabel sent her maid to look after him but Pen rejected her and would not even go with Arabel herself though he appeared to like and trust her. There was no suggestion that Robert should take him over. Elizabeth might applaud a man who was not ashamed to rock a cradle but she seemed to think Robert could not replace Wilson: that was her responsibility. She fulfilled it conscientiously, though doing so reduced her to "a tremble" and her thoughts to "a crumble". She was alarmed to see that in spite of her care Pen looked pale. He announced that he wanted to go back to Paris, and so did she. Her cough had grown worse: "the lungs seem to labour in the heavy air," she wrote to Mrs Martin, adding, "oh, it is so unlike the air of the continent." England was "dear" because of her family and friends but otherwise "detestable". The climate, she vowed, was even worse than she remembered it (though in fact weather statistics for the period do not justify her damning verdict: there was some sunshine, no sharp drops in temperature, and no excessive rainfall).

There was no doubt that Robert would have preferred to stay in London. Elizabeth confided in Mrs Jameson that it was "pure joy to him". He loved seeing so much of his father and sister and adored being with his literary friends. She went so far as to estimate "I do believe he would have been capable of never leaving England again had such an arrangement been practicable for us . . ." But it was not: Robert could see how she was suffering. He knew he had to get her out of London before any fog arrived and he made arrangements accordingly. Wilson had long since returned to them and on 26th September 1851 they departed for Paris travelling in the company of Carlyle (who used Robert shamelessly as a dogsbody to save himself the trouble of having to see to luggage and fight for seats). Robert was sick on the crossing, as was everyone, and was as exhausted as his wife by the time they reached Paris. Elizabeth's spirits immediately rose. Robert's sank. The moment she reached Dieppe, Elizabeth stopped coughing with miraculous (but also suspicious) ease. It was, she announced, due to the change of air. French air was "very light and clear" and that is all there was to it. Robert trudged around Paris in this light clear air trying to find lodgings in the Madeleine district, to be near Kenyon on his approaching visit, but everything in that fashionable quarter was too expensive. Elizabeth reported back to Miss Mitford that they were like "doves turned out of a dovecote". But by mid-October they had found "a very pleasant apartment" on the Champs-Elysées. Elizabeth wrote enthusiastically of the "pretty sitting room full of comfortable chairs" to Henrietta – another of England's faults had been, apparently, that it lacked "sympathetic" chairs. The room had two big windows through which the sun poured and a terrace "big enough to be a garden" upon which she could watch "all the brilliant life of Paris sweep to and fro". Robert was amused at her home-making instinct – "the very instinct of making a sympathetic

[257]

home that works in me" – and teased her because she bustled about the apartment pushing "about the chairs and tables in a sort of distracted way" until she felt satisfied she had made them her own. Pen was a reformed character, happy to have Wilson safely back. To complete his happiness there were "four Punches in the immediate neighbourhood! There's civilisation for you!"

It was civilisation to which Elizabeth was looking forward. It might be argued that London was just as civilised as Paris but from her point of view it was not. In Paris, she went out without coughing, firmly believing the air was safe for her. She adored Parisian street life every bit as much as Pen did, finding it in many ways more colourful and varied than that in her beloved Florence. All her regular correspondents – her sisters, Miss Mitford, Mrs Jameson, Mrs Ogilvy, Mrs Martin and now also her brother George – were treated to lively descriptions of everything she and Pen saw and heard. There were "dancing dogs, turn-about horses", wonderful shop windows, magnificently dressed people and every kind of crowd to mingle with. Elizabeth brought her sister Henrietta up-to-date with that most Parisian of all attractions – fashion – knowing it would appeal most to her. The novelty of the season was "point behind" (a sort of bustle) and the general style of the moment "basque dresses". It was considered "utterly barbaric . . . to wear over full petticoats". Elizabeth never missed an opportunity to show that she thought caring for fashion was frivolous, and hid her own interest in the subject by saying she had to buy new clothes only because Robert liked her to be well and modishly dressed. But her pleasure in her purchases that autumn was obvious and had little to do with Robert's opinions. She bought a bonnet – "a drawn maroon satin trimmed with velvet of the same shade, with purple flowers inside" – and, because she had been imprudent and yielded to an impulse to buy it from "a shop in a fashionable situation", it cost a scandalous sixteen shillings (or roughly Wilson's wage for one whole week's work). She also bought a new dress – "very pretty . . . black merino polka". But it was on Pen's behalf that she was most extravagant. She bought him a white felt hat with white satin ribbons and feathers and trimmings of blue, and a pair of "such ridiculous tiny trowsers up to his knees" and long white gaiters. Wilson said people turned in the street to look at her charge, to Elizabeth's gratification.

They also tended to turn in the street when they heard Pen speak. He had now added a smattering of French to his imperfect English and quaint Italian and the result was made even more bizarre because of the slight lisp which increased the puzzling effect of his peculiar mispronunciations in every language. Miss Mitford, meeting him in London, had been outraged that the child was being brought up, if not encouraged (which she suspected), in such linguistic confusion. Elizabeth was unperturbed. She simply admired the way her son made every language his own. She also thought it amusing that he dispensed with pronouns, as she herself had done as a child. It fascinated her to try to work out what Pen actually meant and her letters became full of examples that had baffled her but which she had finally solved. Her whole attitude was quite un-Victorian. The only doubt in Elizabeth's mind about the licence she allowed Pen remained over the tricky question of permitted excitements. She had to admit that there was growing evidence that Robert and Wilson were right: Pen did get over-excited and then became ill. That autumn and winter in Paris he had what sounds, from his mother's alarmed description, like a series of slight fits. As a consequence, Elizabeth conceded that perhaps Pen should lead a quiet life, a little more like that of the conventional child's (though only a little) and keep more suitable hours. Wilson was relieved. She had long believed Pen would profit from a more mundane and stable routine.

Elizabeth, too, would have benefited from such a routine but that autumn in Paris she gave way to the other side of her nature, the side that craved to walk among the stars. From the moment of their arrival she was impatient to explore Parisian literary society and for once did not pretend this was wholly for Robert's sake. She knew that unless she was very lucky she would be confined inside once the winter set in so she was eager to get out and about. On October 29th they both went to a soirée at Lady Elgin's. Lady Elgin had one of the best houses in Paris where she held Monday evening receptions. Elizabeth wanted to go for one purpose only: to meet celebrities. She was disappointed to find few present that particular Monday. She chatted to some "notables" but nobody exciting. She had instructed Robert to keep near her, in a fit of nerves at what might happen and who might come her way, but she eventually realised it was all going to be very staid and predictable. She reported to Miss Mitford with some disgust that the only refreshment seemed to be cups of "infinitesimally weak tea". It was "pleasant enough" and "no fuss" but disillusionment spoke in every line of another account to Henrietta. Elizabeth had not come to Paris to take weak tea with bores when she knew the great George Sand was breathing the same air as she was.

Elizabeth was absolutely determined to meet George Sand and expected Robert to arrange for her to do so. They had a letter of introduction, provided through Carlyle, but the problem was to have the letter delivered to her. Robert refused to leave it at a theatre where one of George Sand's plays was being performed in case it became mixed up with fan mail for the leading actress. Elizabeth had never heard of anything so ridiculous in her life – all that mattered to her was the end, not the means. Robert dithered, Elizabeth bullied and then they heard that George Sand had left Paris altogether. Elizabeth was furious and blamed Robert: "I am so vexed," she wrote to Miss Mitford, "she came, she has gone, and we haven't met!" When George Sand returned, early in 1852, Elizabeth insisted on direct action. She told Miss Mitford, "I pricked Robert up to the leap for he was inclined to sit in his chair and be proud a little." She told him "you *shan't* be proud . . . and I *won't* be proud – and we *will* see her." Robert, unable to locate George Sand's precise residence, brought himself to entrust the letter of introduction to a friend of a friend who promised to deliver it. Next day, to Elizabeth's delight, a short note came back saying that George Sand would be happy to receive them on Sunday at 3 rue Racine but that she could not absolutely guarantee to be there; she was to let them know. If Robert's troublesome pride was hurt by the offhand tone, Elizabeth's was not. She was ecstatic and pronounced the unmistakably grudging note "graceful and kind". The weather was by then bitterly cold but she announced defiantly that she intended to go "at the risk of my life". Robert found this kind of adulation only a little short of repugnant. Elizabeth did not care what he thought. At her command, he wrapped her up in shawls, with one of them completely covering her head, and rushed her into a closed, heated carriage. She took her respirator with her in case either excitement or cold air brought on a fit of coughing.[5] George Sand received them in a room with a bed in it but Elizabeth was not as shocked as Robert, maintaining sensibly, "it was the only room she has to occupy I suppose". She greeted them "very cordially", considering she was a world famous author and Elizabeth then not well known outside her own country and Robert, of course, even less well known. She kissed Elizabeth on the lips which almost made her faint. Every detail of her appearance was afterwards relayed to Miss Mitford, who was as eager as Elizabeth to discover if writer matched writings.

The answer was no. Elizabeth was surprised to find George Sand not very much taller than her own extremely small self and "a little over stout for that height". She tried hard to find something noble in George Sand's forehead and thought the eyes "dark glowing eyes as they should be". She had to admit the lower part of the face was "not so good": the teeth stuck out, the chin receded, the complexion was too sallow and the cheeks too fat. It was a relief to examine the hands and discover they were commendably small and well shaped. As for George Sand's clothes, Elizabeth was at something of a loss to describe them. Certainly, the woman did not know a "point behind" was the current thing. She had on instead "a sort of woollen grey gown with a jacket of the same material". Expectations of dress as dramatic or bizarre as her work went unfulfilled. Nor did George Sand's personality fit her novels. Elizabeth described her as lacking in animation though unaffected and natural. It sounded very much like wishful thinking when she added, "under all the quietness . . . you are aware of an intense, burning soul".[6]

Robert was aware of less exalted things. As far as he was concerned, George Sand turned out to be a rather ugly, offhand, badly dressed woman surrounded by a seedy collection of raffish young men, the sort into whose company he would not normally consider it proper to take his wife. He was also aware of being patronised, which he found insufferable. Elizabeth heatedly denied this, arguing (in a letter to her brother George) that there had not been "the least intention on her part of being otherwise than most cordial to us", admitting only that George Sand had not been very kind about her respirator which she had looked at "with disdain". It was true that no conversation of note had taken place and that there had been no feeling of rapprochement – in fact the reverse – but Elizabeth chose to interpret the encounter as a success and was glad to have made it. Robert often thought he understood his wife so completely that he had nothing more to discover about her, when the vehemence of some desire of hers, such as this passion to meet George Sand, would reveal to him that he was mistaken. But this strengthened rather than weakened their marriage, bringing them closer together rather than driving them apart. Their marriage, five years old, was still an exciting voyage of continuing discovery.

Robert received a forceful proof of this that winter. Elizabeth had never been able to talk to him fully about the death of Bro. She had written about it, sparingly, during their courtship but she had never been able to take him through the agony she had suffered. He had never pressed her. He was therefore horrified to hear that a lecturer in Paris, in delivering a talk on Elizabeth's poetry, was quoting from her friend Miss Mitford's new book, *Recollections of a Literary Life*, in which she apparently gave intimate details of how Bro was drowned. In it, Miss Mitford said of Elizabeth, "I have so often been asked what could be the shadow that had passed over that young heart . . . it seems to me right that the world should hear the story of an accident in which there was much sorrow and no blame." She then told the story of Bro's accident and its effect on Elizabeth, including one telling sentence that Elizabeth had had "a natural but a most unjust feeling that she had been in some sort the cause of this great misery". Robert could hardly believe it, since neither he nor Elizabeth had yet seen the book. Informed of what was going on by Uncle Hedley, he went to a repeat of the lecture himself. He was appalled to have the rumour confirmed and, which was worse, the lecturer also threw in entirely untrue details including "a tragedy about a fiancé" which, Elizabeth quoted Robert as saying, would have done credit to Dumas himself. There was also an unspeakably banal description of "waving of handkerchiefs" and such like: it was "lie upon lie . . . lies heaped up, pressed down, running over" and amounted, Elizabeth declared, to "a hideous fake". She did not care what anyone said about her work – "cut up my poems and welcome" – but she thought "my *me* should be safe till I am dead". Elizabeth wrote to Miss Mitford, "*you* have pained ME," and said she was "miserably upset". Perhaps Miss Mitford could not understand this but she had "lived heart to heart (for instance) with my husband these five years and have never yet spoken out in a whisper even what is in me – never yet could find heart or breath . . ." The whole subject of Bro was taboo and Miss Mitford had cruelly broken it. Elizabeth was prepared to believe her friend had had only the best of motives but it made no difference: the offence was inexcusable. Miss Mitford, distressed and embarrassed and more than a little guilty, wrote explaining, justifying and apologising. Elizabeth promptly forgave her.

Chapter Sixteen

D ESPITE Elizabeth's plans that she and Robert would work in Paris, in the autumn and winter of 1851–52 the city was far too exciting to permit either of them to concentrate on poetry. The political situation was potentially explosive. Three years before, when a republic had been declared (much to Elizabeth's joy), Louis Napoleon, nephew of the great Napoleon himself, had been elected President. In the autumn of 1851, when the Brownings had arrived, it was being rumoured that Louis Napoleon was going to impose himself, contrary to the 1848 Constitution, as President for a second term. Part of that "brilliant life of Paris" which Elizabeth so enjoyed watching from her Champs-Elysées window was due to the spectacle of magnificently dressed soldiers on horseback endlessly parading backwards and forwards. "People say," she wrote to Miss Mitford, "that the troops which pass before our windows every few days through the Arc d'Etoile to be reviewed will bring the president back with them as Emperor some sunny morning not far off." She told her friend that there was "a great inward agitation but the surface of things is smooth enough". At the end of the paragraph she added "Vive Napoleon III", commenting with unmistakable relish, "What a fourth act of a play we are in just now!" She openly admired Louis Napoleon's ambition and would not have it that, "as yet", he had done anything dishonest.

On 4th December came the anticipated *coup d'état*. From her windows, Elizabeth watched the "pouring in of the troops, to music, to trumpets and shouting", unable to tear herself away from this grandstand view of history in the making. She saw Louis Napoleon himself at last and heard "the great thunder of a shout" which hailed him; she would not, she swore, have missed it for anything. But her passionate support of Louis Napoleon now landed her in trouble with her husband and her brother, both of whom pointed out that her hero had definitely broken the law as enshrined in the Constitution. Her defence of the

President was based on shaky logic. She would not have it that he was bad, only "bold", and it was this boldness which attracted her instinctively: "I confess myself carried away into sympathy by the bravery and promptitude of his last act. Call it perjury, usurpation of rights, what you will – call it treason against the constitution which it assuredly is . . . de facto, the assembly opposed the wishes of the people instead of representing the people."[1] This was the unsound argument she presented to Robert and George: that the people had elected Louis Napoleon in the first place and the Assembly in rejecting an amendment that would have given him a second term, was not carrying out the wishes of the people. For good measure, she also defiantly alleged, "there's a higher right than a legal right" and even that "the living people are above the paper constitution." Evidently aware that lawyer George was likely to be less than convinced, she admitted finally "my sympathy with his audacity and dexterity is rather artistical sympathy than anything else." Elizabeth's enthusiasm for Louis Napoleon obviously contradicted her proclaimed republicanism but she obstinately denied that it did so. She acted as though the Emperor was a republican himself, writing to Miss Mitford that she simply did not see why he could not "head the democracy" and still "do his duty to the world".

"Artistical" or not, her sympathy with the Emperor profoundly irritated Robert as well as George. Robert discussed Elizabeth's attitude in a letter to his brother-in-law, finding it a relief to share his exasperation. "Is it not strange," he wrote, "that Ba cannot take your view, not to say mine and most people's, of the President's proceedings? I cannot understand it." What particularly annoyed and even genuinely angered Robert was his wife's disputation of *facts* – "things that admit of proof" as he put it to George. In a simple but effective metaphor he compared Louis Napoleon to a man who realised a clock was wrong so he stopped it in order to put it right. This was permissible and even praiseworthy but, when the same man proceeded to pocket the clock and say to people they did not need it because from now on he would tell them the time, then, as Robert wrote to George, "this won't do at all". When he tried to explain this to Elizabeth, and confronted her with "facts", she made only one reply: the people had chosen Louis Napoleon and therefore he could do no wrong. The fact that the people were by no means free to choose because the Emperor suppressed opinion and used the army to override them escaped Elizabeth. In her over-identification with "the people" Elizabeth had as usual become both obstinate and emotional and was blind to any rational assessment of the situation. She saw herself as a democrat, the supporter of the oppressed, and therefore the champion of anyone whom she judged to have taken up their cause.

Elizabeth sat up on the night of the *coup d'état*, crouching over the fire in her dressing gown listening to the distant sound of gunfire and shivering at the realisation that men were killing each other. She told Miss Mitford that whatever the rights and wrongs she "could not escape the emotion of the situation". The following day she was horribly scared when Robert was turned back from a walk by a passerby who had just been narrowly missed by a ball from a gun. Elizabeth was distressed to think of the suffering the "revolution" caused and yet could not help boasting to George of the "interesting position" in which she found herself. It made being confined indoors by the weather less frustrating – Paris had failed her by turning out to be bitterly cold. She could not conceal her disappointment, though professing "the air is decidedly LIGHT" if freezing. Warm and snug in her apartment, she was avid for details of the action outside and felt guilty that hearing about it was a welcome distraction. From her fireside position she was given to making sweeping generalisations, such as "one thing was clear . . . the sympathy of the people of Paris went fully with the President". Yet she had access to none of these "people of Paris" except Désirée, the maid who helped Wilson. It was no wonder that Robert, who knew her sources, was infuriated by his wife's pontificating. "Robert and I have had various domestic émeutes on the subject," Elizabeth wrote to Mrs Ogilvy without embarrassment. She was proud of holding her own point of view and even added, "I expect him to come round in time" (though she agreed that Robert probably expected her to do the same). They were both fascinated that they could argue and differ so hotly, breaking their "usual harmony" and yet feel no rift. Elizabeth felt it was a triumph to hold such opposing views and yet not come to blows. But she realised that intellectual differences were absurdly unimportant compared to emotional ones; if there had been any weakening, any failing, of their mutual love, of their emotional understanding and interdependence, then Mrs Ogilvy would not have been entertained with it.

Elizabeth's confidence that these were unimpaired was justified. Robert, that autumn and winter, had good cause to know how deep was the bond between him and his wife: she answered his great need of her during a period when his sensitive nerves were severely lacerated. That summer, when Robert had gone to his old home to confront his mother's absence and console his grieving father, he had discovered a most painful and unexpected set of circumstances. His father had found consolation in the company of another woman. Robert's initial reaction to this astounding news is not known, nor are Elizabeth's letters enlightening: she mentions nothing about her elderly father-in-law's infatuation. He was seventy years old and cared for devotedly by his daughter Sarianna and yet he seemed to have set his cap at a middle-aged widow shortly after Robert's mother died in 1849. The widow in question was a Mrs Von Müller, forty-five years old and considered distinctly attractive. Mr Browning senior had apparently noticed her at her window as he passed her house each day on his way to work at the Bank of England and had fallen into the habit of waving to her. She waved back. Soon he was stopping when he met her in the street and begging leave to accompany her home. Within a very short time indeed he was said to have proposed marriage. Unfortunately for Robert's desire to represent the whole thing as a misunderstanding of his father's kindness and politeness, and to imply that Mrs Von Müller had taken shameless advantage of him, his father had committed himself to paper. There were a great many letters, all couched in the most extravagant language, in Mrs Von Muller's possession. At the beginning of November 1851, Sarianna and her father suddenly turned up in Paris in a state of some distress. It seemed Mrs Von Müller had mentioned to Mr Browning that she might have married her second husband before her first was dead without knowing it. This, he had decided, was "a crime or gross error" and made Mrs Von Müller an undesirable woman. He had come to Paris to consult with Robert as to what he should do. On 1st November Robert himself wrote on his father's behalf to Mrs Von Müller saying that his father had told him of "the manner in which she had annoyed him and of the persecution he had undergone". Following on the son's self-righteous missive came his father's sanctimonious communication, in which he withdrew his offer of marriage on the extraordinary grounds of Mrs Von Müller's "misconduct from the time she was a girl". Not unnaturally, Mrs Von Müller was furious but even more furious was her son-in-law (she had three grown-up children) who decided she had grounds for a breach of promise case.

It was a nightmare of the very worst kind for Robert. Nothing appealed more to the press of the day than this sort of case which would be sure to attract plenty of attention. If there was one thing Robert loathed it was any invasion of his privacy and he knew there would be no escaping it. His beloved mother's memory would be besmirched, his father would become a laughing stock whatever the outcome. He had held up his family to Elizabeth as a model: unlike the Barretts, they did not fight amongst themselves, were endlessly understanding and loved each other to distraction. Now they appeared differently. In one respect at least Mr Barrett suddenly seemed more worthy than that most perfect of fathers, Mr Browning. Elizabeth's father had pride, dignity, enormous reserves of strength; it was inconceivable that he could ever be involved in a breach of promise case. He had been widowed when still young, handsome and in charge of eleven children, the youngest only four years old, and yet he had not turned to another woman. But not a word of criticism of her father-in-law crept into Elizabeth's correspondence. She wrote to George in December, after Sarianna and her father had returned home to London, only that Robert had been "absorbed between his father and sister (whom he had to carry about Paris from morning to night when they were here)". The veiled hint that she was annoyed that Robert had been put under such a strain was not present in her letter to Miss Mitford who was simply told, "Robert's father and sister have been paying us a visit during the last three weeks. They are very affectionate to me and I love them for his sake and for their own and am very sorry at the thought of losing them . . ." She was careful to present a united family front, emphasising that Sarianna was "full of accomplishment and good sense . . . devoted to her father as she was to her mother", but made the telling observation that "the father appears the child of the child" (and a very naughty child she knew him to have been). What concerned her most was the way in which the situation came between Robert and his work – how could he write poetry in the midst of such emotional distraction? All he could do was to edit and write a preface for a collection of Shelley's letters (which later proved to be forgeries).

But on 1st January 1852, Robert made a New Year resolution to write a poem every day. On that day he wrote "Love Among the Ruins", on the next "Women and Roses" and on the following day "Childe Rolande". Then, after such a splendid beginning, he gave up; there was just too much to do in Paris, too many attractions he could not resist. Elizabeth, though she wanted him to work during the day, encouraged him to go out in the evening. That winter saw the beginning of Robert's forays alone into society, something he had resisted up to then and indeed had not missed. In Pisa and in Florence during those winters when she could not herself venture forth, Elizabeth had always begged Robert to go alone but he had refused, saying he wanted only her company. But in Paris circumstances were different and demanded a different response. It was Elizabeth herself who wanted to sample vicariously the delights of Paris society through Robert. It was a source of great anguish to her that she was not well enough and the weather not mild enough for them both to participate in the social life. But Elizabeth was always quick to blame the weather for any ill health, and with her strange theories about the properties of air could always find something to blame, but this time there was evidence to support her opinion. It was an exceptionally cold winter in Paris – an east wind blew and it was extremely wet too – and anyone with a bronchial condition suffered. But it was also true that from now on Elizabeth's cough is mentioned much, much more frequently in her letters, whatever the climate, and that the winter of 1851–1852 saw the beginning of a real decline in her health, a decline all the more marked because of the robust period enjoyed from 1846 to '51. No doctors were called in so there are no medical reports at this juncture but the frequent accounts of a cough, breathlessness, congestion, occasional chest pain and attacks of fever would indicate acute bronchitis verging on bronchopneumonia.

There was nothing pathetic or martyred about her desire that Robert should go out alone nor was it in the least an indication that Robert was bored by her. She wrote to Mrs Ogilvy that Robert could "breathe just as well in the cold as in the warm" and that therefore she had insisted he should go into society. It would have been "absurd" she added if both of them had remained prisoners.[2] And in many ways she actually preferred Robert to go alone: she was able, with no loss of energy, to share in all he had seen and heard without any difficulty at all. But once the worst of the winter was over, she managed to get out a little. She went, for example, to the theatre to see the sensation of the season, *La Dame aux camélias*. Ever a lover of gossip, Elizabeth had heard that the play, by the son of one of her heroes, Alexandre Dumas, was based on a true story – the story of Marie Duplessis with whom Dumas *fils* had fallen in love. She had been in love with a count, had borne his son and had been forced to give him up by the count's father. The heroine of the play is the eternal victimised woman, the pawn of powerful and uncaring men against whom she has no protection. Watching it, Elizabeth said it "almost killed" her. She sobbed until she was blind with tears and had "a splitting headache" for the whole of the next day. Robert cried too, as did most of the audience at every performance (there was a contemporary cartoon showing people in the pit holding up umbrellas to protect themselves from the showers of tears). When she had recovered, Elizabeth felt outraged that the acting had been so "exquisite", it had passed "the bounds of Art". She thought it not right that life and death should be handled like that and wrote to Mrs Jameson "art has no business with real graveclothes". But she was extremely proud of having seen the play and boasted to George of her daring, because in England it was thought of as an immoral, indecent production.

Elizabeth had wanted to be in Paris for just such occasions, to be at the centre of literary and artistic events. Her great sense of the power of the present, that strong interest in the contemporary which even at her most withdrawn she had always had, made her relish her role as a spectator of history as it was being created. It was this eagerness to be part of momentous events that made her go on an extremely exhausting outing to a military fête with Mrs Jameson who was passing through Paris in May 1852. Afterwards, slightly shamefaced, Elizabeth tried to justify her trip to George on the grounds that it was "the significance of the whole event that I cared to study and understand".[3] The fête was held in the Champs de Mars and Elizabeth frankly confessed she had been "anxious to go in proportion to the difficulty of getting tickets". She set off with Mrs Jameson expecting the ride to take its usual ten minutes. It took three and a half hours. Mrs Jameson thought they should turn back half way but Elizabeth would not hear of it. The crowds were frighteningly dense and noisy but they managed to get to their seats which turned out to be poor ones. They then witnessed the restoration to various regimental standards of eagles – nothing more than a display of military pomp. The heat was dreadful. Trying to get home was an adventure in itself: they could not find a carriage and Elizabeth soon announced that her strength was at an end. The frantic Mrs Jameson (terrified of "What Browning would say") managed to support her friend as far as the boulevard des Invalides where they both collapsed at a pavement café. Here a cabman, tired of waiting for two other ladies, offered to take them home for an extra three francs on top of his regular fare. Elizabeth reported to George that, although "ashamed to confess our baseness", they snapped up the offer. In spite of the exhaustion, she announced, "I am glad I went." She gloried in her escapade, experiencing a delicious tinge of guilt about the whole day because "Robert would not have let me [go] if he had had an idea of the state of things".

Her cold and cough were still "horrid" when the cold weather ended so even then she was dependent on visitors to cheer her. The Ogilvys came to Paris, which she enjoyed, and so did the Hedleys on their annual progress. Elizabeth had little in common with them but felt for them a deep family love since they were her most valued link with her happy childhood. She was especially fond of Ibbit, second of the Hedleys' five children, whom at four she had described as "the very dream of a lovely child" and now found, at thirteen, to be utterly delightful. But life in Paris, however pleasant, had to end. Another visit to London was necessary because Robert's father's breach of promise case was due to be heard in the High Court in July. After that ordeal, they would return to Italy.

The Brownings returned to London on 6th July. When they arrived the weather was hot. Elizabeth grudgingly acknowledged this but condemned the atmosphere as "heavy and strangling". They stayed in "very comfortable rooms" in Welbeck Street, running parallel to Wimpole Street, which were even nearer her old home than Devonshire Street had been. Henrietta came up from the country for a week and stayed "twenty doors away". Elizabeth was well aware of the effort and expense entailed and very grateful to her sister who was expecting another baby in September. She was perfectly open about her envy of Henrietta: she herself had given up all hope of having the daughter she would have loved, writing a little bitterly to Miss Mitford that rumours that Pen was to have a little brother or sister were lies. "Too glad I should be to say 'yes'" she commented "but 'no, no' it must be instead". The rumours were "*bosh* . . . I have not any prospects, nor have had since the bad illness in Florence nearly two years ago . . . so now I give up the hope of it."[4] Considering she was forty-six, it was not before time.

Fond thoughts of another baby in the family, and Henrietta's conviction that it would be a girl, cheered a gloomy beginning to Elizabeth's stay in London. As soon as they arrived, Robert promptly had to turn round and go back to Paris again to find permanent lodgings for his father and sister. The breach of promise case had been heard and had gone disastrously. *The Times*, as was its habit, reported the case in minute detail exposing Mr Browning to ridicule. It was hard to decide from the report who had made more of a joke of the old man, the prosecuting or the defending counsel. The counsel for the prosecution said that, whereas there was usually "more or less romance" involved in breach of promise cases, there was none at all in this one; his client was suing not for compensation so much as to recover her reputation. He then proceeded to go over Mr Browning's pursuit of Mrs Von Müller, producing letters at every stage. There were fifty of them, beginning in December 1850. The entire court laughed hysterically when they were read out because of the absurdly extravagant openings – "My dearest, dearest, dearest, dearest, dearest, dearest much-loved Minne". Mrs Von Müller's character appeared irreproachable. Mr Browning's allegations as to her "misconduct" were proved quite unfounded when the death certificate of her first husband was produced in court to show he had died a full two months before she married again. The only resource for the defence was to argue that this was "an idle and trumpery case" and to disparage his own client by calling him "an old dotard in love". Lord Campbell, the Judge, called attention to Mr Browning's hitherto exemplary character but nevertheless did not find the case so idle. It seemed to him that Mrs Von Müller had not "held out any lure to this old gentleman" and that "his folly was his own folly". Even worse, Lord Campbell's opinion was that Mr Browning had conducted himself "in a most cowardly manner" and that far from being "trumpery" this was "a very gross case".[5] Damages of £800 were awarded to Mrs Von Müller and her name cleared. The humiliation for the Brownings was total. Mr Browning's salary was £320 a year: he could not pay the damages. Nor could Robert. The only solution was to leave the country and escape the jurisdiction of the court. So Robert took his father and sister to Paris, made them "tolerably comfortable" and returned to Welbeck Street exhausted. Elizabeth confided to Henrietta that "the vexation of it all is immense".

Once this distressing business was over, there was some pleasure to be had out of London. All of them (including Flush) went on several pleasant outings, once to Wimbledon to see Kenyon and on another particularly enjoyable occasion to Farnham where they met Charles Kingsley. In Welbeck Street itself they had a constant stream of callers – John Ruskin, Mazzini, the Carlyles, Richard Monckton Milnes and, most interestingly in retrospect, Florence Nightingale, Monckton Milnes' friend. Miss Nightingale was not yet in the least famous but was renowned in Monckton Milnes' circle for her knowledge on health policy. Elizabeth found her interesting but when she described the visit to Mrs Jameson chose to comment only on Miss Nightingale's face, manner and charm. It was a lost opportunity; Elizabeth never did understand Florence Nightingale's aims and saw her desire to make nursing into a profession as a retrograde step, "a revival of old virtues", which it most certainly was not. All these visitors naturally tired her as well as stimulated her and to Mrs Ogilvy she announced herself "worn out" by "the toils of London". It was almost a relief to be approaching the date for Wilson's visit home to Sheffield, leaving her mistress "tied and bound" to Pen and therefore unable to accept invitations. But before Wilson left she made a request that shocked Elizabeth: she asked for her wage of 16 guineas a year to be raised to twenty. She had never, in all her ten years of service, had a rise in wages nor had she asked for one, although her duties had trebled. Engaged in 1842 as a lady's maid, she had become, after Elizabeth's marriage, part housekeeper and seamstress and after the birth of Pen a nursemaid too. She said she thought it was time for this to be taken into consideration and intimated that, if it were not, she doubted if she would want to return to Italy.

Elizabeth was distraught. She seemed to think Wilson's request greedy and outrageously ungrateful. Once more, when put to the test in her private life, her publicly expressed concern for "the people" seemed a sham. Furthermore, she saw it as a sign that Wilson was not as devoted as she had appeared. To Mrs Ogilvy she wrote that the "inconvenience" of Wilson's decision was as nothing compared to the "disappointment of . . . I may say the affections. I thought she cared more for me and the child than to leave us so". But neither she nor Robert were prepared to pay the paltry sum Wilson requested: "we hadn't in our power to do", wrote Elizabeth. What Wilson had not appreciated, in her opinion, was how munificently she was paid in love, beside which money was nothing. The atmosphere in Welbeck Street was icy for the next two weeks and then suddenly, on the eve of her departure, Wilson capitulated. On 3rd September Elizabeth wrote triumphantly to Mrs Ogilvy that she was feeling "in spirits" because Wilson was to stay at the same wage – "there was a misunderstanding or something like it". She said she could not bring herself to leave her mistress or her charge. Elizabeth felt this was exactly as it should be. There is no suggestion anywhere in her correspondence that she saw Wilson as the victim of a system she herself professed to abhor, that she recognised her maid for what she was, a working girl with no bargaining power. When Wilson was first engaged, Elizabeth had complained to Miss Mitford that she was "a very expensive maid at £16 a year". Even if she had been right, Wilson would have been more than entitled ten years later, and doing two jobs, to more money, but in fact Elizabeth was wrong. Wilson's wage was exactly on a

20. Mary Russell Mitford   21. John Kenyon

22. Anna Jameson

23. Robert Browning by Dante Gabriel Rossetti

24. Facsimile of the penultimate sonnet "from the Portuguese"

25. Robert Browning, Senior

26. Sarianna Browning, Robert's sister

27. Interior, Casa Guidi

28. Pen Browning aged 9

29. Elizabeth with Pen in Rome, 1860

30. Exterior, Casa Guidi

31. Robert Browning in Rome, 1860

32. Elizabeth in Rome, May 1861, a month before she died

33. Drawing by Elizabeth, signed "1860. Oct. 7 - Villa Alberti Siena - My fig tree - E B Browning". Robert added "Drawn the last time she ever sat under it. We left, the next day. R.B."

par with the average wage for a lady's maid when she began and by 1852 this had risen to £18.[6] There is no escaping the fact that she was underpaid. Nor was it as though Wilson performed her duties grudgingly or did not give satisfaction. Elizabeth continually congratulated herself on her own luck in having her. And Wilson was generous: that very spring, on Pen's third birthday, Elizabeth had written to Arabel of how "kind Wilson" had bought her over-indulged son "two magnetic swans". What that represented as a proportion of her maid's wage she never thought to calculate. When she told Wilson she thought she had loved her more, Wilson could equally well have replied that she thought the Brownings loved *her* enough to see that her wage was increased at least to what it should be without her having to beg for a rise. The Brownings were not by any means rich but another two if not four guineas a year for such a maid would not have been beyond their means.

Wilson, defeated, at least had the sense to take three weeks' holiday instead of the agreed two. No sooner had she departed than Elizabeth was made acutely aware all over again of her value. Pen was "good and precious" she told Mrs Ogilvy, and she would rather "wait on him than on the grandees literary or otherwise of this world" but he was also exhausting. Robert wanted to engage a temporary nursemaid (funds were miraculously available for that kind of expense) but Elizabeth judged this would be more bother than it was worth. Pen was so devoted to his "darling Lily" that he would tolerate no rival. So Elizabeth looked after him herself, which meant rising at six, even though she was coughing, and never having a moment's rest all day. But she took advantage of Wilson's absence to do something of which her maid disapproved: she taught Pen "eight or nine poems" and "some two hundred nursery rhymes". Wilson's theory was that this over-stimulated Pen. "She never likes his learning anything for fear of over-excitement," wrote Elizabeth scornfully to Mrs Ogilvy.[7] The over-excitement duly arrived but it was worth it to hear Pen recite so charmingly. He was full of "enormous spirits" and George thrilled his sister by asking her if her child "*ever* cried; it seemed out of his nature". This time he went quite willingly to Wimpole Street and played with "mine untles" who made a great fuss of him. Elizabeth went with him, with the usual mixed feelings of dread and fascination. "For my part," she wrote to Henrietta, who was back in Taunton in Somerset awaiting the birth of her baby, "I do really wonder sometimes how I can bear to do it – but then I go again, just as if I didn't wonder at all." At first, she was careful to leave No. 50

Wimpole Street well before her father was due back but with every visit her departure grew nearer to the hour when he returned from the City. It was as though she were quite deliberately trying to precipitate a confrontation. "Horribly frightened, too, I get," she confided in Henrietta but fear made her increasingly bold. Once, she saw her father coming down the street as she left the house and only just escaped in time round the corner into Weymouth Street. Her panic communicated itself to Pen, who became convinced some hideous monster lurked in his mother's old home. Minny Robinson, the old housekeeper, was angry with Elizabeth for letting Pen have such foolish ideas but she defended herself on the grounds that the truth would terrify her son even more.

Elizabeth knew that her father was well aware of her presence in London and even of her visits to his house. She could not help feeling that it was a little hopeful that he had not barred her from it or forbidden the rest of his children to see her; perhaps this was his own strange form of concession. It occurred to her that an "accidental" meeting might solve everything. But there was no meeting or communication, accidental or otherwise. She wrote another letter, forgetting that writing was not her father's medium as it was hers. To her joy, a reply came, a letter addressed to her in her father's unmistakable hand. Her hopes rose so high that she delayed opening the letter the longer to cling onto them – wisely, because once opened she was revolted by the contents. "It was, I confess to you, with a revulsion of feeling that I read that letter," she told Henrietta, " . . . written after six years with the plain intention of giving me as much pain as possible. It was an unnatural letter and the evidence of hardness of heart . . . is unmistakable."[8] His letter (never found) obviously contained exhortations to repent of her supposed sin because she told Henrietta "certainly the effect of it is anything but to lead me to *repentance*. Am I to repent that I did not sacrifice my life, and its affections, to the writer of that letter?"

Her misery over her father's cruel letter left her feeling low and depressed but she was a little cheered by the news of the birth of Henrietta's baby, a girl, born on 28th September, named Mary after their mother. "Since she is yours I won't covet her," Elizabeth wrote to her sister but to Mrs Ogilvy she cheerfully admitted she was "up to the brim with covetousness". Fingering the tuft of hair she had been sent, Elzabeth longed to see her niece but there was no time. The first fog of the autumn had reduced her to a coughing wreck; she was obliged to leave England as quickly as possible, without seeing Miss Mitford who had been ill and unable to visit her. There was a final flurry of farewells and the Brownings left on 12th October, Elizabeth declaring to Miss Mitford that she was "almost mad with the amount of things to be done". Her heart ached, she wrote to Henrietta, to leave "our poor beloved Arabel". It was purely for this sister's sake that she would ever again brave "this climate that will not let me live".

Elizabeth was sure that "once I am *gone*", she would recover. She expected to enjoy, as she usually did, the long journey back to Florence but it began badly with one of the worst Channel crossings they had ever experienced. They had planned to pass straight through Paris but found they had left behind in London some "valuables" and had to wait for them to be sent on. This involved Robert in trying negotiations but Elizabeth could not help enjoying the delay, though she knew it was "rather dangerous to let the charm of Paris work". She told Kenyon that if they had to wait very long "the honey will be clogging our feet . . . and make it difficult to go away". She desperately wanted to see the newly created Empire in and would have insisted on doing so "if I were a little less plainly mortal with this disagreeable cough of mine". At least she managed to see "the grandest spectacle in the world, the reception of Louis Napoleon . . ." It was a brilliantly sunny day in which the glitter of uniforms and weapons was so magnificent that it was "difficult to distinguish between the light and the life". She was full of barely suppressed emotion as she watched Louis Napoleon showing "his usual tact and courage by riding on horseback quite alone". Pen definitely saw him take off his hat just to him and went into uncontrollable "ecstasys" shouting over and over "very loud" his "Vive Napoleons". Elizabeth waved her handkerchief energetically and said to herself, "God Bless the People". She was thrilled to have been yet again in another drama of history.

The rest of the journey was disastrous. It was almost November by the time they left Paris but they chose "to cross the Mont Cenis". It was bitterly cold and through a mistake about booking inns they were obliged to travel "three nights without once undressing". Elizabeth coughed and coughed, sometimes barely able to catch her breath between paroxysms of coughing. By Turin, she was "nearly extinct" and thought herself in danger of suffocating. They were forced to stop for two days at Turin but the rest did her little good. Robert was frantic with worry and nursed her so tenderly it brought tears to her eyes. She wrote to Arabel, "for a man to love a woman after six years as he loves me

could only be possible to a man of very uncommon nature such as his
. . ."⁹ They managed to reach Genoa before she "broke down entirely".
Robert was terrified, he had never seen his wife so ill. But then, at Genoa,
a miracle took place before his eyes revealing to him once and for all the
power of warmth and sunshine in his wife's case. Elizabeth, "just fit to lie
on the sofa by an open window through which poured the full Italian
summer" (even though it was November), felt that "every breath
brought the life back to me". The suspicion that Elizabeth's dramatic recovery means that her illness was psychosomatic is unjustified.
Chronic bronchitis, even without spreading to the lung tissue and
becoming bronchopneumonia, has a direct, acknowledged connection
with wet, cold weather and even with city life (especially city life in
Victorian times.) The kind of journey the Brownings had undertaken,
most of it in draughty carriages, quite obviously exacerbated Elizabeth's
condition. Without modern antibiotics the only beneficial treatment for
this condition was to remove the patient to a warm, dry atmosphere
which was precisely what Robert did. But of course her recovery was
more apparent than real. The likeliest diagnosis is that patches of
infected tissue remained scattered throughout her lungs, dormant but
ready to become inflamed at the slightest provocation.

She was soon well enough to travel on to Florence. Arriving back at
the Casa Guidi was rapture. To every one of her correspondents she said
the same thing: she loved Italy, she loved Florence, she loved the Casa
Guidi. Relief made her light-headed. Their apartment was in excellent
order and she recovered her health quickly. She stopped coughing and
Robert stopped worrying. All that disturbed her, safe and well once
more, were her dreams. These were full of her father. Until now, she had
throughout her marriage managed to adopt a most sensible and prag-
matic attitude to her father's intransigence and she had never quite given
up hope of his eventual forgiveness. After his apparently brutal letter of
September 1852 this changed. She was tormented by the most awful of
conundrums: if her father had loved her as she knew he had loved her,
how could such a love disappear, and if it could, did this mean she had
been deluded and it had never existed? She could not bear the thought
and yet could not stop thinking along these lines.

But by the end of November her nerves as well as her health were
stronger. She boasted to Arabel "I am quite myself again . . . getting
fatter even". Robert, on the other hand, was she reported "a demoral-
ised man". He found winter in Florence duller than ever after two in

Paris. But Elizabeth thought his boredom no bad thing; they could turn
the dullness of Florence into an asset by working, knowing there were no
distractions. She was the prime mover in insisting they should both
establish a new routine and stick to it. They had always planned to write
side by side, separate but together, and the time had come. She was well,
not too enveloped in maternity that she could think of nothing else, and
in Florence there was peace and quiet. This would be the winter of work.

Chapter Seventeen

FOR once, it all turned out exactly as Elizabeth had planned. All winter, taking pride in their strict new routine, both she and Robert worked hard and to such good effect that even before it was over this was labelled "the happy winter". Nothing and nobody vexed them or interrupted their creativity. Her health continued to be good, helped by the exceptionally mild and sunny weather, and there was even the additional security for Robert of not having to worry about money since the rent from letting the Casa Guidi in the past year formed a solid basis to their always precarious income.

There was a great deal in Elizabeth's letters about her reformed life style but significantly little about the content of what she was working on. She and Robert both got up at seven and were dressed and breakfasting by nine. Then Wilson took Pen out while both poets used "the bright ribbands of morning time" to write until three o'clock when they dined. Robert worked in the little sitting room and Elizabeth in the drawing room. The dining room was between them, with the doors firmly closed. Robert sat at a desk writing lyrics for a collection to be called *Men and Women*; Elizabeth sat in an armchair with her feet up writing *Aurora Leigh*, the long prose poem she had contemplated for so many years. Neither showed each other the day's output nor did they discuss it. Elizabeth had firm ideas about this: no matter how close people were, their intimacy should not extend to work. "An artist must, I fancy, either find or *make* a solitude to work in, if it is to be good work at all," she once wrote to Chorley, and meant it. There had to be, for her, an element of secrecy about what she was engaged on once it was begun. For years, during the gestation period, she had referred to her projected "long prose poem" which would be on a contemporary subject, but now she wanted to keep it to herself. To George, she confided that she meant it to be "beyond all question my best work" and to Mrs Jameson she wrote this was "the novel or romance I have been hankering after for so long".

Beyond that, she revealed very little, except that her heroine was "an artist woman" and her subject "intensely modern". Not even to Miss Mitford, who had known of her idea from the beginning, did she say more.

Part of the success of the new régime in the Casa Guidi was that the Brownings had acquired a new servant which made the running of their household smoother. Alessandro had gone, to Wilson's immense satisfaction. She had never liked him, and the friction this generated had not been conducive to the kind of domestic harmony essential to any homebound writer. Henrietta was given the full story of the new servant, a man called Vincenzo, who was extremely efficient and, even more vital, in awe of Wilson. Elizabeth commented tartly, "Wilson professes to be satisfied and comfortable – which means more than if we professed the same thing." On the other hand, she was herself "vicious enough to feel a little ashamed of him – he looks so like a groom – by no means of the chambers", another example of the importance she placed on civilised standards while declaring herself a Bohemian at heart. Robert, whose eyesight was deficient in any case (he was short-sighted in one eye and long-sighted in the other), had hired Vincenzo in the evening when the light was poor and had failed to notice the man's seedy appearance. Though disreputable looking, he performed his duties so well that there were no grounds for dismissing him – but Elizabeth minded his appearance.

That winter there were three favourite visitors. Frederick Tennyson, the poet's brother, physically a large, impressive man but with a shy, refined nature, married to an Italian and father of four; Robert Lytton, son of Sir Edward Bulwer-Lytton, who was "very young but full of high aspirations" and an attaché at the British Embassy; and Hiram Powers, whose sculpture Elizabeth admired as much as his "great spiritual eyes". When these gentlemen came to tea Elizabeth presided over the conversation while she sewed frocks for Pen, well aware of the charming picture she made. She had by now bought her own thimble and endlessly made fun discovering her new "feminine" talent. Robert, as ever, talked most, of which Elizabeth approved: talk was good for him. In fact, a lot of the talk at such sessions was not good for him because it touched again and again on a topic in which Elizabeth had always been interested. This was spiritualism. Lytton, Tennyson and Powers were, like their hostess, believers and spent hours regaling each other with "evidence of supernatural happenings". Robert was, Elizabeth wrote to Arabel, in a "glorious minority". She wrote that he tried hard "to keep his ground . . ." but had difficulty against the combined onslaught. His ground was that until he had seen for himself he would give no credence to moving tables and such like. Elizabeth wrote to her brother George, who of course shared Robert's scepticism, that it was foolish of Robert to need personal confirmation before he could admit spiritualism was a fact: "he and all of you must come into it . . . why wait to embrace a truth with the servants of the age?"[1] She did not deny that there were dishonest mediums: "I for one have always been aware . . . of the fallacies which might and did conceal themselves in various of those operations, that a very slight and unconscious muscular movement . . . would move a rather heavy table." But there were now reliable reports of objects moved entirely without touch. This excited Elizabeth tremendously. She was always producing wonderfully naive examples of such happenings to corroborate what she said. There was, she told George solemnly, even an underwriter in an insurance company who had had to hold down a table that moved without assistance. "You will set me down as an unmixed idiot George," she wrote. "Nevertheless, you will change your views and I shall not change mine." George, who had heard that tone of authority all his life from his father, could not be persuaded. Neither could Robert. But when Elizabeth and friends began to experiment with moving tables he made sure he was there. Elizabeth described to Arabel how Tennyson, Lytton, Robert and she all tried to move a table "and failed". They tried for twenty minutes then gave up, blaming Robert who had been "laughing the whole time". Irritated by his levity, and extremely jealous of Mrs Trollope who at the other end of Florence was having great table-moving success, Elizabeth was comforted to find an ally in her sister-in-law. Sarianna, famed for her commonsense, had attended a séance in Paris in the same spirit of sceptical enquiry as her brother and had been converted. Elizabeth recounted triumphantly to Miss Mitford how Sarianna had seen a table move and heard it "knocking with its leg responses according to the alphabet" and had checked for all possible trickery before being "bound to speak the truth". Robert remained unimpressed. He was uneasy, too, about the effect of his wife's enthusiasm for spiritualism on Pen. Elizabeth swore to George, "I do not instruct Penini in these things I assure you," but Robert saw that she did not need to: Pen was highly impressionable and inevitably absorbed what was around him. Elizabeth herself related to George how Pen had asked if she had been knocking at his door and when she denied this he had replied, " 'Well' – turning a face radiant with satisfaction – 'then it *muss* be *pinnets*'." She thought this very funny; Robert did not.

Pen, these days, was everywhere, though his parents quarrelled amicably over how involved he should be in their social life. Elizabeth told Henrietta that Robert wanted "to keep the nursery in decent shadow on social occasions" and so would not let her take their son on morning visits. She had never heard anything so silly in her life and was "in revolt". She would do as she pleased. Pen was "a fairy King of a child – and is intended to be looked at accordingly".[2] She adored to see how, when he was in the street, Pen was always being "stopped and kissed and sometimes has a circle of ladies around him." She thought Robert was absurd to disapprove of Pen's narcissism and pointed out that their child was "extremely fond of society", so much so that "two minutes" after anyone called he was in the drawing room to entertain them, having begged Wilson to "do mine hair velly pretty". That winter of 1852 the entertainment he provided for startled visitors, used to the prevailing dictum that children be seen and not heard, was the tambourine. Robert accompanied him on the piano while he twirled about, in all his golden three-year-old glory, making up dances to his own beat. This, as far as Elizabeth was concerned, was what small children should do: play, amuse themselves, be natural. She considered formal education at that age to be an abomination. "Mental precocity may mean just nothing," she wrote to Mrs Ogilvy and even rebuked Henrietta for teaching her little son the Lord's Prayer. She asserted, "Play is the occupation of a child – a child learns most when he plays – and an active vivacious child never feels the time hang heavily on his hands . . ."[3] Certainly Pen never did. By now she admitted Pen would be her only child and recognised in herself a slightly defensive tendency to try to keep him a baby as long as possible.

Nor was it only to keep Pen young that she wished time to stand still. The years were galloping past for herself, too, and she wished desperately that they would not. All references to ageing were extremely irritating to her. Mrs Ogilvy, innocently making a remark about how wonderful Miss Mitford was "for her great age", was sharply pulled up. Miss Mitford was *not*, at sixty-five, a great age: "she is as young . . . in the spirit as you yourself are."[4] (Mrs Ogilvy was thirty.) She hated the outward appearance of ageing, the "putting on of a mask", the erection of what she thought of as barriers between the real self and the visible self. She did not like attention being drawn to white hair (her own, at almost forty-seven, remained mercifully black, untouched even by grey) or to wrinkles or other tell-tale signs. It made her angry when people remarked on such unimportant things. During the "happy winter" of 1852–53 her tendency to try to arrest time became markedly stronger. She told Mrs Martin "the rust of time" was "hideous and revolting" to her and confessed she had "a worse than womanly weakness" on the subject. It made her less adventurous than she had been during the previous seven years of her marriage: she found it difficult even to think about going as far as Bagni di Lucca for a holiday. She wrote hesitantly to George that there was "something painful in breaking the thread and letting our pleasant friends roll off like lost beads." Goodbyes upset her more than they had ever done. Yet she would not have it that these feelings arose from an awareness that time was running out, that she was on the threshold of old age herself. She told Mrs Martin, "I, for my part, never felt younger." For good measure, she threw in some scathing comments about "women who throw up the game early (or even late) and wear dresses 'suitable to their years' (that is, as hideous as possible . . ." People who reminisced about the good old days were, she announced, "pests of society".

But in July 1853, when Florence as usual "began to blaze", Elizabeth was forced to agree with Robert that they must go somewhere for a couple of months. She was still "sorry to go" and repeated to Mrs Ogilvy what she had already said to George about fearing to tempt fate by breaking up their household. The beads, she added, keeping to the same metaphor, might never be strung together again. It was a long time since she had given way to the morbid streak within her. Just before they left Florence, she and Robert went to a soirée at Lytton's Bellosguardo villa. They sat on the terrace with Tennyson and Powers, looking down "on that purple wonder of a vision" which was Florence, lit by stars and fireflies. Elizabeth was acutely conscious, as she poured tea and joined in the conversation about Michael Faraday's recent denunciation of spiritualism, of how happy she was. "Seldom have I had a pleasanter evening," she commented and was nostalgic about it almost before it was over. She realised her happiness, caught it, marked it, appreciated it and was sad to let it go.

Once at Lucca, her mood became more optimistic. This time, the Brownings were not at the top of the three hill villages but in a much larger house lower down, a house "withdrawn from the village". The only trouble was that there was at first no congenial company and since the place was so familiar it needed human stimuli to make it more attractive. The Brownings were glad to discover a pleasant couple, whom they had met briefly in 1849, staying nearby. William Wetmore Story was an American lawyer, poet and sculptor with a pretty young wife, Emelyn, and two lively children, Edith who was nine and Joe, aged six, ideal companions for the four-year-old Pen. Edith and Joe were the brother and sister Pen craved (Elizabeth often told Henrietta how desperate Pen was for siblings, even going so far as to suggest buying some). He managed to overcome his reluctance to leave his parents and Wilson to go and spend all day with the Storys. There was "a great deal of mutual strawberries and cream" and "coming and going in both generations". It was the sort of holiday atmosphere in which friendships of a particular kind flourish but, though Elizabeth enjoyed its benefits, she did not confuse it with the deeper intimacies she had left behind in Florence. The Storys were "sympathetic and charming" but they were no substitute for the intellectual companionship of Lytton, Tennyson and Powers. But at least she had the sense to rejoice over how much better this kind of social intercourse was for Pen. In fact, everything at Lucca was better for Pen, especially since he also had another new adult friend. This was Ferdinando Romagnoli, engaged before they left Florence to replace Vincenzo who had conveniently fallen ill and could therefore decently be paid off. Ferdinando was a hero to Pen. Tall, strong and handsome in a rugged way, he had fought for the unification of Italy as a volunteer in 1848. He enslaved Pen by showing him the gun with which he had fought. Pen's enthusiasm and awe were enough to indicate to his mother that, although she liked to think there was "much of the girl nature" in her son whom she struggled continually to bring up against society's ordained edicts as to what was masculine or feminine, there was also an aggressively conventional male part which could not be suppressed. She described to Henrietta how Pen followed Ferdinando everywhere. It was Ferdinando who took him to the river and would have taught him how to swim if Wilson had not demurred. Wilson always went with them and not entirely to keep an eye on Pen: she was secretly deeply attracted to Ferdinando herself although, with memories of Signor Righi's faithlessness, inclined to indicate otherwise.

In this pleasant outdoor life of picnics and walks, Elizabeth did not forget work. She described herself and Robert to Mrs Ogilvy as "doing work in a lazy sort of way" even though they had abandoned their fiercely strict winter timetable. She always had her little sheets of paper handy while she was sitting in the garden and, in the time-honoured tradition of women writers everywhere and in any age, took up her pencil and scribbled if her child was occupied elsewhere. Robert worked too, but was easily distracted (Elizabeth never ceased to be amazed at how easily he was distracted). Even Pen "worked" a little. Elizabeth was teaching him to read. She was on the defensive to Henrietta about this, knowing it appeared to contradict everything she had said about formal education for the young, and assured her sister she had not "the least notion of beginning a course of education". It was just that Pen had clamoured to be taught to read. Both parents told him it would be very hard work, but he solemnly announced he was prepared to "do mine lessons evelly day". The lessons lasted five minutes each which was sometimes twice as long as Pen would concentrate. Surprising herself as well as him, Elizabeth told her small son rather sharply that, if he was not going to be good, the lessons would stop. Pen, on one occasion, stalked off only to return later and enquire "You dood now, Mama?" (His mother said she thought she was and Pen said in that case they could start the lesson again. They kept pegging away all the time at Bagni di Lucca with simple, one-syllable words until both Robert and Elizabeth were going mad with the boredom of it. D-O-G Elizabeth spelled out again and again while Robert groaned and commented "What a slow business.") Robert privately thought it could be a lot quicker if Pen was disciplined more: he lacked any kind of self-control. Elizabeth was shocked at the suggestion. Pen was only four and the most delightful child in the world. What on earth did Robert want to "discipline" him for? Why and how did he propose to do it? Robert showed her. She watched, aggrieved and contemptuous, while Robert tried to demonstrate to Pen the virtues of obeying. If Pen disobeyed a reasonable order, Robert thought he should be punished. The exact nature of the punishment was difficult to decide but finally Robert made up his mind to deprive Pen of a pleasure the next time he was naughty. Pen was informed, when the moment arrived, that he was not to be allowed to eat any of the delicious pears hanging on the trees all round the garden. Elizabeth reported to Mrs Ogilvy that "the victim couldn't believe at first that anything so cruel was seriously intended but, on becoming alive to the full horror of the situation, he burst into sobs of anguish and exclaimed with the tears running down his cheeks, 'Oh naughty Papa! What I do *if the peaches are too sour*?"[5] Elizabeth thought this the most wonderful riposte in the world and that it served Robert right. She added, sarcastically, that she was glad Robert "suffered in his soul . . . for seeking to impose any punishment at all". To "discipline" such an unintentionally witty angel was an absurdity.

All the time she was at Lucca, even while writing or reading delicious novels newly arrived from England (Charlotte Brontë's latest novel, *Villette*, and Mrs Gaskell's *Ruth*, both of which she greatly enjoyed and admired), Elizabeth felt hanging over her the prospect of going to Rome. It was not that she did not want to see Rome – she had always longed to – but that once more she was afraid of the untried and untested. They had been so happy, so productive during the last winter in the Casa Guidi – why leave it, why risk the unknown? But Robert wanted to go. He had heard that the winter society of Rome was almost equal to that of Paris. Dickens and Thackeray were rumoured to be Rome-bound, as were Fanny Kemble, the Storys, and a friend to whom they were becoming increasingly close, Isa Blagden. Isa had settled in Florence the year Pen was born. She had a rented villa near Lytton's up at Bellosguardo where she managed to entertain most hospitably on a very small income. Nobody knew much about her: she was about ten years younger than Elizabeth, unmarried, born in India, and wrote novels without much success. She was small, like Elizabeth, with dark hair and eyes and had such an olive skin it was conjectured her mother might have been Indian. By 1853, Robert was visiting Isa sometimes four times a week, with or without Pen, and Elizabeth often urged him to go to see her. The thought of Isa in Rome was a great comfort to her as they returned first to Florence in October then set out on 15th November. The journey took eight days but was wonderful and Elizabeth's spirits soared. They went via Assisi and Terni and the scenery all the way was "exquisite". Arriving in Rome was one of the happiest ends to a journey Elizabeth had ever had: Robert and Pen sang, the sun shone brilliantly, she hardly felt tired at all and, when they reached the apartment the Storys had kindly taken for them in the via Bocca di Leone, it was to find "lighted fires and lamps as if we were coming home". Elizabeth felt ashamed of her previous reluctance to come.

Next morning, she changed her mind again. Robert started their stay by shaving off his beard and whiskers, on a sudden whim. Elizabeth screamed at the sight of him and declared that until he grew them back "naturally everything was at an end between us". Hardly was she over this trivial upset than, as they sat down to breakfast, a message came from the Storys asking them to come quickly because Joe was ill.

Elizabeth and Robert rushed round to the Storys' apartment where they found little Joe in a fever and unconscious. That night, he died in convulsions. It was the first death Elizabeth had ever witnessed. Often, she had said how she envied those allowed to bid farewell to their loved ones, how she had felt cheated to be spared the experience. Joe Story was not a loved one, he was not family, she had only known him for a few months and yet seeing him die made death assume a reality for her which it had never had before. Faced with a dying child and then a six-year-old corpse it was difficult to be resigned, to accept God's will and refer to it as "but an incident in life". It needed no effort of Elizabeth's very considerable imagination to substitute Pen for Joe in the coffin. To her own shame, her feelings of distress and sympathy for the Storys were overtaken by a much stronger and more primitive emotion. She wrote to Miss Mitford, "I fell into a selfish human panic about my child." She begged Robert to take her away from Rome at once, without delay, pausing only to collect Pen and their things; she wanted to leave within the hour in case what Joe had died of was contagious. Robert was disgusted and told her she had lost her head. The doctor had assured everyone Joe's fever was not contagious and besides there were the poor parents, their friends, to comfort and help – how could she talk of running to the ends of the earth with Pen in her arms? The next day, when both Edith Story and her nurse succumbed to the mysterious, supposedly non-contagious fever, Elizabeth's panic, with surely some justice, intensified. Edith, removed from the apartment where her dead brother lay, was lodged in the same house as the Brownings, in rooms below them. In Elizabeth's opinion, this was far too close for comfort. She became almost hysterical when the child of the family with whom Edith was lodged also fell ill but Robert, though worried, refused to run. Nobody else died. Gradually, Edith began to improve, but Elizabeth was still nervous.

In an act of what she saw as almost superhuman heroism, Elizabeth drove with Mrs Story to the cemetery to lay flowers on Joe's newly dug grave. As she looked out of the carriage window, "the mountains and great campagna" all around the ancient city seemed "slurred over by ghastly death fingers, smelling of fresh mould". Entering the cemetery was the most terrible ordeal. She told Miss Mitford, "I flinch from corpses and graves and never meet a common funeral without a sort of horror."[6] This cemetery was the real, the "earth-side of death" and she recoiled from it. For years and years she had written poems thickly strewn with corpses, graves, shrouds and dust, assuring her readers that all these things were merely part of a transitional stage in life and not to be feared. Now, she feared. On their recent Bagni di Lucca holiday, she and the Storys had laughed together as they struggled to communicate with the dead through table-movings and spirit writings. Now such experiments were put in a different perspective as she stood with the bereaved mother looking at the grave where her son was buried. Her religion did not fail her – on the contrary, she never faltered in her belief that everything was God's will – but she experienced in the days following Joe's death a sudden doubt in her own philosophy. Was death just "a mere incident" in life? Were the trappings of death, "the earth-side", meaningless? Was the transition as painless, glorious and immediate as she had supposed? Rome was overnight abhorrent to her, covered as it was with "the ghastly flakes of death". The sight of young Edith's pitifully white face distressed her and she found the grief of the Story parents oppressive. She could not comfort them because her own theoretically lesser anguish overwhelmed her. The thought of spending the approaching Christmas with her friends appalled her but Robert said that, if friendship meant anything, they must. Elizabeth confessed to Henrietta that, on Christmas Day when they dutifully went to the Storys, "I did not like it but, poor things, we had agreed it should be so."

She remained shaken, telling Miss Mitford it took a while "for the light to break through," but by the middle of January she was sufficiently recovered to be able to report that "when I look deathwards I look OVER death". She had "arrived at almost enjoying some things". But both she and Robert were far too emotionally disturbed to do any work. Elizabeth wrote to Mrs Ogilvy, who herself had just written a long poem while one of her own children was gravely ill, that "I hear with unaffected wonder of anyone's being able to write verses with brain and heart torn to pieces as yours must have been . . ." She herself could not do this because "the first effect of grief upon *me* is the striking of me dumb – and it is the same with Robert. We, both of us, wait for calms before we do anything with Art. Perhaps melancholy calms – but the state of calm is necessary to most artists, I think."[7] Rome, quite apart from its associations with death, was anything but calm. It was hectic. Elizabeth detested what she saw of the general Roman society life, sneering that "it rains lords and ladies for the especial benefit of Thackeray perhaps". She told Arabel the kind of dinners and parties Thackeray thrived on pained her: it was "intolerable to me – relays of young ladies at the piano singing and playing in that sixth rate amateur manner . . ."[8] As ever, Elizabeth was far too ready to accept as true the standard gossip; Thackeray, far from being dissipated, was for once spending most of his time in his lodgings partly because he had no one with whom to leave his two young daughters, Anny and Minny, aged fifteen and thirteen, and partly because he was ill. When he did go out, it was very often to visit the Storys to whom he displayed great tenderness. Mrs Story was amazed at how he came "again and again, listening to our tale of grief . . ." But Elizabeth had not yet seen behind what Mrs Story correctly described as Thackeray's "cynical exterior and manner".

But there were some people in Rome she liked. Fanny Kemble was one and her sister, Mrs Sartoris, another. She liked even better a remarkable young woman she met for the first time, an American sculptress called Harriet (Hatty) Hosmer, who lived in the house where Isa lodged. Hatty was only twenty-two and lived, Elizabeth told Miss Mitford, "the eccentric life of a 'perfectly emancipated female'". She lived alone and dined and breakfasted "at the cafés precisely as a young man would". But Hatty also worked hard – from six in the morning until dark – and was, according to Elizabeth, "pure". She was attractive rather than conventionally pretty – her forehead was apparently too broad by Victorian standards for real beauty – with lovely, dimpled, rosy cheeks. Hatty was very much Elizabeth's ideal young woman, combining as she did hard work and artistic aspirations in a way of life quite beyond the reach of the average girl and yet not losing any of her femininity in the process. Hatty's friend, a Miss Hayes, was equally remarkable and fascinated Elizabeth. She wore men's clothes "to the waist" as Elizabeth described it – "there's the waistcoat . . . and the collar, neckcloth and jacket", everything except for the "wag-tail behind" of the jacket. (Robert had once suggested, in Paris, that Elizabeth might wear such a waistcoat, which many fashionable women adopted, but she had de-murred.) Elizabeth thought Miss Hayes, who had the added distinction of having translated George Sand, looked marvellous but had not the nerve to copy her. She was not only strictly conventional in dress herself, whatever she might write to Henrietta about keeping up with the latest styles to please Robert, but had also become, without realising it, rather old fashioned. That winter in Rome people who noted such things were beginning to find her hair style – still bunches of thick ringlets – a trifle démodé, to say the least.

Robert, of course, went out far more than Elizabeth. They were in

Rome partly for Elizabeth's health. She had been coughing before they left the Casa Guidi and it was obvious she needed an even warmer climate than Florence could promise. She was back to taking great care not to deplete her energies unnecessarily and while not an invalid in the strict sense of the word was nearer to leading an invalid life than she had ever been since Wimpole Street days. What energy she had was to be saved for Robert, Pen and her work; it could not be squandered on socialising. But the other reason for being in Rome was to provide amusement for Robert: Elizabeth wanted him to have agreeable company and encouraged him to take what was on offer, just as she had encouraged him during the winter in Paris. She herself had plenty of company at home if she wanted it. William Page, an artist who lived below, was delighted to come up and see her and so were Thackeray's daughters, who became regular visitors in the evening (very convenient for Thackeray who was feeling better and needed a babysitter). But Elizabeth was not desperate for distraction while she waited for Robert to return: she had a new, secret one at home. A great many evenings were now spent with Wilson absorbed in a pastime of which Robert strongly disapproved: Wilson had turned medium. Elizabeth told George all about it, endlessly seeking to convert him, though knowing perfectly well she never would. Wilson had gone one day with Pen to visit Isa Blagden. Marianne, Isa's maid, was a friend of Wilson's and had just discovered she could "do" spirit writing. Wilson watched a session and, according to Elizabeth who was relying on Wilson's own testimony, "laughed at these things". Then, "on a sudden impulse", she asked to be given a pencil and "in half a minute the pencil seemed to leap as she held it". When she came home she told all this to Elizabeth but added sceptically, "I think there's something in that pencil of Miss Blagden's." Elizabeth could not wait to put her maid's newly discovered psychic powers to the test. The two of them set up their own little séance when Robert was out and to Elizabeth's delighted astonishment Wilson's hand went "stiff and cold, while the pencil moves and vibrates itself . . . she has not the least consciousness of what she has written." What she had written was the name "Mary Barrett" and then "Mama". Elizabeth told George she knew he would laugh at her excitement but she did not care; she had never felt "saner or less excited". She and Wilson held more intimate séances and she herself tried spirit writing though with little success. Then, on 9th January 1854 she received an instruction through Wilson's spirit-propelled pencil to try again. "I took the pencil and sat down," she wrote to George, ". . . after five minutes for the first time in the course of all my experiments I felt the pencil move in a spiral sort of way, the fingers growing numb at the ends — but the force was not sufficient to produce a stroke even much less a letter."[9] But she was so inspired she gave George a lecture on this "new development of Law". She was not, she wrote, claiming miracles but merely the opening up of something always there but never recognised. "Rational people should not put away these things without examination" was her opinion. She thought herself extremely rational. There was the distinct impression that she wanted George to believe in spiritualism with her, not as any way of harking back to the past but as a kind of insurance policy against the future. She was concerned only with preparations for that future. She had done with the past.

By the time spring came, Elizabeth was announcing to Mrs Ogilvy that "the present and the future are strong within me till I am all in flame . . . you cannot think how eager I am about every step we take upwards." It was an uncharacteristic expression, an unusually strong sign of confidence in life after a winter dominated by Joe Story's death. Good health helped Elizabeth to be so optimistic. The Roman winter had proved as mild as she had been promised and she had even been able to go out in January. Robert's longer excursions were still beyond her strength but she managed several shorter ones and by April had been on five picnics (Robert had been on nine). The Storys finally left with the fully recovered Edith, freeing Elizabeth from the continuing distress she had felt every time she saw them. But hardly had they departed for Naples, leaving Elizabeth with a guilty sense of relief, than a message came back saying Edith had had a relapse and was very ill again, and asking if Robert would come. Robert responded instantly, rushing around to collect his things ready to set off at once. Elizabeth was furious: she did not see why Robert had to go at all. He had spent the whole winter helping the Storys, and she could not see what good he could do if Edith were ill. He would merely become embroiled in the Storys' affairs yet again. And she was afraid, too, of whatever illness Edith had: Robert ought not to risk catching it, it was irresponsible of him. But Robert, as Elizabeth perfectly well knew, was a man of compassion and principle with a particular tenderness for the weak and sick. Elizabeth's objections were ignored and so were Pen's "most piteous screams and sobs". Their son had become quite hysterical listening to that rare occurrence, a real quarrel between his parents. Intuitively, Pen sensed that this argument was different from previous discussions on politics or spiritualism, however heated those had been. For Elizabeth and Robert to disagree on this emotional level was unprecedented. Robert departed and Elizabeth was left behind, angry and defeated. It stunned her to think that for once Robert had not put her first and that somebody else was, for the moment, of more importance. It hardly mattered that, as it turned out, Robert was back within twenty-four hours bearing the glad tidings that it had all been a false alarm and Edith was better again. Elizabeth had meanwhile not slept. She wrote to Arabel that she despised William Story who had not shown the "manliness and fortitude" he should have done. He had his wife with him, two excellent servants, three doctors on call and plenty of money – why could he not manage with such help, why had he needed Robert? It came as a profound shock to her to realise that Robert could even consider going against her wishes to the extent of leaving her when she begged him not to. In this attitude of hers there were many parallels to her father's reactions on similar occasions in the past when he too, in much the same way, had been incredulous that his wishes were not paramount among those he loved and who he believed loved him. Elizabeth seemed to have no memory of this; she did not recall her fathers' outraged "what for?" which had so upset her when she had said, in her youth, that she was going to see Boyd, or any of the other times when her fathers' selfishness had distressed her. What need had ever been seen to match his? What need could now be alleged to match hers? The coldness of her tone was exactly like her father's, concerned with logic and facts and making no allowance for emotion. To Mrs Story she wrote hypocritically that she had been only too glad to "play her part" in doing without Robert (though she could not resist some sharp words about the folly of not sticking to the advice of *one* doctor) but everything she wrote to Arabel contradicted this assertion. She had always said she loathed "masculine men" but now she scorned Mr Story for not being masculine and Robert for acting with "feminine" warmth and sympathy. It was only when the whole episode was over that she began to feel proud of her husband.

But it was another black mark against Rome. She wrote to Miss Mitford at the beginning of May that "to leave Rome will fill me with barbarian complacency – I don't pretend to have a rag of sentiment about Rome." Pen had just been ill – "more unwell lately than ever I saw him" – and they had had to call the doctor three times. Instead of looking his usual "radiant" self, he was now "a delicate, pale little creature".

Robert was feeling pulled down by the unexpected expense of their winter there: Elizabeth wrote to Henrietta that Rome had been "enough to ruin us with its dearness". They were obliged to "live upon woodcocks, snipes and hares and turkey because of beef and mutton being so high in price". They had spent so much money that once back in dear, cheap Florence they would have to economise strictly to be able to visit England, as planned, in the summer. On May 28th, they left Rome with Pen still suffering from diarrhoea. Elizabeth announced the climate was "pestilential" and that she was leaving "with joy". What was worst of all about the past winter was how little work had been done: *Aurora Leigh* had remained untouched for two months after Joe Story died and then she had made only halting progress. Robert had not fared much better. The only good work to come out of Rome were the poems they had contributed to an album for Arabel's Ragged Schools Charity and to another called *The Keepsake*, again for a charity. One of the two short poems Elizabeth sent for *The Keepsake* was "Amy's Cruelty". This saw men as never giving love for nothing: they, unlike women, sought to dominate and always wanted the whole of a woman's world without ever being prepared to let women have all of theirs.

The projected visit to London was the next landmark in their lives. It was essential for professional reasons. Robert's poems, copied out by Isa, were ready for publication and, though Sarianna would see them through the press, it would be better if Robert himself supervised. Elizabeth hoped that by the time they left Florence she would have *Aurora Leigh* ready but was not very confident; it had grown very long and she had reached a difficult stage in its composition. She was more glad than sorry when, in July, Robert, to his own acute disappointment, said they would not be able to go to England at all. The money from the *David Lyon* had not arrived and so expensive had Rome been that they did not have enough even to go to Bagni di Lucca. They had to stay in blazing Florence. "If you could see me here," wrote Elizabeth to Henrietta, "low armchair – feet on the sofa – costume – as little as possible, and chiefly expressed by negatives – no stays, no gown, scarcely any petticoat – a white dressing gown – dimity jacket, I mean!" But she was happy and well, working steadily on her poem without even a cough to interrupt her. A period of retrenchment in Florence, hot as it was, pleased her.

Chapter Eighteen

T HE routine in the Casa Guidi throughout the summer and autumn of
1854 was the same as during the "happy winter" although, because
of the heat, not so rigorously imposed. Elizabeth and Robert wrote in the
mornings, rested in the afternoons (or sometimes Robert walked) and
then congenial visitors were invited to tea. Old friendships were resumed
and new ones begun (for instance with Brinsley Norton, Caroline
Norton's second son who had married an Italian peasant girl), but only
with Isa Blagden did they feel really close. Isa was now a favourite with
Pen as well as with his parents and shared their passionate interest in his
development.

Elizabeth was still trying hard to reveal the joys of learning to Pen,
now five, but with little success. She was determined to keep to her
resolution never to force learning on Pen but what was beginning to
perplex her was that her son seemed to have no natural desire, rising
unbidden as it had done in both his mother and father, to learn. Her
lessons with him were far from satisfactory and so were the dividends.
His writing caused her less concern than his reading: Elizabeth proudly
told Mrs Ogilvy that Pen's Grandfather Browning treasured a book of
his handwritten compositions, "all perfectly genuine". But his reading
irritated her. She told Mrs Ogilvy that Pen could read aloud from
"childish books" very well "and with great animation" but then criti-
cised him for his "want of . . . application" when it came to any text the
least bit difficult. He would not keep still and try to work out problem
words. He hopped about like a bird, and "played at omnibus for
instance on the arm of my chair". If she brought herself to scold him he
would say, "Oh you darling pet Ba – be dood," and as she said to Mrs
Ogilvy, what could she do "half-strangled in the little hugging arms".

Robert was unkind enough to suggest that she could do quite a lot.
Elizabeth taught Pen reading but Robert taught him music and in his
department he was quite determined there should be a disciplined

approach. He taught Pen how to play the piano through the traditional method of constant practising of scales and chords which Elizabeth told Henrietta was a "system rather dry for such a young child". Robert did not think so and pressed on regardless. Pen did his scales and the sight of him sitting with his music book solemnly reciting "*tot*chet, sharp etc." was described by Elizabeth as too sweet for words. What amazed her was the young piano player's quite open anxiety "to get on". He clearly wanted not only to succeed but to please his teacher. It was a salutary lesson for Elizabeth and gave her pause for thought. She realised that Pen did indeed benefit from an element of compulsion and that loving indulgence only encouraged him to think he could give up when anything was difficult. He often made Elizabeth laugh but he also made her sad: no matter how hard she tried to keep Pen a baby he was growing up fast and he was growing into a boy. Her attempts to keep him young and delightfully "neuter", as she had once put it to Henrietta, were only just this side of ridiculous and already doomed to failure because Pen wanted them to fail. She had hoped to carry on dressing him in pretty, delicate fabrics until he was twelve, an age she had fixed for having his curls cut off. But Pen suggested having his hair cut now – the curls got in his way – and she had to compromise by having it trimmed, but "only the ends to prevent splitting". She could still coax him into his "long crowned black velvet hat and feather". It pleased her that as his sixth birthday approached he asked for a doll that squeaked and could sleep with him, and thanked God that he was still "peculiarly infantine" and was never thought even to be six. Six was "dreadful enough" and she confessed, "I grudge the six years old."[1]

Unfortunately, there were more telling reminders of time passing than small boys growing up: at the other end of the time scale, old friends were dying. As soon as they had returned to Florence from Rome, Flush, aged fourteen, had died. Elizabeth was brave about it, telling Arabel, "he was old you know . . . He had scarcely a hair on his back." It had been comparatively easy explaining to Pen, who had witnessed the dog's dying, that Flush was so old and tired that he could no longer enjoy life and his death was a natural and merciful release. Pen was quickly consoled, especially by the purchase of more rabbits, for whom Ferdinando built hutches on the now dangerously overcrowded balcony, and by the ceremony of burying Flush in the Casa Guidi courtyard. Other shadows cast in 1854 were not so easily dispelled and, even when they passed over without fatal results, Elizabeth was left trembling. In

Pen's sketch of his father, 1853: "I done this for please Papa"

September her father had a serious accident. He was thrown from a cab and broke his leg. At almost seventy years of age this was a frightening incident, even though he made a good recovery, and made Elizabeth more aware than ever that her father was likely to die without forgiving her. Knowing that the sight of her handwriting would prevent him opening any letter from her, she cunningly had Pen address the envelope and then sent it to a friend in London to post so that there would be no Italian postmark. This would give her desperate plea "a chance of being opened". Whether it was opened or not, she never knew: certainly, her father did not reply. Her worry and distress about him overshadowed her eighth wedding anniversary. Robert, to cheer her, gave her "a beautiful malachite brooch . . . mystically marked and as deep a green as the Elysian ghosts walk in when the poets glide them". They both bought Wilson a "very pretty" new silk dress.[2]

But in January 1855 another expected death was not averted. Miss Mitford died. Arabel had written in December to say Miss Mitford was very seriously ill and not expected to recover but Elizabeth, still receiving her friend's vigorous letters, did not believe her: they were written in such a firm hand and were so resolute in tone that it was inconceivable the writer was dying. She wrote Miss Mitford a flurry of letters during her last illness, full of religious comfort. She reminded her friend of "that ineffable tenderness" of our Lord Jesus Christ which would make the human love left behind "strike you as cold and dull by comparison". She assured her, "He means well by us," and that "when we suffer . . . he often makes the meaning clear." Death was once more "a mere incident in life – perhaps scarcely a greater one than the occurrence of puberty." It was as though Joe Story had never died, so complete was her re-affirmation of her earlier convictions, with no sign that they had been dramatically shaken such a short time before. The "body of the flesh" was "a mere husk" and Elizabeth repeated that she believed "in no waiting in the grave" but in "an active HUMAN life, beyond death as before it, an uninterrupted human life". At the end of a passionate rather than compassionate résumé of her creed she added a little self-consciously, "But you'll be tired with 'what I believe'."

Once Miss Mitford was dead, Elizabeth found it much harder to believe in her own comfort. She tried to tell herself that her friend was better off and that, as she assured Henrietta, death was "gain to her". But she could not bring herself to look through Miss Mitford's last letters; they were put with all her others in a box which was closed. It was a bad time for her to have received such news, because she was ill herself. A happy, cosy Christmas had been followed by a dreadful month during which she was ill as she had never before been ill in Italy. Her cough was racking, her breathing difficult. Their apartment had been arranged for the winter into a huge bed sitting room but even so it was not easy to keep the combined bedroom and drawing room warm – the ceilings were high, the windows vast, the floor area enormous. Her illness began with a cold and developed rapidly into "my old illness" (to which no single name was ever given) with scarcely a pause between violent, prolonged paroxysms of coughing: clearly, the chronic bronchitis had returned. Robert, with Wilson's help, nursed her night and day. It was he who sat up all night to see that the fire was kept up and to feed Elizabeth tiny, hot, reviving spoonfuls of coffee. Elizabeth blamed the weather, which was unusually frosty with a bitter wind, and was quick to assure Sarianna, "I have escaped some bad symptoms. No spitting of blood . . . no loss of voice and scarcely a threatening pain in the side." She was not, she said, as "wasted away" as she used to be in the old days after such attacks. What was striking was her absolute determination to get better. She wrote to Mrs Martin that she need not worry: "you needn't exhort me – I don't give up. I mean to live on and be well."

As she told Mrs Ogilvy, she had a child and a husband to live for. The idea of welcoming death, as once she had done, was abhorrent to her. She forced herself, in February, to write a long letter to Henrietta, "lest you should be anxious, all of you, about this silence of mine". And to convince her sister she was well she discussed a wide range of topics to show she was not comatose but able to take her usual lively interest in the world. She was indignant that she had been asked if she was concerned about what was happening in the Crimea (where war had begun the year before between England and France, on the one hand, and Russia, on the other). Certainly she was concerned and, as for Robert, he was "frantic". They were both "sick" at accounts of what was happening, even though she wrote that the war was "a most righteous and necessary war". She thought what was at stake in the Crimea was "the liberty and civilisation of all Europe, the good of the world for centuries". It made her "blood creep" to think of the sufferings of the soldiers and of their relations (including the Hedleys who had a son, her cousin, there). But she was pleased at one aspect of the war – the alliance between England and France – even if she could not resist praising the French for "how well and magnanimously" they had behaved and criticising the English for "errors of organisation". She wrote with such vigour that she left her sister in no doubt that she was recovering "for love's sake".

But it was not only "for love's sake" that she fought to recover: it was for work's sake too. The *David Lyon* had finally yielded the sum of £175 and the plan was to go to England in the summer to see both her work and Robert's published but, whereas Isa had finished transcribing Robert's *Men and Women*, Elizabeth had neither finished her own *Aurora Leigh* nor copied a single line ready for printing. She wrote despairingly to Mrs Ogilvy in March, "here are between five and six thousand lines *in blots*." Until she was fully recovered she could not make any progress but in April the sun returned to Florence and the wind vanished and at once her strength began to return. "I am on my perch again – nay, even out of the cage door," she reported and was moved to reflect that she was like a cat with nine lives. By the time Hatty Hosmer and two other Americans, Mr and Mrs Kinney, visited her at Easter she was so full of high spirits that she actually took part in an extraordinary escapade (though it never ran its full course). Hatty suggested that she and Elizabeth and Mrs Kinney should dress up as men so that they could get into a monastery barred to women, in order to see some pictures

Robert had been describing. He and Mr Kinney could take them, pretending to be their tutors. A week later the plan was carried out. All three women began dressing as men, in a state of high excitement, while a reluctant Robert and Mr Kinney condescended to go and get a closed carriage. The arrangement was that they would bring the carriage into the doorway of the Casa Guidi and the three disguised women could jump quickly in without being seen. But Elizabeth, ready first, went downstairs to wait, got carried away with her own daring and began testing her disguise by walking up and down the pavement in full view of some Florentines who were puzzled by this strange looking "man". Robert and Mr Kinney arrived back with the carriage just in time to bundle her into the house. Robert was furious, Elizabeth tearful with remorse. He was terrified her disguise had been penetrated, her identity established and that a story would appear in a newspaper. Mrs Kinney and even the bold Hatty thought Elizabeth had gone off her head: it had not escaped Mrs Kinney's notice that Elizabeth had had "an extra dose of opium".[3]

At least such exuberance showed Elizabeth capable of making the trip to England, even if her energy was drug-induced and more apparent than real. This time she had a not unpleasant feeling of urgency about going to London. She thought *Men and Women* a brilliant collection and fully expected Robert to have his genius acclaimed. It was important to her more than to Robert that it should be: the year before, when a play of his, *Colombe's Birthday*, had been briefly revived she had been barely able to read the reviews because of her feverish hope that they would be magnificent, which they were not. She wanted him to be acknowledged by his peers as a significant poet. Of her own still unfinished poem and its possible impact on the public she thought little. By the time they left the Casa Guidi in June 1855 she had completed "six or seven thousand lines" but felt she had at least another two thousand to write. This seemed to cause her no distress; she was optimistic that she would somehow be able to work on *Aurora Leigh* in transit though she ought to have remembered that past experience suggested the contrary. She needed to be settled to write, not travelling or in limbo. What caused her more anxiety as they set off was a domestic matter: Wilson and Ferdinando had just announced their engagement. With still vivid memories of Crow's duplicity, Elizabeth was gratified that everything was open and above board but she saw hideous complications looming ahead. Wilson was English and Protestant, Ferdinando Italian and

Catholic. Ferdinando did not see the problem – he would agree to any conditions, marry in any church – but both Elizabeth and Robert felt that, as the couple would be living in Italy, their marriage must be valid in the eyes of the church there. For a Protestant to marry a Catholic needed a dispensation, and an agreement from the Protestant that any children would be brought up in the Catholic faith. Elizabeth took this far more seriously than the betrothed couple and was annoyed when Ferdinando said he would turn Protestant if necessary, and with Wilson when she appeared not to care in which religion her children were brought up. What Elizabeth did not know was that her servants were in no position to argue the finer points: Wilson was four months' pregnant when she announced her engagement. The trip to England came at a disastrous time for her. She wanted to marry immediately but her employers had so far only obtained a dispensation from the Archbishop of Florence as a provisional step. As far as they were concerned, there was no hurry and Wilson did not dare enlighten them. Both Brownings liked Ferdinando: he was excellent, Elizabeth told Arabel, and vowed "a better man more upright and of a more tender nature it would be difficult to find". The Brownings were not like Mr Barrett nor did they rule their establishment as he ruled No. 50 Wimpole Street but, all the same, Wilson, like Crow, did not have enough confidence in her employers' sympathy to tell them the truth till she was safely married.

The Brownings, together with their two engaged servants, went first to Leghorn and then by ship to Corsica where they picked up another ship to Marseilles, a route they estimated less tiring than the overland one. At Marseilles they were extremely surprised to find Alfred Barrett, who, they knew from Henrietta and Arabel, was about to take the momentous step, at the age of thirty-five, of marrying his cousin Lizzie Barrett, his father's ward for the last thirteen years. Alfred knew, of course, that he would be instantly cast off by his father as his sisters had been.[4] His position would be perilous because, like all the Barretts except Elizabeth, he had no money of his own and his income was small. This did not stop him buying lavish presents for Pen, who announced his "Untle" was nearly as nice as his mother and father. To Elizabeth's relief, her brother did not try to solicit her support for his marriage. She did not want to be involved – no Barrett ever did in events of this troublesome sort – but in any case she was not sure she approved any more than her father. Lizzie's branch of the family had mental instability in it and Alfred's lack of money was more of an obstacle in her eyes than it had been when she announced long ago to Miss Mitford that she adored people who married for love. But no confessions marred their time together in Marseilles which was lucky because, in Paris a week later, Elizabeth needed Alfred's help to retrieve a box she had left behind. The box was valuable not because it contained the manuscript of *Aurora Leigh*, which it did, but because it held "all my Penini's pretty dresses, embroidered trousers, collars, everything I have been collecting to make him look nice in . . . isn't it horrible?"

The stay in Paris, meant to be short, took an extra week because of Wilson's marriage. Elizabeth reported to Arabel that Ferdinando was behaving very oddly – "Ferdinando keeps saying 'Why won't they (meaning Robert and me) let me turn Protestant?'" She announced self-righteously to Arabel that "he may turn Protestant when he pleases afterwards but it's our duty *first* to make his marriage legal in his own country."[5] After another few days Ferdinando was described as "desperate" and to Elizabeth's astonishment he "resolved to . . . renounce his country and set up a *fiacre* (of all vocations adopted through melancholy!) in Lyons . . ." It did not come to that. On 10th July a liberal priest was found and Wilson and Ferdinando were married the day before they all left for England (Alfred Barrett married his cousin Lizzie in Paris, too, three weeks later). After "a hideous, rolling, heaving passage" to Folkestone they all reached London at three in the morning. This time they were lodged in Dorset Street, still within Barrett territory but further to the west of Wimpole Street than before. The apartment was tolerable but the weather was not: it was another chronically bad English summer. Within a week Elizabeth was claiming that due to the "heavy air" Pen was horribly pale. Ever since their arrival it had been "very uncertain, cloudy, misty and rainy". Ferdinando was found staring out of the window in a depressed state. Elizabeth had no idea that he was depressed about something more than the rain.

But of course the weather was irrelevant to the purpose of their visit which was to supervise the printing of *Men and Women*. By the middle of August, the first half volume was done and Elizabeth was helping Robert read the proofs of the rest as it came off the press. She found it totally exhausting. "I assure you," she wrote to Mrs Martin, "I am stuffed as hard as a cricket ball with the work of every day." Her own *Aurora Leigh* did not stand a chance, so pressing was the need to concentrate on Robert's collection which she was more convinced than ever would astound the world. Pleasant times with her sisters were rare. Arabel was suddenly told the whole household was moving to Ramsgate three weeks after the Brownings had arrived, and Elizabeth was in despair. Robert said he thought they could manage some time there, too, but they could find no lodgings. As it turned out, this was just as well because Occy, unable to find lodgings for the Barretts, had gone on to Eastbourne instead. Arabel said she would refuse to go but was obliged to give in, though she defiantly returned for a visit to see Elizabeth. It was doubly distressing not to have Arabel in Wimpole Street because Pen was quite happy, this year, to go out with her – very useful when Mama and Papa were busy with proofs. While his aunt was still in residence at No. 50 Wimpole Street, he made one visit which ended dramatically and thrilled his mother "to the roots of my heart". George, also at home, had been playing boisterously with Pen in the hall while his father was in the dining room. It is inconceivable that George did not know his father was at home – everyone was always extremely aware of Mr Barrett's presence – equally inconceivable that Mr Barrett would not hear a child's laughter and screams, sounds quite foreign to the house. It was elementary for him to connect such a noise with the presence in London of his estranged daughter's small son. He duly heard, as presumably he was intended to, and came out into the hall. He looked at Pen, then aged six and reputed to be the image of Bro at that age. He watched the child (according to Elizabeth's account drawn from what George told her) "for two or three minutes", then he turned and went back into the dining room. George was called for. His father asked, "Whose child is that, George?" to which George replied, "Ba's child." There was no explosion of wrath. Mr Barrett merely looked at George and asked, "And what is he doing here, pray?"[6] George's answer is not recorded. Pen was taken home. Soon after this encounter, the order to go to Eastbourne was given. But one of Elizabeth's dearest wishes had been granted, if in a roundabout way. Her father had seen her child.

He had never seen Altham, Henrietta's son, nor was he likely to. That summer, Henrietta could not manage to get to London (she had had a miscarriage in the spring) and Elizabeth could not leave it. The frustration of being so near to each other and yet so far deepened. By the middle of August, Elizabeth was writing to Henrietta, "I know I am behaving just infamously to you" but that she need not doubt "if I *could* go to you, you would not need to ask me". Apart from Henrietta's health, money was a genuine obstacle to the Cooks' coming to London but Surtees finally agreed to send his wife and son on their own on a quick visit. Unfortunately, this was just at the point when Arabel had to leave for Eastbourne and by the time Henrietta had decided she would just have to miss Arabel she fell ill again. The three sisters gave up hope of the longed for reunion. But soon confusion of a different but equally maddening kind followed. Wilson, unable by the end of August to hide her condition any longer, told Elizabeth she was expecting a baby in a few weeks' time. Elizabeth was appalled. She wrote to Henrietta on September 6th that she was not only "shocked" but "pained". Clearly, the baby had been conceived in the Casa Guidi by the unmarried couple. She does not appear, for all her acknowledged recognition of the power of sexual attraction, to have thought back to the living accommodation in the Casa Guidi, to that room of Wilson's next to the even smaller one where Ferdinando slept. The proximity for two people in love was irresistible. As usual, it was not only the immorality which shocked Elizabeth, that admirer of George Sand, but the *deceit*. She hated to think Wilson had not confided in her. She had never given Wilson the least cause to be sure of her sympathy and tolerance in such a situation but she was angry that she had not been naturally trusted. But at least her affection for, and gratitude to, Wilson was sufficient to make her try hard in this crisis to "think chiefly of her many excellent qualities and of what she has done for me . . ." as she put it to Henrietta. Quite what *she* was prepared to do for Wilson in this hour of her need was not at first clear. Obviously, Wilson would have to go somewhere to have her baby: she certainly could not give birth in her employers' lodgings. It was arranged that she would go to her sister's who lived in East Retford (her mother had died two years before). Equally obviously, Elizabeth would need a new maid: managing on her own during Wilson's annual two week holiday was one thing, managing for a possible six months another. But these were trivial decisions compared to the underlying major one: would Wilson come back after the birth of her baby? Could she come back? Could she bring her baby with her? The Brownings' answer to that last question dictated all else: No, Wilson could not take her baby back to the Casa Guidi. The apartment was too small, they could not afford another mouth to feed and Wilson would be unable to perform her duties properly. So they gave Wilson a choice: either she remained in their service, leaving her baby with her sister, or she left their service and kept her child. Where her husband Ferdinando fitted into this choice was for Wilson to work out. If she stayed in England, she lost him, unless he could miraculously find employment and support her and her child; and if she went back to Italy, she kept him but lost her child. She left for East Retford with no illusions, still undecided. Nobody had offered her the only truly compassionate alternative: to keep both husband and baby, return with them to Italy, board the baby out nearby and continue working. Victorian employers thought such magnanimity absurd. Elizabeth was a creature of her time in sharing what they saw as an entirely justifiable viewpoint: her peers would not have expected her to behave in any other way. But the author of *Aurora Leigh*, so concerned with the plight of poor working women, so close to a servant who had proved her loyalty over and over again at considerable personal risk, cannot be judged by conventional standards. Elizabeth failed Wilson as Wilson had never failed her. To take Wilson and her baby back to Italy would have been impractical, inconvenient, unreasonably charitable – but it would not have been impossible for people as resourceful and courageous as the Brownings.

The Wilson crisis was the last straw. Elizabeth condemned the whole visit to London as "most uncomfortable and unprofitable". Even the socialising, enjoyable though much of it was, had been too much. "It's the mad bull and china shop," she complained to Mrs Martin, "and we are the china shop. People want to see if Italy has cut off our noses, or what!" They received invitations from all over the country and "we have had to say 'no, no, no' everywhere". Not quite everywhere; she made time, though "pulled on all sides" and "in a state of distraction", to go to a séance conducted by the famous medium, Daniel Dunglas Home. He was Scottish born but his family had emigrated to America where, by the time he was in his twenties, he had made a name for himself as a medium who could call forth spirit hands and music. Elizabeth had heard about him from American friends in Florence and when told he was in London wrote to Henrietta, "He's the most interesting person to me in England out of Somersetshire and 50 Wimpole Street." She was as passionate to attend a Home séance as she had been to meet George Sand and Robert was subjected to the same kind of bullying until he had arranged for her to attend one. Home was staying in Ealing with a lawyer called Rymer who had recently lost a twelve-year-old son, Wat, with whom the medium claimed to be in touch. Mrs Rymer was a lady of irrefutable character, a friend of the inestimable Mrs Jameson. On the evening of 23rd July the Brownings both went to the Rymers' house, with Robert disapproving and uneasy while Elizabeth was excited and expectant. Since it was summer it was not dark by the time the séance began at nine o'clock but with the heavy curtains almost drawn and only one dim light from a lamp it seemed dark enough. Home, the Rymers, the Brownings and five others sat round a table. The table soon moved, faint, weird music was heard and then the rappings began. The one lamp was put out. The company waited. Elizabeth, in the account she later gave to Henrietta, felt "perfectly calm, not troubled in any way". She was absolutely certain some spirit was present but "*no spirit belonging to me*". She felt her dress blow as though in a wind and then saw a hand "white as snow" coming from underneath the table. She "put up my glass to look . . . proving it was not a mere mental impression". Another hand then appeared and, picking up a clematis wreath lying on the table, placed it on Elizabeth's head. She asked if it could be transferred to Robert's head. As it went from Elizabeth's head it passed under the table towards Robert and he felt several pats on his knee. He tried to grasp what he imagined was a hand but it disappeared too quickly. Home announced that it belonged to a relation of Elizabeth's. The name would be rapped out in a code. To Robert's extreme satisfaction, it was a name unknown to Elizabeth. Home then went into a trance and spoke as Wat, the dead Rymer child. Elizabeth admitted this was "such twaddle", but it did not invalidate the rest of the séance for her. She pronounced it as "wonderful and conclusive" and was careful to keep the clematis wreath.[7]

Robert had never felt so disgusted – with Home, with the Rymers, with Elizabeth, with the whole charade. What disgusted him most was his wife's willingness to be made a fool of, to be party to what he termed "a vulgar fraud". He did not know how the effects had been managed but of one thing he was certain: they *were* stage effects, human ones. No sooner had he left the Rymers than he was chastising himself for not exposing the blatant trickery he had witnessed. He realised that Home had relied on his respect for the grieving Rymers: such sensitivity was what all mediums depended on. The highly charged emotional atmosphere was an effective way of controlling interference from sceptics: people like Robert did not want to be cruel, did not want to embarrass. Robert's hatred of Home grew in proportion to the pity he felt for those desperate to be duped, among them his wife. Nothing would persuade Elizabeth to admit that there had not been one single piece of solid evidence of contact with a spirit world. Music, rapping, table-moving, ghostly hands (which had not felt ghostly to Robert) – none of these so-called "manifestations" were anything of the kind. Robert could not explain how any of it was done but he saw no need to; the onus of proof was on the other side. Elizabeth denied this. She said she did not need proof, that only sceptics did. Communication with a spirit world was "undeniable" and "has been from first to last". They quarrelled and to her surprise she found Robert was not prepared to agree to differ. On the contrary, he was prepared, after a night's restless sleep, to go and confront Home and the Rymers and tell them what he thought. Elizabeth begged him not to, but he refused and sent a message demanding an interview with Home at once. Home said he was ill but then snatched the advantage by turning up unannounced with the Rymers to visit Elizabeth. She was in agonies over what would happen. Robert, with a fine display of contempt, shook hands with Mrs Rymer but acted as if Home were not there. Elizabeth (but this is according to Home's account) stood "pale and agitated" until he went up to her. Robert, who could not bear such an odious man to touch even his wife's hand, launched into an offensive diatribe against him. Home tried to defend himself, Mrs Rymer took his part, Robert continued to rage and Elizabeth to tremble. It was a most humiliating and painful scene ending with no one the victor.

Yet distressed as she was, Elizabeth still believed. She made no cheerful remarks, as she had once done, about converting Robert or about everyone being entitled to their own opinion. There was a real rift and she recognised it as such. It shook her: she did not toss her head or announce with glee that she knew she was right. From now on, she wrote to Henrietta, anything whatsoever to do with spiritualism was "a *tabooed* subject in this house". Her sister was not even to mention it, or any aspect of it, in her letters. Robert and she had "completely different views" and all compromise was out of the question. Elizabeth turned secretive, for the first time in her marriage, instructing her correspondents to hide any spiritualist information she sent them. When a Mr Jarves in America wrote and told her how the spirits were becoming bold and were making themselves "partially visible" she passed this gem on to Henrietta but warned her, "the subject is still *in suspense* in this house". The atmosphere in the house was tense and when Wilson revealed her condition it became worse. Wilson trudged round the Dorset Street lodgings, packing Elizabeth and Pen's clothes in readiness for their departure to Paris and instructing Harriet, her replacement, as to the finer points of caring for them. She was worried about Ferdinando being on his own without her in Paris, not knowing when they would be reunited. She still had not made her "choice" by the time she left London for East Retford in the first week of October. The Brownings left, with Ferdinando and Harriet, on October 17th. Four days before, on Saturday October 13th, Wilson gave birth to a son, Oreste. From Paris Elizabeth wrote to Henrietta that they had fallen "upon evil days and yellow satin sofas in the rue de Grenelle". There was no sunshine because it was "due east in aspect . . . with draughts flying around like birds". Almost immediately she caught cold though this was somehow not the fault of Parisian "draughts" but "through London". Pen moped for Wilson, Ferdinando moped for Wilson and Elizabeth herself moped a little for her too, now that she was without the comforts Wilson brought. Everywhere she looked was "*black*".

The only cheering news that autumn in Paris was that *Men and Women* had been published on 11th November and that in the first three days it had sold enough copies to cover costs. Elizabeth's hopes soared: at last Robert was to get his due. But sales soon fell off (though compared to Robert's previous pitifully small sales they were still healthy). The critics did not hail his genius as Elizabeth had anticipated. *The Athenaeum* grieved instead over his wasted energy and chastised him for his old fault, obscurity. Some individual poems were praised but the general tone was carping. The other magazines were hardly more enthusiastic. At first, Robert dismissed the reviewers as crass but then he grew angry and bitter. The critics, he decided, were not just fools but animals. He wrote to his publishers that he had stopped up his ears – "Whoo-oo-oo-oo mouths the big monkey" – and that he felt like giving them a brutal dig with his umbrella.[8] Elizabeth suffered for and with him. The injustice of such a reception for the beautiful *Men and Women* collection pained her. She watched the reviews make Robert steadily more unhappy – all he did, she wrote to Henrietta, was "smoulder over the fire" and torture himself by going to Galignani's, the reading-room well stocked with English papers which abused his work. Their position, in the uncomfortable apartment with its "hateful" yellow sofas, was "wretched". But Robert refused to go off without her to the Holy Land as she had suggested; she had been spitting blood for the first time for years and he was seriously alarmed. This spitting of blood looks like evidence of TB but, since yet again the stethoscope revealed none, it was not as significant as it seemed. Prolonged, violent coughing can easily cause traces of blood in the phlegm – many a Victorian woman (Caroline Norton, for example) considered herself fatally ill because she was spitting blood only to discover that the blood came from gum disease or from this kind of rupturing cough. But Robert, of course, had never seen Elizabeth spit blood before and was naturally afraid. Their mutual apprehension together with their misery at the reception of *Men and Women* made them tender with each other. Robert promised to be "meek as a maid" if he met Home, who was rumoured to be in Paris, and even brought himself to read letters from the Storys in Florence, about mediums walking in the air over heads, without exploding. They were, Elizabeth wrote to Arabel, like "the lion and the lamb" over spiritualism now, lying together on the sofa in total harmony.

Elizabeth needed such harmony desperately: she could not afford any more calls on her depleted energies. *Aurora Leigh* was still not finished. She must finish it and take it to England before she could return to Italy and make herself well again. To her relief, the raw edge of Robert's bitterness was soon blunted and he absorbed himself in drawing. His father, now permanently resident in Paris with his daughter Sarianna, was currently in the habit of going to the Louvre to draw (he was an accomplished artist) and Robert began to go with him, quite content to spend most of every day sketching, too. Then there was another cause for rejoicing when they managed to move into an apartment in a street off the Champs-Elysées where Elizabeth immediately felt better. She was so ill when they moved in the middle of December that Robert had to carry her to a carriage, "swathed past possible breathing" in shawls. The concierge, alarmed at the sight of this "struggling bundle", was told by Robert that it was only the body of a woman he had murdered but that it was easy to carry because there was nothing there but a pair of lungs. The lungs adapted well to the new apartment. By Christmas, for which Pen was given the strange present of an iron and stone fireplace, Elizabeth was hard at work. She boasted bravely to Henrietta that she weathered storms "in a miraculous way", and so it seemed. The new apartment was taken until 15th June, when they would visit London once more before returning to Florence. She had not quite six months to finish what she knew would be her greatest work.

Chapter Nineteen

THE New Year of 1856 brought "a plague of industry" for Elizabeth in Paris. She was so busy she left a precious English newspaper on the table "three days . . . before I could read it". She was experiencing, she wrote to Mrs Martin, "a sort of *furia*" in her efforts to finish *Aurora Leigh*. By the end of February she told Mrs Jameson she had "put in order and transcribed five books, containing in all above six thousand lines". This left another book ready to transcribe "and then must begin the composition part of one or two more books I suppose".[1] The "I suppose" was revealing. It indicated that, like many an author at this stage of composition, Elizabeth was in difficulties with her work. It was not that she was bored by it, nor that her creative energy was flagging, but that she was unsure which direction to take as she neared the end of her immensely long poem. A look at the finished *Aurora Leigh* shows why. When she made this comment to Mrs Jameson about supposing she had one or more books still to go, she was at the end of Book VI.

These first six books of *Aurora Leigh* race along with such exuberance that no one needs to be told that the author found them pouring out of her with the greatest ease. Everything she wrote up to the end of them had been pent up inside her for a decade – it was a joy to find her feelings and opinions emerging so effortlessly and with such force that the only problem was to curb and shape their impetuosity. Elizabeth told Aurora's story as though intimately acquainted with it. Aurora was born in Italy to an Italian mother and an English father. Her mother died soon after her birth and her father when she was thirteen. She was sent to England, where she was brought up by a strict, cold aunt whose main concern is that Aurora should marry her cousin Romney who wants her to help him in his idealistic social experiments when she grows up. But Aurora has a different view of marriage as well as a strong desire to fulfil her vocation and be a poet.

It took Elizabeth 1,248 lines (Books I and II) to establish her subject matter. The next three books of her poem saw her developing her main theme: can women be happy with only their art to fulfil them or do they need men? She explores this question within an intricate plot concerning her cousin Romney's projected marriage to a poor girl, Marian Erle. The marriage never takes place because Marian jilts Romney. Book VI reveals why: Marian has been tricked, raped, and has borne a child. Aurora, discovering Marian in Paris, where her captors took her, becomes her saviour. She takes her and her son to Italy to live with her. In Books VIII and IX, in which Aurora tries to bury herself in her work, there is a dramatic dénouement. Romney, blinded in a fire which destroyed the hall where he had housed his new social community, arrives in Florence and marries Aurora.

No summary could reveal how hard Elizabeth worked on the construction of this melodrama. She was determined that *Aurora Leigh* should have a strong narrative drive but found this more difficult than she had envisaged. By February 1856 she was at the end of Book VI – where Aurora has discovered Marian and heard her sad story – and facing great technical problems. The main one was what to do with the ruined Marian. The poem could end in one more book if Aurora were to take Marian under her protection. The point of the poem would then be both a diatribe against worthless men and in praise of work as a way of life for women instead of so called love and marriage. This would make a sensational text – certainly that "thoroughly modern" poem she had wanted – but it would also be a betrayal. Elizabeth wanted to defend the Marians of the world and to indict a society which could exploit their need but she had no desire to condemn the entire male sex. In some ways, at the end of Book VI she realised she was only just engaging with the issues which obsessed her. She was "so anxious" to make her poem "good" and now was the testing time when the making mattered. It was no longer a question of catching and arranging her own ready words as they tumbled out, but of stopping, thinking and above all making vital artistic decisions. It was a calculated, cold-blooded affair and it worried her. For the first time she envisaged *Aurora Leigh* as a failure and wrote, "if it's a failure, there will be the comfort of having made a worthy effort, of having done as well as I could."[2] The responsibility sat heavily upon her as she contemplated alternative endings. By the end of March, she knew "one or two" books would not be enough: she had embarked on an ending so complicated she would need at least three to work out the destinies of Aurora and Romney who were to be brought together in Italy. If she missed a single day's composition now she announced herself "lost". This, she admitted, was "too close a rate" and made her feel "nervous".

In the midst of this exhausting daily labour – and it was both noticeable and significant that in the last three books there was much more effort than pleasure – normal life went on. Elizabeth was relieved that Robert, although not writing poetry, was still engrossed in drawing and also in Paris social life. He often went out to dinner and made himself useful to old friends like Lady Elgin who was now paralysed and needed company. There was no need to worry about Robert's welfare. Pen caused her more concern. He still missed Wilson. Partly because she knew this, Elizabeth made sure she continued his lessons even though they took up such a lot of her precious time. She confessed to Henrietta that Pen "tears me to rags sometimes . . . inattention, talking nonsense, dawdling in finding his books . . . and kissing me instead of pleasing me" but she did not want to burden Robert with Pen's reading, since he already taught him music, nor could she trust Harriet, Wilson's replacement. Pen never lost his temper with Wilson but he did with Harriet who had the temerity to read faster than he could and told him he was naughty. Elizabeth described, half admiringly, how Pen "with flashing eyes" snatched the book from Harriet and threw it down when he was insulted. Still, it made for "a full life", as Elizabeth commented a little wearily to Mrs Jameson: "the secret of life is in full occupation, isn't it? The world is not tenable on other terms."[3] She only wished she had a little more strength to make the fullness less wearing. This Parisian winter was fortunately mild but she was still confined indoors a great deal and found "the small rooms and deficiency of air resulting from them" not good for her. In the Casa Guidi, with its "acres of apartment", this kind of enforced seclusion had never been a problem. She tried to go out in the fresh air but it made her "a good deal tired". Her faith in being able to "get strong again easily" was waning.

She was resolute, all the same, about going to England in June, whatever the state of her health. The year before, Robert's work had made it imperative to go, this year it was hers. There was no discussion about whether she would be up to it; she *had* to be. She stirred herself to go shopping before they left to buy new clothes but found it almost too much for her. So did Pen. He commented laconically, "It's really enough to mate one dead, to sit a whole hour in shops looting at dresses."[4] They inspected two shops before she had to give up; and she came home looking like a ghost. On 29th June they left for London, at least spared the fag of looking for rooms because Kenyon, who was lying gravely ill in the Isle of Wight, had insisted they went to his empty (and magnificent) house in Devonshire Place. They both felt uneasy about accepting his kind offer but did so, appreciating the comfort of it while "rather afraid of moving our elbows for fear of breaking something". One of the greatest pleasures in arriving there was that Wilson joined them, leaving her baby with her sister. It did not seem callous to either Elizabeth or Robert that no sooner had their maid been reunited with her husband, Ferdinando, than they were taking her away from him again: Wilson was to go to the Isle of Wight with them, Ferdinando to stay in Devonshire Place.

Aurora Leigh was finished and they were free to leave London. Elizabeth's decision had been to make Aurora take Marian and her child with her to Italy. She settles in Florence and soon hears that her latest book has been a great success. This does not cheer her. She feels apathetic and cannot work. In Book VIII, Romney suddenly turns up. It emerges that his social reforms have ended in disaster: the villagers burnt down the hall where he founded his idealistic colony. In front of Aurora, Romney asks Marian to marry him. She refuses: all her love is for her child. Romney, released from his moral obligation, declares his love for Aurora and confesses he was blinded by the fire. Aurora falls into his arms and they resolve to love and work together. It was the end of what had become a cumbersome and often banal plot in which Elizabeth had come down on the side of a convenient and melodramatic climax. Love wins through and in the process much of what she believed, and expressed elsewhere in her poetry, was contradicted. Aurora's independence and bravery count for little; Romney, sanctified by fire, is made her saviour. No one was left in any doubt that Aurora was after all unable to reach complete self-fulfilment through creative work alone. It was Elizabeth's own conclusion. She had found, in her own life, that she could not in all honesty claim she had been entirely fulfilled only through her work or only because of Robert: both were essential.

Her work done, Elizabeth was free to think of fitting in a visit to Henrietta whom she had not seen at all on her three month visit the year before. In the interval, Henrietta had had her third child, Edward, and Elizabeth longed to see him. The minute she arrived in London, she began scheming to make quite sure of a reunion with her sisters. However, just as he had done the year before, as soon as the Brownings arrived, Mr Barrett ordered Arabel to accompany the rest of the family out of London. It was, as Elizabeth remarked bitterly to Henrietta, "hard, – almost inhuman". Arabel's position enraged her sister. She was now a woman of forty-three who was entirely subjugated to the will of a father who did not begin to appreciate her. She had made a life for herself helping the Ragged Schools Charity but her charity work was treated with scant respect. What appalled Elizabeth was the knowledge that, should Arabel offend or defy her father, "he would turn her out at a moment's notice". Many times she wished he would, so that Arabel would be free to come to her. As it was, she would never leave him, however harshly she was treated. Of all the Barrett children, Arabel was the most dutiful and the most religious. But she had enough sense of justice that summer to be angry with her father and, though she obediently left London, she openly expressed her resentment and went, according to Elizabeth, "in bad spirits, distressed and angry . . . determined to dislike it accordingly". The only silver lining to this cloud was that Mr Barrett had chosen the Isle of Wight for that year's exodus and of course the Brownings planned to go there, too, to see Kenyon. It was easy to visit Arabel in Ventnor while her father was still in London. They spent "a happy sorrowful two weeks" with her before going on to Cowes, at the other end of the island, to see Kenyon. Pen, happy once more with Wilson in charge, had adored Ventnor, surrounded as he was by "mine untles" (George, Henry, Sette and Occy) who set themselves to toughen him up. They introduced him to English notions of "pluck" and were delighted when, after three weeks' coaching, he squared up to a twelve-year-old boy, telling him not to be impertinent or he would "show you *I'm a boy*". Elizabeth was annoyed with her brothers for reinforcing a stereotyped notion of masculinity she hated, but there was a flash of maternal pride in her letter to Mrs Martin when she commented, "So you will please to observe that in spite of being Italians and wearing curls we can fight to the death on occasion . . ."[5]

It was as well that Pen had this kind of boisterous fun with his uncles because the rest of the Isle of Wight stay was gloomy. The Brownings went to stay in the house where Kenyon was dying of cancer at Cowes, naturally, "a melancholy visit" with Pen having to be as quiet as a mouse. Elizabeth tried to persuade herself Kenyon was not dying but, even then, "witnessing his pain and weakness was distressing enough". She was deeply affected by her friend's visible suffering. "The breath is very difficult," she wrote to Sarianna, "it is hard to live. He leans on the

table saying softly and pathetically 'My God! My God!'" Elizabeth
herself had many times suffered breathing difficulties but this kind of
pain was different. It was impossible to know what to say or do
confronted with it. On paper, she could have offered, fluently but with
feeling, the same kind of comfort she had given Miss Mitford but with
Kenyon there, in front of her, in mortal agony, she could find no words.
This of course was a common predicament for her. Extrovert and
confident on paper she found herself inarticulate in person. This was
why she had been happy only to write to Robert without meeting him:
her paper self was not only fluent but in control, presenting her thoughts
and masking her emotions as and if she wished, whereas her physical self
was a dumb, helpless creature. The two sides of herself rarely merged;
long after she had made a bosom friend on paper she was capable of
being constrained in his or her company. It was a matter of inhibition in
the end. On paper Elizabeth was protected by distance and was therefore
uninhibited, once she had tried and tested a correspondent, but in
person, except with Robert and her family, she never could relax. She
watched, judged, analysed and generally exhausted herself picking up
every nuance of the conversation.

Depressed and miserable, she was embarrassed in Kenyon's presence
to find herself coughing and needing attention. It was "the piercing east
winds," she said and they reminded her "how late in the year it was
getting" (it was only the beginning of September). She must get back to
warm Florence as quickly as possible.

But first there was Henrietta to see. Plans to bring her to Ventnor had
failed and she felt she could not ask her sister to come to London,
commenting to Sarianna, "she has no means for the expense . . . she has
done it twice for me and can't this time (the purse being low)". It was
plainly her turn to go to Henrietta. She pleaded with Robert to agree to
going to London via Somerset, which, as she said to his sister, was
"something like going round the earth to Paris". But Robert counted his
pennies and decided such an expensive circuitous route could be managed. There were hopes that Arabel would be able to slip away and join
them – "she swore she would go, too, if she *could*" – but her father
arrived in Ventnor and made this impossible. The Brownings went from
Cowes to Southampton and then through Yeovil to Taunton where they
arrived at Henrietta's house the last week in September. Elizabeth had
been a little nervous about her sister's ability to house them comfortably
and had warned her, rather offensively, that Robert *must* have "some

little closet to dress in". But she need not have worried: Robert got his closet. The three of them, plus Wilson, were very happy in a cottage in the grounds of Henrietta's house. It was a delightful visit; the whole atmosphere of her sister's home struck Elizabeth forcibly as "precious". The place was entirely child-orientated and, with a father as genial as Surtees presiding over it and a mother as gentle as Henrietta, the whole family seemed to live in "a nest of love". There had always been a lingering doubt at the back of Elizabeth's mind about her sister's marriage: was Henrietta *really* happy? Could it be believed that there was more than one blissfully happy couple in the world, more than one perfect marriage? Elizabeth's attitude to Surtees had always been patronising: he was the solid soldier who would do for her sister but must not be compared, as a lover, with Robert. Now, staying among her sister's children and observing her with her husband, Elizabeth realised that Henrietta and Surtees loved each other deeply and were every bit as well matched and happy as she and Robert. Afterwards, she wrote in her thank you letter to Henrietta that she felt for Surtees "real sisterly love . . . Tell him so – tell him that I rejoice to know that you belong to him! and *that's* the fullest of compliments as it is the tenderest of truths."[6]

Leaving Henrietta was painful. Elizabeth wrote that she "could not go through all the pain of the goodbye over again". She was so upset that when they arrived back in London she ignored the feast Ferdinando had prepared and went straight to bed. When she woke up, after a fitful night, sunny Somerset seemed a golden myth; London was "very uninvitingly" wrapped in fog. She felt tired, Pen clamoured for his cousins, and there was *Aurora Leigh* waiting to be proof-read before she could return to Italy. A letter waiting for her from Arabel plunged her into further gloom: their father was ill in Ventnor. "May God help us all," Elizabeth wrote to Henrietta, adding that Robert wanted to leave at once but she still had eighty pages of her poem to correct. She knew she was making mistakes as she read her proofs: "the work presses almost too much when one is not well – and coughs half the night by way of preparation for a laborious day – and so omissions *will* happen."[7] Her opium mixture, which she was again taking in the daytime as well as at night, did not seem to be having its usual effect and she suspected the chemist was not making it strong enough. She sent Robert back to her old chemists. He provided what she used to have and expressed surprise that she was still alive – presumably indicating that the tincture he made up was a strong one – which afforded her some wry amusement. She kept herself going, even when her cough grew to "house-rending proportions", by thinking of Italy. Once back there, she would be well again. Finishing the proofs brought her to the edge of total collapse. In her last letter from Devonshire Place to Henrietta, she regretted she was not going to be able to stay to say goodbye to Arabel but consoled herself with the thought of "the badness of the goodbyes". Going away this time "will be sadder than usual after all". She no longer had any hope of a reconciliation with her elderly father. That summer, she knew both her Aunt Jane and Mrs Martin had written to him begging him to forgive her and his other cast-off children. He had replied to Mrs Martin that he *had* forgiven them and that he prayed for their families, but he failed to communicate this welcome news to the children. Elizabeth felt he had been more unforgiving than ever in his blatant attempts to keep Arabel from her.

There was one farewell Elizabeth was thankful not to have to make: Wilson was coming with them. She had at last made her "choice". A year alone with a baby in East Retford had most effectively decided her. (In fact, she had made her decision within two months of the Brownings' departure for Paris the year before and had told them so but they had said they considered they were bound to her replacement, Harriet, until they returned to London.) After the return from the Isle of Wight and Somerset, Wilson had her baby Oreste brought down from East Retford for a final leave-taking before committing him to her sister's care. Elizabeth described him as "a pretty, interesting baby . . . with great black Italian eyes". His parents proposed sending part of their wages back to East Retford each month to support him until they could be reunited. When that would be, or how it would come about, nobody was optimistic enough to speculate. Nowhere in Elizabeth's correspondence at the time did she express any compassion for Wilson's agony. The mother who adored her own child and had been overwhelmed by the violence of maternal feeling, and the poet who was about to publish a poem full of the tenderness of women for children and a defence of the exploited working-class girl, both seemed untouched by her own maid's anguish. This was a severely practical matter. Nobody had exploited Wilson, nobody had forced her into marriage or motherhood. She was a servant, she had married, she had had a baby: the rules of the game were laid down and Elizabeth abided by them. But it is not, strictly speaking, true that she was obliged to do so. It was not even true that *no* Victorian family could take in a servant's baby. Josephine Butler, soon to be famous for the campaign she led against the Contagious Diseases Acts, wife of an Oxford don, had already done so: she took in an unmarried girl who had been seduced by a Balliol man and had borne his child. There are enough isolated examples of that kind of courage, that sort of deliberate flouting of social convention, to suggest that Elizabeth could have taken Wilson's baby home with them if she had really wanted to, if her compassion had been large enough.

The Brownings left London on 23rd October, not even staying for the publication of *Aurora Leigh* scheduled for 15th November. Getting back to Florence and curing Elizabeth's cough was far more important than waiting to see how her greatest work would be received. Her cough "dropped off somewhere along the road" between Marseilles and home and, in spite of some unseasonably cold weather on their return, did not reappear. It was bliss, as ever, to be back in the Casa Guidi, where once more they found their tenants had looked after the place beautifully. The minute they settled in, Elizabeth felt as if they had "dropped suddenly down a wall out of the world". Old routines were resumed, old friends picked up and only the gossip was new. It was mainly about Home, who had recently been in Florence causing sensations among believers. She rested, and waited quite calmly for news of the reviews of *Aurora Leigh*. The first she received, among them the influential *Athenaeum*, were good. She thought "the press astonishing in its good will" but cautioned Sarianna not to be too complacent: "patience! In a little while we shall see the other side of the question and the whips will fall faster than the nosegays." The sales at least could not be disputed: they were phenomenal. The first edition sold out in a week and the second in a month. Copies could not be printed fast enough (certainly not fast enough to satisfy Robert). None of this went to Elizabeth's head. She responded gratefully and graciously to the congratulations of her friends but maintained a strong sense of perspective and proportion. Sales were welcome, praise pleasant, but what she cared about was whether her poem had been properly *understood*, which she very much doubted. She thought the critics, even the kind ones, appeared to have an "absolutely futile" idea of her work and that its "metaphysical intention (was) entirely ignored". It also annoyed her to be accused of copying *Jane Eyre*. Since it was eight years since she had read it, she sent to the library for the book "to refresh my memory", but on re-reading it could not see any real foundation for the allegation. (Edward Bulwer-Lytton's *Ernest*

Maltravers and Mrs Gaskell's *Ruth* both were more likely sources of acknowledged inspiration.) Other charges, of poor taste and of a lack of humour, disturbed her not at all. She had expected them. She knew she could not write about the Marian Erles of the world without being abused but this had been an added incentive: she wanted to rouse people to disgust, but a disgust with what was done *to* Marian not by her. She was proud when she heard that mothers thought her poem too shocking to allow their virtuous daughters to read – which she saw as proof that she had made an impact and that the daughters would be all the more determined to read her. But the best part of her success was Robert's delight. A year ago, he had suffered at the hands of many of the same critics who now praised his wife's work but there was not a scrap of resentment in him towards her success. He was far more excited, it seemed to Elizabeth, than if this success had been his own. Anyone who slammed *Aurora Leigh* was marked down by him for revenge: he promised a friend he would "rub their noses in their own filth one day" with a viciousness that alarmed his much more philosophical wife.

The odd thing was that both Robert and Elizabeth seemed genuinely to believe that the reviews as well as the sales of *Aurora Leigh* had been excellent. For once, Elizabeth's acute sense of what lay behind apparent flattery failed her. She did not appreciate how very critical a great many reviewers were. Partly, this was because the reviews came late to Florence and separately, so her overall view was a little distorted, and, partly, it was because almost every review was divided. Lavish praise was mixed with strong condemnation to an unusually confusing extent. For the first time in her career, Elizabeth took in the praise but underestimated the criticism. She picked out the applause she liked and this deafened the jeers. *Blackwood's*, for example, said, "this is a remarkable poem . . . it more than sustains that high reputation which by her previous efforts Mrs Browning has so honourably won." This was precisely the kind of compliment Elizabeth had always prized – she wanted above all else to believe she *had* a reputation and that she was improving it all the time – and she seemed not to be disturbed by the rest of the review in which she was attacked for the length, the style and the plot of her poem. She was also pleased with the reaction of the popular *Daily News*, which informed its readers that in *Aurora Leigh* she had produced "a faultless unity". Elizabeth wrote to Mrs Martin that extravagances of this nature were enough to make one laugh but she was clearly not disposed to be contemptuous of either a popular press which praised her or of a public who bought her.

The financial significance of Elizabeth's best-seller was not as important as it would have been in any previous year because on 3rd December Kenyon died and left money to both Brownings. He left Elizabeth £4,500 and Robert £6,500, a distinction for which Elizabeth was deeply grateful. This made them financially secure for the first time in their marriage and no longer in need of the profits from their poetry. Both of them were immensely grateful but at the same time so deep and genuine was their grief that they were appalled by some of the letters they received when Kenyon's legacies became known. Several people were insensitive enough to congratulate the Brownings on their luck, which disgusted Elizabeth in particular. Kenyon, for the last eleven years, had stood in the place of father to her. How could she take the smallest pleasure in his death, whatever its apparent benefits to her? But she herself indulged in a little of the speculation over the dead man's money that she condemned in others, wondering whether Henrietta would get any of it, and hoping desperately that she would. (She did, but only £100 which dismayed Surtees who had hoped for more.)

With the success of *Aurora Leigh* assured and financial worries a thing of the past, the winter of 1857–58 ought to have been another happy one, but it was not. Elizabeth's cough returned and was troublesome. She could not get rid of it in spite of holing up in her draught-proof bed-sitting room with the fires kept permanently stoked. She felt not only tired but "done in", as she put it, lacking in every kind of energy. Part of the trouble was that she was not writing. Though the physical act of writing exhausted her, the process as a whole lifted her both emotionally and spiritually. Only twice before had she written nothing for a long period – once soon after her marriage and again after Pen's birth. In both cases she had not felt the lack of it because she was inspired by her new role, first as a wife, then as a mother, and there was no room for anything else. But now the situation was different. The completion of her greatest work bred a sense of anti-climax which depressed her. For the time being, she had no idea where she wanted to go next. Her love for Robert and Pen grew every day but it was not all-consuming, not sufficient in itself to satisfy every part of her. Lying on winter afternoons in the Casa Guidi, while Pen was out visiting with Wilson and Robert was attending life-drawing classes, she had hours and hours in which to brood now that she no longer snatched such time to write. Her books fell from her hands; no narrative seemed to hold her attention for long. More and more she thought of her father and the inexplicable nature of his rejection. Time, instead of making it easier for her to accept his cruelty, made it harder. She found the resolution made straight after her marriage, not to let her father's intransigence ruin her happiness, was weakened beyond repair. She realised she had never really thought, in spite of anything she might have said, that her father would *never* forgive her, that he would move not one jot from his declared position of 1846. She had expected it to take years and years, she had expected to have to keep pleading, she had expected only a small measure of forgiveness; but what she had been too terrified to expect, she now saw, was his complete abandonment of her, his complete denial of love. She wrote to Henrietta that she had "many sad and heavy thoughts this winter, many". They were all about her father. Most of all, she found herself wondering what he would make of *Aurora Leigh*: "I think so much of these things in reference to him," she confessed to Arabel, "but I daresay he is absolutely indifferent to me and my writings."[8] It was this indifference which, in her weak and idle and uncreative state, reduced her to tears.

Robert was patience itself but had no solution to offer. No amount of reasoning was going to explain Mr Barrett. He knew, of course, that in her present condition Florence was as bad for Elizabeth as it was dull for him but it was clearly out of the question to move to Rome or anywhere else warmer and more lively. In the spring, when she was well, they would seek ways of diverting her from her pointless, tortured but pitiful thoughts. But it proved a long, dreary winter and its end was eagerly looked for. This was marked by a carnival with street processions and balls. Usually, the Brownings watched from their little balcony but this year they became participants. Pen was the prime mover. He had always wanted, Florentine fashion, to wear a mask and a domino costume in the streets. Elizabeth described to Sarianna how he "persecuted" her and "with tears and embraces" told her he had "*almost never* in all his life had a domino". He wanted "a blue one trimmed with pink! that was his taste". Clad in his pretty costume, he ran round the streets from morning to night with Wilson in hot pursuit. Florence was "one gigantic pantomime" Elizabeth told Sarianna, and the "universal madness reached me sitting by the fire (whence I have not stirred for three months)". Her spirits lifted in spite of her cough and gloomy pre-occupations. She had begun to wish she could join in the fun, too, when the bitter winds dropped, the sun shone and Robert waved a wand, declaring she *should* go to the ball. The ball in question was "the great opera ball" where Robert had amazed himself by extravagantly taking a box. The decision that Elizabeth should go to the ball was so sudden that there was no time to have a domino made so she hired one. They left the Casa Guidi on the night of the ball and went straight to their box, which Elizabeth was relieved to find more like "a pretty room" than the claustrophobic cubicle she had feared. She had intended just to sit quietly and watch but after an hour or so the lure of mingling with the crowd proved irresistible, particularly as she was feeling perfectly well. Down she went with Robert and "penetrated every corner of the theatre". Everyone else was doing the same, "all the grandees in their boxes coming down every moment among the people". She was thrilled to see the Grand Duke himself rub shoulders with Ferdinando. Somebody actually "smote me on the shoulder" with their fan and cried out 'Bella mascherina!'" She felt entirely Italian, part of this brilliant, friendly, classless mixture and could not resist boasting to Henrietta afterwards, "such things would be impossible in England". She vowed that for that night at least there was "perfect social equality". Her pleasure was complete when, at one in the morning, she presided over a supper prepared by Ferdinando – "gallentina, sandwiches, rolls, cakes, ices and champagne." She stayed until two thirty and came home feeling "disabled about the chest (not cough – only oppression)". Robert stayed on, following her home at four o'clock when the ball ended.[9]

Writing letters about this happy occasion Elizabeth's regret that such events were not regularly enjoyed came over clearly. One large and permanently frustrated part of her wanted to be forever whirling around the world sampling its "characteristic things" and witnessing its important moments. The only consolation, one that came to her the morning after the ball, was that if she had been able to indulge this side of herself "one would lead such a useless life" because no work would get done and what would life be without work? She was beginning to think she knew the answer: it would be unsatisfying. She had not worked for nearly a year, Robert for nearly two. It was not enough excuse, that summer, to tell herself she was weak or that she was still worn out after finishing the mighty *Aurora Leigh*, though people who saw her at the time would certainly have accepted such an excuse. Catherine Winkworth, who accompanied her sister and Mrs Gaskell to see Elizabeth, said she looked "very delicate". Catherine did not know how lucky she was to be permitted a glimpse of Elizabeth at all. Another of her rare visitors was Mrs Harriet Beecher Stowe whom Elizabeth allowed to come and see her only because she had adored *Uncle Tom's Cabin*. She was very glad to have done so because it emerged that Mrs Stowe was a fervent believer in spiritualism and an instant bond was forged between them. It was a bond she had need of because she had heard in March that Treppy had died. Treppy's great age (over ninety) made this less of a shock and sorrow, but she had provided a link with the past, with Elizabeth's happy childhood, and Elizabeth was saddened. She wrote to Arabel, in her usual vein, of death being but a bridge to cross but she had a new reflection to make. "As long as I *grow*, I desire to live," she wrote, ". . . but when the principle of growth is arrested . . . then I would willingly be removed."[10] Seven years previously she had written rather differently to Mrs Ogilvy.

All thoughts of resuming her writing and forging ahead poetically were banished by the news that on 17th April Mr Barrett had died of erysipelas, or St Anthony's fire, an acute skin infection which can lead to blood poisoning. Elizabeth had known he was ill but not how ill: neither the doctor nor Arabel had realised he was dying. There had been no opportunity for death-bed reconciliations or last words of forgiveness. George, as the eldest son in England (Stormie was in Jamaica), organised the funeral. The body went by train to Gloucester then by carriage to Ledbury where it was buried beside his wife's and his child's. Surtees Cook was amazed to see all the Barrett sons openly weeping at the graveside. Far from there being any grim satisfaction that a tyrant was dead and they were free, it was evident how much they had loved him. Elizabeth, when she received the news, was, said Robert, "sadly affected at first; miserable to see and hear". As on all other occasions of devastating loss, she did not cry. She lay on her sofa, silent and deathly pale, with Robert struggling to comfort her. He was relieved when after a few days the tears began and even more so when they were not followed by the remorse he had dreaded. He approved of the way Elizabeth was "reasonable and just to herself . . . does not reproach herself at all; it is all mere grief . . . that this should be *so*."[11] For several weeks, she wrote only to George and her sisters, expressing the most obvious religious sentiments about their father's death. God, she assured Henrietta, "does what HE can" and their part was over. A great deal of her grief was mercifully deflected into a more constructive channel, the question of what was to happen to Arabel.

Elizabeth assumed Arabel would make her home with her, as she had always warned Henrietta. It came as a shock to discover that Arabel herself assumed no such thing. She intended to live alone, in London. Elizabeth was sure everything would continue as normal in Wimpole Street for some time – "they won't break up everything at once in Wimpole Street" – but she could not have been more mistaken. The old Barrett home was broken up at once, by mutual agreement of all in it. Elizabeth wrote indignantly to Henrietta that nobody was showing poor Arabel any consideration. But Arabel wanted none. She was in perfect control of her own destiny. She ignored all advice from Elizabeth, who told her that of course she would be leaving London and her charity work with it and going to some quiet country place. "London is *not good*," Elizabeth wrote, but Arabel disagreed. Elizabeth promptly tried to bring pressure to bear, writing that she did not think Stormie and George, now head of the family, "will ever agree to Arabel's living by herself in London" and they would be quite right: so much for the supposedly emancipated author of *Aurora Leigh*. Convincing herself that she wanted only what was best for her sister, Elizabeth was actually trying in the most blatant way possible to run her life. Arabel was quite capable of realising this and resisting it. In time, Elizabeth acknowledged she had been at fault. She wrote to Henrietta that she was "moved in the spirit always to get up and meddle and put everybody in the place I want them to stand in – which is foolish and very provoking I dare say".[12] Foolish, provoking and very like her father. The difference was that Elizabeth had more insight and eventually brought herself to use it. She knew she had tried to dominate Arabel, who at forty-four years of age had only just escaped a life-time of domination by her father, and was ashamed. "Isn't Arabel vexed with me?" she asked Henrietta, anxiously, and swore she would reform and "keep my place and be silent. Then she will forgive me for having pushed and pulled and teased . . ." But she still hoped Arabel would choose to come to her, at least for a holiday away from "that Refuge" where she insisted on working. Otherwise, they would not see each other for another year because the Brownings were not going to England – the thought was obnoxious.

Florence that summer of 1857 dazzled with its beauty – "the trees stand in their green mist as if in a trance of joy" – but Elizabeth knew she would find release only in work. She wished for some "hard, regular work" but was not capable of it. Instead, she reported to her sisters that she lay on her sofa "and [I] never stir nor speak." She had no energy, physical or psychic, for anything. Only Pen roused her intermittently from her depression and it was for his sake that she made the effort to go once more to the Bagni di Lucca but with no enthusiasm at all. Suddenly, her life which had been for the last twelve years so ambitious and forward-looking, in every sense, lacked direction.

Chapter Twenty

Going to Bagni di Lucca did not at first improve either Elizabeth's health or her spirits. The minute she arrived, she wrote to Henrietta that she was "half-sorry" they had come, in spite of the fact that it was so much cooler. What worried her most was the dullness of Bagni di Lucca in general. They had now spent three long summers there and knew it too well. It was beautiful but familiar. Elizabeth had tried hard to persuade George to come and also Henry but remarked bitterly to Henrietta that of course they wouldn't and "I don't waste myself hoping". She urged old friends to join them. To her great delight both Isa and Lytton agreed to come, "all for our sake" as Robert told Sarianna, adding "they not otherwise wanting to come this way".[1]

It was a pity they allowed themselves to be persuaded. Lytton arrived feeling vaguely unwell and the next day was prostrate with what was thought to be sunstroke. It turned out to be gastric fever. He was very ill indeed and Elizabeth became frantic because Robert insisted on helping Isa nurse him. He was irritated by her selfish anxiety and the unreasonable way his wife not only resented Lytton's illness but implied that it was his own fault for returning to Florence after a four year absence at the hottest time of year "perfectly unacclimated". Lytton lay ill most of August and Robert, keeping himself healthy with daily plunges into the ice-cold mountain stream, stayed at his side. Elizabeth, discontented and resentful, wrote to Fanny Haworth that this was "a summer to me full of blots, vexations and anxieties". She was not good at dealing with any of them.

Wilson was a considerable vexation. She was pregnant again, an entirely predictable but nonetheless annoying circumstance. This time she could not be packed off to her sister's. Half way through August, Wilson collapsed and had to be put to bed. Nobody knew whether she had caught Lytton's fever or whether, since she was unsure of the date of her expected confinement, she was about to go into premature labour.

Whatever her true condition, she was useless as a maid. Not only could she not look after Elizabeth and Pen but she needed someone to look after her. Robert was worried about the justice of separating Wilson, in such a state, from Ferdinando and subjecting her to the ordeal of returning to burning hot Florence alone and ill, but he could see no alternative. Apart from any other considerations, Casa Betti, the house they were renting, was not big. There was no room for another maid to look after Wilson as well as themselves. So, on 29th August, "all in tears, poor thing", Wilson was packed off, seven months pregnant and sick. She cried not only because she had nobody to go to in Florence (even East Retford looked rosy by comparison) but because she was leaving her husband in the company of her extremely pretty, young, vivacious replacement, Annunciata. Elizabeth called this Italian girl "one of those enchanted new brooms" but Wilson was less than charmed. Jealous and worried, she rented a lodging house next to the Casa Guidi as soon as she reached Florence with a loan the Brownings had given her. Elizabeth feared Wilson "may have expected more" but thought she had been generously treated as in this respect she had. The lodging house provided her with the means of making an income as a landlady, once she had recovered from the birth of her second child. The news from Bagni di Lucca was reassuring, too: Annuciata fell ill with gastric fever as soon as Wilson left and was in no position to flirt even if, as Wilson judged, she was bound to. She was ill only four days but Elizabeth was worn out "running backwards and forwards night after night" because the sick Annunciata naturally could not look after Pen, who had also sickened.

Pen was never very ill, but both parents acted as though he were at death's door. His spirits, once the initial, short-lived delirium was over, were high enough to make Pen a difficult patient, though his mother continued to think him "so sweet and good". He wanted Wilson and, failing her, would accept Annunciata but would have none of the local girls willing to replace her in turn when she was herself ill. Grudgingly, he learned to like some of them but refused point blank to be dressed by them. It alarmed his mother to see her nine-year-old son becoming so conscious of his masculinity but she was bound to admit there was other growing evidence of it. On holiday his satin and silk clothes were frequently torn on passing bushes as he rode his pony, and he demanded "proper" trousers. Elizabeth wrote to Henrietta that she had been obliged to concede that Pen would wear "white jeans" for riding only and that she hated to see him in them – "so ugly, Henrietta." It was almost a comfort to have her son out of the hideous jeans and looking angelic and sexless once more in bed, instead of a burgeoning male of the species, especially when he was soon out of danger and laughing at the amusing antics which Annunciata performed to please him. Elizabeth, watching the new maid sing and dance for Pen's entertainment, told Henrietta how satisfied she was with the girl. Unlike the heavily pregnant, tearful Wilson, Annunciata was fun: "Her activity and intelligence are really great and her good nature and kindness not less." Elizabeth liked her even more when she discovered she was quite happy to accept a wage three pounds less than Wilson had been paid.[2]

The summer at Bagni di Lucca had only one other mark in its favour and that was the making of a new friend for Elizabeth. This was Sophie Eckley, the sweet and charming young wife of a wealthy American, David Eckley, whose additional attraction was that she was "a powerful medium". David Eckley went riding with Robert; Doady Eckley, roughly Pen's age, came to play with him; and Sophie stayed with Elizabeth and "talked spirits". Sophie told Elizabeth that spirits "grew faster" in the spirit world, something Elizabeth was quite prepared to accept as "a fact". Since her father's death she had been more interested than ever in the idea of change-beyond-the-grave and Sophie Eckley encouraged her to believe in its possibility. Their friendship, nurtured on spiritualism and poetry (Sophie deeply admired Elizabeth's poetry and was herself a poet), blossomed suspiciously fast. Elizabeth was not normally given to sudden friendships: she liked to proceed cautiously, usually along intellectual paths, before she succumbed completely. But there was no doubt that the speed with which Sophie Eckley established herself reflected the crying need Elizabeth had at the time for a female confidante who was all her own. Isa, whom she liked and trusted, was not her own but shared with Robert and, in any case, Isa's idea of friendship was not quite of the "slip-slop" type which Elizabeth craved. Sophie was adept at the kind of gossip she loved, though a far less worthy person than Isa, and Robert had no wish whatsoever to share her. He did not even really like her, though she was hard to resist with her sweet, pretty looks and air of innocence.

They were all glad to return to the Casa Guidi in October 1857, where the big event in Pen's life became the birth of Wilson's and Ferdinando's second son, Pilade, on 11th November. Ferdinando was still cook to the Brownings but since Wilson lived next door was not totally apart from his wife with whom he shared wages and expenses. These finances were complicated. Wilson sent all but £4 of her wages, while she was in the Brownings' service, to her sister Ellen in East Retford for Oreste's upkeep. When she stopped working and began to run a boarding house, Ferdinando sent his wages. The living arrangements between him and Wilson were also complicated but seem to have worked fairly satisfactorily because the two houses were next door: Ferdinando and Pen were in and out of both houses all the time. Having a new baby so near was Pen's idea of heaven. He was at Wilson's side a mere two hours after the birth and Elizabeth described to Arabel his "enchantment". It was as if "he were the mama and papa in one".[3] Pilade was the baby brother Pen had never had. Elizabeth was touched but also made a little wistful, remembering her own thrill at being allowed to be "nurse for a day" to her baby brothers. Those brothers still kept their distance and so, more hurtfully, did Arabel. She admitted to Henrietta, "I have always held that people should choose their own lives and live them clearly," but she returned to trying to influence Arabel's. She was still convinced that London was "specifically bad" for Arabel and begged her to come and winter in Florence. It was painful to realise that Arabel was now free and had money, and yet did not choose to come. Elizabeth was jealous of Henrietta who received visits from, and herself visited, Arabel. Yet the thought of going to England and becoming part of the inter-family exchanges was anathema to her: "the very name of London makes me sick and sad."

"Sick and sad" was how she had felt since April when her father died and a summer holiday had done little to change her mood. Christmas jollifications had no appeal either but Pen's enthusiasm proved enough for them all. Elizabeth wrote to Henrietta that their Christmas was not merry "except for our Peni" who decided to host his own party in his room. She was fascinated by her son's ingenuity, relating to Henrietta how he had illuminated his room with "hundreds of little wax torches . . . stuck all over the high stove and walls, all ablaze . . . you never saw anything so fantastic – really pretty and quite absurd." The guests were "heaps of Italian girls" as well as some boys and Wilson was the only adult (his parents were summoned to admire but not as proper guests). Compared to Robert's preoccupations that Christmas, Elizabeth found Pen's wonderfully cheering. Robert was drawing skeletons. Twice a week he attended classes to learn to draw from the nude, and now, early in the new year of 1858, he brought home his own skeleton so that he could study it and draw better. The mere sight of it made Elizabeth feel

[327]

"sick and dizzy". Robert lectured her nevertheless on how beautifully the bones fitted together and demonstrated "the facility with which the head comes off and on". She thought it disgusting and Robert's interest far more morbid and unhealthy than hers in spiritualism. She was prepared to strike a bargain, "saying, that if I tolerate Robert's bones in the house, he should my spirits . . ." Robert did not agree to any bargain but he did go as far as to tolerate Sophie Eckley who came to the Casa Guidi almost daily and he knew for what. She was more devoted than ever to Elizabeth who, though slightly embarrassed by the degree of devotion, and its sometimes extravagant manifestations in the way of gifts, was not averse to it. Sophie could communicate freely with the spirit world and Elizabeth, low and weak and confined indoors in one of the coldest winters ever known in Florence, needed the comfort of her "messages". She ignored Robert's warnings to beware.

There was surprisingly little in her letters about her health that winter: to all her correspondents she was now curiously reticent on the subject. She merely mentioned that she felt some "vital fluid" had been drained from her but maintained she would doubtless soon recover her strength in the summer. But there was a thin black thread of fear running through all the bright colours of the anecdotes she was so good at telling and to Mrs Ogilvy, significantly not in touch with her family and therefore unable to alarm them, Elizabeth wrote a more revealing health report than to anyone else. "For a year past," she wrote, "I have been slow . . . After some blows, one takes up the burden of life again, but one staggers a little at first and then creeps. Then the nerves strengthen, one walks nearly as usual perhaps. The end is not so far."[4] For twelve years she had banished death from being an ever present shadow, but now she was back to acknowledging its presence. No amount of pretence or forced optimism could conceal the fact of her decline.

People who saw her that winter were shocked. Visitors to the Casa Guidi tended to hold their breath and wonder how such a weak, frail, insubstantial creature could survive. Nathaniel Hawthorne and his wife had met Elizabeth very briefly once before but regarded themselves as strangers. When they went to her home to meet her again they privately wondered if she was anything but a ghost. Mr Hawthorne thought the kindest word he could use to describe her was "elfin". His wife thought she looked as though she were only just hanging on to life. But whatever she looked like and however she felt, Elizabeth told Henrietta that, in spite of an eye infection and though "a rag of a woman", she was getting stronger and was eager for the visit to France they were planning.

Elizabeth had a great deal invested in this trip to France, planned for the summer of 1858. She hoped to persuade not only her sisters but if possible all her brothers to join Robert and her, and Robert's father and sister, in some convenient and attractive holiday place. Her excitement at the idea of such a grand double family reunion gave her the energy to contemplate the journey: throughout June her spirits at last soared at the prospect of seeing Arabel and George for certain and probably Henry, and with the possibility of seeing the Surtees Cooks too. She began to look so well that three artists were allowed to paint her and, as she remarked drily to Arabel, "You may be certain I am respectable in the face or Robert would not consent to it." Robert himself wrote on the back of the envelope, "Ba is decidedly better." The coming trip, with all it promised, was the kind of diversion she needed. Robert needed it too. He was eager to see his father and sister and to sample once more the delights of Paris where they were bound to go for at least a short time. For once, they both looked forward equally to going away and could share each other's sense of anticipation. It had been a difficult winter for both of them. Inevitably, the kind of adjustments married couples have to make in such circumstances were forced on them. Robert was healthy, strong, energetic; Elizabeth was ill, weak, listless: the plain truth was that they could not live their joint life at the same pace. They had to agree to live increasingly separate lives which, to those who did not appreciate the depth of their relationship, appeared to signify that their marriage was becoming less successful. But it was not: this was simply a way of dealing with a situation that dictated its own terms. Because Elizabeth loved Robert she was not afraid to encourage him to leave her in pursuit of distraction from the misery of seeing her so ill and because Robert loved her he had the courage and the commonsense to see that, if he left her and enjoyed himself, she could more easily endure her own helplessness. Elizabeth's poor health made a difference to the way in which she and Robert lived but it was not the totally destructive force it so often is in a marriage. Spiritually and emotionally they were as close together as ever and both of them knew it.

They left Florence in July, just before it became too hot. Only Pen was upset to be leaving, sobbing "with his shoulders" as Elizabeth described it because he could not take Wilson or Ferdinando or their adorable baby with him. The high spirited Annunciata was accompanying them instead. They went by train to Leghorn, then caught a ship to Genoa. Elizabeth had the adventure of sleeping on deck which pleased the side of her nature she had always felt was pulling her towards life as "a vagabond". Robert was amused: "fancy Ba, the luxurious chair lover, 'pricking for a soft plank' as the sailors call it". After that it was "fast express trains" all the way to Paris. Both of them loved it. Elizabeth claimed she felt "less tired throughout the journey" than she had sometimes felt staying at home beside the fire. Naturally, holding as she did weird theories on the properties of various kinds of air and their relationship to her health, she attributed her sense of well being to French air. Robert suggested that maybe they should just travel on "for ever so" and she could think of nothing more agreeable. Both of them were "very nearly sorry" to arrive in Paris but when they did, Paris was rated "more splendid than ever", even if it seemed rather cold for July and Elizabeth found herself "looking wistfully at the grate". They took an apartment for a week in the Hôtel Hyacinthe near the Tuileries. It was Robert's father's birthday on 6th July, the day they arrived. Robert thought his father looked ten years younger than his seventy-five and Elizabeth was moved to see the old man "radiant with joy" at the sight of Pen. But though she loved the week in Paris, she was impatient for her Barrett reunion.

The Brownings were never good at finding places to stay but this was quite one of the worst searches they ever made. At the end of two weeks "a-wandering, a-wandering", Elizabeth wrote to Mrs Jameson that it had been futile as well as exhausting. Robert was attracted to Etretat but, though she admitted it was pretty, Elizabeth disliked the bay and its popularity which would make her feel "like a fly in a microscope". Robert, overruling her fussiness, took a house there but Elizabeth forced him to give it up by pointing out that the view was "a potato patch". All very well for Robert, who would never be there to notice it, but she would be doomed to look at it day after day during her enforced rests. So on they went, meaning to investigate Dieppe but ending up in Le Havre. Here they settled, both embarrassed and apologetic about their choice of venue. Elizabeth told Mrs Jameson they were "ignominiously settled" and admitted that a week before they would have scorned Le Havre, "a mere roaring commercial city". At least the house they took was near the sea, had a garden, was "quite away from a suggestion of streets" and had good bathing in front. There was a post office and a reading room nearby, the only marks of civilisation to which Elizabeth liked to cling.

Bravely, she said they had come for the sea and the sea was what they had got. But Robert wrote to Isa that Le Havre was "hideous" and the house they had taken "in a hideous angle" without even a view of the sea. He and Pen swam every day and his temper improved. Even Elizabeth had her hip bath filled with sea water and immersed herself for five minutes a day.

The arrival of Arabel and George did not bring Elizabeth the joy she had expected. She had never experienced that strange phenomenon of inter-family reaction and had naively assumed that Barretts and Brownings would effortlessly fuse together in one warm, loving embrace. They did not. No amount of goodwill could disguise the strain of trying to pretend they were all one family, joined by Robert and Elizabeth. Mr Browning and Sarianna had their own apartment in the rented house but shared meals with Robert and Elizabeth. When George and Arabel came, they were there for meals and a good deal of the rest of the day, too, if the weather prohibited the beach. Making this assortment of people comfortable in relatively cramped conditions was hard work and when Henry arrived with his new wife the surprise was delightful but the pressure increased. Elizabeth's head stopped aching, however, long enough to be vastly amused by her brother Henry's infatuation with "his dear Millikins" (he had married a widow, Amelia Morris, in April). She wrote to Henrietta that he kept telling her that "Millikins is a most wonderful woman! Impossible to put out of humour." She would have liked to devote more time to test the perfect Amelia but was endlessly distracted by having to attend to everyone else as well. Robert was not as much help as he might have been. He liked the Barretts but found them boring. It was a relief when George took himself off to Heidelberg, saying he would see them again in Paris, and when Robert's old friend Milsand came for ten days providing immensely congenial company. When Milsand left, Robert did not attempt to conceal his boredom, writing to Isa, "What is to say about such a dull daily life as this daily one of ours! I go mechanically out and in and get a day through – whereof not ten minutes has been my own . . ."[5]

It was perhaps fortunate that Sette and Occy did not arrive (though Elizabeth did not forgive them, saying she knew perfectly well they could have done if they had wanted to) and nor did the Surtees Cooks because the children had whooping cough. Elizabeth was sad not to see Henrietta, but relieved when the disastrous holiday came to an end and they returned to Paris. As she wrote to Henrietta, in Paris,

"Robert's family will separate from us and go to their own domicile," while Arabel would stay and "the gossip time will be enlarged". There was so much she wanted to show Arabel, who had never been to Paris, and so many things she wanted to do with her as well as the essential gossiping. She took Arabel round the Parisian shops and together they bought Elizabeth a bonnet, a parasol and a black and red petticoat of which the staid and demure Arabel did not quite approve. All the time the sisters were together they talked, going over and over minute details of family life, analysing and discussing the behaviour of friends, reminiscing endlessly about the past. There was no pause, ever. Elizabeth teased Henrietta, "don't you feel how we talk of you – we do you on one side and then turn you like a knead cake!" She wrote that she squeezed Arabel "drop by drop like a sponge till I get everything out and even now I haven't done squeezing."[6] Robert was mystified. He could only deduce that there was some invisible, natural bond between sisters which made his intellectual, mentally exacting wife able to tolerate the slow, uninspiring Arabel with whom he would have said she had nothing in common.

They had decided to stay in Paris till the cold drove them away. Elizabeth hoped they might stay until well into November but they were obliged to seek the warm south by the middle of October. The euphoria had gone in any case; that surge of energy that had carried her towards her family reunion had disappeared as soon as Arabel returned to London. Elizabeth felt weak and listless. The journey home contrasted horribly with the journey outwards; she went into no more rhapsodies over the bliss of travelling. There was confusion over various connections they were supposed to make and did not, and at sea, between Genoa and Leghorn, there was a terrifying storm. The crossing took eighteen hours and when the ship finally docked Elizabeth was prostrate and unable to continue. They were so late arriving back in Florence that Annunciata's sister had spent three days in tears convinced they were all dead. Elizabeth was "so glad, so glad" to be back in the Casa Guidi but Robert was determined to get out of it as soon as possible. He did not need any sharp-eyed visiting Americans to tell him his wife looked terribly ill, he could see it. He intended to take her even further south before the winter came. To his horror, winter came early and with a vengeance: it snowed the second week they were back, "enough to strangle one", wrote Elizabeth to Sarianna. It did not last, but though the snow turned to rain Elizabeth reported that she was "languid" and "wretched". The last thing she wanted to bear with in such a condition was Wilson's problems. Wilson knew the Brownings would take Ferdinando to Rome and also Annunciata. She did not like the idea at all, so she suggested to Elizabeth that her sister Ellen could be brought from East Retford, with Oreste, to Florence. Ellen could look after Pilade, too, and run the boarding house, miraculously freeing Wilson to go to Rome with her husband. Elizabeth expressed amazement. She said she appreciated that wife and husband should be together but said that, even if such a scheme could be brought off, it would be "unfair" to Annunciata.[7] Ferdinando was sent off, ahead of his employers, to Rome, taking their plate and linen. That was the end of the matter.

The Brownings and Annunciata followed a week later. "Our journey was most prosperous," Elizabeth wrote to Sarianna. It was also extremely comfortable because the Eckleys had insisted that the Brownings should use one of their own luxurious carriages. Robert, still suspicious of the fawning Sophie Eckley, did not want to accept the offer but for the sake of his wife's comfort could not bring himself to turn it down. Elizabeth was also reluctant – she commented to Sarianna that the Eckleys "humiliate me with their devotion" – but was similarly tempted. Normally scathing about flatterers, she managed to excuse Sophie's effusiveness by persuading herself that Sophie had a great need to be of use to people and that it would be ungracious to reject her help. So the Brownings left Florence in style in the Eckleys' beautiful upholstered closed carriage, with pretty Annunciata on the coachman's box, prominently in Wilson's view as she waved goodbye. She was left to winter on her own, looking after the Casa Guidi, with Isa's help and occasional company, as well as her boarding house. The Brownings travelled forty miles a day, stopping at noon each day for two hours. Along the way, Elizabeth translated a poem of Heine's which ended "Madam, I love but thee?" and inscribed it, "Ba for Sophie".

They arrived in Rome on 24th November, after several adventures on the last leg of the journey. One day the horses almost pulled the carriage into a ditch and on another two of the drivers of the oxen teams, which had replaced the horses for the pull up a steep hill, had a knife fight. Robert was a hero. He jumped out and separated the fighters. "I did not shriek," Elizabeth wrote to Arabel, "but did the next best thing and fainted . . . It really was frightful."[8] In spite of the comfortable carriage, she was very tired, though not quite "up to the point of pain". They rented the same apartment as on their previous visit in 1853, but it was newly painted and "universal carpeting" made it "snugger". Rome seemed much more attractive than she had ever had a chance to discover. Robert liked it immediately. He got up at dawn most mornings and rode with David Eckley for an hour. In the evening, he found there was plenty of social life. "It's like a great roaring watering place," Elizabeth wrote, with more than a hint of disapproval. She reported to Mrs Ogilvy that there were "balls, receptions, squeezes in every degree" and that Robert availed himself of them all. She wrote sarcastically that he had become totally dissipated and that she was reduced to making appointments to see him. But there was neither resentment nor bitterness in her joking allegation. She did not want Robert always with her, watching, observing, *feeling* her frightening weakness. She did not want to read despair in his eyes nor for him to catch it in hers. They were both working hard at pretending she was recovering, when both had secretly acknowledged she showed no signs, this time, of doing any such thing. "It pleases me that he should be amused just now," Elizabeth wrote frankly to Henrietta, ". . . and I think it is good for him." She went nowhere. Sometimes, Robert brought particularly interesting people home to meet her but even this exhausted her.

In January 1859 Elizabeth was revitalised by the astounding news that Napoleon III seemed prepared to do something at last for Italy, just as she had always hoped and prayed he would. She had not deviated from her opinion that Napoleon III was to be the saviour of Italy as well as of France nor from regarding him as the people's hero. Ever since December 1851 when she had so staunchly defended his *coup d'état*, she had been able to see in the constitution he granted only his desire to do his best for the people (whereas everyone else saw that it gave him absolute power for ten years and thought Elizabeth's interpretation strange to say the least). Now, she felt justified in crying, "I told you so." To Sarianna she wrote, "Always I expected this from Napoleon . . . I said it long ago," and to Isa she wrote that the prime minister of Piedmont was right in declaring Napoleon was the leader of "the march of civilisation". Once more, the dream of a united Italy free of Austrians seemed to obsess her. On 10th January Victor Emmanuel, ruler of Piedmont, said he could no longer turn a deaf ear to the demands for liberty and he was going to answer them. The question was, would Napoleon help him? War with the Austrians, supported by the French, seemed inevitable. There was no other talking point in Rome and Elizabeth could not get enough of it. She wrote to Henrietta at the beginning of February that she was "breathless with emotion" and that she and Pen, who thought of themselves as Italians (Robert stayed stoutly English), were "all trembling with expectation". She devoured the newspapers and was delighted when the information in them gradually brought Robert round to thinking more kindly of Napoleon III. He also came to agree that England was a little ignoble in being more interested in maintaining the European peace than in the rights and wrongs of the Italian cause. Throughout that spring, Elizabeth was in a fever, but it was a fever which had two good results. It gave her an illusion of strength and energy and this in turn inspired her to write poetry. In "Casa Guidi Windows", nearly a decade before, she had written a political poem but now she produced a different kind of political verse – shorter, sharper, much more controlled. She demonstrated a knowledge of the issues at stake which, even if in the opinion of others at the time (and since) misguided, was nevertheless informed and sincere. She was using poetry as she thought it should be used, as a means of calling attention to, and influencing, burning issues of the day.

Robert, who was not quite "of one mind" with his wife (though she told Henrietta he was), felt his way very carefully indeed. While pleased to see Elizabeth so animated and productive, he was uneasily aware of the dangers of this particular kind of vitality. The last time she had been in such an exalted state because of Italy she had been at her strongest both physically and emotionally. When paradise was not gained she bore the disappointment well, consoled that there would be another chance in the future. Now the chance had come, circumstances had altered. Her health was in a downward spiral and her emotional state was still unstable after her father's death which she could not seem to accept. She lived more and more in the spirit world and less in the real one. Mixed up with politics in her letters were rambling accounts of spirits appearing during séances with Sophie to tell her that "the veil between life and death is very thin". Robert, with justification, thought her perilously close to being unable to distinguish between the two. This time, if Italy failed to become free, no comfort could be offered in the shape of promises that there would be another opportunity soon. "Soon" would be insupportable, meaningless. Robert instinctively appreciated this. He did not stop to analyse why his wife chose to identify herself so completely and passionately with Italy's cause; it was enough that she did and that because she did she was in danger if it failed.

He tried his best to restrain her ardour. His caution and commonsense were reins on her impetuous, headlong gallop towards the certainty of Italian victory. He was not so foolish as to antagonise her by suggesting Napoleon might be involved for his own ends but he tried to get her to appreciate Napoleon's viewpoint and to desist from some of her more exaggerated hero-worship. She told Sarianna that she and Pen were, in Napoleon's case, "agreed to kneel down and kiss his feet", but Robert tried to show her that Napoleon was only a man, only human.

The highlight of this suddenly exciting spring was a visit from Massimo d'Azeglio, the Piedmontese ambassador to Rome. Elizabeth was far more impressed by this man coming to see her than by any other of her often distinguished visitors. D'Azeglio excited her even more by assuring her that it was a case of "1848 over again with matured actors" and that this time Italy would not fail. This put Elizabeth into a state close to euphoria. When, in April, it was reported that French troops were pouring into Piedmont she thought Napoleon "sublime". Robert thought it a signal for them to return home to Florence before they were unable to do so because the country was engulfed in war. They set off at the end of May with Pen clutching a French tricolour, ready to hang on the Casa Guidi balcony. Elizabeth for once did not try to curb his "masculine" enthusiasm for war, though she had been trying hard all winter in Rome to keep him from adopting masculine fashions. He wanted more than ever, now that he was ten, to have his curls cut off but Elizabeth still saw twelve as the demarcation line between "neutral" infancy and real boyhood. His other constant request had been for heavy shoes – hard, leather, *boys'* shoes – instead of the soft slipper-like sandals his mother wanted. She did not care how warlike he was, so long as he ran after soldiers in the streets (as he did) in pretty velvet slippers, his blond curls streaming in the wind. She maintained, most unconvincingly, to Mrs Ogilvy that "all artists (including my husband, I am glad to say) applaud me for not translating him into prose before the time of prose comes".[9]

It was immediately remarked upon by everyone in Florence who knew her that on her return from Rome she looked better than she had done for the last two years. She said she was tired of hearing it. But she had no doubts about why she suddenly was blooming: it was because she felt as if she "walked among the angels of a newly created world" and had "scarcely" in her life been so happy. In that one phrase, her marriage to Robert and the birth of Pen were incongruously equated with the impending liberation of Italy. On 12th May the French troops had joined the Italian armies and together they had won victories over the Austrians at Magenta and at Solferino. Elizabeth was triumphant and then, almost at once, exhausted by the violence of her joy. She tried to explain why she felt as she did, but failed to enlighten. To her father-in-law she wrote that "if ever there was a holy cause it is this; if ever there was a war on which we may lawfully ask God's blessing, it is this". She saw no sordid political opportunism: the war had taken on for her the complexion of a crusade and the fervour of her letters was becoming as intensely religious as her father's had been on any political subject. The starting point had been emotional – love of the warm, sunny country where she was so happy, love of the freedom (in every sense) that she enjoyed there which made her want to fight for the oppressed every-where – and emotion continued to govern her reactions. Her general state of health did not help her state of mind. Because of her worsening health she had been increasing her opium dosage since the previous winter and was no longer leading an exemplary, healthy life. She could not eat or sleep because she was so happy. Her old friend William Story was alarmed to find she verged on the hysterical. He described her voice as "insistent" and her eye as "fixed". When Henrietta tentatively enquired whether, if she was so much recovered, Elizabeth was planning to come on a visit to England that summer, she was told it was "out of the question". The only strong temptation, apart from that of wanting to be with her sisters, was that she would dearly have loved to meet Occy's wife, Charlotte Mackintosh, whom he had married on 19th March. But she could not leave Italy when every day there were new sensations. After Solferino the Austrian-nominated Grand Duke of Tuscany abdi-cated, and then Napoleon and Victor Emmanuel entered Milan together. Robert gave two guineas a month to the war effort and Pen worked at his lessons zealously because he was bribed with the promise of his own *scudi* to donate if he did so. Ferdinando pined to be an unattached young man again so that he could go and fight; the whole of the Casa Guidi lived, talked and dreamed of the war. In June the temperature soared (one day it was 102° Fahrenheit in the shade) but that year there was no summer exodus: the need for access to twice daily war bulletins precluded holidays in remote areas.

The only person not completely besotted by the war seemed to be Wilson. Even in the midst of her own "excitement and exultation" Elizabeth could not escape noticing that Wilson seemed to have gone mad. She wrote an enthralling letter to Arabel telling how "after a cheerful meeting with Wilson the night of our arrival she came to me afterward in my room and I found her to be *quite mad*". The nature of Wilson's alleged insanity appeared to be religious. In the winter, apart from her husband, alone with her baby, Wilson had sat brooding about what she imagined were the evil designs of the pretty Annunciata on Ferdinando in Rome, and to console herself had turned to close reading of the Bible. From it she had gleaned that the world was about to end and that her two sons were "in the first fruits of the resurrection" as she described it to Elizabeth. As she talked, her face was demented and her voice was strange. Elizabeth was horrified. Wilson's susceptibility to religion had revealed itself many years before, when she first arrived in Italy and was confronted by the vast Italian religious pictures. At the time, Elizabeth had made jokes about her maid feeling faint and had suggested it was her modesty that was outraged. Robert thought a word in Ferdinando's ear might not go amiss but that otherwise nothing could be done: Wilson was harmless. If she was indeed mad, a crisis would approach and they could act.

A crisis came first for Elizabeth. No one could have been more confident about the outcome of the war than she was. The war was "a holy crusade" against evil, and good would win because "souls are stronger than bodies always".[10] She was made so restless by the war activity that she rushed around Florence in a most uncharacteristic way, writing to Sarianna that she accompanied Robert into the city daily "after the bulletins and to hear and give opinions". She went out in the evenings, too, "going several times" to the theatre. Staying quietly on her sofa was impossible: "there's something that forbids us to sit at home." It was, she wrote to Sarianna, a case of *"we live or die"*. Her energy was a false energy – she was no better than she had been for some months – but she was forcing herself on, deliberately ignoring all the symptoms of illness to which in other less exciting circumstances she succumbed. Those who saw her were not fooled but marvelled at how mind could, on this occasion at least, triumph over matter. It was at great cost. On July 8th Napoleon negotiated with the Austrian emperor Franz Joseph at Villafranca. Austria gave Lombardy to France and France ceded it to Piedmont in return for the promise of Nice and Savoy at some future date. Elizabeth, on hearing this and having it confirmed as true, collapsed, abandoning all pretence that she was well.

Chapter Twenty-one

I N her own opinion, Elizabeth came as near to dying that summer of 1859 as she had ever done. She wrote to Mrs Ogilvy, "I have been very ill – nearly as ill as I could be, to come back again to the natural world . . . I constantly felt on the edge of a precipice."[1] She told Mrs Ogilvy that although "lungs and heart were out of order" it was the violent "agitation of the mind on account of public affairs" which made her "susceptible" to disease. To Henrietta she wrote that the news of Villafranca made her "dizzy with grief" and that she "fell that day from the mountains of the moon where I had walked hand in hand with a beautiful dream". Sarianna received a more restrained account in which a "blow on the *heart*" was mentioned and her attack was attributed to a combination of the effects of the terrible heat, over-activity and too much talking. She made the onset of her illness sound like a fit – "I was struck, couldn't sleep, talked too much . . ." – and added that she had had not only severe palpitations but also a dreadful pain which had made her think of angina.

She was unable to move from her bed for three weeks. Robert, as ever, was the perfect nurse, not moving from her side except to attend to her needs. Little by little, as she grew stronger, he brought her to see that Napoleon was not necessarily a traitor and that all hopes of Italy's unification and freedom need not be abandoned (even though, in a fit of rage, she had made Pen take his Napoleon badge off and did not want to see it back). But she needed a scapegoat and chose England – England who, according to her, helped "Prussia and confederated Germany by a league of most inhuman selfishness to prevent the perfecting of the greatest Deed given to men to do in these latter days". It seemed to make her feel better to say, with a flash of Mr Barrett-like brutality, "*I never will forgive* England." Robert did not argue. Her illness had left her body even more broken than before. Lack of proper food, heavier doses of opium and total inactivity had reduced her to a wreck. He did not need a doctor to tell him a change of air was vital but nevertheless sought the backing of Dr E. G. T. Grisanowsky, a friend of Isa's and one of the few doctors left in war-threatened Florence. Dr Grisanowsky understood only too well how politics had made Elizabeth "mad". He shared her distress and was so anxious for her welfare that, after advising she should be taken to Siena, he followed her, helped Robert find a villa and then administered to his patient free of charge.

William Story, staying in Siena himself, saw Robert carry Elizabeth into the Villa Alberti and thought her just a shadow in his arms. But slowly, infinitely painfully, Elizabeth did begin to put on a little weight and became marginally more substantial. Being in the Villa Alberti helped. It was a beautiful villa, two miles out of Siena, with "great rooms with beautiful views". These views, Elizabeth wrote to Henrietta, were over "pretty dimpled ground" and the freshness of the constant breeze was both reviving and soothing in the heat of an Italian summer. The villa was sparsely furnished but the simplicity and coolness of the stone floors and white stucco walls greatly attracted the invalid. Those "political dreams" which had plagued her – she was always following a woman in white, whom she knew to be Italy, down long corridors – finally ceased. Her mind, instead of seething in perpetual and pointless turmoil over events she could not control, was filled instead with poetry. For the first time since Bro's death she found the writing of letters repugnant, telling Fanny Haworth, "one soul has gone from me, at least, the soul that writes letters". Instead, lying in the cool villa, perfectly peaceful and silent, she began to write out the poems she had begun before Villafranca, simple poems but eloquent and moving. This, more than anything else, healed her. She was working again, doing something for Italy in the only way she could, taking the bitterness out of her grief with exactly that "hard regular work" she had sought but not found after her father's death. The recuperative power of creative writing astonished her. She gave thanks as she had not done since her youth for her gift. She only wished Robert would work, too, but he was too busy supervising Pen's riding. He had bought the boy his own pony after much agonising. Elizabeth enjoyed relating to Sarianna how Pen had "coaxed" his father for a pony and how he had entreated her "if Papa spoke . . . about the pony, not to *discourage* him". Elizabeth promised not to, and when Robert committed himself to this extravagance she had great fun teasing him – "Robert never spoils him; no, not he, it is only *I* who do that!" But she loved to see, from her window, the golden-haired

Pen galloping past on his Sardinian pony: his happiness made her happy. Pen was having a wonderful holiday, riding, driving grape-carts, chasing sheep and catching stray cows. In Edith Story, he even had a friend with whom to share all this. Naturally, he was neglecting his lessons but Elizabeth did not care. She told people that Pen was not "in the least studious" and left it at that.

By the beginning of October Elizabeth was recovered enough to be going for short drives with Robert and even extremely short walks (more like staggers) round the garden. The thought of returning to the Casa Guidi did not, this year, make her feel as enthusiastic as usual. She was not, in any case, likely to be there long: in her weakened state another winter in Rome was considered essential. Robert would have preferred to go even further south, to Palermo, but the thought of organising accommodation there daunted him. He also had another problem to resolve before going to Rome: what he was to do about Walter Savage Landor whom he had taken under his wing and brought to Siena. He had found Landor wandering the burning streets of Florence before they left, saying his wife had thrown him out and he had nowhere to go. Landor had always been a vocal admirer of Robert's and now Robert, who liked the old man and never forgot a debt of gratitude, felt obliged to look after him. This was not an easy task. Landor had grown intractable in his old age and had developed charming habits such as hurling food on the floor if it was not to his liking. Elizabeth described him to Arabel as a "poor headstrong old man" but there was a degree of disassociation from him in the way she added "altogether it is a very anxious affair for Robert". Indeed it was. Landor came to Siena with them but was lodged with the long suffering Storys who treated him so well that he was quite docile. But a more permanent solution had to be found – Robert had no intention of trailing Landor to Rome with them – and Elizabeth was curious to see what the compassionate Robert would come up with.

Robert's solution was on the surface both obvious and marvellously convenient: Wilson could take Landor. Her boarding house was doing well (well enough for her to be employing a maid herself) and she was thinking of expanding. Robert suggested that he should lend her some more money to rent a bigger boarding house on condition she took in Landor as a paying guest. Wilson thought about it. She had given up begging to be taken back into the Brownings' service (a suggestion Elizabeth found ludicrous, especially as she now preferred Annunciata) and knew her future lay in being a landlady. She was desperate to be reunited with Oreste, now four years old and still in East Retford. Landor would pay her £30 a year and this could go towards the cost of bringing over her first son. But, on the other hand, these material advantages were offset by her certain knowledge of Landor's temperament: she had witnessed several of his tantrums. Elizabeth herself appreciated that Wilson would be faced with considerable difficulties if she accepted Robert's offer, writing to Sarianna, "Wilson will run certain risks and I for one would rather not meet them." But Wilson decided she would risk it. She moved into a house in the via della Chiesa, not too far from the Casa Guidi, and let the first floor to Landor for £1 a week, in addition to the £30 a year for his keep. Considering what her wage had been with the Brownings, she was obviously much better off if she could make this arrangement work. Elizabeth privately wondered about this. Wilson had begun muttering about visions again and had taken to haunting churches where she saw the strangest things. She was missing her first child more, not less, since the birth of her second: looking at Pilade, now almost two, reminded her of Oreste. Elizabeth, sympathetic in theory, had neither the mental energy nor the will to help Wilson achieve her dream of bringing Oreste to join his family in Italy. Before she left Siena, she had promised Robert she would keep calm, that there would be no more "impotent rages". The only way she could try to keep her promise was by detaching herself from anything that troubled her and, frankly, she was only too willing to detach herself from Wilson's troubles.

It was much harder to detach herself from Italy's. A visitor had only to make a faintly derogatory remark about Italian bravery to be challenged by her, if in a weak and quavering voice. She still had an emotional reaction to certain words which she found difficult to control. For example, she wrote to Isa, "the word Venice makes my heart beat".[2] Was there any hope for Venice? Would the city she adored ever be free? What had been agreed about the fate of Venice at Villafranca? Her desire to know the facts grew as "the tide of life seemed fairly set in" once more. Things were "still going on" and it was hard to keep her promise not to become passionately involved again. After only a few days back in Florence, she sensed "an expectation . . . of fighting but only with the Pope's troops . . . or with such mongrel defenders as can be got . . ." Both Sicily and Naples were expecting "an outburst". On the whole, she told Fanny Haworth, "affairs in Italy seem to be going well". Few other foreigners shared her confidence. Rome, when they eventually arrived there (complete with Pen's pony) on 3rd December, was empty. This was lucky in that it meant rents were low and rooms plentiful but it was worrying in that it suggested that the winter would be socially dull. Robert had hardly anyone to visit. Elizabeth felt guilty about having dragged him there, all because of her wretched health. What deepened her guilt was knowing that Pen, for the first time, had not wanted to come. He said if they had to leave home he would prefer Paris. Part of the trouble with Rome was that he was "put to Latin" there and even worse was to be taught it by an Abbé. Elizabeth described this Abbé as "young and gentle" and "one of the most innocent and amiable of men" but Pen was resentful. He had no wish to learn Latin, but his parents thought that now he was nearly eleven the time had come. His younger cousin Altham, it was pointed out, had been learning Latin at school for years.

While Pen struggled to apply himself, Elizabeth completed her new volume of poems and prepared them for publication in the spring. It was a slim volume of only eight poems, all about Italy. Originally she and Robert had been going to bring out a joint volume next – "Robert's own suggestion!" she assured Sarianna – but he had torn up his only poem, about Napoleon. She told George that, if Robert had not approved, she would have torn up hers too: "Robert would not have let me print what he considered below my own mark," she told her brother. But Robert thought her political poems good and even important. Elizabeth expected English critics to savage them when they came out (in March 1860). She promised Mrs Jameson *Poems Before Congress*[3] was "a very thin and wicked brochure" and explained to Isa that "the abuse of the press" would be "the justification of the poems" because they were so pro-Italian and anti-English. She saw it as a kind of war work, telling Mrs Ogilvy, "the further I walk into life, the louder grows the battle, the quicker beats the drum in my heart . . . Not on personal subjects indeed. But what difference does it make if the emotion is personal?"[4] The preface (always a most important part of any volume of hers) was thick with this personal emotion. She spoke of her admiration of the Italian people and their "heroic constancy and union" and said that if patriotism meant the flattery of one's own nation then this made the patriot little better than a courtier, which she had no intention of being. Nor did she think patriotism should lead to total self-love and lack of intervention in the affairs of another country: "non-intervention in the affairs of neighbouring states is a high political virtue; but non-intervention does not mean passing by on the other side when your neighbour falls among

[343]

thieves." What she dreamed about was "the day when an English statesman should arise with a heart too large for England . . ." She made it plain that Palmerston certainly was not such a man.

Her first poem was a long ode to the greatness of Napoleon III who had come to deliver Italy and whose name, whatever then happened, would always be one "to applaud and cherish". The seven other poems were different in tone. "A Tale of Villafranca", which had already appeared in *The Athenaeum* in September 1859, was strongly sarcastic and written in such a straightforward way that the obscurities of Elizabeth's earlier poetry seemed a distant memory. A woman sits her son on her knee and tells him what happened at Villafranca, arriving at the contemptuous judgement, "In this low world, where great Deeds die / What matter if we live?" An August Voice" was full of the same despair. Supposedly written by a soldier, it was an indictment of the Grand Duke. But it was none of these poems, nor the two charming lyrics, "The Dance" and "A Court Lady", which attracted all the attention. It was the last poem in the volume, "Curse for a Nation", on to which the critics fastened . This was a strange, powerful piece of work both in style and content, which had already appeared in America, but was new to most readers in England. Half of the poem takes the form of a prologue in which an angel directs the narrator to write down a curse. The narrator refuses, saying she loves the nation against whom the curse is directed, but the angel insists, saying this love will make the curse more effective. The best kind of curse is "from the depths of womanhood" because then it will be "very salt and bitter and good". So the narrator agrees. The curse is written. It is a curse against the strong for attacking the weak, against the prosperous for not caring about the poor and against those who boast of their own goodness. Elizabeth said the poem was meant to be about slavery: the curse was directed against slavery and therefore against America where it was practised. But when this old poem was included in *Poems Before Congress*, Chorley, her former champion on *The Athenaeum*, interpreted it as being about England, cursed by Elizabeth for not helping Italy. He attacked Elizabeth savagely for such an anti-patriotic gesture, referring to her poem as "a malediction against England – infallible, arrogant . . ." A long correspondence ensued between Chorley and Elizabeth which spilled over into her other correspondence as she defended herself. She told Isa, "Mr Chorley's review is objectionable to me because unjust." But in another letter to Isa she confessed, "the fact is, between you and me Isa, certain of those quoted stanzas do fit England as if they were made for her, which they were not though . . ." She hinted at a deliberate confusion built into her poem about her target. It was, after all, rather strange to include this poem, if it was against slavery, in a volume specifically devoted to the cause of the freedom of Italy.

Elizabeth wrote to Mrs Ogilvy, after she had digested all the reviews, that Robert was "furious" because she had been treated with "great ferocity". But she was not upset – quite the reverse. She wrote to George (who was angry with her himself for the tone of her poems) that "the weight given to the book . . . has on the whole rather flattered me than otherwise".[5] It was no mean feat, she considered, to be given "three columns of abuse for instance in the Saturday Review . . ." Right from the beginning of her career she had craved attention of any kind because without it she would be crying in the wilderness. Her poems were written for a purpose and that purpose was unfulfilled if they were unread and ignored. Abuse attracted attention even more than praise sometimes and she felt she would gain a readership because of it and would find, without necessarily knowing it, "some generous chords in minds open to such an influence". She accused George of not having the least idea what he was talking about in objecting to her poems and with a fine sisterly arrogance advised him to ask himself, "What makes Ba hold these opinions so tenaciously . . . May not . . . these 'political mistakes' of Ba's, as I call them, be nearer the truth than I fancy? May she not know the real colour of things better in Tuscany and Rome than Mr So and So who sees them in Brompton?" At any rate, she was proud of her poems, whatever reception they had, writing to Mrs Ogilvy, "I have delivered my own soul in speaking – and if I had destroyed my popularity in the process I would have spoken out equally." She wanted to suffer for Italy but her popularity, far from being destroyed, was increased. *Poems Before Congress* sold remarkably well for such a volume and, because of the renewed interest in the author, *Aurora Leigh* went into yet another edition (its fifth). It was of course unusual for a woman to write political poetry. *Blackwood's* pointed this out, saying, "it is a good and wholesome rule that women should not interfere in politics . . . the case is worse when women of real talent take part in political affray."

While all this "vituperation" as she called it was going on in England, Elizabeth was passing a quiet and pleasant spring in Rome. She felt better but had not noticeably recovered her strength. She wrote some peotry (not political) but her great delight was that sheer boredom had driven Robert to start writing, too. She wrote to Fanny Haworth that "he deserves no reproaches for he has been writing a good deal this winter – working at a long poem which I have not seen a line of and producing short lyrics which I *have* seen and may declare worthy of him". Once more, as in that "happy winter", they were working at the same time, just as they had always intended. But the crucial difference was that the buoyant atmosphere of that previous "happy winter" could not be recreated. Elizabeth was too ill to enjoy anything properly. It depressed her terribly to hear that Mrs Jameson had died on 17th March, aged sixty-six: the shock was such that she could not discuss it in letters beyond mentioning her distress. Nor could she bear to discuss another shock which had laid her low, one of a very different kind: there had been a rift with Sophie Eckley. The reasons for this are still obscure. It has been suggested that Sophie was exposed as a fraudulent medium but also that she had disgraced herself in some extra-marital affair. She wrote to Elizabeth begging forgiveness, for whatever reason, but this only made the breach worse. Elizabeth could not bear to have Sophie's treachery, whatever it was, mentioned.[6] Robert, of course, was not surprised and indeed thought his wife had brought a good deal of it on herself. It hurt him to see her so low, grimly conserving what little energy she had. Terror of catching cold in her weakened state kept her away from such outings as were available and the occasional visitor brought by Robert gave her little pleasure. The only visitors she liked to hear of were Ferdinando's. Their man servant had friends who did not have access to the newspapers which could tell them what was happening in the rest of Italy – seditious information was banned in the Papal States – so they came to the Brownings' apartment to read them. Isa sent newspapers from Florence inside innocent-looking books brought by the diplomatic courier and these were handed on to Ferdinando and his cronies. Elizabeth loved this – it made her feel like a revolutionary – and referred to her "café". She and Robert agreed with those below stairs that the summer of 1860 *must* see a victorious final struggle in Italy.

It was no time to be travelling but they wanted to get home again and also to escape the southern heat and the fever it had brought. It was a journey Elizabeth did not enjoy but it was mercifully quick: they left Rome on 4th June and were in Florence on 9th June. It was a pity that they agreed not to go straight to Siena, where they intended to spend another summer. All the old problems were waiting to greet them in the Casa Guidi. They had hardly unpacked before Landor burst in, a terrible

Lear-like figure, roaring that Wilson had thrown a dish at him. Wilson followed soon after with the explanation that it was Landor who had thrown his dinner out of the window because it was eight minutes late. He had hurled the soup, then the vegetables, but when it came to the mutton, Wilson could bear it no longer – she snatched it from him. Robert talked to Landor, Elizabeth to Wilson. Landor was finally persuaded "to pardon" Wilson but would not apologise. Wilson agreed to try to rise above the old man's madness but could not guarantee she would manage it. Landor had said Wilson's eyes "flashed fire" at him and she acknowledged "something entered into her" when he provoked her. It was not as though she did not have other provocations: her maid had just walked out on her without giving notice. But Wilson had no choice. If she wanted to bring Oreste over she needed to keep Landor as a tenant. As a concession, it was agreed that if Landor was brought along, too, Wilson and Pilade could come to Siena. This would mean that Wilson would be with Ferdinando, the husband from whom she had been parted all winter. They would not be in the same house – there would be no peace for the Brownings if Landor lived with them – but only "a lane separating" would keep Wilson and Ferdinando apart. Elizabeth did go so far as to admit to Mrs Ogilvy that this was "not perfectly conjugal, after all, I must allow".[7]

As soon as they arrived at the Villa Alberti, which they had once more secured, Elizabeth began to fancy she really could get properly better after all (something she had been doubting for the last two years). But then news came from England that made her faint with foreboding. Henrietta was ill, very ill. Surtees and Arabel both wrote to say that her sister had cancer of the womb. The prognosis was poor. Henrietta had experienced appalling "floodings" and was in terrible pain. She had been up to London to see a specialist who had examined her, said there was nothing to be done, and sent her home. It was the thought of Henrietta's pain that tortured Elizabeth. Throughout her many illnesses she had always known herself to be fortunate precisely because she suffered so little actual pain – weakness, nausea, light-headedness, congestion, but rarely the kind of sharp, acute, sustained pain which now tortured Henrietta. "The thought of that pain," Elizabeth wrote to George, "is the worst thought I have to bear." Her power of empathising had always been remarkable – that ability to feel herself into other people's physical sensations whether in novels or real life – and now it became a curse. She sat and thought about her sister's pain and as she thought the reality of it, the mirroring of Henrietta's agony in her own body, became unbearable. It made her write in a way which sounds selfish but was not. What she wrote to George was precisely true. She told him that every time she found herself smiling at some pleasant sight or event – "the blue hills . . . Penini's musical chatter" – she suddenly remembered "my precious Henrietta is in great pain at this moment perhaps" and the smile was wiped off her face. She was with her sister all the time "in my power of loving and suffering". She felt "soul to soul" and incapable of being separated. Frantically, she begged George to make sure Henrietta was getting the best attention: "Is Stone the first man? Was there not another, famous in these special disorders?" She wanted every possible remedy tried – "tell me whether *caustic* is used in any form" – and every specialist consulted. Most of all she wanted to hear that some means had been found of controlling the pain.

When George wrote and said something that did alleviate Henrietta's suffering a little had been found Elizabeth wrote to Mrs Ogilvy, "the least breath of a word about diminished pain soothes the burning at the heart which devours me." Waiting for letters from Surtees was unbearable: "My anxiety is . . . (when letters are expected) DREADFUL." Her "best state" was patience "under the weight of a stone". She began to do a curious thing which she herself noted and tried to explain. In every letter about Henrietta she followed, without any break, paragraphs and pages expressing her agony with long screeds about the political situation in Italy. She could go straight from breaking her heart over her sister to enthusing about Garibaldi (who was poised, with his Red Shirts, for attack). The juxtaposition seemed offensive but she could not help it, telling George, "I put down something, not to send you an echo of your own sadness – and nothing is at hand but this."[8] Mrs Ogilvy was given another explanation: "Private cares have been broken through for me by the press of public events on all sides."[9] Here again was a statement open to misinterpretation. The average person finds the opposite to be true: public affairs are rarely of importance in the midst of private tragedy. Most people discover they do not even know what is going on outside the confined space of their own immediate suffering. But Elizabeth, in reversing the position, and thus running the risk of seeming callous, was only revealing once more her extraordinary state of confusion. In her mind, she was making Henrietta's illness a metaphor for Italy's struggle. She could not think of the suffering of her sister without confusing it with the suffering of "her" country. All the images she used were those of war. Waiting for letters from Somerset was "as if for the signal to be shot through the heart". When, towards the end of September, she reported to Mrs Ogilvy her joy at hearing Henrietta was well enough to be carried round her garden, she was equally ecstatic that Piedmontese troops were sweeping south. Henrietta was being brave, Garibaldi was a hero: it was as if she were searching for a link. If the Italian patriots succeeded in uniting Italy, then maybe Henrietta would survive; if they failed, she might die.

She longed, of course, to go to Henrietta, if just to hold her hand. Lying under the fig tree in the garden of the Villa Alberti, surrounded by beautiful countryside, her mind was full of memories of how Henrietta had nursed her years ago. It struck her as one of fate's most cruel twists that Henrietta, "the strong one", should now be dying first, instead of her feeble self, unless a miracle happened. Henrietta and illness did not go together. Pictures of her as the bustling, energetic wife and mother on their visit to Somerset in 1856 were impossible to reconcile with the account of her as pale and wasted and unable to walk. It made Elizabeth weep to realise how useless she had always been to those she loved. Whom had she nursed and comforted? Nobody, except occasionally Pen, and Robert, very rarely and briefly indeed. The day-to-day total care of someone she loved who was suffering terribly had never fallen to her. It made her see her role in life as a passive one, hers to receive in time of need, but never to give. Her thoughts returned to Henrietta's children, to Altham, Mary and Edward, all younger than her own son. She could not bear to think of them motherless. She had been twenty-two when she lost her mother and the blow had been severe enough. How would Henrietta's children survive? How did anyone survive such loss? There were no answers. She wrote to Mrs Martin that "the spiritual world gets thronged to us with familiar faces till at last, perhaps, the world here will seem the vague and strange world even while we remain." Half of her felt already there, with her parents and Bro and Sam and Treppy and Miss Mitford and Mrs Jameson and Mr Kenyon. Robert and Pen, so bursting with vitality and health, were the ones who seemed remote, to whom she barely seemed to belong.

All summer, Elizabeth was in a trance, roused only by news of the fortunes of Garibaldi or of the manoeuvres of the statesman from whom everyone now hoped so much, Cavour. What Elizabeth liked best about Cavour was that, as she wrote to Mrs Ogilvy, he was "*at one* with the Emperor from first to last". It was Cavour, after all, whom Napoleon III had supported when he went to the aid of Piedmont against the Austrians in 1859. To George she wrote that Cavour was the only Italian politician with any real vision and that she expected much from him. But, although still following the fortunes of the Italian fight for freedom and unity, and ever anxious to hear what Cavour was doing, her concentration was poor. She was alone most of the time – Robert and Pen rode far and furiously – except for Wilson. Wilson came every day, usually with Pilade (Elizabeth thought him "a fine child"), and they grew closer. During the last five years, the bond between them had been severely damaged until Elizabeth had begun almost to resent her former maid's presence but now, united in their grief over Henrietta, it was discovered still to be strong. Wilson's concern for Henrietta, the Barrett sister who had interviewed and engaged her in the first place, was genuine and deep. She was the only woman near Elizabeth who both knew and loved her sister. Instead of pushing Wilson off, Elizabeth was glad to have someone with whom she could share her sorrow without needing to explain. Inevitably, she saw Wilson's own troubles in a different light now that she felt warmer towards her. Wilson had still not managed to bring her first-born Oreste to Italy: she had now not seen him for four whole years and it seemed to occur to Elizabeth for the first time that this was a monstrous deprivation. She told Mrs Ogilvy that Wilson "ought to have her own child". Mrs Ogilvy agreed and actually came up with a means of getting Oreste from East Retford to Florence. She was in Scotland at the time and had with her an Italian servant girl, Gigia, who was about to return to her native Florence where the Ogilvys had engaged her. She could act as courier for Oreste. Wilson was ecstatic. Arrangements were duly made for Gigia to collect Oreste and to take him by ship from Liverpool to Leghorn where Ferdinando would go to meet them. Elizabeth gave Mrs Ogilvy written authority for the collection and guardianship of Oreste and Wilson also wrote to her sister Ellen explaining what she should do. But when Ferdinando met the ship at Leghorn he found Gigia but no Oreste. His aunt had refused to hand him over. Her side of the story is not known but it hardly needs imagining. Ellen had raised Oreste from a baby. He knew not a word of Italian and she could hardly be blamed for not wanting to entrust him to a girl she had never seen who was taking him to a country with whose language and customs the child was totally unfamiliar. Oreste knew Ellen as his mother; his real mother was only a name, someone who had deserted him. For both selfish and unselfish reasons Ellen had a justifiable point of view. Elizabeth did not see it. She thought only of the shock to Wilson at first – Wilson almost "dropped to the ground" when Ferdinando returned empty-handed – and then of the waste of the Ogilvys' time and trouble which she was embarrassed to have caused. She moved on later to blaming Wilson herself, telling Mrs Ogilvy that she had always been "weak in character" (clearly forgetting her own remark in 1846 that she had been amazed how strong the apparently timid Wilson was when necessary). She reckoned that Wilson's "letters to her family must have encouraged them to assume that attitude of choice and possession . . . as if the boy belonged to them and not to his mother".[10] She approved of Ferdinando's reaction which was immediate and practical: Ellen Wilson would get no more of his wages. Elizabeth commented "for which I commend him" when passing this news on to Mrs Ogilvy. Her final judgement on this episode was that Wilson had "not grown stronger under the responsibilities of her married life". These were harsh words considering the nature of Wilson's married life – her husband had disappeared with the Brownings for roughly six months of every year of it.

By the time autumn came, Siena had not proved as beneficial to Elizabeth's health as she had thought it would. She wrote to Fanny Haworth that, although she loved the place, "circumstances of pain and fear walk in upon me through windows and doors . . ." Henrietta's illness coloured everything and dragged her down. Nor was she much happier about some of the other Barretts. George was paining her because he had announced he was retiring from the law and buying a country estate. Elizabeth was outraged. He was only forty-three and far too young, she told him, to be "sewing up your life in a bag". She protested that there were "positions open . . . with your legal antecedents where you might do moderate and useful work with satisfaction to your country and yourself – I tell you clearly."[11] He was talented and to waste one's talent wilfully, Elizabeth said, was a crime. George ignored her. She was equally annoyed with Stormie, who had been briefly in England, because he had returned to Jamaica taking Sette with him. On the death of their father Elizabeth had assumed that all connections with the West Indies and its hateful slave history would be severed; she did not care about the financial investment. But her brothers did and there was nothing she could do about it. Only Occy pleased her because of his marriage. She hoped he and his wife Charlotte would come to Florence, but was not optimistic, noting that journeys to Italy appeared too difficult for any of her brothers to arrange while truly hazardous trips to Jamaica were seen as easy. It still hurt her deeply that not a single member of her family had ever visited her in her home. She was tired of tempting them, but had another go at George, writing, "We could and would make ever so much room for you . . . we should open our doors and arms to you – and have books for you from the Florence Library, and you could go to sleep undisturbed when the sun was overhot – to say nothing of stray fans and water melons – what could you want more?" George did not say, but he never came.

George, all the same, was useful to his sister that autumn. He handled a legal matter over which both she and Robert were fretting. Fourteen years before, when Robert had insisted on a marriage settlement, one of the trustees had been Sir Joseph Arnould who now wrote that he wished to give up his trusteeship for various personal reasons. The brief time the Brownings spent in Florence between Siena and another winter in Rome was taken up with wondering what to do about this. They asked George if a new trustee could be appointed and if so how (they would have liked George himself appointed). Discussing this brought up the whole question of money in general and of their wills in relation to it. It made Elizabeth impatient to think that even after fourteen years Robert must be legally prevented from absconding with any money of hers. She was at her most hard-headed and unemotional when she commented to George, "Agreed that Robert will survive me – agreed even, on my side, that he may re-marry . . . being a man . . . nay 'being subject to like passions' as other men, he *may* commit some faint show of bigamy – who knows? But what is absolutely impossible for him is that under any temptation or stress of passion he could sacrifice what belongs to Peni . . . for Robert to fail *here* is IMPOSSIBLE."[12] It was a great relief to her when Arnould was persuaded not to relinquish his trusteeship and the distasteful and, in her opinion unnecessary, legal fussing could stop.

But the incident was immensely significant for the light it threw on Elizabeth's state of mind. She had no illusions about her health. Even more, she did not want to have any. She no longer wrote to anyone of her determination to get better for the sake of Robert and Pen. Instead, her letters were littered with pathetic references to being "fit for nothing", "only a rag", "only a shadow" of a person. Robert and Pen's health and energy were strange and marvellous to her. She was not depressed by their vitality, did not contrast it enviously or bitterly with her own apathy, but on the contrary gloried in it. Their obvious closeness pleased her too: it meant she need not worry about them because they could sustain each other. When she died, they would suffer and grieve but they were so clearly in love with life, so resilient because of this, that they would recover together. She would be destroyed if Robert or Pen died: they would not be if she did. There ran through her letters from now on, though it was never explicitly stated, a feeling that her husband and son, however much they loved her, might be better without her. The nearest she came to expressing this was when she wrote to Sarianna that she was "like a drag chain" on Robert. She had no will to do anything: everything was suddenly "duty". She wrote to George in November, "Anyway, Robert says it is a duty for me to go to Rome," so she would have to go when all she wanted to do was lie by the fire in the Casa Guidi and withdraw from all pretence of an active life.

Robert had motives other than his wife's health for wanting to go to Rome as quickly as possible. He knew, as she did not, that Henrietta was near death. George had told him there was no longer the slightest hope. The letter containing the dreadful final bulletin was expected by him any day and he was convinced that if Elizabeth were in a different environment she would withstand the shock better: "the change of scene and necessary exertion would do good." Unfortunately, it did not. As luck would have it, this journey was one of the worst they ever had and when they arrived in Rome it was to find no letter from George. Robert suspected the reason but Elizabeth was frantic with anxiety. All the way there she had been preparing herself for the next report on her sister's condition: "the blood of my heart *must* be left in stains on the stones of the road,"[13] she wrote to Arabel. There followed "four or five days of suspense till it became unbearable" and Robert decided to send telegrams both to England and Florence. It turned out that the fatal letter had "been kept back through the infamous negligence of the officials". Robert had to tell Elizabeth that Henrietta had died on 23rd November, a whole week ago. She bore it well, if bearing it well was lying on the sofa without moving or speaking. Robert, who had seen all this before, was not fooled. Wearily, he wrote to George that "the wounds in that heart never heal altogether". It did not escape his attention that other people, especially "poor Surtees", had wounds too. Elizabeth's thought for him was not as tender, or at least as tenderly expressed, as it could have been. She wrote, with what reads like monumental egocentricity, to Surtees, "Your loss is greater (seeing that she was closer to you and loved you above all) yet mine goes further back into the past and devastates my memories of life and youth."[14] She underestimated how devastated her brother-in-law was. In his diary for the night Henrietta died, Surtees, lacking any of Elizabeth's eloquence, recorded in simple and direct language that his love for his wife had not been ordinary, that she had been his idol and that God in taking her from him could only have thought such human love too great. Nor did Elizabeth appreciate how the bereaved father felt about his children. It appeared that Arabel wanted to take Mary, aged five. Elizabeth was all for this. She wrote to Mrs Ogilvy, "Arabel pleaded hard for the little girl . . . one lonely little girl – but she was refused by the poor father. He could not, he said."[15] Why she thought he should let Mary go to Arabel is a mystery. When her own mother died, the idea of her father "giving" Sette or Occy, aged six and four, to any of their willing aunts, especially spinster Bummy, was never mooted because unthinkable: he adored all his children, they were all his family, they would of course all stay together. Elizabeth's crude assumption that because Mary was a girl, and because Arabel had no children, they should automatically be brought together was offensive to Surtees. The strength of the ties between a daughter and a father were ones Elizabeth was well positioned to understand. Her unforgivable insensitivity was revealed in a phrase to Mrs Ogilvy, when telling her she would try to persuade Surtees to think again, "for the child's sake and Arabel who longs to have it". Mary, it seemed, was a commodity, an "it", not even a "her".

And yet there was no doubting her feeling for her sister's children. She could look at her own child only "through a mist since then". She told Fanny Haworth that she had "to struggle hard to live on". To Mrs Ogilvy, she tried to explain the apparent contradiction in her behaviour, "how it is that I do not believe in loss and yet am overwhelmed as if by loss". She sincerely believed that deaths were only "apparent separations", that when "beloveds" died they merely slipped "between the natural and the spiritual", but then, when they did slip, she found herself distraught: "I am inconsistent and very weak . . . *without excuse*." Her only escape from the terror that filled her was the old, familiar one of reading. "Now I read on," she wrote to Arabel a month after Henrietta's death. "Reading is so part of my life that I suffer horribly when I don't read – the soul eats itself." Robert was immensely grateful that Christmas for the recuperative powers of *The Mill on the Floss* – George Eliot was able to do what he could not and he was not disposed to find this any failing in himself. Increasingly he and Elizabeth found their own ways of facing what they saw approaching but which they could not admit to each other. Miracles had happened before in their lives; but that was all they could look for, a miracle. Meanwhile, it was safer and wiser for Elizabeth to read a novel and for Robert to ride a horse than for either of them to dwell on the future.

Chapter Twenty-two

ELIZABETH did not leave her room in the via Felice throughout the whole of the winter. Robert was rarely there. Unlike the previous winter, there was plenty of stimulating company in Rome. He made the most of it, trying hard to distract himself from the reality of his wife's condition. He did this, as ever, with her full approval and encouragement but, whereas before it had seemed merely sensible, and the best way for both of them to enjoy whichever city they were wintering in, it now began to be desperately sad. To all her correspondents (through death greatly reduced in number) Elizabeth confessed she was "weak and languid" and that she was "very little up" to any kind of effort. To George she wrote, "I feel more fit for going to Heaven sometimes."[1] Heaven was once more a deeply attractive place, as it had been after Bro's death, and she had to struggle to resist the idea of "joining the angels" who "there stand thicker" as she told Mrs Ogilvy.

Her angel, Pen, grew less angel-like every day. In spite of still having curls and being dressed exquisitely (or absurdly, whichever your point of view) he was turning into a man before her eyes. As he approached twelve, his physique changed rapidly. He was no longer slim and delicate in build but distinctly stocky and broad. Twelve, of course, was the age Elizabeth herself had fixed long ago as being the time when poetry would turn into prose, for the curls to be cut off, the long trousers and tail-coat to be put on, and the once fairy feet to be encased in tough leather shoes. It was also to be the signal for Pen to move out of his parents' bedroom where he had slept ever since 1856 when Wilson returned as Ferdinando's wife. Even Elizabeth realised that it would not be appropriate for an adolescent boy to sleep with his parents. As she wrote to George, ". . . all this must end as other sweet things do . . . fencing and sleeping in Mama's room don't go well together."[2] Pen's *bons mots* were no longer relayed in his lisping style. She reported them in proper English and had begun to parade his intelligence and maturity rather than his charm and innocence. She wrote rather coyly of her son's "love affairs", approving of his passion "for the pretty sad Queen of Naples" and making facetious remarks about his future as a lady's man. One change she was not planning to have forced on her was in his name: "He cries out . . . to be called Robert," she told Mrs Ogilvy but she would not allow it. Pen, she wrote, was a wonderful name because it was "declinable . . . as Penini, Peni, Pen . . ."

Tucked up on a sofa, Elizabeth spent the days reading and doing some "pedestrian work" (as opposed to that work of "the flying imagination" to which she often referred). But the imagination still managed to fly occasionally, even in her miserable condition. Thackeray, who had just astonished himself by setting up as editor of a new literary magazine, *The Cornhill*, had asked her to contribute a poem. She sent "Lord Walter's Wife" which was daring enough for Thackeray to think it unsuitable for family consumption. It was certainly a curious poem for her, a happily married woman, to write. It showed that Elizabeth's personal experience of love and marriage had not blinded her to the general status of women with regard to both. In the poem, Lord Walter's wife appears to be trying to seduce a friend of her husband's who has previously shown interest in her. As she becomes more blatantly flirtatious, he turns on her and denounces her wickedness in tempting him. She laughs at him and says she was only showing him what it felt like to be a woman: every single thing she had said to him could have been said by a man with impunity. Thackeray, in a witty and delicate letter of rejection, which he was greatly embarrassed to have to send, described his public as too squeamish for it. He pointed out that, although "the moral [was] most chaste pure and right", she had in fact written "an account of unlawful passion" and it would be found offensive. Elizabeth was quite proud to have been rejected on such grounds. She told Thackeray that she felt "the corruption of our society requires not shut doors and windows but light and air: and that it is exactly because pure and prosperous women choose to *ignore* vice that miserable women suffer wrong by it everywhere."[3]

To prove she was "not sulky" Elizabeth sent Thackeray another poem, the innocuous "Little Mattie" which was quite one of the worst she ever wrote, opening with the sort of line she wrote thirty years before when at her most morbid ("Dead! Thirteen a month ago!"). *The Cornhill* readers loved it, full as it was of maudlin sentiment with its description of a mother mourning the dead child who has known nothing of life. Even its vocabulary was a return to the old days – "dead", "death" and "shriek". But fortunately "Little Mattie" was an aberration. That winter and spring Elizabeth wrote several poems fit to stand with "Lord Walter's Wife", such as "Void in Law". This was a bitter exposure of men who give women rings, make them pregnant, and then desert them, leaving them to discover that society does not rate the ring they thought so significant. At the same time, Elizabeth chose to celebrate sexual passion in "Bianca Among the Nightingales", though even here, while glorifying sexual love in all its beauty, she exposed men as unworthy of it: Bianca is cheated in the end by the false lover with whom she has felt the earth move ("We paled with love, we shook with love/We kissed so close we could not vow").

All the time she was writing, Elizabeth's poor health was ruining her happiness. She was determined not to feel bitterness – there is not a single bitter remark at this time in any of her letters – but to a certain extent she could not help it. No amount of philosophising or bravery could conceal the fact that she was leading a strictly curtailed life when it might have been so full. The only wistful reflection she allowed herself was that she *could* have been so happy when she had Robert, Pen, many friends, work, plenty of remaining ambitions, hopes and schemes. But illness threatened to rob them all of meaning. She tried hard not to be self-pitying and succeeded brilliantly. A lesser woman, a greedier woman, keeps her younger, attractive husband chained to her sick bed, determined he should suffer as she does. She allows him out only to persecute him with jealous fantasies when he returns. Not Elizabeth. She was content to go to bed at eight o'clock, kissing Robert goodbye as he prepared to go out to dinner and admiring his good looks (she thought him even handsomer now than when she had met him). The next day, there were no tearful recriminations because he had not returned until four in the morning. She liked to hear where he had been and who had said what but she was not as eager to hear every detail as she had once been nor as willing to share Robert's social pleasures vicariously. His world was no longer her world. Instead of this being a source of regret to her it was one of relief: he was happy and occupied and that was what she wanted him to be. After talking, drinking and sometimes carousing till the early hours Robert would take a carriage with his companions to see the Colosseum by moonlight while at home his wife slept, not in the least resentful. It was an astonishing display not only of selflessness, but also of self-control on Elizabeth's part. Robert was now forty-eight years old and yet he was behaving more like an excitable young student: there was something inescapably manic about his excessive restlessness. Naturally, the gossips concluded he had tired of his sick wife. What they did not know was that carousing helped Robert deal with the strain of Elizabeth's ill health and that she recognised that this ebullience gave the physical side of him an outlet she could no longer provide. If, as she had told Sarianna, she was indeed "nothing but a drag chain" on Robert, then it was remarkable how rarely she applied that chain herself. But though it was true that, inevitably, she did hamper Robert's movements quite literally, because of her inability to travel, she was still able to fulfil the most important function she had in his life. Their relationship was based not only on the deepest attraction and admiration, but on *talk*. Robert could still talk to his wife, whatever her health, and he said he talked to her as if to another part of himself. It was Elizabeth who explained to Sarianna what this meant: " . . . the peculiarity of our relation is that even when he's displeased with me he thinks aloud with me and can't stop himself."[4] Robert was perfectly aware how precious and extraordinary this was. "Ba and I," he wrote that winter to George, "know each other for time and I dare trust eternity. We differ . . . as to spirit-rapping, we quarrel sometimes about politics and estimate people's characters with enormous difference, but, in the main, we *know* each other . . ."[5] It was this mutual knowledge of each other which made that difficult winter bearable. As long as they could be together, talking, communicating, the misery of Elizabeth's illness could not ruin their marriage. This was affected by it but not to the point of destruction: their love remained strong and enduring.

By the spring of 1861 Elizabeth was still too weak, in spite of warm weather, to go out but not too weak to receive a few choice morning visitors (afternoon or evening visits to her were now quite out of the question). Her favourite visitors remained those who could either discuss spiritualism or, better still, Italian politics. She was thrilled when Sir John Bowring, who was in Rome on his way to Turin with "a mission from the English Government . . . on commercial affairs" came to pay his respects. Sir John had known Napoleon III "well by personal relation" and agreed with Elizabeth that he was "perfectly misconceived of . . . in England". Unfortunately, after only one visit, Sir John fell ill and Elizabeth was deprived of hearing any more about Napoleon III being "frank and loyal . . . and full of great ideas for the world". She had to make do with the new English consul with whom she was bored until she found he had held the dying Keats in his arms: "I made him tell me the most minute details." Occasionally, she had a literary visitor of real repute, like Hans Andersen whom she found "very earnest, very simple, very childlike", even if he did have too much of "a general verve for embracing".[6] The Storys, also wintering in Rome, gave a children's party for him where he read "The Ugly Duckling". Pen came home in a state of great excitement because of this and also because his father had recited his own "Pied Piper" while Story played the flute to conjure up the magic atmosphere.

There was no mention anywhere of Elizabeth seeing any doctor. She seemed to think that there was nothing any doctor could do. She merely felt weak, was weak and all else was the fault of her wretched weakness. Her cough she dismissed as nothing and she was not in any pain. She put her limited faith in time, care and rest. When a winter spent entirely resting failed to restore her, she was depressed but resigned. She did mention sometimes that perhaps she was never going to improve appreciably, that she might have to settle for the state she was in. She herself was more alarmed at her failure to recover emotionally than physically. In April 1861 she wrote to Mrs Martin that she would "like to go into a cave for the year" but that this remark should not be repeated. The desire to hide was strong in her: she was horrified to hear Robert suggest they go to visit his father and sister in Paris. Every spring they had discussions about where they should go in the summer (and every summer about the winter lodgings) but this spring planning ahead was unbearable. She did not contest Robert's right to see his family, and of course she might see some of her own, too, if she were in Paris and so near to England, but the sheer strain of going anywhere appalled her. She might manage the Florence-Siena-Rome triangle but the thought of greater distances sickened her. She did not want to leave Italy: "every-where else seems too loud and light," she wrote, curiously, to Mrs Ogilvy. It was the only place where she felt she could "live here my own way and work my own work and enjoy my own silence". However, she admitted that the trip to Paris had to be faced because "the *duty* of it is clear". To Sarianna she wrote, "I confess to shrinking a good deal about the noise of Paris" and suggested to her sister-in-law that perhaps they could go to Fontainebleau where, "in the picturesque part of the forest", she hoped it would be quieter. She even suggested Le Havre again, in spite of the less than successful previous stay there, because at least it was on the sea. To Mrs Martin she repeated her remark about it being her duty to go but added, "you would pity me if you could see how I dread it." The only thing to do, she told Mrs Ogilvy, was "shut my eyes and leap" (a strange image for a person confined for months to a sofa but one of which Elizabeth was always fond). Then it occurred to Elizabeth that, since it was Robert's family they were to visit, she could be excused: Robert and Pen could go without her. She would stay quietly in the Casa Guidi translating Italian poetry, perfectly well cared for by Annunciata and by Wilson and Isa nearby. Robert would not even discuss such a ridiculous plan. If she was not fit enough to go then she was not fit enough to be left. They had always stayed together, except for the three-day emergency trip with his father to Paris, and they always would.

Before they left Rome, at the beginning of June, Robert made arrangements to return in the autumn, which was unusually far-sighted of him. It made him feel secure to think that everything was for once arranged, so that, however exhausted Elizabeth became during their proposed summer travels, they would be sure of a most desirable and comfortable apartment (the Storys' old one) in which she could recuperate. Elizabeth could not manage to look as far ahead as the autumn; it was all she could do to contemplate the journey home to Florence that month. But she survived the trip better than she had expected, so much so that Robert began to think the old trick would work, that the general stimulus of travelling and the change of air would do his wife more good than remaining cooped up in one room as she had been ever since Henrietta's death. She admitted she did indeed feel "a little stronger". Suddenly, a trip to France seemed a real possibility in her own mind. After a week or so resting in Florence she was prepared to agree that setting off for Paris might be feasible. But then on 6th June, the day after the Brownings arrived back in Florence, Cavour died. The shock to every Italian patriot was profound: Cavour was only fifty and of all the current Italian statesmen by far the most respected. Elizabeth, who had at various times voiced doubts about all the Italian leaders, even Garibaldi and Mazzini, had had none about Cavour. She was enraged when in England the popular *Daily News* "printed a shameful notice of Cavour" (at the height of Garibaldi's popularity) and told George the English did not know how to honour a truly noble man. Two months before Cavour's entirely unexpected dramatic death she had written to George, "if Cavour had died suddenly within the last year or so all would have been ended for Italy – the event would have been awful."

When he did die the event was no less awful than she had predicted. Elizabeth wrote to Sarianna on 7th June, "I can scarcely command voice or hand to name *Cavour*." She felt as though she could "hardly comprehend the greatness of the vacancy" and added that Cavour had been worth "a hundred Garibaldis". Her only forlorn hope was that he and Napoleon III had secretly arranged things so well that "certain solutions" to Italy's problems would just "slide into their grooves". She had barely the energy to follow the actual aftermath of Cavour's death. Robert saw that the apparent ease with which she had withstood the trip home and the better health she had seemed to enjoy since were both illusions: she was broken. In Rome, just before they had left, he had thought he noticed some congestion of her chest – "I think I foreboded evil in Rome" – but when he "reasoned about it" with her he was told it was nothing. Within hours of Cavour's death that "nothing" was visibly something. Grief once more prostrated her, mind once more dominated body and that mind was black and hopeless. If her reaction seems, as it is so often bound to, melodramatic, then it must be emphasised how ill she now was. For weeks she had driven herself on, determined to rejoice because Italy's finest hour had dawned, but all the time she had been doing so she had been fighting her own physical condition. She had not been well for six years; every one of those winters she had suffered from bronchial attacks, of varying severity, which a mild climate could no longer entirely cure. Her small store of energy had been depleted in travelling from Rome even though excitement had buoyed her up so convincingly that she had appeared well. What was remarkable was not that she collapsed when she did but that she had staved off such a collapse for so long. Even Casa Guidi came under a cloud. Usually, Elizabeth was ecstatic upon her return home where she had always been happiest: nowhere was ever more spacious, more comfortable, more attractive to her than her beloved Casa Guidi. Now, for the first time, she seemed to notice how dark and gloomy the apartment was. She also maintained that it was cramped and that if, as planned, Pen were to move into a room of his own now he was twelve, there was none suitable for him. Robert seized on her discontent as a welcome and manageable distraction: they would move to somewhere bigger, lighter, perhaps with a garden. Relieved to have a practical mission, he began to make enquiries.

One thing was certain: there would be no trip to Paris or anywhere else that summer. Elizabeth's letter of apology to Sarianna showed her pitifully aware of the disappointment caused. She vowed she "did really wish and do my best to go" and that she had "touched the line of vexing" Robert in insisting that she could travel but he had been adamant. She promised they would come next year when "the lions in the path will be all asleep" by then. Meanwhile, it was back to the usual invalid routine. She lay in bed or on a sofa all day, took morphine, ate virtually nothing.[7] Wilson came to see her and, though shocked by her pallor, agreed with Elizabeth that her illness was in no way different from the many others they had both witnessed. But Robert, while tempted to agree, felt he would like a doctor's opinion. Elizabeth was averse to this. She said she did not want a doctor, that there was nothing a doctor could do, that she was perfectly capable of doctoring herself when it was merely a case, as this was, of her old ailments. She admitted that perhaps she did have a little congestion, but said it would soon clear. She had no interest in what was wrong with her; she was utterly remote, locked up in herself as she always was in a state of extreme grief. All Robert could do was what he had always done, be with her, soothing and comforting and most of all understanding. Pen came and went, but for once Elizabeth hardly responded to his charm. She wrote no letters – Robert would not let her – and saw no visitors except Wilson and Isa. Isa came to sit with her when Robert went out, which he did usually only to read the newspapers at the reading room so that he could bring back a report on the progress of Italian unity, the only subject in which Elizabeth showed the slightest spark of interest. When Isa came, in the afternoons, she was helped out of bed and put into a chair where she sat listlessly listening to Isa valiantly trying to amuse her. She would rather have remained in bed but Robert insisted (rightly) that it was better for her chest if she sat up. She yielded, but could not please him further by taking two steps on the balcony: that required more strength of will than she could command.

Witnessing this daily régime, which Elizabeth clearly found an ordeal, Robert found himself horribly confused. On the one hand, he wanted to believe his wife when she said this illness was the same as all her others but, on the other, his instinct told him it was not. He did not know which to follow, reason or instinct. Over and over he went through Elizabeth's symptoms and explained them away to his satisfaction – she was incredibly weak: naturally, because she had refused solid food for a long time now. She was wandering in her mind, having hallucinations: naturally, since she had increased her daily dose of opium. There were answers for everything. Most reassuring of all, the invalid herself was perfectly sure she felt exactly the same as she had always done during such an attack; there were no new pains or aches, no sensation with which she was not familiar. So Robert tried not to be alarmist and, when day after day went by and Elizabeth grew no worse, he stifled his nagging worry that in some way he could not define she was much more seriously ill than she realised. But on Thursday 20th June, two weeks since Cavour's death and her collapse, Robert's nerve gave way and his instinct conquered reason. It was a fiercely hot day, one of those "cauldron days" from which they had always fled if they could. The windows, shutters and curtains were all tight closed to keep the rooms as cool as possible. Robert went down to the reading room, leaving Elizabeth propped in a chair with Isa sitting beside her. The streets were still hung with black flags, for Cavour's death, and the heat was oppressive. He found the atmosphere claustrophobic and depressing. It suddenly seemed to him that the best thing he could possibly do was what he had done after the shock of Villafranca – bundle his wife up and take her to Siena, away from a Florence that was uncharacteristically hateful.

While Robert was out, Elizabeth requested that the windows be opened a little. They were not usually opened until the evening, when a welcome breeze blew through them refreshing the apartment once she was in bed and away from any draught. Uneasily, Isa obliged but worried immediately that Elizabeth might catch cold. She was quick to explain to Robert, on his return, that she had been against the invalid having the windows opened and sitting near them. Robert ordered tea. The three of them sat there, with some semblance of normal socialising, until Elizabeth suddenly said she had a sore throat. Isa was sure it was the fault of the open window. Elizabeth was put to bed but slept only fitfully in spite of a heavy dose of morphine and the next day she clearly had a cold. By that night, a cough had developed and Robert had done with reason. At one in the morning the violence of the coughing made up his mind. He roused Annunciata to sit with his wife who was trying to bring up phlegm and being frighteningly unable to do so, and went in search of a doctor. Unfortunately, their friend Dr Grisanowsky was not in Florence so he went to a Dr Wilson, who was currently rated highly for the treatment of chest complaints. He had great difficulty in knocking him up but finally succeeded and brought him back to the Casa Guidi. There Dr Wilson immediately applied a poultice to Elizabeth's chest and made her sit up with her feet in a hot mustard bath. He stayed the rest of the night, closely observing his patient. By dawn, she was rid of the troublesome phlegm and breathing easier. Dr Wilson was agreeably surprised by her resilience. But when he sounded her lungs he regretfully reported that he was sure the right lung was congested and might have an abscess on it. An abscess could burst, with fatal consequences, unless it could be dispersed and that was no easy matter. The patient must be kept calm and take some medicine. He increased her already strong dose of morphine slightly, then departed saying he would return each day.

In one way Robert was inclined to think the doctor's verdict good: a specific ailment had been diagnosed and could therefore be treated. Elizabeth agreed but remained unimpressed by Dr Wilson's diagnosis. According to her, he had confused her lungs: it was the *left* with which she had always had trouble, ever since the days of Dr Chambers. She even said, contemptuously, that Dr Wilson clearly did not understand her case. She was the expert, the one who had listened to every doctor tapping and sounding and pontificating and, like him, getting it mostly wrong. They had made her tired, all her life, with their gloomy prognoses. She had defied them all and would do so again. But Robert was pleased to have Dr Wilson in attendance. He was also pleased to find the good doctor approved of Elizabeth being made to sit up in a chair some of the day. This she continued to do until Friday 28th June, when their old friend Lytton called. Robert was going to receive him in the drawing room so Elizabeth said it would be easier if she stayed in bed. Robert agreed. Her voice had almost disappeared and she was weaker than ever after a month on broth and ass's milk only. Even the short distance from bed to drawing room chair, carried in his arms, exhausted her. She seemed happier that day, spent in bed, and that evening, when Isa called, was quite animated. Isa had snippets of political news. Robert, watching Elizabeth's eyes brighten and her face flush slightly as she heard them, was annoyed with Isa for exciting her. Excitement, he knew, was dangerous. He shushed Isa and turned the conversation at the bedside into a more harmless channel. After Isa had gone, Wilson came in for a few minutes and thought the invalid so much improved that she was sure the corner had once more been turned. Robert felt more optimistic. When he joined his wife at her bedside that night he noticed her breathing was easier. Pen, when he came to say goodnight, asked his mother three times if she was really better as he had heard Wilson say she was. She replied, "*Much better.*" The doctor, who had come to see her before she went to sleep, had broken in to say cautiously, "Perhaps a little better."

Robert, in spite of his relief, did not go to bed himself. He settled himself to sit in a chair and watch over his wife. He saw her sleep, then waken, then drift to sleep again. Sometimes she said his name, sometimes she smiled. Once she told him to get into bed himself instead of sitting there like a sentinel when there was no need. Robert, ever watchful, always checking, found her feet were icy cold even though the night was sweltering again and both bed and room could not have been warmer. Then, at half past three, in that eerie hour before the dawn, Elizabeth suddenly exclaimed, her eyes wide open and staring, "What a fine steamer – how comfortable." Robert immediately panicked. He woke Annunciata, not wanting to leave his wife in this state even for a few minutes, then roused the porter and sent him for Dr Wilson. While they waited for the doctor to arrive, he and Annunciata bathed Elizabeth's feet with hot water and then he raised her up and managed to get her to take some chicken jelly, convinced she must have some nourishment. "Well, you do make an exaggerated case of it!" she teased him, smiling. She kissed him and kept her arms round his neck. She had once more closed her eyes and Robert was not sure if she was awake or asleep. "Do you know me?" he whispered. She smiled again and murmured, "My Robert – my heavens, my beloved!" and kissed him again and again, saying, "Our lives are held by God." Gently, Robert laid her on the pillow but still she tried to go on kissing him. When once she was lying down she could not reach him and instead kissed her own hands and raised them up towards him as though trying to shower him with kisses. He asked her, "Are you comfortable?" and she replied "Beautiful." She seemed to fall asleep again. Suddenly, Robert remembered she ought not to be in a lying position when, as he could see, the struggle to cough was beginning. He lifted her up to ease the cough. He felt her try to expel the phlegm and then stop. He thought she had fainted with the effort or fallen asleep now that she was comfortable. He looked at her face, held against his own chest, and saw her forehead contract in a spasm of pain, then clear. All at once, she looked like a young girl. It was Annunciata, hovering anxiously in the background, who realised Elizabeth was dead and said so in Italian: "Quest' anima benedetta é passata!" It was true. Her last gesture a kiss, her last thought of their love.[8]

*   *   *

Nobody dared to imagine how Robert would bear the death of a woman he had loved so much that he felt her to be a part of him. Everyone who had anything to do with him waited, in terror, for his breakdown, for the tears and agonies of grief he would surely suffer. Hardly less terrible was the prospect of Pen's reaction. No son had ever been closer. It was expected, and dreaded, that he would be inconsolable. But all expectations were confounded. Both Robert and Pen were in perfect control of themselves, at least initially. In Robert's case, his astounding composure came from a failure to appreciate that Elizabeth *was* truly dead even though he had held her as she died. He told William Story that when he looked at his wife's face, somehow mysteriously "rounded and filled up" in death, she seemed to have a smile on her lips and looked "so living", so young and lovely, that all traces of ill health were wiped out. Her death was easier to bear because it looked like happiness. It was a great consolation to Robert that his wife had not known she was dying and that the manner of her death was peaceful; she had not died screaming with pain or contorted with agony.[9] He thought of this as a privilege and awareness of it gave him courage. Pen gave him even more. He seemed literally to grow up in a day. Putting his arms round his father, Pen kissed him and talked to him and Robert found it quite uncanny how his twelve-year-old son seemed to behave so like his mother, even using the same words she used. He told Sarianna that Pen was "perfect to me". Far from adding to his burdens, his son lightened them. Isa was in charge of him, taking him up to Bellosguardo with her, but hardly needed to be.

But of course there were burdens which could not be avoided. Chief among these was the funeral. If Elizabeth herself had had a phobia about cemeteries, Robert, in spite of his love of skeletons, had an equal horror of the paraphernalia of death. Story would have been only too willing to relieve his friend of this miserable task but arrived too late. Arrangements had already been made and he was surprised and disapproving because he did not think Robert had made them splendid enough. But Robert did not care about splendour. Story might relate later that the funeral service had been "blundered through" and that hardly anyone turned up but all Robert remembered was "a flash of faces". Elizabeth's coffin was carried along a special route, permitted only to the honoured, through streets still hung with black crêpe for Cavour, to the Protestant cemetery. Here she lay next to Leigh Hunt's wife, Fanny. No Barrett was there to see her buried. Even if they had wanted to come to Florence for the funeral, to the city they had avoided visiting while their sister was alive, they could not have got there in time. She died on 29th June and was buried within three days, on 1st July, partly because the intense heat made it necessary. But although no Barrett was present, their presence was nevertheless felt by Robert who dreaded what they might say about a death of which they had received no warning. George and Arabel were naturally the two most in his thoughts. They had been sent a stark telegram but writing to them at length was the major task Robert faced after the funeral. On 2nd July, the very next day, he sat down at Isa's villa, where he and Pen were now staying, and wrote to George. He asked his brother-in-law not to hate him for "giving . . . any pain anybody else might have spared you" and then related in full how Elizabeth had died. He described her collapse after Cavour's death, how she had caught cold, how they had all assumed the resulting illness was merely one of her usual attacks. He wrote of the manner of her death, of how serene it had been, of how she "in some perfectly gracious way was allowed by God" to suffer no pain. Again and again in this account Robert repeated that no one had known Elizabeth was dying. He brought in all sorts of detail to demonstrate how all the evidence had suggested she was recovering, telling George how his sister that last night had "sat up by herself, cleaned her teeth, washed her face and combed her hair without the least assistance". Going over it all proved too much for him. "This is all I can bear to tell you now of it," he told George and then, after concluding with a description of the funeral and of the tributes paid, he added a postscript saying, "I must write no more letters like this." George would have to tell his brothers what he had been told: "all brothers and relatives *must* forgive my not attempting to write to them . . . I cannot go over this again and again in letters." Not only was doing so agonising but it destroyed his self-control. If he dwelt on the past, he could not face the future.

In common with other lovers whose loved one dies, Robert was experiencing that strange sensation of suspended belief. He knew Elizabeth was dead, but he did not *feel* she was. He had seen her lifeless body, he had buried it and yet he found her still alive within him. It was not that he shared any of her own ideas – he did not for one moment think she had become a spirit who was communicating from the other side – but that the truth of what he had always alleged was proved: she was part of him and that part would live as long as he himself lived. Nor was it just a trick of memory, of remembering too well how she had looked or what she had said, but something much more subtle. He found he carried her within him, that he listened to her constantly, that he was perfectly able to hear her replies even to questions never asked in her lifetime. At first, this was an immense comfort and explained his apparent bravery but then as the days passed and still Elizabeth was as alive as ever, within his heart but not his grasp, he began to be tormented by her presence and burst out to Isa, "I want her! I want her!" At last the tears came. When he had wept he found that the notion of Elizabeth still being with him was no longer unbearable; once more, it was a comfort. Part of the comfort was having a feeling that he was under direct orders. He had a mission – Pen. He and Elizabeth had spent hours and hours discussing and deciding how they would bring up Pen and had been on the threshold of making many changes. Nothing Robert did with Pen during the days following his wife's death was his own idea. He did not seize his son and brutally cut off his curls and divest him of his pretty clothes in any desire to react against the way Elizabeth had liked to see him; what he did was in accordance with her own wish, if a most reluctant one. There was neither cruelty nor revenge nor rebellion in Robert's decision to let Pen grow up at once: it had all been agreed.

But he had another mission, too. This was to publish Elizabeth's last poems. He had her own list of everything she had written since her last collected edition, leaving aside major works like *Casa Guidi Windows*, *Poems Before Congress* and *Aurora Leigh*, some of which had already appeared in magazines. There were more poems than Robert had realised and some of the best, like "Lord Walter's Wife", had never appeared. Arranging them and seeing them through the press was the kind of "pedestrian work" Elizabeth herself had craved at times of great grief and Robert now found the same release in doing it. The poems were published in February 1862, entitled *Last Poems*, with a dedication of Robert's to "Grateful Florence". Among the poems was "My Heart and I" in which Elizabeth effectively wrote her own epitaph. All that mattered in life, the poem said, was to have been loved. The last verse ran:

> Yet who complains? My heart and I?
> In this abundant earth no doubt
> Is little room for things worn out:
> Disdain them, break them, throw them by,
> And if before the days grow rough
> We once were loved, used – well enough,
> I think, we've fared, my heart and I.

And she had thought so and Robert knew it. She had achieved, by the time she died at the age of fifty-five, all she had longed to achieve when as a restless, ambitious young girl she had thought herself trapped forever within the narrow confines of the kind of life women of her time and class were doomed to lead. She had longed to fulfil the talent she knew she had and which, when she was beginning as a poet, found such imperfect expression. In *Aurora Leigh* she did so: it was a great work. *Sonnets from the Portuguese* were the great love poems Robert judged them and, even if not highly praised when they appeared, have been so virtually ever since. But of course Elizabeth did not really care what critics thought or the public said, even though she enjoyed the appreciation of both. She cared what Robert thought and most of all what she herself thought. She died judging she had not failed her own talent, that she had produced some good poetry fit to stand, some of it, near the work of those gods of poetry she so revered. She wanted to make a significant literary contribution to her age and she did so. It was in fact much more significant than she realised because she had no means of knowing, for example, how she was influencing, *before* she died, Emily Dickinson[10] and after it would influence a long line of other modern poets.

But as well as "faring well" in her work, Elizabeth had done so even more remarkably in her personal life against all expectations. She had loved a man who returned her love and through him had experienced a far more elusive kind of self-fulfilment. Her love for Robert was the great illuminating force in her life and her luck in finding him and finding this love grow and be reciprocated was so incredible that she never ceased to marvel. All her bitter youth she despised women who traded themselves in marriage and had known she would never do so, no matter how strong the lure of children and a home of her own. She had settled, long before 1845, for being a woman whose work was central to her life, as did so many nineteenth-century women – Florence Nightingale, Emily Davies, Elizabeth Blackwell and hundreds of other less well-known women who "gave" themselves to their careers at a time when doing so meant making a straight choice. Women, then, did not expect to have it all: it was a career *or* marriage and motherhood. Elizabeth, at thirty-eight, had made her choice without much difficulty. It did not displease her. No man tempted her, no marriage seemed enviable. She was a poet and that was enough as well as a far, far better thing than being a wife. But then she met Robert and fell in love and was half terrified to find herself so blessed. Once she was safely married to him and was living with him, there was nothing else to wish for except, greedily (she felt), a child. The birth of Pen when she was forty-three pushed her happiness over the brim into an excess of joy. Of the three roles she, as a woman could have, she had all three: wife, mother, poet. She never, even in her darkest days, forgot that.

Robert also drew strength after her death from knowing this. His wife had been happy. Given good health she would of course have been even happier; but he was no more disposed than she to emphasise what she had *not* had – when she had had so much. The unfairness of the acute ill health of her last three years and of her sudden comparatively early death had to be balanced by the realisation that she had enjoyed twelve years of great happiness which she had never thought to have. Robert did not need to mourn wasted talent, lost opportunities, broken promises: Elizabeth had fulfilled herself even if there had been still more to give. It was he who had not yet done what he could, not completely. He had not put himself at full stretch as she had done in *Aurora Leigh*. This he had still to do, as she had urged: another mission. Yet he was aware that in another way he had no more to give. He knew that he and Elizabeth had shared a love extremely rare. Theirs had been that union of two souls which love should be and so rarely is. He was grateful for that privilege. He knew he was to be pitied because he had lost Elizabeth but he also knew that he was to be envied that he had ever had her.

Robert treasured what he had known, what Elizabeth had been in herself and to him, and found the courage from her inspiration to strike out and make the mark she had wanted him to make. She had already made her own mark, becoming one of those literary "grandmothers" she had looked for in vain when she was young: it is precisely how she wished to be remembered.

Afterword

Robert and Pen, accompanied by Isa Blagden, left Florence on 27th July 1861. They went first to Paris then to Saint-Malo before arriving in London in September. For nine months they either stayed with Arabel in London or lived in rented accommodation but then Robert settled down with his son at No. 19 Warwick Crescent. He stayed there for twenty-five years, never returning to Florence. At first he was wretchedly lonely until he picked up the threads of his old London literary life and was soon on the way to becoming a literary lion, especially after *Dramatis Personae* was published in 1864. The reviews and acclaim, which Elizabeth had hoped and prayed for and predicted, arrived: Robert Browning was at last hailed as "a great dramatic poet".

In his personal life, Robert was not as fortunate, though he was far from unhappy. His father died in 1866 and his sister Sarianna came to run his household. He never remarried. He died in 1889, in his son's house in Venice.

*　　　*　　　*

Pen Browning has suffered from gross misrepresentation. He has been portrayed as a wastrel, a dilettante, the disappointing failed son of brilliant parents. What he in fact became was a good artist and a popular, kind man but certainly he failed academically. Robert was determined to get him into Balliol College, Oxford – ironic in view of his own lack of academic training and his dislike of the little he had – but Pen could not make the grade and went instead to Christ Church. Never remotely intellectual, which his mother had always recognised and acknowledged, he spent most of his time rowing and inevitably finally dropped out. Robert was, most unfairly, upset but relieved to find Pen becoming serious about art if about nothing else. He accepted with a good grace Pen's decision to study painting and sculpture (under Rodin) on the Continent. Pen made great progress and exhibited in both Paris and London galleries.

In 1887, when he was thirty-eight, he married Fannie Coddington, an American heiress, and bought the Palazzo Rezzonico in Venice, devoting himself to its restoration. His marriage failed three years later, soon after his father's death. There were no children, although Pen had one illegitimate daughter whose mother was a peasant girl whom he met on holiday in Brittany. This daughter, Ginevra, came to live with him during his marriage and continued to do so afterwards until she herself married. Pen never left Italy after Fannie deserted him. He died in Asolo in 1912.

* * *

Wilson stayed in Florence looking after Landor until his death in 1864 but her son Oreste was able to join her in 1862 when he was seven. For a few years Wilson had the happy family life she had wanted but then abruptly returned to England where she set up a boarding house in Scarborough. It failed. She returned to Italy, destitute except for the £10 a year Robert allowed her for old times' sake. When Pen bought the Palazzo Rezzonico, it is gratifying to record that he remembered his beloved "Lily" and took her in. She lived with him and went with him to Asolo where she died in 1902. Her husband Ferdinando seems to have parted company with her in the late 1870s but turned up in Paris in 1885 and afterwards was also taken in by Pen. Ferdinando died in 1893.

* * *

Of the Barretts, only Arabel was close to Robert and Pen. Arabel died in Robert's arms in 1866. Most of the brothers lived to a good old age except Septimus. He died at the age of forty-eight in Jamaica, where he had gone to manage the family estates but mismanaged them so spectacularly that he left immense debts. Stormie (Charles John) was left to try to sort out the mess. He ended up a relatively poor man (by previous Barrett standards, that is). Stormie married and had one daughter. He too died in Jamaica, in 1905.

* * *

The other brothers lived and died in England and France. George, who never married, died in his Pembroke home in 1895, and Henry a year later. Alfred, who had two daughters and two sons (from one of whom the present Edward Moulton-Barrett is descended), died in France in 1904.

Chronology

1806   6th March – birth E B B at Coxhoe Hall, Durham.
1809   Barrett family move to Hope End, nr. Ledbury, Herefordshire.
1815   June – ⚔ Waterloo.
         October – EBB and parents spend month in Paris.
1817   EBB starts *The Battle of Marathon* while on holiday at Ramsgate.
1820   6th March – 50 copies of *The Battle of Marathon* privately printed.
1821   May – EBB's first magazine publication (*New Monthly Magazine*).
         June – sent to Gloucester Spa.
1822   c. May – returns to Hope End.
1823   Holiday in Boulogne.
1825   EBB goes for long stay with paternal grandmother in Hastings.
1826   25th March – *An Essay on Mind, with Other Poems* published.
1828   7th October – death of Mary Moulton-Barrett, EBB's mother.
1830   December – death of EBB's paternal grandmother – leaves her money.
1831   EBB keeps a diary for a year.
1832   Hope End sold – Barretts leave for Sidmouth, Devon.
1833   May – translation of Aeschylus' *Prometheus Bound* published.
         August – Parliament votes to abolish slavery.
1835   EBB and family settle in London.
1837   20th June – Queen Victoria ascends throne.
1838   6th June – *The Seraphim, and Other Poems* published.
         August – EBB goes to Torquay to convalesce.
1840   Bro drowned.
1841   EBB returns to London.
1844   *Poems*, 2 volumes, published.
1845   January – Robert Browning writes first letter to EBB.
         May – RB makes first visit to EBB.
1846   12th September – EBB marries RB.
         19th September – leave secretly for Italy.
1847   Brownings move from Pisa to Florence.
1848   EBB begins *Casa Guidi Windows*.
1849   9th March – birth of Pen.
1850   *Poems*, new edition, published.
1851   May – Brownings set out for London.
         – *Casa Guidi Windows* published.
         Winter – go to Paris.

1852   July – second London visit.
       October – return to Florence via Paris.
1853   EBB begins *Aurora Leigh*.
       Summer in Bagni di Lucca.
       Winter in Rome.
1854   May – return to Florence.
1855   January – EBB ill.
       July – third London visit.
       Winter in Paris.
1856   *Aurora Leigh* completed.
       June – fourth London visit.
       October – return to Florence.
       December – death of Kenyon leaving legacies to Brownings.
1857   April – death of Edward Moulton-Barrett.
1858   July – holiday in northern France with both families.
       Winter in Rome.
1859   June – return to Florence.
       Napoleon III signs armistice at Villafranca.
       EBB very ill.
       Winter in Rome.
1860   March – *Poems Before Congress* published.
       June – return to Florence.
       Summer in Siena.
       November – winter in Rome.
                   – death EBB's sister Henrietta.
1861   EBB confined to room during winter.
       June – return to Florence.
             – death of Cavour.
             – collapse of EBB.
       29th June – death of EBB.
       1st July – buried in Protestant cemetery, Florence.

Notes and Sources

All quotations from letters (up to 1840), unless otherwise stated, are from Volumes 1 to 5 (1809–1842) of *The Brownings' Correspondence* edited by Philip Kelley and Ronald Hudson (pub. Wedgestone Press). Since the 966 letters in these volumes are chronologically arranged, and make all identification simple, I have not thought it necessary to note them.

Chapter One

1. 13th July 1850 to Mrs David Ogilvy.

2. Financial details about John Graham-Clarke come from the nine boxes of Graham-Clarke Papers deposited in Gloucester Record Office.

3. EBB's father did not use the hyphen and neither did she. It was after her death that her brothers began to use it. (See *The Brownings' Correspondence*, Vol. 1, p. xxvi, for details.)

4. Mary Trepsack was about five years younger than Mrs Moulton. She was the daughter of a white Jamaican planter and a female slave. When her parents died during her infancy she became a Barrett ward and from 1782 lived at Cinnamon Hill. She was Elizabeth Moulton's lifelong friend, and lived with her until 1830 (when E. Moulton died). She was known as both "Treppy" and "Trippy" and was adored by all the Barretts. (See *BC*, Vol. 1, p. 301.)

5. John Kenyon was only a year older than Mr Barrett and had a similar background. His great-grandmother was EBB's great-grandfather's sister, making him a distant cousin. He became a poet and philanthropist, travelled widely, and was prominent in London literary society.

6. Philip Kelley has established that Coxhoe Hall was leased by Edward himself, and not by his mother, as previously thought.

7. *BC*, Vol. 1, p. xxi.

8. Since Charles was the name of Edward Moulton-Barrett's father, it would seem that his feelings towards him were not as hostile as the history of their relationship would otherwise suggest. Charles Moulton corresponded with both his sons, as adults, and they do not seem to have cut him off or held against him either his treatment of their mother or the fact that he had fathered two more families (in England) since she left him.

9. The MP for Hereford had died and the seat was hotly contested. The candidate the Barretts favoured got in. Mr Barrett was always very active in all local affairs (in both 1812 and 1814 he was elected Sheriff of Herefordshire).

10. By the 1820s, there were hundreds of establishments in England calling themselves girls' schools; but what they taught was mainly "accomplishments": sewing, piano playing, singing, and drawing. The teachers in these places were entirely untrained. It was not until the late 1840s that any girls' schools worthy of the name were founded, and not until the Taunton Commission (1868) that the generally appalling state of girls' education was exposed.

Chapter Two

1. EBB began *The Battle of Marathon* at Ramsgate in the summer after her eleventh birthday. Two years later she was referring to it as "my DARLING project" in a letter to her mother. There is a copy in the British Library.

2. *Adonais*, verse xxxii.

3. Printed p. 347, *BC*, Vol. 1, from the original manuscript.

4. "Glimpses into My Own Life and Literary Character", printed p. 348, *BC*, Vol. 1, from the original manuscript.

5. EBB varied the age at which she read Mary Wollstonecraft – at one point she said she was twelve, at another even younger. This letter at least proves she was no more than twelve.

Chapter Three

1. Mary Trant (née Barrett) was the first cousin of EBB's paternal grandmother. She was a widow with three sons, one of whom, Dominick, particularly annoyed EBB because he teased her.

2. There is no death certificate extant for Mary Barrett. The only disease mentioned as diagnosed (soon after her last son's birth in 1824) was rheumatoid arthritis. The suddenness and unexpectedness of her death suggest a heart attack (and the heart is, of course, affected by all forms of rheumatism).

Chapter Four

The quotations used from EBB's diary in this chapter are taken from *Diary by E.B.B.*, edited by Philip Kelley and Ronald Hudson (Univ. of Ohio Press, 1967).

Chapter Five

1. The Reverend George Barrett Hunter's age is not known. In spite of his name, he was not related to the Barretts. His wife Mary was alive but, according to EBB in a letter to Miss Mary Russell Mitford, mad.

2. *The Family of the Barrett* by Jeannette Marks (Macmillan, 1935), p. 443, letter 8th Aug. 1834 from Edward Moulton-Barrett to his brother.

Chapter Six

1. At a meeting of the Browning Society in 1985, two eminent doctors – one arguing in favour of undiagnosed TB at some stage, and one against – both agreed

Dr Chambers was proficient with the stethoscope and that he could not have failed to detect a tubercular condition at this time if it had been present.

2. Whether or not her father *made* EBB pay for her own household is not absolutely clear. Even if he did, this was not exactly unfair of him. EBB was an adult of independent means, not a child whose illness was a responsibility her father had to accept. Mr Barrett had not been mean on other occasions about maintaining another household (eg for Arabel).

3. The fact that some nights "even opium" did not make EBB sleep indicates either that she was extremely resistant to the drug, or, as I have suspected, the dosage was low.

4. Sam's tombstone at Cinnamon Hill reads thus:

S. M. BARRETT

Whose remains rest beneath until the last trumpet
when this corruptible must put on incorruption and
this mortal must put on immortality

Jan. 13 1812 – Feb. 1840

Being the 2nd son of E.M. Barrett of Cinnamon Hill
whose only consolation under this bereavement is that
his son died in the faith of Jesus for the remission
of his sins.

5. *The Letters of Elizabeth Barrett Browning to Mary Russell Mitford*, edited by Meredith B. Raymond & Mary Rose Sullivan, Vol. I, p. 235. (All quotations from EBB's letters to Miss Mitford from now on are from this three vol. edition and are usually dated in the text.)

Chapter Seven

1. Raymond and Sullivan, Vol. I, p. 336 (hereafter R & S).

2. Cornelius Mathews was very important to the promotion of EBB's fame in America. It was thanks to him that her 1838 volume was reviewed (in a magazine edited by him) and it was to him that she sent four sonnets that appeared in *Graham's Magazine* in Dec. 1842.

Mathews was only in his twenties, a poet himself, and was backing a hunch that EBB would soon become popular; he was right.

3. R & S, Vol. II, p. 59.

4. R & S, Vol. II, p. 281.

Chapter Eight

1. R & S, Vol. II, p. 411.

2. R & S, Vol. II, p. 404.

3. EBB's contributions to *A New Spirit of the Age* were, like everyone's, anonymous, but through her correspondence, it is possible to identify the essays on Carlyle and Monckton Milnes as hers, together with most of the essay on Landor

and half the essay on Wordsworth and Leigh Hunt. She also added notes to the essay on Tennyson (written by Horne himself).

4. The American edition was published by H. O. Langley. Cornelius Mathews arranged the publication and negotiated 10% of the net sales for EBB.

5. *The Letters of Elizabeth Barrett Browning*, ed. F. G. Kenyon Vol. 1, p. 176 (hereafter K).

6. K, Vol. 1, p. 213.

7. *The Letters of Elizabeth Barrett Browning to Richard Hengist Horne*, ed. S. R. Townshend Mayer (1877), Vol. II, p. 115.

8. K, Vol. 1, p. 183.

9. R & S, Vol. II, p. 449.

10. R & S, Vol. II, p. 441.

11. All information given by Surtees Cook comes from the manuscript copy of his diary kindly loaned to me by Mary Altham.

12. R & S, Vol. III, p. 49. This is the first unmistakable description of what was to become *Aurora Leigh*, though EBB did not even begin it for several years afterwards.

Chapter Nine

1. Alfred Domett, a year older than Robert, was born in Camberwell too. He went to Cambridge then became a barrister and emigrated to New Zealand in 1842, where he was Prime Minister 1862–3. Domett was a poet himself and Robert valued his criticism. (See *B C*, Vol. 4, p. 316.)

2. André Victor Amédée de Ripert-Monclar, five years older than Robert, got to know the London Brownings because he was a neighbour of a relation who lived in Paris. Monclar was a royalist who held office under Charles X. Robert met him in 1834 when he came to London, possibly on a royalist mission. (See *B C*, Vol. 3, p. 321 for further details.)

3. *B C*, Vol. 3, p. 256.

4. All quotations from Robert's and Elizabeth's letters are taken from *The Letters of Robert Browning and Elizabeth Barrett Browning 1845–1846*, ed. I. G. Kenyon, 1899, and are usually dated in the text.

5. R & S, Vol. III, p. 75.

6. *B C*, Vol. 3, p. 327.

Chapter Ten

1. Haydon committed suicide in despair after the failure of his latest exhibition when his two great pictures, "Aristeides" and "Nero" failed to win the acclaim they deserved. A contributory factor was his fear that he was about to be arrested yet again for debt (he had already been arrested 7 times in 25 years). (See *A Sultry Month – Scenes of London Literary Life in 1846* by Alethea Hayter.)

2. It has been used ever since, even by biographers who ought to care more about the inaccuracy of the term when applied to EBB's marriage.

3. *Elizabeth Barrett to Mr Boyd*, ed. Barbara P. McCarthy, p. 280.

Chapter Eleven

1. *Letters of the Brownings to George Barrett*, ed. Paul Landis, p. 149.
2. Vol. 5, *Browning Institute Studies* (1977), p. 21.
3. *Love and Work Enough – Life of Anna Jameson* by Clara Thomas, Chap. 17.

PART TWO: 1846–1861

Chapter Twelve

1. *Elizabeth Barrett Browning – Letters to her Sister 1846–1859*, ed. L. Huxley, p. 12 (hereafter H).
2. R & S, Vol. III, p. 209.
3. Ibid.
4. H, p. 15. EBB quotes Wilson as saying "I never saw a *man* like Mr Browning in my life."
5. Vol. 5, *Browning Institute Studies*, p. 23.
6. Ibid., p. 24.
7. On 7th December 1843, R & S, Vol. II, p. 356.
8. *B C*, Vol. 3, p. 282 – 28th September 1837.
9. Since EBB was passionately anti-slavery, she was only too eager to oblige the American request for a poem to help their cause. She sent the "Runaway Slave at Pilgrim's Point" in December 1846, but it was not printed until 1848, when it appeared in *The Liberty Bell*, a publication sold at the National Anti-Slavery Bazaar in Boston. The English public did not read it until 1850, when it appeared in EBB's new volume of collected poems.

Chapter Thirteen

1. *Casa Guidi Windows*, ed. Julia Markus (*Browning Institute* 1977), Appendix p. 65 (Huxley omits more than half the text of this letter in his edition of EBB's letters to Henrietta, including this account of the wedding day. cf EBB's appreciation of Wilson).
2. Robert's theory is not quite so absurd as it sounds. There were many days in EBB's life when she wrote four long letters one after the other. I have test-written them myself and found it exhausting. The total number of words (in four letters to Henrietta, Mrs Mitford, Mrs Martin and Mrs Ogilvy) was 8,000, and it took me 5 hours.
3. H, p. 83.
4. K, Vol. I, p. 363.
5. H, p. 73.
6. H, p. 60.
7. It is impossible to establish this. EBB and Robert write only of steadily diminishing the drug, although Robert *implies* it was diminished to the point of being totally dispensed with. But in a letter in the Harry Ransom Humanities Research Center (Univ. of Texas at Austin), written by EBB, soon after her son's birth, to Fanny Dowglass, *she* implies she never did quite give it up and speaks of the

"unspeakable rapture" she felt when her son was pronounced perfect, because she had worried about the effects of taking opium during her pregnancy. (EBB to F. Dowglass, 16th May 1849.)

Chapter Fourteen

1. *Twenty-Two Unpublished Letters of Elizabeth Barrett Browning and Robert Browning Addressed to Henrietta & Arabella Moulton Barrett* (New York, 1935), p. 63.
2. EBB's son was not called Pen until he himself started to use the name at the age of two. Since by no perversion of sound in either English or Italian could "Wiedemann" come to be "Pen" or "Penini", it seems more likely the child was somehow twisting the Italian for "little one". I have used "Pen" from the beginning for the sake of consistency and to avoid calling him "the baby" all the time.
3. *Elizabeth Barrett Browning's Letters to Mrs. David Ogilvy*, ed. Peter N. Heydon and Philip Kelley, p. 31 (hereafter O).
4. Margaret Fuller's husband, Giovanni d'Ossoli, was a radical aristocrat who helped set up a Republic in Rome in 1848. When Rome was besieged by the French, the d'Ossolis organised relief, but could not prevent the Republic being overthrown. It was because they were fleeing police persecution for their part in assisting the Republic that they were now in Florence and about to leave Italy altogether. It was embarrassing for EBB to have to admit that her hero Louis Napoleon was responsible for restoring power to the Pope (because he believed it was in the best interests both of the Catholic Church and of France).
5. Surtees Cook *was* poor by Barrett standards, and could not even afford the £1,000 needed to buy himself into a Guards or Cavalry regiment, which was why he was in a Yorkshire one.

Chapter Fifteen

1. O, p. 205 (Appendix – the whole of EBB's letter to Arabel is printed here).
2. O, p. 44.
3. K, Vol. II, p. 15.
4. These are the letters that have never been found, but are believed still to exist. Philip Kelley tracked down a desk, sold in the West Country, to its last-but-one owner, and has every reason to think these letters are in it.
5. A respirator was a primitive version of an asthma inhaler.
6. This was one of the occasions upon which EBB wrote descriptions of the same event to many correspondents. The best and most complete was to Miss Mitford, on 16th February 1852.

Chapter Sixteen

1. *Letters of the Brownings to George Barrett*, ed. Paul Landis, p. 155.
2. O, p. 67.
3. Landis, p. 179.

4. R & S, Vol. III, p. 371.

5. *The Times* for 2nd July 1852.

6. See Appendix (Domestic Servant Wage Rates) to *The Rise and Fall of the Victorian Servant* by Pamela Horn.

7. O, p. 88.

8. Huxley excised this letter which is quoted in *The Book, The Ring and The Poet – A Biography of Robert Browning* by William Irvine and Paul Honan, p. 299 (Houghton MS, EBB to Henrietta, September 16).

9. *Browning Institute Studies*, Vol. 5, p. 36.

Chapter Seventeen

1. Landis, p. 190.

2. H, p. 182.

3. H, p. 200 (EBB here sums up her own philosophy as to the upbringing of children and shows herself a century ahead of her times – the whole of modern nursery education is based on similar beliefs).

4. O, p. 76.

5. O, p. 108.

6. R & S, p. 401.

7. O, p. 115.

8. *Browning Institute Studies*, Vol. 5, p. 37.

9. Landis, p. 214.

Chapter Eighteen

1. O, p. 132.

2. Servants in Victorian times often had their clothes bought by their employers as part of their wages, so it may well have been merely time for Wilson's annual dress, and not quite the generous present it appears – but at least the dress was "very pretty", and silk, which presumably it need not have been.

3. The Kinney story is taken from the enthralling account of this episode by Ronald A. Bosco – *The Brownings and Mrs. Kinney: A record of their friendship* – in *Browning Institute Studies*, Vol. 4. Mrs Kinney only *suspected* EBB had taken another dose of opium, but it certainly sounds as if she was "high", and as if, from now on, she was using opium in a way she never had before. I am indebted to Edward McAleer for directing me to this article.

4. Mr Barrett had made it plain that no child, son or daughter, of his would have his blessing to marry if the match was not suitable in every respect. Alfred's was not suitable in his eyes in any respect, since Alfred had no income worth mentioning and Lizzie's mother had gone mad.

5. The story of Wilson's marriage is told in three letters to Arabel, *Browning Institute Studies*, Vol. 5, p. 40.

6. Another letter entirely omitted by Huxley from his collection of EBB's letters to Henrietta. This is quoted, from the Huxley typescript, by Betty Miller in *Robert Browning: A Portrait*, p. 154.

7. For EBB's account of this séance, see H, p. 218; for Robert's, see Irvine & Honan, p. 333.

8. For Robert's reaction to his reviews, see Irvine & Honan, Chap. 19.

Chapter Nineteen

1. K, Vol. II, p. 228.
2. Ibid.
3. K, Vol. II, p. 230.
4. H, p. 248.
5. K, Vol. II, p. 238.
6. H, p. 256. Extraordinary though it may seem, this was the first time EBB and Surtees had actually come face to face. Surtees' diary reveals he saw EBB once, in a carriage, in 1845, but did not then meet her. His diary has the year 1846 removed, and for the year 1856 there is no record of the Browning visit.
7. H, p. 259.
8. *Browning Institute Studies*, Vol. 5, p. 41.
9. H, p. 269. Much has been made by some of Robert's biographers of this kind of incident, in which he appeared to desert EBB and chose to enjoy himself without her. But there is overwhelming evidence that she was eager he should, and did not feel in the least betrayed.
10. *Browning Institute Studies*, Vol. 5, p. 42.
11. K, Vol. II, p. 263.
12. H, p. 272.

Chapter Twenty

1. K, Vol. II, p. 267.
2. Edward C. McAleer, *The Brownings of Casa Guidi*, p. 65.
3. Ibid. p. 66.
4. O, p. 136.
5. *Dearest Isa: Robert Browning's Letters to Isabella Blagden*, Edward C. McAleer, p. 17.
6. H, p. 300.
7. McAleer, *The Brownings of Casa Guidi*, p. 69.
8. *Browning Institute Studies*, Vol. 5, p. 45.
9. O, p. 141.
10. K, Vol. II, pp. 313–319 for a series of letters in which EBB expresses repeatedly her views on the war.

Chatper Twenty-one

1. O, p. 143.
2. K, Vol. II, p. 340.
3. The congress for which EBB named her volume never took place. In November 1859, a peace treaty had been signed between France, Austria and Piedmont, to

reinforce the terms agreed at Villafranca, and at the same time Napoleon III invited representatives of the major powers to a congress in Paris the following January. EBB had already named her volume before it became obvious that the congress was indefinitely postponed.

4. O, p. 149.

5. Landis, p. 225.

6. The exact nature of Sophie Eckley's treachery is still under dispute. It has always been supposed that the Brownings discovered she had been a false medium, deliberately inventing messages from the other side. But now it is suspected that the betrayal may have been a moral one, in that Sophie may have had an affair while posing as a virtuously married woman.

7. O, p. 166.

8. Landis, p. 238.

9. O, p. 159.

10. O, p. 162.

11. Landis, p. 241.

12. Landis, p. 253.

13. *Browning Institute Studies*, Vol. 5, p. 47.

14. BM typescript, EBB to Surtees Cook, December 1860.

15. O, p. 168.

Chapter Twenty-two

1. Landis, p. 258.

2. Landis, p. 261.

3. These were very nearly the exact words used by Josephine Butler ten years later when she led the fight against the Contagious Diseases Acts (an attempt, in fact, to legalise prostitution for the use of the army in selected towns). It was Mrs Butler's whole argument that prostitution only flourished because "pure" women pretended it had nothing to do with them, that it was a matter for choice on the part of the wanton women involved, when really it was an attack on the whole female sex. In writing in this strain, EBB placed herself firmly in the vanguard of feminist opinion — but of course she did so privately and "Lord Walter's Wife" did not appear publicly at the time.

4. K, Vol. II, p. 435.

5. Landis, p. 256.

6. It was to Hans Andersen that EBB wrote her last poem "The North and The South", published after her death in *Last Poems*, 1862.

7. As usual, the exact dosage is impossible to state, but since EBB now refers to morphine and not to "my opium mixture", it does sound as though she may have been taking grains of morphine undiluted in alcohol — that is, straight morphine and not laudanum — which would almost certainly mean she was taking opium in a stronger form. This would tally with the hallucinations, which she had never experienced while taking opium as laudanum.

8. Landis, p. 270–271.

9. The exact cause of EBB's death is not known; there is no extant death

certificate or doctor's report. Modern medical opinion holds that, although she may have had a heart attack, it is more likely that heavy doses of morphine paralysed her breathing (morphine attacks the nerve cells in the brain). It is extremely unlikely that her death was the result of a burst abscess in the lung, as Dr Wilson diagnosed.

10. The tributes to the influence of EBB on Emily Dickinson are to be found in her letters as well as her work – see *Emily Dickinson: Selected Letters*, ed. Thomas H. Johnson, pp. 172, 174, 179, 210, 214.

Selected Bibliography

LETTERS AND DIARIES

The Brownings' Correspondence, 1809–1842, ed. Philip Kelley and Ronald Hudson, Volumes 1–5 (pub. Wedgestone Press).

The Letters of Elizabeth Barrett Browning to Mary Russell Mitford, 1836–1854, Volumes 1–3, ed. and introduced by Meredith B. Raymond and Mary Rose Sullivan (pub. jointly by The Browning Institute, Wedgestone Press, Armstrong Browning Library of Baylor University, and Wellesley College).

Diary by E.B.B.: The Unpublished Diary of Elizabeth Barrett 1831–1832, ed. Philip Kelley and Ronald Hudson (pub. University of Ohio Press).

The Letters of Elizabeth Barrett Browning Addressed to Richard Hengist Horne, 2 volumes, ed. S. R. Townshend Mayer.

Elizabeth Barrett Browning: Letters to her Sister 1846–1859, ed. Leonard Huxley (pub. John Murray).

Letters of Robert Browning and Elizabeth Barrett Browning 1845–1846, 2 volumes (pub. Harper Bros.).

Twenty-two Unpublished Letters of Elizabeth Barrett Browning and Robert Browning Addressed to Henrietta and Arabella Moulton-Barrett (pub. New York, 1935).

Elizabeth Barrett to Mr Boyd – Unpublished Letters of Elizabeth Barrett to Hugh Stuart Boyd, ed. Barbara P. McCarthy (pub. John Murray).

Dearest Isa: Robert Browning's Letters to Isa Blagden, ed. Edward C. McAleer (pub. Austin, Texas).

Letters of the Brownings to George Barrett, ed. Paul Landis with the assistance of Ronald E. Freeman (pub. University of Illinois Press).

Invisible Friends: The Correspondence of Elizabeth Barrett Barrett and Benjamin Robert Haydon 1842–1845, ed. W. B. Pope (pub. Harvard University Press).

The Letters of Robert Browning and Elizabeth Barrett Barrett 1845–1846, 2 volumes, ed. Elvan Kinther (pub. Harvard University Press).

Browning to his American Friends: Letters between the Brownings, the Storys and James Russell Lowell 1841–1890, ed. Gertrude Reese Hudson (pub. Barnes & Noble).

Elizabeth Barrett Browning's Letters to Mrs. David Ogilvy 1849–1861, ed. Peter N. Heydon and Philip Kelley (pub. John Murray).

The Barretts at Hope End: The Early Diary of Elizabeth Barrett Browning, ed. Elizabeth Berridge (pub. John Murray).

Browning Institute Studies, Volumes 1–14.

The Brownings of Casa Guidi, Edward C. McAleer (pub. Browning Institute).
Elizabeth Barrett Browning. Hitherto Unpublished Poems and Stories, ed. H. Buxton Forman, 2 volumes (pub. Boston).

SECONDARY TEXTS

The Life of Elizabeth Barrett Browning, Gardner B. Taplin (pub. John Murray).
Elizabeth Barrett Browning, Dorothy Hewlett (pub. Cassell).
The Book, the Ring and the Poet: A Biography of Robert Browning, William Irvine and Park Honan (pub. Bodley Head).
Mrs Browning: A Poet's Work and Its Setting, Alethea Hayter (pub. Faber & Faber).
Opium and the Romantic Imagination, Alethea Hayter (pub. Faber & Faber).
A Sultry Month – Scenes of London Literary Life in 1846, Alethea Hayter (pub. Faber & Faber).
Robert Browning: A Portrait, Betty Miller (pub. John Murray).
Life and Letters of Robert Browning, Mrs Orr (pub. Smith, Elder & Co.).
The Courtship of Robert Browning and Elizabeth Barrett, Daniel Karlin (pub. University of Oxford Press).
The Tragi-Comedy of Pen Browning, Maisie Ward (pub. Browning Institute).
William Wetmore Story and his Friends, Henry James (pub. Boston).
My Browning Family Album, Vivienne Browning (pub. Springwood Books).
The Family of the Barrett, Jeannette Marks (pub. Macmillan).
Love and Work Enough: The Life of Anna Jameson, Clara Thomas (pub. Macdonald).
A New Spirit of the Age, 2 volumes, ed. R. H. Horne (pub. Smith, Elder & Co.).
Elizabeth Barrett Browning, Angela Leighton (pub. Harvester Press).

WORKS OF ELIZABETH BARRETT BROWNING

The Battle of Marathon. A Poem, by E. B. Barrett (printed for private circulation, 50 copies, W. Lindsell, 1820).
An Essay on Mind, with Other Poems, [unnamed] (printed James Duncan, 1826).
Prometheus Bound – Translated from the Greek of Aeschylus. And Miscellaneous Poems, by the translator, author of An Essay on Mind (pub. A. J. Valpy, 1833).
The Seraphim, and Other Poems by Elizabeth B. Barrett (pub. Saunders & Otley, 1838).
Poems by Elizabeth Barrett Barrett, 2 volumes (pub. Moxon, 1844).
Poems by Elizabeth Barrett Browning, new edition, 2 volumes (pub. Moxon, 1850).
Casa Guidi Windows. A Poem, by Elizabeth Barrett Browning (pub. Chapman & Hall, 1851).
Aurora Leigh by Elizabeth Barrett Browning (pub. Chapman & Hall, 1857).
Poems Before Congress by Elizabeth Barrett Browning (pub. C. & H., 1860).
Last Poems by Elizabeth Barrett Browning (pub. posthumously C. & H., 1862).

UNPUBLISHED SOURCES

The Diary of Surtees Cook.
The Graham-Clarke Papers, 9 boxes, Gloucester Record Office.
12 letters in University of Texas

Index

friends visit Brownings, 346; separated from Wilson, 347; and Ellen Wilson, 351; later life and death, 373
Romagnoli, Oreste (Wilson's son): born, 306; left in care of aunt, 315, 333, 342; mother takes back, 342, 347, 350, 373
Romagnoli, Pilade (Wilson's son), 326–7, 333, 342, 350
Romantic Revival, 35
Rome: Brownings winter in, 285–92, 333–4, 343, 345–6, 353, 356, 358, 361
Ruskin, John, 271
Rymer family, 303–4

Sand, George: EBB admires, 125; Hunter criticises, 149; Mme d' Ossoli meets, 240; Brownings meet in Paris, 260–1; Miss Hayes translates, 288; *Leila*, 114
Sartoris, Adelaide (*née* Kemble), 288
Scully, Dr William, 97, 104, 106–7
Shelley, Percy Bysshe: Browning edits (forged) letters, 267; *Adonais*, 28; *Queen Mab*, 35
Sidmouth, 65, 68–76
Siena, 242–3, 340, 346–7, 351
Silverthorne, James, 180
Solferino, Battle of, 1859, 337
Somers, John Sommers Cocks, 1st Earl of, 34
Soulie, Frédéric, 83
Spectator (journal), 245
spiritualism, 279–80, 282, 287, 289–90, 303–5, 321, 326, 328, 335, 359
Staël, Anne Louise Germaine de, Baroness: *Corinne, or Italy*, 67
Steers, Frances, 57
Stendhal (Henri Beyle): *Le Rouge et le Noir*, 150
Stone, Dr Thomas, 348
Story family: in Rome, 285–8, 290, 307, 361; entertain H. C. Andersen, 360
Story, Edith, 283; illness, 286–7, 290–1, 341
Story, Emelyn, 283, 286, 288, 291, 341
Story, Joe, 283; death, 285–7, 290, 296
Story, William Wetmore, 283, 291, 337, 340–1, 367
Stowe, Harriet Beecher, 321
Sue, Eugène, 83

Taunton Commission, 1868, 378n10
Taylor (dog-snatcher), 118, 136, 176
Tennyson, Alfred, 1st Baron, 88, 139, 246, 251–2, 380n3 (Ch. 8)
Tennyson, Frederick, 275–80, 282–3
Terni, 285

Thackeray, Ann (W. M. Thackeray's daughter), 288–9
Thackeray, Minny (W. M. Thackeray's daughter), 288–9
Thackeray, William Makepeace, 285, 287–9, 357
Torquay, 92–8, 104, 157–8
Trant, Dominick, 61, 378n1 (Ch. 3)
Trant, Mary (*née* Barrett), 378n1 (Ch. 3)
Treherne, Elizabeth *see* Crow, Elizabeth
Treherne, Mary Elizabeth, 127
Treherne, William, 123–6
Trepsack, Mary ("Treppy"), 6, 10, 15, 32, 110, 183; death, 321
Trollope, Frances, 280
Turner, J. M. W., 120
Tuscany, Grand Duke of *see* Leopold

Vallombrosa monastery, 212
Valpy, A. J. (publisher), 76
Venice, 247–8
Victor Emmanuel, ruler of Piedmont (*later* of Italy), 334, 337
Victoria, Queen of Great Britain, 92, 97, 109, 120
Villafranca, Peace of, 1859, 338, 339–40
Vincenzo (servant), 279, 283

Waddell, Hope, 97
Wardlaw, Dr Ralph, 75
Ware, William, 224
Westwood, Thomas, 128
Wight, Isle of *see* Isle of Wight
Wilson, Elizabeth (*later* Romagnoli; EBB's maid): appointed, 126–7; and mesmerism, 132; attends EBB, 151, 176; and EBB's marriage, 178–80, 214; travel preparations, 184; accompanies Brownings to Italy, 185–7; relations with Browning, 186–7, 199; life in Italy, 196, 213; illness, 197–8; and EBB's pregnancies and miscarriages, 198–9, 216–17; cheated in Pisa, 206; in Florence, 206–7; relations with EBB, 209; visits Vallombrosa monastery, 212; given brooch, 214; room in Casa Guidi, 222; and Righi, 224, 249; life and friends in Florence, 224–5; sews baby clothes for EBB, 228; and Pen's birth, 230–1; cares for Pen, 234, 256, 258, 278, 318–19; in Lucca, 235–6; return visit to London, 247–8, 256; and Pen's upbringing, 248–50, 259; depression and weight loss, 249; holiday in England, 256, 272–3; return to Italy, 257; denied wage rise by Brownings, 272–3; and